JS331.S28
Local political surveys

1 906 069 744 9

JS   56703
331
S2.8   Schattschneider

	DATE DUE	

JS   56703
331
S2.8   Schattschneider, Elmer

AUTHOR
Local political surveys

TITLE

DATE LOANED	BORROWER'S NAME	DATE RETURNED

LOCAL

POLITICAL

SURVEYS

E. E. Schattschneider
and
Victor Jones

Holt, Rinehart and Winston, Inc.

LOCAL POLITICAL
SURVEYS

E. E. SCHATTSCHNEIDER
Wesleyan University

VICTOR JONES
University of California
Berkeley

HOLT, RINEHART AND WINSTON
New York

PREFACE

This is a book for teachers and students, especially those who enjoy working together in the fabulous social complex known as American local government and politics. It can be used by individual students working independently on projects of their own, or by whole classes or groups, in or out of college, that want to make cooperative surveys.

No rational person would ever want to try to do everything suggested in this volume. We have suggested a great variety of things to do, because the raw materials of the subject are wonderfully rich and diverse and because data available in one town may be nonexistent in the next. If the reader cannot find one kind of data, we suggest that he try the next and the next, until he finds something that is appropriate to his needs.

There are an almost infinite number of kinds of surveys, and the requirements of each kind are unique. Our aim has been to help the student pick and choose according to his own needs and opportunities. We have not tried to prescribe a single correct procedure, because we do not think that there is such a thing.

Anyone attempting to make a survey is likely to be confronted with a baffling array of difficulties. Where does he begin? What is he looking for? Where is he likely to find the information he wants? Whom does he go to see? What questions does he ask? How can he evaluate the data he collects? We have tried to help the reader find the answers to such questions by directing him to library materials and to other public and private sources and by giving him clues to the analyses of a great variety of problems and leads to help him "size up" situations. We have, in addition, placed some red flags along the pathway to mark a number of booby traps.

Throughout this volume the reader will find specific applications of a position with respect to political research: politics can be understood only by putting together (1) all we can find out about the participants—who they are, their condition, and the circumstances of their lives; (2) how they vote and otherwise affect the political process; and (3) what is going on in the government.

A glance through this guide should convince the reader that the purpose of the authors has not been to encourage anyone to suppose that field work is a substitute for the more conventional kinds of learning. The bibliographies and book notes throughout this volume emphasize the need for heroic reading and hard library research as integral parts of any good survey. We believe that the combination of hard book work and hard field work will produce miracles of scholarship.

Finally, the authors wish to express their profound gratitude to the Falk Foundation for the generous interest and assistance that made the preparation and publication of this volume possible.

Middletown, Conn.
Berkeley, Calif.
February 1962

E. E. S.
V. J.

CONTENTS

Chapter *I*

INTRODUCTION

This is the age of surveys. Everybody is making surveys of the local community. Surveys are made by an incredible number of organizations and agencies for a great variety of purposes. Some of the more common types of surveys are: housing, traffic, highways, urban redevelopment, planning, public health, marketing, zoning, crime. In addition, school authorities, new industries, political parties, merchants, churches, governmental agencies, and public utilities make surveys for purposes of their own.

This book is designed for use by students, teachers, businessmen, civic groups, politicians, labor leaders, public officials—for anyone who wants to get a better understanding of his own community.

So many kinds of surveys are made for so many reasons, using so many techniques, that only a general introductory discussion is likely to meet the needs of any substantial number of people. One of the objectives of this book is to inform the reader about the great wealth of raw materials that are available to him. The reader is invited to select the material, references, concepts, and techniques best suited to his interests and needs and to work with these materials for his own purposes.

This is therefore a book for nonspecialists. It is not designed for students who are interested in developing special techniques of social inquiry, and it cannot, therefore, take the place of books such as Key, *A Primer of Statistics for Political Scientists* (1),* Parten, *Surveys, Polls, and Samples: Practical Procedures* (2), or Young, *Scientific Social Surveys and Research* (3). These books and others cited in them should be used to supplement this text, to sharpen the analytical tools that the student must employ in studying social phenomena. Especially valuable for this purpose is Duncan, Cuzzort, and Duncan, *Statistical Geography* (4).

The survey contemplated here is the learner's research project. It is designed to bring about a confrontation between the theory and practice of local politics. It is assumed that the field work involved in the survey is going to be based on a great deal of reading, and that the project as a

whole may invite the reader to use books to help him reexamine the world of reality in which he lives.

A general survey of the community is probably the best point at which to begin. A general survey of the community forces the beginner to draw on all of the social sciences and to try to use a wide range of research techniques. It forces him to look at the community as a whole and to become aware of the relations of its parts to the whole.

STUDYING THE SOCIAL SCIENCES THROUGH THE LOCAL COMMUNITY

Some experience with amateur political surveys indicates that it is necessary to organize the surveys around some hypothesis in order to avoid the accumulation of great quantities of miscellaneous information. The proposition underlying the surveys suggested in this volume is that political attitudes are related to the circumstances in which voters live. This proposition is used as something to be investigated, not as an established dogma. It has the advantage of leading the student to relate some of the materials of demography, urban sociology, and urban land economics to local political statistics. It is hoped that the student may be able to get some insight into the relative political significance of the kinds of data with which he works.

WHAT IS A COMMUNITY SURVEY?

Not all surveys can be called community surveys in the sense in which we use the term. A public opinion poll is a survey. A factual inquiry into the collection and disposal of garbage and trash is a survey. Many surveys are made by professionally trained surveyors. Recently community "self-surveys" have been devised and made in a number of communities. See Wormser and Sellitz, *How to Conduct a Community Self-survey of Civil Rights* (5).

This book is an introduction to community political and governmental surveys; that is, it brings together in a single project two different kinds of surveys, a community survey and a political-governmental survey. It calls for an examination of the community as an economic enterprise and social structure in order to prepare the student

---

*The numbers within parentheses correspond to the numbered references at the conclusion of each chapter.

for a study of the political and governmental dynamics of the community. This procedure is based on the assumption that the social, economic, and political aspects of the life of the community are inseparable, and can be understood only when seen as parts of the whole. One of the objects of the survey is to help the student understand that data about occupations, employment, wages, housing, income, social stratification, segregation, and standards of living are filled with political implications.

A social survey is a necessary preliminary of a political survey because it sheds light on what people need, what politics is about, how people are likely to divide, how they are likely to line up in conflicts of opinion, how social status and politics are related, what kinds of services people want the city to provide for them, what their grievances are, who is liked and who is resented, why people work more easily with some kinds of people than they do with other kinds. These are the raw materials of politics.

It is necessary to investigate these materials (i.e., to get as much accurate and reliable information as possible and formulate it as understandably as possible) because things are not always what they seem.

A preliminary social survey is essential, in the second place, because the student is being asked to interpret the political data for his city, and one of the best ways to test his interpretations is to check them against his conception of the community as a going economic and social concern. Do people act politically the way one might expect them to act in view of the circumstances of their lives? The hypothesis that there is some kind of relation between the social status, income, economic condition, and associations of people and what they do about politics is something to be tested. It is not a proposition that has already been demonstrated so conclusively that a uniform and universal relation can be taken for granted. Whether the hypothesis stands up or not, it gives the student something to begin with in formulating his own interpretation of the political data for his city.

This hypothesis is therefore the initial focus for the studies suggested in this volume. One proposition that can be taken as axiomatic is that the community includes a great diversity of people. People differ as to status, income, origin, occupation, associations, way of living, education. The question is: Do these differences have any significant relation to the politics of the community?

Our concern is specialized in that we are interested in politics and government. We believe that politics and government should be studied in a social context. One such context that is almost universal in our society is the local community.

The community survey outlined here is designed to be a teaching tool. It is a way of learning and can therefore be used by the student or the adult citizen without formal instruction. We hope that the student will learn how to teach himself and that he will look upon his instructor as a partner in a joint study of his local community.

A community survey is a means of weaving together the insights of social, economic, and political research. The student will find many assertions, assumptions, and hypotheses in text books, monographs, and periodicals. The richness of his experience in making a community survey will depend in large part upon his ability to pick out the generalizations in the textbooks and adapt them into questions about his own community, questions that he can investigate for himself. The assumption made in these survey projects is that no student really knows what the textbooks have to say until he has tested the propositions laid down in them against his own observations in the community.

It is probably wise to begin your study of the community by making a general survey in order to get an over-all view. Thereafter more specialized studies may be made. Paradoxically, a general survey is probably easier to make than a more intensive survey. The purpose of this book is to get you started on a study that might conceivably be continued throughout your life, because no one will ever know everything about any one community. What the beginner needs first is a perspective on the whole community. The general survey is recommended here as an introduction to the subject, not as a substitute for the intensive, specialized, technical survey.

Because all people live in communities, all disciplines dealing with people have a bearing on the community. This is true of economics, sociology, history, political science, geography, public administration, law, statistics, demography—to say nothing of engineering, architecture, sanitation, etc. Nobody can master all of these disciplines, but the amateur student of the community should not hesitate to draw on all materials available to him; even if he makes some mistakes, he will learn in the process.

Almost anyone will get more out of living in a community and will be a more effective member of the community if he knows more about it. He will be a better businessman, citizen, politician, journalist, labor leader, teacher, lawyer, clergyman, or physician if he understands what is going on in the community in which he lives.

It is amazing how little most people know about the communities in which they live, even after many years of residence. They know the route to and from their place of work, where the post office is, where to shop, where places of amusement are to be found, and perhaps where the good and the bad residential areas are located. But that is nearly all they know about the town. Even a careful reading of local newspapers may reveal very little about the power structure or organization of the community, or about the tensions, conflicts, political alignments, and social cleavages in the population. It is obviously unintelligent to live in a community in this condition of innocence and ignorance.

Because it is possible to live in a town or a city for many years without ever having <u>seen</u> it, the questions must naturally arise: How do you learn to <u>see</u> the community that is all about you? What do you look for? Where can the information be found? Where do you begin? How do you interpret what you see?

The very best way to begin to see the world about you is <u>to read some good books about the community</u>, books dealing with the social sciences. A book is a way of seeing the world in which we live; every book is a voyage of exploration. Anybody who has read a good book about any aspect of the life of the community ought to be able to see something in the community that he was unable to see before he began to read.

One reason for the kind of intellectual blindness from which many people suffer is that they do not use books to the best advantage. <u>They do not use books to see something new; they do not follow through from their reading to discover for themselves the world of reality about them</u>. They are like someone who reads travel literature but never travels to see for himself the strange places he has read about. It is probably no exaggeration to say that the student who reads books but never insists on seeing things for himself has learned nothing. It is the divorce of reading from seeing that accounts for the blindness of people who live in communities but know nothing about them.

A local community survey is a wonderful learning device. Nowhere is the gap between reading and seeing crossed so easily. The raw materials surround us in tropical abundance. The community is therefore the best laboratory of the social sciences. We follow up some hard reading, by going out to take a hard look at one aspect of the community, turn to the books for further elucidation, then return to the community to test the bookish propositions. This alternation of reading, observation, testing, rereading, proving and probing is the process of learning to which this volume is devoted. It is very much like the relation between theory and practice in many disciplines.

Fortunately, the literature and the raw materials for testing in community studies are abundant.

This guide to local political surveys includes many alternative techniques and procedures for the study of the community. It is not supposed that anyone is going to use all of them. Many procedures are suggested because in communities where one kind of data is unavailable, it is necessary to substitute another kind of data or another procedure. This is apt to be true of census data which have not been compiled for many of the areas which students may want to survey. Students who get into difficulties because one kind of data is unavailable should try first one, then another, then still another of the alternatives listed in this text.

Above all, do not be so impressed by statistical materials that you are defeated if the statistics you want cannot be found. You can often make your own statistics. (Always remember that census enumerators are probably less inventive and skilled than you are; what they can do, you can probably do better.)

In the last analysis, statistics are only a somewhat stilted and artificial substitute for the things you can see for yourself. There is never an adequate substitute for what you can see with your own eyes, what you can learn by talking to people, or what you can smell with your own nose. A camera is a wonderful research tool; a picture of a house, a street, or a person may be as instructive as a graph or a table of statistics.

What has been said about statistics is equally true of maps. If there are no maps available, make your own. Your maps may be extremely useful, even if they are not as accurate as surveyor's maps; they do not have to be as accurate for most of your purposes.

The situations any student is likely to encounter are so diverse and so unpredictable that no set of instructions could provide a plan for all circumstances. Research is always a process of invention. Everyone gets along with what he can find and adapts his methods to the conditions with which he must cope. It is hoped that the suggestions made in this text will help the student devise his own methods and define his own objectives to suit his own needs.

Never regret the fact that it is possible to test a proposition several different ways. Your confidence in your results will be greatly increased if you can check one kind of data against another kind. As a rule, you ought to test all other data against your own personal observations and see if you can verify your conclusions by interviewing people who are in a position to know the facts.

HOW TO START A COURSE OF READING

It is first necessary to understand in a general way how an urban community is organized. This requires an initial familiarity with general texts in urban sociology, urban land economics, local government, local administration, and local politics. The beginner may choose one of several texts in each of these fields. We suggest the following books for the best over-all view of the American local community:

Anderson, W. A., and E. W. Weidner, *American City Government*. rev. ed. New York: Holt, Rinehart and Winston, Inc., 1950.

Queen, S. A., and D. B. Carpenter, *The American City*. New York: McGraw-Hill Book Company, Inc., 1953.

Ratcliff, R. U., *Urban Land Economics*. New York: McGraw-Hill Book Company, Inc., 1949.

In the second place, the student ought to read works on the special phase of community life that he plans to emphasize in his survey. If, for example, he is going to make a local political survey, he should first read the following books (as well as others suggested in the footnotes and bibliographies found in them):

Berelson, B., P. Lazarsfeld, and W. N. McPhee, *Voting*. Chicago: University of Chicago Press, 1954.

Key, V. O., Jr., *Politics, Parties, and Pressure Groups*. rev. ed. New York: Thomas Y. Crowell Company, 1953.

Lazarsfeld, P., B. Berelson, and H. Gaudet, *The People's Choice*. New York: Columbia University Press, 1944.

Schattschneider, E. E., *Party Government*. New York: Holt, Rinehart and Winston, Inc., 1942.

If, as another example, the student is especially interested in housing and urban redevelopment, he will already have acquired some background from Ratcliff. This should be supplemented by *The Future of Cities and Urban Redevelopment* (6) and *Urban Redevelopment: Problems and Practices* (7).

The Encyclopedia of the Social Sciences (8) is a good place to start when compiling a subject bibliography. This encyclopedia does not contain items published during recent years, but it does list many standard references. The essays are themselves good introductions to many phases of urban life.

The bibliographies at the end of each essay may be brought up to date by using the standard bibliographical aids. Other standard bibliographical aids are the *Readers' Guide to Periodical Literature*, the bulletins of the *Public Affairs Information Service*, the *International Index to Periodicals*, the *Education Index*, the *Industrial Arts Index*, and, of course, library card catalogs.

Each annual volume of the *Municipal Year Book* published by the International City Managers' Association, Chicago, lists selected standard references on public personnel, municipal finance, local government and administration, city planning, public welfare, public health, housing, public works, municipal utilities, public utilities regulations, fire protection, police, traffic, recreation, education, public libraries, municipal law, and the local judiciary. Other special bibliographies will be referred to in subsequent chapters of this text.

Although it emphasizes material on metropolitan communities, the student will find many general references to urban government and politics in Government Affairs Foundation, *Metropolitan Communities: A Bibliography* (9). A supplement covering material published 1955-1957 has been compiled by Jones, Hudson, and Johnston (10). Both volumes contain references to many items published by sociologists, demographers, and economists, as well as by writers on governmental functions and problems, governmental organization, and metropolitan politics. For a critical evaluation of works on local government see two articles published in the *American Political Science Review:* Daland, "Political Science and the Study of Urbanism" (11) and Herson, "The Lost World of Municipal Government" (12). See also Anderson's comments on the Herson article in the September issue, 1957, pp. 776-783.

The third step is to read some books on research methods and techniques in the social sciences. Examples of such books are those by Key, Goode, and Hatt, or Parten, Young, and Duncan cited elsewhere in this chapter. Students will need to refer to them frequently during their surveys, but they should become sufficiently familiar with them before they start their surveys to know when to use them. Other works in which the student will find methodological suggestions are classified in Junker, *Field Work: An Introduction to the Social Sciences* (13).

The fourth step is to read several published community surveys. Perhaps the best known of the American surveys are the two volumes about Muncie, Indiana, by the Lynds, *Middletown* (14) and *Middletown in Transition* (15). An extensive bibliography of English and American surveys will be found in Parten. See also Eaton and Harrison, *A Bibliography of Social Surveys* (16). Sociological studies of the community are critically reviewed and evaluated in Stein, *The Eclipse of Community: An Interpretation of American Studies* (17).

THE VALUE OF FIRST-HAND OBSERVATION

Before starting the systematic collection of data, it might be wise for the student to talk with one or two people who can give him a general view of the town. A good reporter on a local newspaper, a politician, an alert schoolteacher, a clergyman, or the secretary of a civic association may be willing to talk about the community, to describe what kind of community it is and how it got that way. It is important for the student to find out who knows most about the special aspects of the community that interest him and where he is likely to find secondary materials about the community.

It is assumed that the student will also make a personal reconnaissance of the community. The student must learn to use his own eyes, ears, and nose, as well as his own shoe leather in making a survey and the best time to begin is the day before yesterday.

A reconnaissance should be helpful in planning a survey. Some kind of plan is necessary before work on the survey is actually begun. Such a plan will undoubtedly be changed many times before the project is finished, but the surveyor will save himself and the people who help him many hours of unnecessary trouble and frustration if he defines his objectives and plans his procedures carefully.

The principal danger in making a community survey is that the surveyor will feel certain that he already knows the community. This is especially true of students who are surveying communities in which they have lived all their lives. The student will either fail to ask relevant questions or he will construct answers from inadequate evidence. As Goode and Hatt say in their *Methods in Social Research*:

What most of us feel is a kind of at-homeness with... close acquaintances, so that we fill in or ignore those facts or dimensions of the persons which are really unknown to us.

This danger, then, is one which the observer himself creates.

The consequences of this feeling of certainty are many but most of them can be grouped under one main heading: a temptation to ignore basic principles of research design. Since the observer feels so very certain about the area of experience he is investigating, he feels no need to check the overall design of proof. (18)

Read carefully Chapter 19, "Some Problems in Qualitative and Case Analysis," in Goode and Hatt. The remainder of this volume will bring to the attention of the student the many facets of his community that he might otherwise ignore or never see. This is not, however, a manual on social research methods. We must again emphasize, therefore, the importance of supplementing this text with training in the methods of analyzing political, economic, and other social data.

You ought to make up your mind to do a vast amount of shoe leather research. Start taking long walks to take a new look at the city. Make a point of seeing all that you can about all of the neighborhoods in the city. Note what kinds of people live in the various neighborhoods and where they work; note factories, places of business, etc. There is no substitute for this kind of basic research.

If you assume that people buy or rent the best kind of housing they can afford, you can get a fair impression of the conditions of life of the people of the city by making a kind of housing survey of your own. Even if census block statistics are available, they should be checked against your own observations. You can find out about congestion by noting the number of mailboxes at the front doors of dwellings (as evidence of the number of families living in them), or by observing the size of building lots (judged by distance between houses, distance from street), the age and condition of dwellings, and by a rough valuation of the properties. (A real estate dealer can help you in estimating property values. See the tax assessor.)

You can use the street lists in your city directory to find out which of the residents on any given street own the houses in which they live. A shortcut to locating the best residential areas in your city is to plot on a street map the addresses of the physicians listed in the yellow pages of your telephone book.

Before you get through with your survey you will need to make and use many maps. (See Chapter VI for possible sources of maps but keep your eyes open for other sources also.) You may be sure that somebody has maps of your town because it is impossible to run a local government, i.e., to build streets, lay sewers, water mains, assess real estate, keep land records, or adopt a zoning ordinance, without maps.

The people who make and use maps also know how to reproduce them. Get enough copies so that you can mark them up for your special purposes.

For some purposes a freehand sketch of a map will do. With a little practice you can learn to make your own. Begin by making a simple sketch showing the town as a transportation center. All cities and towns are transportation centers, places where people get together. Make a map showing where the principal railways, highways, buslines, waterways, etc. converge. Your sketch will give you one clue to the nature of the community.

After a physical reconnaissance of your city and before you are swamped with details, make a simple profile of the community. How do you divide the people of the community into categories? How do they make a living? Who works for whom? What kind of economic enterprise is the community? What is the makeup of the population? Can you relate your impressions to the map of the city?

You will revise your profile as you proceed with your survey, but this preliminary effort will help you keep your bearings.

REFERENCES

1. Key, V. O., Jr., *A Primer of Statistics for Political Scientists.* New York: McGraw-Hill Book Company, Inc., 1952.

2. Parten, M., *Surveys, Polls, and Samples: Practical Procedures*. New York: Harper & Brothers, 1950.

3. Young, P. V., *Scientific Social Surveys and Research*. Englewood Cliffs, N.J.: Prentice-Hall, Inc., 1949.

4. Duncan, O. D., R. P. Cuzzort, and B. Duncan, *Statistical Geography*. New York: The Free Press of Glencoe, Inc., 1961.

5. Wormser, M. H., and C. Sellitz, *How To Conduct a Community Self-survey of Civil Rights*. New York: Association Press, 1951.

6. Woodbury, C., ed., *The Future of Cities and Urban Redevelopment*. Chicago: University of Chicago Press, 1953.

7. Woodbury, C., ed., *Urban Redevelopment: Problems and Practices*. Chicago: University of Chicago Press, 1953.

8. Seligman, E. R. A., and A. Johnson, eds., *Encyclopedia of the Social Sciences*. New York: The Macmillan Company, 1930-35.

9. Government Affairs Foundation, *Metropolitan Communities: A Bibliography with Special Emphasis on Government and Politics*. Chicago: Public Administration Service, 1956.

10. Jones, V., B. Hudson, and L. D. Johnston, eds., *Metropolitan Communities: Supplement for 1955-57*. Chicago: Public Administration Service, 1960.

11. Daland, R. T., "Political Science and the Study of Urbanism," *American Political Science Review*, Vol. 51, June 1957, pp. 491-509.

12. Herson, L. J. R., Jr., "The Lost World of Municipal Government," *American Political Science Review*, Vol. 51, June 1957, pp. 330-45.

13. Junker, B. H., *Field Work: An Introduction to the Social Sciences*. Chicago: University of Chicago Press, 1960.

14. Lynd, R. S., and H. M. Lynd, *Middletown*. New York: Harcourt, Brace & World, Inc., 1929.

15. Lynd, R. S., and H. M. Lynd, *Middletown in Transition*. New York: Harcourt, Brace & World, Inc., 1937.

16. Eaton, A., and S. M. Harrison, *A Bibliography of Social Surveys*. New York: Russell Sage Foundation, 1930.

17. Stein, M. R., *The Eclipse of Community: An Interpretation of American Studies*. Princeton, N.J.: Princeton University Press, 1960.

18. Goode, W. J., and P. K. Hatt, *Methods in Social Research*. New York: McGraw-Hill Book Company, Inc., 1952.

THE ORGANIZATION AND FUNCTIONS OF LOCAL GOVERNMENT

The role of government in the community cannot be understood in isolation from the work of nongovernmental institutions and agencies operating in and beyond the community. Although this chapter deals with local government, subsequent chapters will introduce you to the nongovernmental as well as to the governmental aspects of community life. Government never exists in a vacuum.

Throughout the study of a local community, you should seek to identify social institutions and bear in mind that these institutions are likely to have an influence upon the government of the community. You should also be aware of the impact of government upon the economic and social life of the community. Government is one of the makers of our way of life. A major function of political leaders is to elicit a sense of community feeling about local problems. The community, if it exists at all, is apt to be a seamless web of interdependent social, economic, and political institutions. Keep all of them in mind.

Government is a logical point of departure for a community survey because the legal governmental structure is the most visible focus of interests in the community. Government is the most inclusive and powerful social institution; it has great resources, it concerns everyone, and it is the only institution that is able to meet certain basic needs of the community. Local government is one of the oldest organized attempts to deal with community problems. It has an enduring concern with maintaining peace and protecting persons and property. Many things are done by local governments because they are customary, but efforts are constantly being made to get the government to regulate some additional activity or to render new services. The role of government in the community is therefore nearly always a controversial subject; indeed, politics very commonly originates in controversies about this very point. It follows that governments are characteristically storm centers; they thrive on conflict; we never get through defining their functions.

In any event, decisions have to be made about the way in which the community uses its government. One way of judging the adequacy of any governmental system is to determine whether emerging problems in the community can be raised to the level of administrative or political issues. Another criterion is the ability of the government to act on pressing problems. The failure of local governments in metropolitan areas to meet these tests is one of the most serious problems of our times.

Every placid, noncontroversial local government should be regarded as something requiring a special explanation. Any active government, alive to the needs of the community, is very apt to be involved in controversy. In a way, your first problem is to determine whether or not your local government is alive or dead. Is it on top of its job and in the forefront of community enterprises or has it lost the initiative and leadership? Local governments differ greatly in morale and in the energy and initiative they display.

What kind of a going concern is your local government? One way to find out is to ask a number of people. Ask different kinds of people and try to get them to tell you why they think as they do. Do they expect the local authorities to take the initiative?

The organization of local communities for effective, popularly controlled government is part of the larger problem of the democratic organization of the nation. As Anderson and Weidner have said:

The long run success of local self-government in the great American cities remains an unsettled question. The theory of local self-government and of its supposed advantages was originally based upon the notion of the small community and the intimate, face-to-face contrasts that it made possible. The rural township and the small village satisfy the requirements well enough, but what about the great city? What about New York, Chicago, Los Angeles, or even Toledo, Indianapolis, or Seattle? In such places the ordinary voter cannot know intimately and pass judgment upon the actions of all his elected officials. He is caught up in large-scale government, in communities where mass movements and powerful pressure groups can conceivably elbow aside the "average citizen." Can local democracy succeed in such places?*

*W. Anderson and E. W. Weidner, *American City Government*. New York: Holt, Rinehart and Winston, 1950, p. 12. Important questions about local government finance and the effect of revenue measures upon the community are discussed in Chapter IX of this text.

The same question might be asked about township and small village governments. As to whether they "satisfy the requirements well enough," see (even if you are not making a survey of one) Lancaster, *Government in Rural America* (1). Vidich and Bensman, *Small Town in a Mass Society* (2). These books will open up the subject for you and help you become aware of the issues in small town politics.

If you are studying a suburb of one of the large cities, you may find it necessary to insist on asking these questions in the face of widespread conviction that none of the faults of the central city are to be found beyond its boundaries. Read Wood's *Suburbia: Its People and Their Politics* (3) for a sympathetic presentation of the widely held image of suburbia and a devastating analysis of its reality and of its promises and dangers. Whether you are surveying an independent city, a suburban community, or even a central city, read Wood's book carefully for propositions to be tested in your survey.

Sayre and Kaufman, *Governing New York City* (4) should also be read in the same manner and for the same purpose. The orientation and methods of the authors can be applied to the study of the local government of any community. The book is an excellent demonstration of the meaningful use of formal documents in studying formal institutions. Even though we realize that government is only one among many "governors" of a community and that much of the politics and administration in government is missed by a formalistic description, it is necessary to remember that the phenomenon we are studying is a formal institution. Sayre and Kaufman show how necessary it is to master constitutions, statutes, regulations, and official reports if we are to understand how governmental officials and their clienteles behave and operate.

The functions of government are so elastic that nothing about the role of government in the community can be taken for granted.

Each chapter in this text discusses government and politics or leads you to material that will help you understand government and politics. In this chapter, we are concerned with how one can find answers to the following questions:

1. What units of local government exist in the community?
2. What are their functions?
3. How are they organized?
4. What are the relationships between governmental units?

It should never be assumed that there is <u>one</u> government which is <u>the</u> government in any community. On the contrary, several different governments have jurisdiction over every community, and sometimes an examination will reveal the existence of a multitude of governments superimposed on each other in a very confusing pattern.

There are 155,000 local governments in the United States, but this does not mean that the United States is divided into 155,000 districts, each with one local government. Because local government jurisdictions overlap, everybody lives under several layers of local governments. In *Government and Housing in Metropolitan Areas* (5), Banfield and Grodzins, cite as an example of this kind of pattern the case of the residents of Park Forest, Illinois, who pay taxes to thirteen local governments. Illustrative of the pyramiding of governments in some local areas is the existence of no less than 1,071 local governments in the New York metropolitan area.

It is necessary to understand the whole system. You may find at the local level a jungle of cities, townships, communities, taxing districts, school districts, judicial districts, and hosts of other special purpose *(ad hoc)* jurisdictions. Authorities are often superimposed in a bewildering chaos of governments and districts. You cannot understand the problem if you do not see the whole complex.

As every survey worthy of the name is an attempt to combine two different kinds of knowledge, the information, analysis, and insights you can find in books and the data you can gather for yourself in the living community from your own observations—from everything you can hear, see, and smell—one of the best places to begin to work is in a library. The volume of published materials on local government is so great that it would be impossible for you to read more than a small part of it. Do not let yourself be defeated by the fact that you cannot read everything that has been published. The library materials have been so well indexed and classified that, with some help from the librarian, you can easily become an expert in finding the data you want. You will first want to investigate the scope of the library materials and, secondly, to find out how to get quickly the material you want. Because you will find it necessary to return to the library again and again, an initial effort to master the various indexes and reference works will be a good investment of your time.

GENERAL SOURCES OF INFORMATION

Consult the card catalog of your library to see whether you can find the following periodicals and books.

Three general periodicals should be consulted for articles about local government.

Public Management, published monthly by the International City Managers' Association, Chicago. (Fig. 2-1)

FIGURE 2—1

PUBLIC MANAGEMENT

JOURNAL OF THE INTERNATIONAL CITY MANAGERS' ASSOCIATION

JUNE · 1961

The Job of the City Manager

By JOHN M. PFIFFNER*
Professor of Public Administration, University of Southern California

*City managers must develop values and goals for their communities
based on research and intellectual analysis.*

THE city manager mov
as a reform device to m
conditions—corruption
agement. It brought into play
values which were often co
early reformers: (1) A high
civic conscience combined wit
a do-gooder complex. It is
many of the early reformers
thropic background. (2) A c
and productive efficiency as
the industrial sector of ou
slogan was to bring business
government.

What Cities Are Doing

To Revise Model Charter

A COMPLETE revision of the *Model City
Charter* has been undertaken by the National
Municipal League with completion scheduled for
late 1961 or early 1962. The work is being financed by contributions from a number of foun-
dations and organizations, including the International City Managers' Association. In addition,
a model state enabling act will be prepared. Legal
afting will be done by the Legis-
Research Fund of Columbia Uni-
iltation with the staffs of the Na-

increment, are withheld until the pro
been paid off. The funds for the Harl
Project and other pilot projects were a
from general city revenues. The retu
made possible the establishment of a re
ment revolving fund which, in turn, h
possible the financing of additional proj
federal grants.

Retirement Reserves Incre

Financial assets of state and local gov
employee-retirement systems rose by $2
during fiscal 1960. accor   to *Fi*

News of the Month

Polygraphs Aid in Choosing
Policemen and Firemen

POLYGRAPHIC tests have been used
since the first of the year in Evanston,
Illinois, as an aid in the final screening for
new policemen and firemen.

The polygraphs cost from $15 to $20 per
applicant and are administered by a private
consulting organization in Chicago. The
polygraphs are combined with psycho-
logical and psychiatric examinations to pro

City Hall Bookshelf

ANALYSIS OF CURFEW ORDINANCES IN MICHIGAN.
Michigan Municipal League, 205 South State
Street, Ann Arbor. 1961. 23pp. $2.

COMPUTER APPLICATIONS IN POLICE MANPOWER
DISTRIBUTION. By R. Dean Smith. Interna-
tional Association of Chiefs of Police, Mills
Building, Pennsylvania Avenue at 17 Street,

LEARNING MORE A
Irving S. Shapiro
Council of Health
257 Park Avenue
24pp. $1.

PLANNING AND THE
ON URBANISM AND

National Civic Review, (formerly the *National Munici-*
pal Review), published monthly by the National Municipal League, New York. (Fig. 2-2)
The American City, published monthly by the American
City Magazine Corporation, New York. (Fig. 2-3)

Take time to examine a number of issues of
each of these periodicals to familiarize yourself
with the coverage, the kinds of articles, news
notes, compilations of data that they publish. How
are they indexed? How can you use these periodicals to get information about specific questions of
municipal policy and administration?

Each of these periodicals contains news notes
about government in American cities and metropolitan areas. Each also carries longer articles
and bibliographies. The references listed in *Public Management*, ''Pick of the Month,'' are consolidated each year into the subject matter bibliographies of the *Municipal Year Book* (see below).
Familiarize yourself with these publications so
that you can quickly locate all useful materials
available. You can get an idea of the scope of any
of these publications by examining its table of
contents and by leafing through the pages. This
will give you an overview of the literature of the
subject.

The Municipal Year Book is a veritable gold
mine of information about municipal government.
Published annually by the International City Managers' Association, Chicago, it is an indispensable
source of information about what is happening in
local government throughout the country, including data about the organization and activities of
individual cities. Examine the following account
of the scope and content of the *Year Book* to see
if you can find ideas that may be useful to you in
making your survey.

The scope of *The Municipal Year Book* is described by the editors:

The chief purpose of *The Municipal Year Book*, now in
its twentieth year (1953) is to provide municipal officials with information on the current problems of cities
throughout the country, with facts and statistics on individual city activities, and with analyses of trends by
population groups. Many of the sections are brought up
to date and repeated year after year, and certain types
of material are published in one edition only. This plan
enables the *Year Book* to achieve continuity and balance
and also to introduce some new material each year....

Illustrative of the coverage of the *Year Book*
are the articles on city planning, special assessments, municipal hospitals, off-street parking,
and many similar subjects. It also contains information on subjects such as fire prevention inspection, mutual aid and fire protection outside
the city, box fire alarm systems, the use of
women in police and traffic work, practices in the
payment of policemen required to testify in court,
data about police departments making use of one-

man patrol cars, and nonproperty tax revenues.
These articles are filled with data useful to you
in planning your survey of your own community;
you can use this material to compare what is
done in your community with what is done elsewhere. At every point, these articles are likely
to suggest questions that you may be able to
bring up in your interviews with local officials
and leaders.

In addition to the foregoing, the *Year Book* contains up-to-date information about metropolitan
and fringe-area developments, the number of
governmental units in various areas, forms of
city government, the manner of selecting the
mayor and council, utilities owned and operated
by cities, salaries of chief municipal officials,
pay rates for certain city jobs, number of city
employees and payroll personnel organization,
working conditions, retirement systems, public
reporting systems, city planning organizations
and expenditures, financial statistics, fire and
police data, directories of city officials, and
model municipal ordinances. Do materials of this
sort suggest questions to ask about your own city?
Make up a list of questions for later use in your
survey.

Data concerning individual cities are presented
in twenty major tables, summarized and analyzed
in articles preceding the tabulations. These comprehensive summaries will enable you to compare your own city with other cities of approximately the same size. Locate the summaries of
these cities in the *Year Book* and look them over
to see what kinds of data are included. These kinds
of data give you wedges for opening up specific
inquiries in your community.

Sources of information are listed at the end of
each section. An explanation of these sources and
how they can be used is presented in the article
''How to Use the Year Book.'' The title page and
part of the table of contents of the 1953 *Year
Book* is reproduced as Figure 2-4.*

In preparing for your interviews, your biggest
difficulty is going to be finding good questions to
ask. Some strenuous reading in the sources listed
here will furnish you with ammunition to be used
as you develop your survey.

Look for references to your own city in the
Year Book. In this way you can learn how to use
the tables and compilations. If you spend some
time familiarizing yourself with the volume, you
can hardly avoid picking up ideas that will help
you with your survey. Look over the whole series
of volumes of the *Year Book* going back as far as
they are available. How has the *Year Book*
changed? Do changes in the *Year Book* reflect
changes in the scope, organization, interests, and
methods of local government?

---

*The foregoing is an abridged version of the state-
ment made by the editors of the *Municipal Year Book*.

News in Review

City, State and Nation   .   .   .

Council-Manager List Passes 1,800

Annual Rate of Growth Continues to Be Strong

THE International City Managers' Association announces it has added 76 communities to its council-manager directory list in 1961 and removed eighteen, for a net gain of 58. This gives a total of 1,814 places—cities, towns, villages and

creased to 4[...]
74 in the 1[...]
for the enti[...]
  In additi[...]
ager comm[...]
and Canad[...]
1,732 comm[...]
Ireland, N[...]
manager p[...]
of 3,546.
  The villa[...]
NESOTA, on[...]
proposal to[...]

Books in Review

Pressure Groups

PRESSURE GROUP POLITICS. The Case of the British Medical Association. By Harry Eckstein. Stanford University Press, Stanford, California, 1960. 168 pp. $3.75.

Concern over the role of pres[...] groups and lobbyists in the [...] process has grown in recent [...] the point where, in many [...] sentatives of such group[...] quired to register and [...] submit expense acco[...] Political scientis[...] directed more [...] study to t[...] starting [...] licati[...]

in [...]
soph[...]
theory [...]
solid case [...]
the British[...]
the socializati[...]
practice.

More important [...] justments of the grou[...]

for the exi[...]
and the sin[...]
tions, so [...]
by the [...]
of [...]
t[...]

The States' Concern

Advisory Commission recommends might help solve metropolitan

By ALLEN D. MANVEL*

IS IT not rather strange that most discussions of metropolitan area problems begin with a recital of the increase in metropolitan area population that has been taking place [...] seems in prospect for the [...] ades? Growth is som[...] ricans traditiona[...] welcomed [...] or ba[...]

NATIONAL CIVIC REVIEW

February 1962   Volume LI, No. 2

Published monthly except August by the National Municipal League

FIGURE 2-2

Second-class postage paid at Worcester, Massachusetts. Publication office, 35B New Street, Worcester 5; editorial and business office, Carl H. Pforzheimer Building, 47 East 68th Street, New York 21, N. Y. Copyright © 1962 by the National Municipal League. Subscription, $5 per year; Canadian, $5.25; foreign, $5.50; single copies 50 cents. The contents of the REVIEW are indexed in *Business Periodicals Index, Index to Legal Periodicals, International Index to Periodicals,* and *Public Affairs Information Service.*

Breaking the Barriers

Efficiency and economy demanding removal of legal bars to intergovernmental cooperation.

By FRANCIS BERGAN†

THE spin-off of population and business activity from the central areas of cities in nearly all sections of the United States in the last ten years has created an acute problem for both the city and the surrounding areas. It is a problem which the constitutional and legal drafts-[...] [...] attempt to solve to create

health co[...]
usually p[...]
same tim[...]
tion and [...]
cities wea[...]
to contin[...]
revenues.
  The p[...]
strengthe[...]

The Fight for Beauty

Los Angeles citizens prove elimination of eyesores good business, contagious example.

By ANDREW HAMILTON*

WORLD War II and the boom of the late 1940s changed Los Angeles into a sprawling industrial

come and go," he said. "I'll give yours just one year."

But Los Angeles Beautiful did not

FIGURE 2-3

These brief summaries are not a treatment of the problems. We hope to help some of them (?). (handwritten)

Trend Toward Regional Schools Noted in Suburban Areas

...IALS and com-
...be pleased
...tion

and often there will be substantial savings to the taxpayer.

Two notable recent school district centralization efforts occurred in Oc... in north Westchester County, ... and in north Bergen ...k, ...ersey. Both were well ...citizens' groups, ...promotional ...

Municipal & Civic Publications

Needed—New Municipal Revenues

By Simeon E. Leland. Published by The United States Conference of Mayors, 730 Jackson Place, Washington, D. C. 1953. 24 mimeo pp. $1.

A summary of this paper on Municipal Revenues, presented by Professor Leland at the 1953 Annual Conference of Mayors in Montreal, was published in the November 1953 issue of THE AMERICAN CITY (page 159). The paper should be studied in conjunction with the 1953 Report of the U. S. Conference of Mayors, on "Municipal and Intergovernmental Finance in the United States: 1932, 1942, 1952."

Climate and Architecture

By Jeffrey Ellis Aronin. Reinhold Publishing Corporation, 330 W. 42nd St., New York 36, N. Y. 1953. 304 pp. $12.50.

The limitations imposed upon man by the climate have always affected his choice of building design. In this book with its numerous tables and illustrations (including weather charts and graphs) the author presents the problems of sun, temperature, wind, rain, lightning, humidity, etc., and offers practical solutions for living with the elements.

How to pick a site, how to keep a dry basement, how to sleep comfortably on hot nights, how to plant trees for protection and beauty—such information is valuable not only to architects, but to homeowners, gardeners, real estate developers, planners, and city officials, as well.

The Cincinnati Area Must Solve Its Metropolitan Problems

By Doris D. Reed and Thomas H. Reed. ...hen H. Wilder Foundation, 921 ...Cincinnati 2, Ohio.

First Progress Report, Committee on Highway Laws

Department of Economics, Finance and Administration, Highway Research Board. Sec., David R. Levin, Chief, Land Studies Section, Financial and Administrative Research Branch, Bureau of Public Roads, U. S. Department of Commerce, Washington 25, D. C. 1953. 47 mimeo. pp.

The First Progress Report on the comprehensive study of the highway laws of the 48 states, now under way, was presented before the American Association of State Highway Officials, meeting in Pittsburgh on November 11, 1953. Modernization of state highway laws to meet today's engineering and financial needs is the Committee's objective.

Attitudes Toward Giving

By F. Emerson Andrews. Russell Sage Foundation, 505 Park Ave., New York 22, N. Y. 1953. 145 pp. $2.

In this new book on giving, the author of *Philanthropic Giving* and *Corporation Giving* studies the motives and attitudes of people making donations. The testimony is based on personal interviews and attempts no statistical measure. The book will be helpful to the fund raiser because it gives people's reactions to various approaches and techniques, as well as their reasons for giving.

Municipal Charter Revision In New Jersey

By Benjamin Baker. Published for the Bureau of Government Research, Rutgers University, by the Rutgers University Press, New Brunswick, N. J. 1953. 27 pp. 50 cents.

The first section of this study provides a brief summary of the Optional Municipal Charter Law of 1950. The second section offers a number of suggestions concerning the organization and functions of charter commissions, which should make the book... ...eful to municipal officials and mem... ...commissions.

Municipal Security Analysis and Bank Investment Problems

Special Bulletin 1953E—Published by the Municipal Finance Officers Association of the United States and Canada, 1313 East 60th St., Chicago 37, Ill. August 1953. 7 pp. 50 cents.

The bank investment problem and the related analytical techniques for judging municipal credit are considered from two angles: (1) to what extent state and local governments rely on commercial banks for credit requirements, and (2) How important the obligations of these governmental units are to the banks. This bulletin is based on a paper by Raymond E. Hengren.

The People's Right to Know

By Harold L. Cross. Columbia University Press, 2960 Broadway, New York 27, N. Y. 1953. 405 pp. $5.50.

Written by a well-known specialist in newspaper law, this book contains a good analysis of state and federal statutes, court decisions, attorney-general opinions, and official regulations that determine rights of public and press access to public records and proceedings.

Important appendices list cases in which newspapers were litigants in this field; set forth statutes defining "public records"; cite judicial decisions on the status of records for a variety of purposes other than inspection, and set forth statutes declaring general rights of inspection.

The book is written with the full understanding of the public's stake in open government. Of particular interest to munic... ...pal officials are four chapters on "Insp... ...tion of State and Municipal Non-Judic... Records." In this section there are se... ...rate chapters on records subject to pu... ...inspection, those not subject, "police rec... ords," and "newspapers as litigants," ...ords," and ...compulsory inspection."

Recreation Leadership

By Walter L. Stone and Char... Stone. The William-Frederick Pre... W. 35 St., New York, N. Y. 1952 $... ...te manual of program plann... ...velopment, and of ... ...the use

FIGURE 2–4

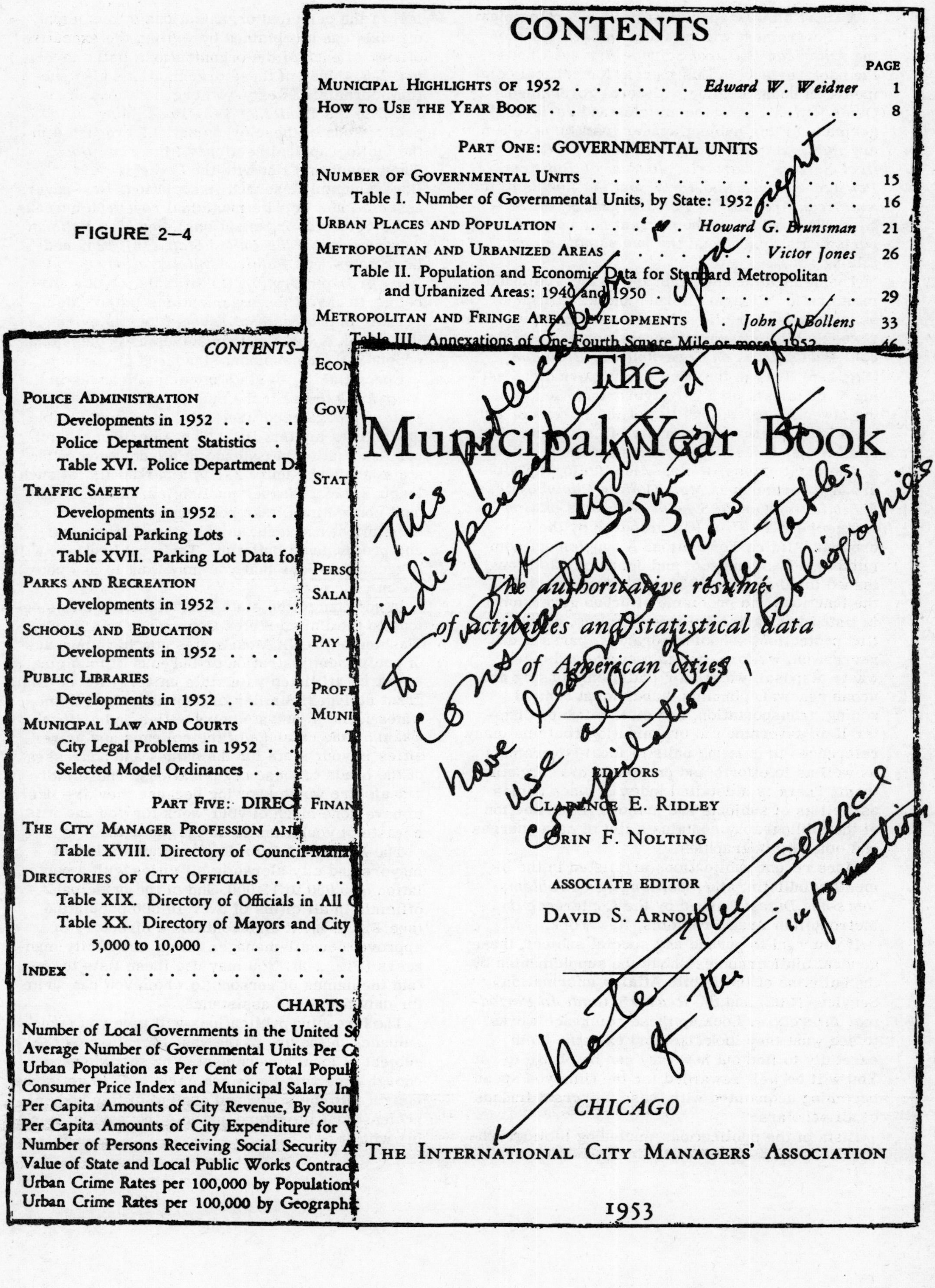

CONTENTS

PAGE

CONTENTS

The Municipal Year Book 1953

The authoritative résumé of activities and statistical data of American cities

EDITORS
Clarence E. Ridley
Orin F. Nolting

ASSOCIATE EDITOR
David S. Arnold

CHICAGO

The International City Managers' Association

1953

A short bibliography of works concerning municipal government will be found in each issue of the *American Political Science Review*. Check the book reviews in this journal for critical comments on books dealing with local government. Other journals in which articles and reviews germane to this subject appear from time to time are *Public Administration Review, Western Political Science Quarterly, Journal of Politics, Political Science Quarterly,* and *the Annals of the American Academy of Political and Social Science*. Take a look at the current numbers of these periodicals to see what the professionals are talking about.

The Joint Reference Library of the Public Administration Clearing House, and its affiliated associations of public officials, Chicago, publishes a weekly bibliography of accessions entitled *Recent Publications on Governmental Problems* (Fig. 2-5). This is the most useful periodical listing of materials on local government. See, also, the biweekly accessions list of the Bureau of Public Administration, University of California. Is a similar list issued from your state university?

The most extensive classified bibliography on urban government is *Metropolitan Communities: A Bibliography with Special Emphasis on Government and Politics* (6), prepared by the Government Affairs Foundation. A supplement compiled by Jones, Hudson, and Johnston has been issued for the years 1955-1957 (7). Material on the functions and problems of urban government is listed in Chapter I: finance, police, courts, fire protection, schools, libraries, parks and recreation, welfare, health, sewage and other waste disposal, water, air pollution, housing and urban renewal, planning, subdivision control, zoning, transportation, and civil defense. Chapter II on governmental organization contains many references to existing units of local government as well as to efforts and proposals to reorganize them. There is a detailed index of place names as well as of subjects and authors. Each section of the bibliography contains a list of data sources and other bibliographies.

More recent publications are listed in the bimonthly bulletin, *Metropolitan Area Problems: News and Digest,* issued by the Conference on Metropolitan Area Problems, New York.

If you want to pursue any special subject, these general bibliographies should be supplemented by the bulletins of the Public Affairs Information Service (PAIS) and the *Reader's Guide to Periodical Literature*. Look up these reference works to see what they look like, and examine them carefully to find out how they can be of use to you. You will be well rewarded for the time you spend becoming acquainted with these universal friends of all scholars.

Lists of the publications, including bibliographies, of the principal organizations of municipal officials can be obtained by writing the executive officer of each of the organizations listed in Figure 2-6. (Many of these organizations also publish journals.) Twenty-two organizations are listed in the *Municipal Year Book*. Many of the publications of these organizations are listed in the bibliographical sections of the *Year Book*. Supplement this list with the *Directory* of the Governmental Research Associations (tax-payers' associations, private municipal research bureaus, and other civic organizations). See also *National Associations of the United States* (8), 1949 and later dates, and *Public Administration Organizations, A Directory* (9). Do officials in your city belong to any of the organizations listed? Membership in professional associations is evidence that officials think of themselves as professional people with professional standards of conduct.

Check the list of state municipal leagues in the *Year Book* to see if the municipalities in your state are organized. (See the *Year Book's* Table of Contents for this list.) The American Municipal Association in Chicago is a federation of the state leagues; Figure 2-7 is a partial list of such leagues. Most leagues publish journals, hold annual conventions, take positions on proposed legislation, and issue informational, technical, and professional bulletins. Their publications will suggest questions that you may want to ask people in your town.

In addition to the state leagues, many cities belong to the United States Conference of Mayors, Washington, D.C.. Most states now have bureaus of public administration or bureaus of municipal research affiliated with state universities or land grant colleges. Similar organizations are sometimes found in private universities and colleges. Examine the catalogs of the colleges and universities in your state for the names and addresses of the heads of these organizations. These individuals are worth knowing because they are likely to have done much of your work for you and it is a waste of your time to do the job again.

The *Municipal Year Book* contains a list of mayors and city clerks in all cities with a population of 5,000 to 10,000, and of the principal officials in all cities of over 10,000 population (see Fig. 2-8). It also contains a directory of approved council-manager cities and of city managers (Fig. 2-9). You may use these lists to obtain the names of persons to whom you can write for data and other assistance.

The foregoing publications will give you some guidance in the use of the vast literature on the subject of local government. You should spend enough time with these scholarly aids to get some insight into the scope and content of this body of professional literature and into the ways of working with it.

RECENT PUBLICATIONS ON GOVERNMENTAL PROBLEMS

compiled weekly by the
Joint Reference Library
1313 E. 60th Street
Chicago 37, Illinois

SPONSORING ORGANIZATIONS: AMERICAN MUNICIPAL ASSOCIATION · AMERICAN PUBLIC WELFARE ASSOCIATION · AMERICAN PUBLIC WORKS ASSOCIATION
AMERICAN SOCIETY FOR PUBLIC ADMINISTRATION · AMERICAN SOCIETY OF PLANNING OFFICIALS · BUILDING OFFICIALS CONFERENCE OF AMERICA · COUNCIL OF STATE GOVERNMENTS
FEDERATION OF TAX ADMINISTRATORS · INTERNATIONAL ASSOCIATION OF ASSESSING OFFICERS · INTERNATIONAL CITY MANAGERS' ASSOCIATION · MUNICIPAL FINANCE OFFICERS ASSOCIATION
NATIONAL ASSOCIATION OF HOUSING AND REDEVELOPMENT OFFICIALS · PUBLIC PERSONNEL ASSOCIATION · PUBLIC ADMINISTRATION SERVICE

ISSUED BY: PUBLICATIONS DIVISION PUBLIC ADMINISTRATION SERVICE · ANNUAL SUBSCRIPTION $10.00 · SINGLE COPIES 25 CENTS

Volume 30, Number 18
FIGURE 2-5
May 1, 1961

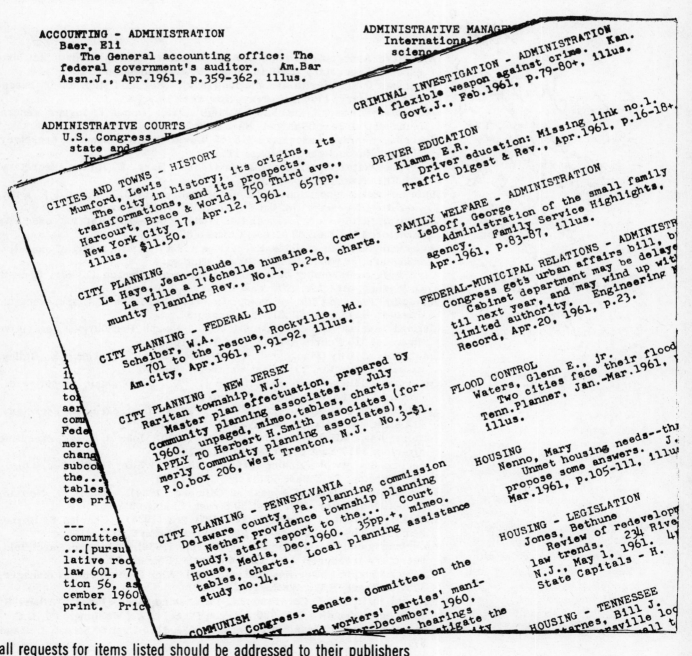

ACCOUNTING - ADMINISTRATION
Baer, Eli
 The General accounting office: The federal government's auditor. Am.Bar Assn.J., Apr.1961, p.359-362, illus.

ADMINISTRATIVE COURTS
U.S. Congress, H
 state and
 In

ADMINISTRATIVE MANAGE
 International
 science

CRIMINAL INVESTIGATION - ADMINISTRATION
 A flexible weapon against crime. Kan.
 Govt.J., Feb.1961, p.79-80+, illus.

DRIVER EDUCATION
 Klamm, E.R.
 Driver education: Missing link no.1.
 Traffic Digest & Rev., Apr.1961, p.16-18+.

FAMILY WELFARE - ADMINISTRATION
 LeBoff, George
 Administration of the small family
 agency. Family Service Highlights,
 Apr.1961, p.83-87, illus.

FEDERAL-MUNICIPAL RELATIONS - ADMINISTR
 Congress gets urban affairs bill, b
 Cabinet department may be delaye
 til next year, and may wind up wit
 limited authority. Engineering N
 Record, Apr.20, 1961, p.23.

CITIES AND TOWNS - HISTORY
 Mumford, Lewis
 The city in history; its origins, its
 transformations, and its prospects.
 Harcourt, Brace & World, 750 Third ave.,
 New York City 17, Apr.12, 1961. 657pp.
 illus. $11.50.

CITY PLANNING
 La Haye, Jean-Claude
 La ville a l'échelle humaine. Com-
 munity Planning Rev., No.1, p.2-8, charts.

CITY PLANNING - FEDERAL AID
 Scheiber, W.A.
 701 to the rescue, Rockville, Md.
 Am.City, Apr.1961, p.91-92, illus.

CITY PLANNING - NEW JERSEY
 Raritan township, N.J.
 Master plan effectuation, prepared by
 Community planning associates. July
 1960. unpaged, mimeo.tables, charts.
 APPLY TO Herbert H.Smith associates (for-
 merly Community planning associates),
 P.O.box 206, West Trenton, N.J. No.3-$1.

FLOOD CONTROL
 Waters, Glenn E., Jr.
 Two cities face their flood
 Tenn.Planner, Jan.-Mar.1961,
 illus.

HOUSING
 Nenno, Mary
 Unmet housing needs--th
 propose some answers. J.
 Mar.1961, p.105-111, illu

CITY PLANNING - PENNSYLVANIA
 Delaware county, Pa. Planning commission
 Nether Providence township planning
 study; staff report to the... Court
 House, Media, Dec.1960. 35pp.+, mimeo.
 tables, charts. Local planning assistance
 study no.14.

HOUSING - LEGISLATION
 Jones, Bethune
 Review of redevelop
 law trends. 234 Rive
 N.J., May 1, 1961. 4
 State Capitals - H.

i
l
lo
to
aer
com
Fede
merc
chang
subco
the...
tables
tee pri

--- ...
committee
...[pursu
lative re
law 601, 7
tion 56, as
cember 1960
print. Pric

COMMUNISM
 S. Congress. Senate. Committee on the
 workers' parties' mani-
 r-December, 1960,
 hearings
 atigate the

HOUSING - TENNESSEE
 arnes, Bill J.
 nsville lo

all requests for items listed should be addressed to their publishers

FIGURE 2—6

THE MUNICIPAL YEAR BOOK

Professional Organizations of Municipal Officials

TWENTY-TWO national organizations of chief municipal officials who generally are appointed are listed in this section. One of them is the American Society for Public Administration which cuts across

Each of these organizations is a potential source of information for you.

American Association of School Administrators (1865). Worth McClure, executive secretary, 1201 16 Street, N.W. Washington 6, D.C.

American Public Health Association (1872). Reginald M. Atwater, executive secretary, 1790 Broadway, New York 19.

International Association of Fire Chiefs (1873). James F. Jagger, general manager, 11 East 38 Street, New York 16.

American Library Association (1876). David H. Clift, executive secretary, 50 East Huron Street, Chicago 11.

American Water Works Association (1881). Harry E. Jordan, secretary, 521 Fifth Avenue, New York 18.

International Association of Chiefs of Police (1893). Edward J. Kelly, executive secretary, 1424 K Street, N.W., Washington 5, D.C.

American Public Works Association (1894). Donald F. Herrick, executive director, 1313 East 60 Street, Chicago 37.

American Institute of Park Executives (1898). Emile Mardfin, executive secretary, 30 North LaSalle Street, Chicago 2.

Civil Service Assembly of the United States and Canada (1906). Kenneth O. Warner, director, 1313 East 60 Street, Chicago 37.

Municipal Finance Officers Association (1906). Joseph F. Clark, executive director, 1313 East 60 Street, Chicago 37.

National Recreation Association (1906). Joseph Prendergast, executive director, 315 Fourth Avenue, New York 10.

International City Managers' Association (1914). Clarence E. Ridley, executive director, 1313 East 60 Street, Chicago 37.

American Public Welfare Association (1930). Loula Dunn, executive director, 1313 East 60 Street, Chicago 37.

Institute of Traffic Engineers (1930). Fred W. Hurd, executive secretary, 212 Strathcoma Hall, New Haven 11, Connecticut.

National Association of Housing Officials (1933). John B. Lange, executive director, 1313 East 60 Street, Chicago 37.

American Society of Planning Officials (1934). Walter H. Blucher, executive director, 1313 East 60 Street, Chicago 37.

National Association of Assessing Officers (1934). Albert W. Noonan, executive director, 1313 East 60 Street, Chicago 37.

National Institute of Municipal Law Officers (1934). Charles S. Rhyne, general counsel, 730 Jackson Place, Washington 6, D.C.

American Society for Public Administration (1939). Laverne Burchfield, secretary-treasurer, 1313 East 60 Street, Chicago 37.

American Public Power Association (1941). Alex Radin, general manager, 1757 K Street, N.W., Washington 6, D.C.

National Institute of Governmental Purchasing, Inc. (1944). Albert H. Hall, executive director, 730 Jackson Place, N.W., Washington 6, D.C.

National Institute of Municipal Clerks (1947), 1313 East 60 Street, Chicago 37.

FIGURE 2—7

124   *THE MUNICIPAL YEAR BOOK*

TABLE VI—STATE MUNICIPAL LEAGUES—Continued

State	Name of League and Headquarters Address	Secretary or Executive Director	Year of First Effort to Co-operate†	Year First Organized‡	Number of Member Cities
New York	New York State Conference of Mayors, 6 Elk St., Albany	Morgan Strong	1910	1910	306
North Carolina	North Carolina League of Municipalities, Raleigh Bldg., Raleigh	Mrs. Davetta Steed	1908	1922	316
North Dakota	League of North Dakota Municipalities, City Hall, Bismarck	Roberta C. Burr	1912	1927	247
Ohio	Ohio Municipal League, 55 East State St., Columbus	Allen E. Pritchard, Jr.	1912	1952	138
Oklahoma	Oklahoma Municipal League, 821 N.E. 25th St., Oklahoma City	David Fudge	1913	1913	112
Oregon	League of Oregon Cities, Johnson Hall, University of Oregon, Eugene	Herman Kehrli	1913	1933	199
Pennsylvania	Pennsylvania Municipal Authorities Association, 1717 Main St., Northampton	Claude C. Fogelman	. . . .	1943	86
	Pennsylvania State Association of Boroughs, Hanover	T. F. Chrostwaite	1900	1936	510
	League of Cities of the Third Class in Pennsylvania, 302 Municipal Bldg., Harrisburg	Walter Greenwood			47
South Carolina	Municipal Association of South Carolina, Old Library Bldg., University Campus, Columbia	James N. Caldwell	1936	1939	232
South Dakota	South Dakota Municipal League, Aberdeen	J. G. Barger	1925	1935	292
Tennessee	Tennessee Municipal League, 228 Capitol Blvd., Nashville	Herbert J. Bingham	1913	1940	198
Texas	League of Texas Municipalities, 108 East 19th St., Austin	E. E. McAdams	1913	1925	563
Utah	Utah Municipal League, Newhouse Hotel, Salt Lake City	Tom McCoy	1907	. . . .	184
Virginia	League of Virginia Municipalities, Travelers Bldg., Richmond	Harold I. Baumes	1905	1921	175
Washington	Association of Washington Cities, 250 Smith Hall, University of Washington, Seattle	Chester Biesen	1910	1910	217
West Virginia	West Virginia League of Municipalities, P.O. Box 3141, Charleston	Pat E. Maloney	1917	1935	102
Wisconsin	League of Wisconsin Municipalities, 30 East Johnson St., Madison	F. N. MacMillin	1898	1898	441
Wyoming	Wyoming Association of Municipalities, University of Wyoming, Laramie	John E. Swanson	. . . .	1952	12

† The date in this column refers in most instances to the beginning of a loosely knit organization of cities on a corporate basis for the purpose of presenting municipal problems before the legislature.

‡ This date is the year when an active service organization, as now known, was established.

§ Approximate date.

Note: According to the records of the American Municipal Association, there are 12 <u>active</u> leagues with an uninterrupted existence: California, Florida, Iowa, Kansas, Michigan, New Jersey, New York, Oklahoma, Pennsylvania, Texas, Virginia, and Wisconsin.

Does your state have a league? look it up.

TABLE XX

DIRECTORY OF MAYORS AND CITY CLERKS IN ALL CITIES OF 5,000 TO 10,000 JANUARY, 1953

Code for Mayor:
B—Burgess
C—Chairman of Council or Board
P—President of Council or Village President

Code for Clerk:
A—Auditor
R—Recorder
S—Secretary
M—City Manager

An asterisk (*) indicates council-manager city.
A dagger (†) indicates acting official.
Letter "t" indicates town and "tp" township.

City	Mayor and Date Term Expires	City Clerk	City	Mayor and Date Term Expires	City Clerk
ALABAMA—26					
Albertville	Floyd Brown 10-56		Prescott	Joe L. Allen 2-55	P. H. Miller
Alexander City	Joe H.		Tempe	Hugh E. Laird	E. M. Barbre
Andalusia	T. B. W		Winslow		
Athens	Elmer				
Atmore	H. H. D	J. M. Cochran			
Attalla	Charles				
Brewton	C. C. F				
Cullman	W. I. N				
Demopolis	N. B. P				
Enterprise	D. H. R				
Eufaula	M. E. E				
Fort Payne	W. H. H				
Greenville	John C.				
Guntersville	E. H. C				
Jasper*	George				
Lanett	Reid Ke				
Mountain Brook*	C. F. Z				
Opp	Ned Mo				
Ozark	Douglas				
Roanoke	K. L. H				
Russellville	Ed J. H				
Sylacauga	Felix E				
Tarrant City	Sam Mu				
Troy	E. J. He				
Tuscumbia	Frank H				
Tuskegee					
ARIZONA—9					
Douglas	H. W. B				
Flagstaff	E. K. Sc				
Glendale*	H. E. Sc				
Globe	Dan. L.				
Nogales	Harry G				

TABLE XIX

DIRECTORY OF CITY OFFICIALS IN ALL CITIES OVER 10,000: JANUARY, 1953

Code for City Clerk and Finance Officer:
A—Auditor
C—Controller
F—Fin. Dir. or Comr.
K—City Clerk
M—City Manager
N—Accountant
R—Recorder
S—Secretary
T—Treasurer

Code for Mayor:
B—Burgess
C—Chairman of Council
P—President or President of Council

Code for Director of Public Works:
E—City Engineer
M—City Manager
S—Supt. of Streets

An asterisk (*) indicates council-manager city, a dagger (†) indicates acting official, "t" town, "tp" township

City and 1950 Population (000 omitted)	Mayor and Date Term Expires	City Clerk	Chief Finance Officer	Director of Public Works	Fire Chief	Police Chief
ALABAMA—20						
Anniston 31	E. C. Lloyd 10-54	L. O. Treadway	L. O. Treadway K	James E. Standridge E	E. E. White	J. L. Peek
Auburn 13	G. H. Wright 9-53	W. Wilson Hill	W. Wilson Hill K	J. A. Baker S	W. E. Pollard	C. E. Ellis
Bessemer 28	Jap Bryant P 10-54	Mrs. Frances C. Jones	Mrs. Frances C. Jones K	R. N. Parsons	Leo B. Hill	Charles T. Mullen
Birmingham 326	W. Cooper Green	Mrs. Eunice S. Hewes	C. E. Armstrong A	J. D. Woods E	Hoyt M. Ayers	E. H. Brown†
Decatur 20	H. R. Summer	Joe Petty	Joe Petty E	J. Elliott	L. F. Elkins	J. B. Whitmire
Dothan 21	J. B. Davis	L. R. Driggers	L. R. Driggers A	C. H. Seele	Floyd Harris	Eddie D. Kelley
Fairfield 13	J. T. McLaughlin 9-56	William F. Pf	William F. P	J. T. Duncan		Lacey Alexander
Florence 24	E. F. Martin 9-54	S. B. Howard	S. B. Howard K	H. M. Hargett E	Donald White	Noah H. Danley
Gadsden 56	Roy L. Wallace 10-54	P. M. McCall	P. M. McCall S	W. R. Hooks E	C. E. Landers	C. Fay Boman
Homewood 16	E. Ray Acton 10-56	Ward Bracken	Ward Bracken K	R. E. Burks A	Edgar Knox	Eli L. Scott
Huntsville 16	R. B. Searcy 9-56	N. M. Payne	N. M. Payne F	R. L. Mann S		J. L. Carroll
Mobile 129	Charles A. Baumlauer	S. H. Hendrix	H. G. Ziegler C			D. E. McFadyen
Montgomery 107	W. A. Gayle 10-56	Silas D. Cater	H. L. Hughes C	O. L.	R. L.	G. J. Ruppenthal
Opelika 12	Forney Renfro P	W. F. Pearson	W. F. Pearson K	N. L. McCrary	G. A. Mitchell	Floyd H. Mann
Phenix City 23	(not reporting)					
Prichard 19	G. V. Dismukes 9-56	Mrs. B. H. Centanne	Mrs. B. H. Centanne K	E. I. Ladd E	W. E. Dickson	E. C. Anderson
Selma 23	Chris B. Heinz 9-56	C. C. Ward	C. C. Ward K	W. P. Phillips S	H. H. Berry	E. W. Mullen
Sheffield 13	C. L. Beard 10-53	E. S. Enoch	E. S. Enoch K	W. C. Tankersley	James E. Tyree	Bob Price
Talladega 13	J. Wallis Elliott 10-53	A. R. Decatur	A. R. Decatur K	H. A. Churchill S	Howard Lanier	R. D. Rutledge
Tuscaloosa 46	J. Hal McCall 10-53	Wallace F. Dalee	George F. Lamb A	A. C. Parker E	Earl Mathews	H. D. Billingsley
ARIZONA—3						
Mesa 17	George N. Goodman 6-54	George N. Goodman 6-54	Marston Richards K	Thomas J. Nesbitt E	Elgin W. McCarty	Gail A. Brimhall
Phoenix* 107	Hohen Foster 1-54	Ann Crawford†	John L. Williams F	K. K. King	George L. Simpson	Charles P. Thomas
Tucson* 45	Fred A. Emery 5-53	Carl M. Hilt	L. H. Wixson C	Neil B. Faunce	J. C. Sievert	Don J. Hays
ARKANSAS—12						
Blytheville 16	Dan A. Blodgett 1-54	W. I. Malin	W. I. Malin K	C. L. Alexander E	Roy Head	C. R. Graves
Camden 11	Walter H. Laney	F. P. Benson	F. P. Benson K	E. A. Rich E	D. M. Teague	G. B. Cole
El Dorado 23	A. C. Neel 1-54	George W. Jackson	George W. Jackson K	William E. McRae T	Fleie M. Methvin	Wm. E. Hickman
Fayetteville 17	Powell M. Rhea 12-53	J. W. McGehee	J. W. McGehee K	Harold Zick A	John E. Mahaffey E	Burl Skelton
Fort Smith 48	Jack Pace	Carl Atkins	Carl Atkins	R. W. Ferguson T	Jay Medlen	R. L. Rudd

FIGURE 2—8

International City Managers' Association, The Municipal Year Book, 1953.

City Manager Profession and Directory

A summary of city manager statistics for the year 1952 furnishes continuing evidence of a definite trend toward a professional career in municipal management.

Appointments. About one-half (49 per cent) of all city managers appointed in 1952 had been managers in other cities, administrative assistants to managers, or interns in council-manager cities. In 1939 less than one-fourth (23 per cent) of the total manager appointments came from these sources. In the decade 1940 to 1949 this figure was 34 per cent and in 1951 it was 55 per cent (see Table 1).

In 1952 more than four out of every five managers appointed were city managers in other cities, assistant city managers, or holding some other governmental position, mainly public works engineers, finance officers, city clerks, and other city department heads. Thirty-four managers (14 per cent) came from nongovernmental positions, the same per cent as the previous year.

With 86 per cent of all appointments going to men trained and experienced in public administration, it would appear that the work of the colleges and universities is really having its effect at the local government level. Out of 245 appointments in 1952, 204 came from governmental backgrounds, 33 from business and industry, one from the private engineering field, and seven unknown.

The trend of appointing managers from outside the city appears to continue. The figure was 71 per cent in 1952, as compared to 74 per cent in 1951. There seemed to be an upsurge in 1952 in the appointment of department heads and other key personnel to city manager positions during the year that had not been so evident in previous years. Since such appointments are, in the main, appointments from within the city and therefore counted as local appointments, it would account for the slight reduction in outside appointments as compared with local appointments.

One-half of the men entering the profession for the first time in 1952 were under 40 years of age. Twenty-one of them were under 29. The predominant (22 per cent) age was the 30-to-34-year age group. Five managers who accepted appointments for the first time were over 65.

Separations. A total of 123 city managers were separated from the service in 1952, representing a turnover of 11.1 per cent as compared to 11.7 per cent in 1951, 12.6 per cent in 1950, and 13.9 per cent in 1949. A classification of the separations follows: 9 died, 7 retired, 6 resigned because of ill health, 3 resigned to accept quasi-public positions, 8 entered governmental consulting work, 8 entered private business, 4 left for further military duty, 10 entered some other governmental position, and for 68 their

FIGURE 2—9   International Managers' Association, The Municipal Year Book, 1953.

TABLE XVIII

DIRECTORY OF APPROVED COUNCIL-MANAGER CITIES, AND CITY MANAGERS

1,131 CITIES AND 15 COUNTIES AS OF MARCH 1, 1953

This directory includes all cities, villages, boroughs, towns, townships, and counties in the United States and its possessions and in Canada that have the council-manager plan. The figure following the city indicates the number of city managers to date. In the column headed "Plan" the letter "E" indicates state optional enabling act adopted by vote of the people; "H" home rule charter drafted locally and adopted by the people; "O" ordinance adopted by the city council and not submitted to people; "Oh" ordinance (initiative or other) approved by voters in local referendum; "Oe" ordinance passed by council putting into effect the provisions of optional state law providing for council-manager plan without local referendum; "S" special charter passed by the legislature without local referendum; and "Sh" special charter passed by legislature and adopted by people in local referendum. After the manager's name (M) indicates Member and (AM) Associate Member of the International City Managers' Association; the figure indicates he has served more than one city. After name of city "pl" indicates plantation, "t" town, "tp" township, "vil" village.

City	Pop. 1950	Plan In Effect	Name of Manager	Year Appointed
ALABAMA—3				
Fairhope (1)	3,354	Oe	C. B. Niemeyer (M)	1949
Jasper (2)	8,589	Oe	James S. Freeman (AM)	1953
Mountain Brook (5)	8,359	Oe	Joseph J. Swenson (AM)	1952
ARIZONA—4				
Eloy (1)	3,580	O	R. C. Sartain	1952
Glendale (3)	8,179	O	E. B. Tucker (M)	1948
Phoenix (25)	106,818	H	Ray W. Wilson (M)	1950
Tucson (6)	45,454	H	D. P. Wolfer (M)3	1952
ARKANSAS—0				
CALIFORNIA—106				
Alameda (9)	64,430	H	Carl Froerer (M)	1948
Alhambra (11)	51,359	H	Edwin A. Ingham (M)3	1945
Anaheim (1)	17,267	O	Keith Murdoch (M)2	1950
Antioch (2)	11,051	Oh	Phil Milner (M)2	1949
Arcadia (1)	28,733	H	William Richards (M)3	1951
Auburn (1)	4,653	O	Willis Endicott	1949
Avalon (2)	1,506	O	Philip W. Storm (M)2	1952
Bakersfield (11)	34,540	H	C. Leland Gunn (M)2	1952
Berkeley (6)	113,805	H	John D. Phillips (M)	1923
Buena Park (1)	6,000	O	Arthur W. Brewer	1953
Burbank (4)	78,577	H	E. J. Friedrich (AM)	1927
Chico (4)	12,272	H	Robert O. Bailey (M)3	1923
Chula Vista (1)	21,578	H	Herbert V. Bryant (M)	1949
Claremont (2)	6,327	O	Kalman I. Dienes (AM)	1948
Compton (8)	55,645	O	Kenneth B. Douglass (M)	1925
Corona (2)	10,223	O	William J. Mount (AM)	1949
Coronado (9)	17,171	O	Glenn Wade	1920
Culver City (1)	19,720	O	M. Tellefson (AM)	1949
Delano (3)	8,717	Oh	Raymond F. O'Hara (M)	1946
Dixon (1)	1,714	O	(Vacancy)	1950
El Cajon (1)	8,653	O	Bernard J. Noden (M)2	1950
El Cerrito (2)	18,011	O	Kenneth H. Smith (AM)	1948
Escondido	6,544	O	Carl Reed	1948

Throughout the course of your survey, you will find it necessary to interpret a great variety of data about your local government and its activities. The best way to get a basis for the evaluation of these facts is to learn how to use the literature of the field. In this literature you will find discussions of problems very much like your own. The more you find out about the experience of other communities and other scholars, the better you are able to understand your own problems. It is not necessary to read everything in sight. You want to know where the information can be found quickly.

NUMBER AND TYPES OF LOCAL GOVERNMENTAL UNITS

Almost everyone in the United States lives under the jurisdiction of at least three governments: federal, state, and county (or its equivalent). Most people are also subject to the authority of a municipality (city, town or village), a township, one or more school districts, and one or more special districts.

An Inventory of Local Governments. One of the first things to do in making a community survey is to prepare an inventory of governments operating within your community. Put the national and state governments at the top of the list (see Fig. 2-10). There are three reasons for doing this: (a) All the activities of these governments have an impact on people living in local communities; (b) Many federal and state activities are carried on within communities; (c) Local governments are intimately affected by their relations with state and federal agencies. For several decades, the federal government and state governments have become increasingly involved in local affairs—particularly in large metropolitan areas. This involvement has reached the point where several states have either created departments or commissions on local government (Minnesota, New York, Wisconsin), or are considering such a step (California). The Advisory Commission on Intergovernmental Affairs was created by Congress in 1959; it is likely that during the coming decade some form of cabinet status will be given to some of the federal agencies operating in urban areas. For background information and some recommendations of this subject see Bollens, *The States and the Metropolitan Problem* (10) and Connery and Leach, *The Federal Government and Metropolitan Areas* (11). Other references will be found in *Metropolitan Communities: A Bibliography*, pp. 244-249, and in the Supplement for 1955-1957, pp. 118-123.

The state is the creator of local governments, the source of local government powers, and the parent and custodian of all local authorities. You need to know how the state exercises its power over local governments and what the local government policy of your state is. It is necessary to have clearly in mind the total governmental organization of the community, a structure within which the state plays a key role.

Many activities of both state and federal governments are carried on within local communities—frequently concurrently with those of local governments. See the latest *United States Government Organization Manual*, issued annually. (Sample pages from the 1951-1952 *Manual* are reproduced in Fig. 2-11), and reports of the state governments for descriptions of such programs and for leads for further investigation. Figure 2-12 illustrates the type of information to be obtained from the reports of the state of Connecticut.

Having made an inventory of governments operating within your community, your next step will be to identify the local government unit which has jurisdiction over the largest area. This will probably be a county, although in some metropolitan areas it may be a large special district. In some states, the next unit to be listed is the township (in New England, the town) or municipality. Now make a list of special districts, i.e., local authorities having specialized functions such as school districts, sanitary districts, tax districts, water districts, etc.

The inventory should cover all units of local government in the area. In some instances it may be impossible to list all local authorities. There are, for example, over 1,000 units of government in the New York-Northeastern New Jersey metropolitan area and over 500 each in the Chicago, Pittsburgh, and Philadelphia metropolitan areas. See U.S. Bureau of the Census, *Local Government in Metropolitan Areas* (1957). Usually, however, the number of these authorities is not so large.

At the very least, all governments operating in the county in which your community is located should be listed in the inventory.

Several reports of the 1957 *Census of Governments*, compiled by the U.S. Bureau of the Census, will be helpful. Although the data for each state have been published in state bulletins (see Figs. 2-13 and 2-14 for examples taken from the California bulletin), you should examine four bulletins in Vol. I of the 1957 *Census of Governments* on governmental organization:

No. 1. "Governments in the United States"
No. 2. "Local Governments in Standard Metropolitan Areas"
No. 3. "Local Government Structure" (for description of the various types of local government in each state and territory)
No. 4. "Elective Offices of State and Local Governments"

It will be very much worth your while to examine one or two of the standard textbooks on

Table 11.—NUMBER OF GOVERNMENTAL UNITS, BY TYPE AND BY COUNTY AREA: 1952—Continued

(handwritten across top: "This is a sample page to compare the year book census data to other state municipal ... other school ... chart")

State and county (or county-type) area	Total (including State and county governments)	Municipalities	Townships[1]	School districts	Special districts	Exhibit: Intercounty units[3] Municipalities	Special districts
TEXAS—Continued							
Kent	7	1					2
Kerr	11	1					2
Kimble	5	1					
King							
Kinney	2						
Kleberg							
Knox	2						
Lamar	21	3		14	3		3
Lamb	15	5					
Lampasas							
La Salle	11						
Lavaca							
Lee							
Leon	18						
Liberty	22						
Limestone	29						
Lipscomb	12						
Live Oak	6						
Llano	4						
Loving	3						
Lubbock	17						
Lynn	11						
McCulloch	9						
McLennan	33	7					
McMullen	3						
Madison	13			3			
Marion	10	1					
Martin	10	1					
Mason	4	1					
Matagorda	18	3					
Maverick	10	1					
Medina	17	3					
Menard	4	1					
Midland	4	1					
Milam	33	3					
Mills	7	2					
Mitchell	8	2					
Montague	19	3					
Montgomery	12	2					
Moore	9	2					
Morris	10	3					
Motley	9	2					
Nacogdoches	31	3					
Navarro	30	5					
Newton	9	1					
Nolan	10	2					
Nueces	32	6					
Ochiltree	5	1					
Oldham	7	1					
Orange	15	1					
Palo Pinto	20	5					
Panola	13	2					
Parker	20	1					
Parmer	9	3					
Pecos	11	2					
Polk	16	2					
Potter	7	1					
Presidio	10	1					
Rains	12	1					
Randall	5	1					

See footnotes at end of table.

State and county (or county-type) area	Total (including State and county governments)	Municipalities	Townships[1]	School districts[2]	Special districts	Exhibit: Intercounty units[3] Municipalities	Special districts
TEXAS—Continued							
Reagan							1
Real							
Red River	51	25					1
Reeves	11				5	1	1
Refugio	10	3					
Roberts	4						2
Robertson	20	3		18			1 2
Rockwall	3						1 2
Runnels	14	3		3	2		1
Rusk	30						

Number of Governmental Units*

THE total number of governmental units in the United States in 1952 was 116,839, as compared with a total of 155,116 in 1942, according to the United States Bureau of the Census. Local school districts numbering 67,442, made up three-fifths of the 1952 total. In addition to the federal government and the 48 state governments, there were 49,348 local governments other than school districts (see Table 1). The average number of governmental units per state was 2,434, but Rhode Island had only 89 while Minnesota had 9,026. Nebraska was next with 7,981 and Illinois third with 7,723 units. Seven other states with more than 5,000 local governmental units were Kansas, Wisconsin, Missouri, Michigan, Iowa, New York and Pennsylvania (see Table I). These 10 states which had over 5,000 governmental units each accounted for more than one-half of the total number of governmental units in the nation. Nine of the 10 have numerous towns or township governments and all have large numbers of school districts.

TABLE 1

TYPES OF GOVERNMENTAL UNITS IN THE UNITED STATES: 1942 AND 1952

Type of Government	Number of Units 1952	1942	Per Cent Change
U. S. Government	1	1	0.0
States	48	48	0.0
Counties	3,049	3,050	(¹)
Municipalities	16,778	16,220	3.4
Townships	17,202	18,919	-9.1
School districts	67,442	108,579	-37.9
Special districts	12,319	8,299	48.4
Total	116,839	155,116	-24.7

[1] Less than .05 per cent.

The number of governments has declined 25 per cent since 1942. The most striking change was the elimination of 41,137 school districts—a re[duction]... (see Table 1). The number of townships decreased ... of special districts, on the other hand, in[creased] ... r during the 10-year period and the number ... per cent.

FIGURE 2—10

International City Managers' Association, The Municipal Year Book, 1953.

... entitled Governments in the United States in 1952 ... ureau of the Census, Governments Division (Allen D. ... pervised by Mrs. Gertrude Whitehouse under the direction of Robert F. Drury, Assistant Chief of the Division. For a more detailed discussion of trends in local government units, see William Anderson, Units of Government in the United States: An Enumeration and Analysis (Chicago: Public Administration Service 1949. 50 pp.

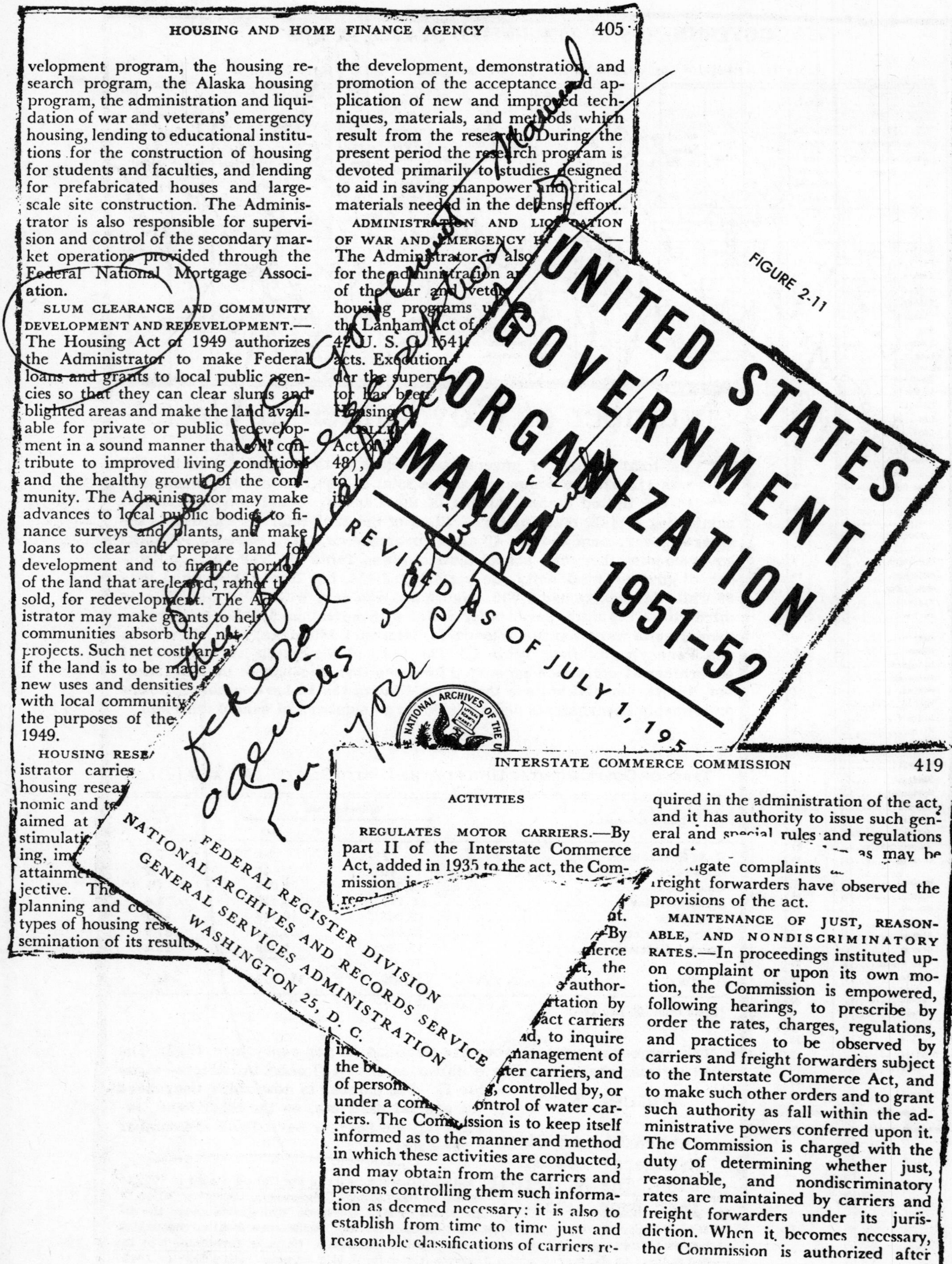

velopment program, the housing research program, the Alaska housing program, the administration and liquidation of war and veterans' emergency housing, lending to educational institutions for the construction of housing for students and faculties, and lending for prefabricated houses and large-scale site construction. The Administrator is also responsible for supervision and control of the secondary market operations provided through the Federal National Mortgage Association.

SLUM CLEARANCE AND COMMUNITY DEVELOPMENT AND REDEVELOPMENT.—The Housing Act of 1949 authorizes the Administrator to make Federal loans and grants to local public agencies so that they can clear slums and blighted areas and make the land available for private or public redevelopment in a sound manner that will contribute to improved living conditions and the healthy growth of the community. The Administrator may make advances to local public bodies to finance surveys and plants, and make loans to clear and prepare land for development and to finance portions of the land that are leased, rather than sold, for redevelopment. The Administrator may make grants to help communities absorb the net projects. Such net cost may be if the land is to be made new uses and densities with local community the purposes of the 1949.

HOUSING RESE istrator carries housing resea nomic and te aimed at stimulatic ing, im attainme jective. The planning and co types of housing res semination of its result

the development, demonstration, and promotion of the acceptance and application of new and improved techniques, materials, and methods which result from the research. During the present period the research program is devoted primarily to studies designed to aid in saving manpower and critical materials needed in the defense effort.

ADMINISTRATION AND LIQUIDATION OF WAR AND EMERGENCY H The Administrator is also for the administration a of the war and vete housing programs u the Lanham Act of 42 U. S. C. 1541 acts. Execution der the supery tor has bee Housing Cl

Act
48),
to l
it

ACTIVITIES

REGULATES MOTOR CARRIERS.—By part II of the Interstate Commerce Act, added in 1935 to the act, the Commission is regu

By
erce
t, the
authori-
tation by
act carriers
d, to inquire
management of
er carriers, and
, controlled by, or
under a com ontrol of water carriers. The Commission is to keep itself informed as to the manner and method in which these activities are conducted, and may obtain from the carriers and persons controlling them such information as deemed necessary; it is also to establish from time to time just and reasonable classifications of carriers re-

quired in the administration of the act, and it has authority to issue such general and special rules and regulations and as may be ugate complaints freight forwarders have observed the provisions of the act.

MAINTENANCE OF JUST, REASONABLE, AND NONDISCRIMINATORY RATES.—In proceedings instituted upon complaint or upon its own motion, the Commission is empowered, following hearings, to prescribe by order the rates, charges, regulations, and practices to be observed by carriers and freight forwarders subject to the Interstate Commerce Act, and to make such other orders and to grant such authority as fall within the administrative powers conferred upon it. The Commission is charged with the duty of determining whether just, reasonable, and nondiscriminatory rates are maintained by carriers and freight forwarders under its jurisdiction. When it becomes necessary, the Commission is authorized after

FIGURE 2-11

UNITED STATES GOVERNMENT ORGANIZATION MANUAL 1951-52

REVISED AS OF JULY 1, 195

NATIONAL REGISTER DIVISION
NATIONAL ARCHIVES AND RECORDS SERVICE
GENERAL SERVICES ADMINISTRATION
WASHINGTON 25, D. C.

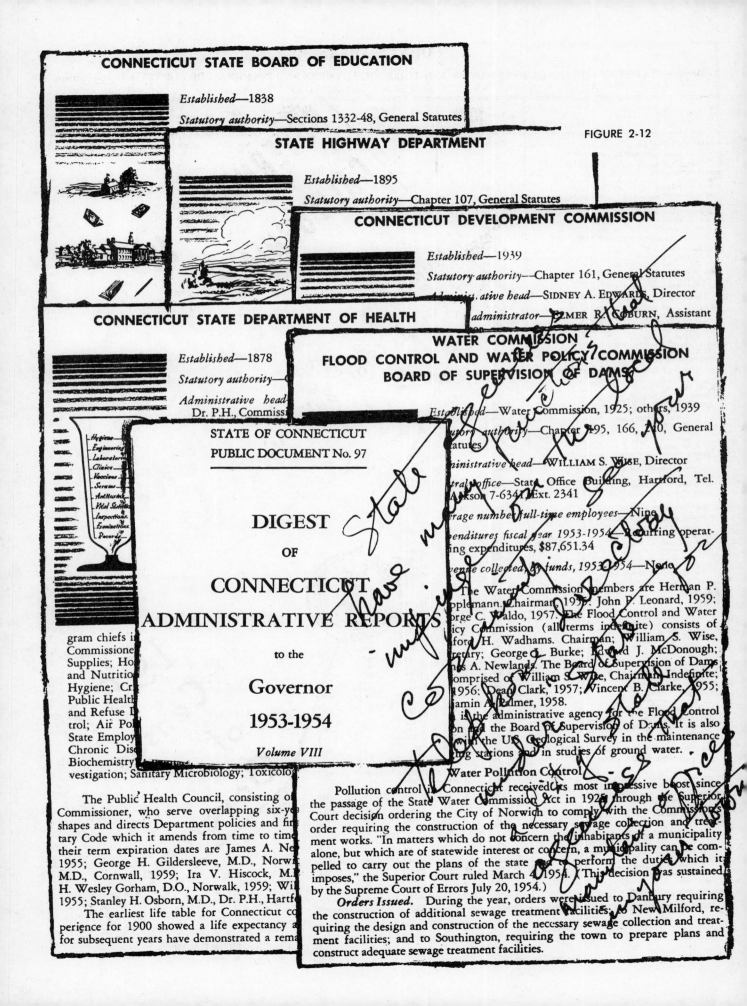

FIGURE 2-12

CONNECTICUT STATE BOARD OF EDUCATION

Established—1838

Statutory authority—Sections 1332-48, General Statutes

STATE HIGHWAY DEPARTMENT

Established—1895

Statutory authority—Chapter 107, General Statutes

CONNECTICUT DEVELOPMENT COMMISSION

Established—1939

Statutory authority—Chapter 161, General Statutes

Administrative head—SIDNEY A. EDWARDS, Director

administrator—ELMER R. COBURN, Assistant

CONNECTICUT STATE DEPARTMENT OF HEALTH

Established—1878

Statutory authority—

Administrative head—
Dr. P.H., Commiss

Hygiene
Engineering
Laboratories
Clinics
Vaccines
Serums
AntiNoxtal
Vital Statistics
Inspections
Examinations
Records

WATER COMMISSION
FLOOD CONTROL AND WATER POLICY COMMISSION
BOARD OF SUPERVISION OF DAMS

Established—Water Commission, 1925; others, 1939

Statutory authority—Chapter 195, 166, 210, General Statutes

Administrative head—WILLIAM S. WISE, Director

Central office—State Office Building, Hartford, Tel. JAckson 7-6341, Ext. 2341

Average number full-time employees—Nine

Expenditures fiscal year 1953-1954—Recurring operating expenditures, $87,651.34

Revenue collected, all funds, 1953-1954—None

The Water Commission members are Herman P. Copplemann, Chairman, 1955; John P. Leonard, 1959; George C. Waldo, 1957. The Flood Control and Water Policy Commission (all terms indefinite) consists of Clifford H. Wadhams, Chairman; William S. Wise, Secretary; George C. Burke; Edward J. McDonough; James A. Newlands. The Board of Supervision of Dams is comprised of William S. Wise, Chairman, Indefinite; ___ 1956; Dean Clark, 1957; Vincent B. Clarke, 1955; Benjamin A. Palmer, 1958.

___ is the administrative agency for the Flood Control ___ and the Board of Supervision of Dams. It is also ___ with the US Geological Survey in the maintenance ___ gaging stations and in studies of ground water.

___ Water Pollution Control

Pollution control in Connecticut received its most impressive boost since the passage of the State Water Commission Act in 1925 through the Superior Court decision ordering the City of Norwich to comply with the Commission's order requiring the construction of the necessary sewage collection and treatment works. "In matters which do not concern the inhabitants of a municipality alone, but which are of statewide interest or concern, a municipality can be compelled to carry out the plans of the state and to perform the duties which it imposes," the Superior Court ruled March 4, 1954. (This decision was sustained by the Supreme Court of Errors July 20, 1954.)

Orders Issued. During the year, orders were issued to Danbury requiring the construction of additional sewage treatment facilities; to New Milford, requiring the design and construction of the necessary sewage collection and treatment facilities; and to Southington, requiring the town to prepare plans and construct adequate sewage treatment facilities.

STATE OF CONNECTICUT
PUBLIC DOCUMENT No. 97

DIGEST

OF

CONNECTICUT

ADMINISTRATIVE REPORTS

to the

Governor

1953-1954

Volume VIII

gram chiefs in ___
Commissioner ___
Supplies; Ho ___
and Nutrition ___
Hygiene; Cr ___
Public Health ___
and Refuse D ___
trol; Air Po ___
State Employ ___
Chronic Dise ___
Biochemistry ___
vestigation; Sanitary Microbiology; Toxicolo

The Public Health Council, consisting of ___
Commissioner, who serve overlapping six-ye ___
shapes and directs Department policies and fi ___
tary Code which it amends from time to time ___
their term expiration dates are James A. Ne ___
1955; George H. Gildersleeve, M.D., Norwi ___
M.D., Cornwall, 1959; Ira V. Hiscock, M. ___
H. Wesley Gorham, D.O., Norwalk, 1959; Wi ___
1955; Stanley H. Osborn, M.D., Dr. P.H., Hartf ___

The earliest life table for Connecticut co ___
perience for 1900 showed a life expectancy a ___
for subsequent years have demonstrated a rema ___

Table 36.—STATISTICS ON LOCAL GOVERNMENTS AND THEIR EMPLOYMENT AND FINANCES, FOR COUNTY AREAS—Continued

(Dollar amounts in thousands)

Item	San Diego	San Francisco	San Joaquin	San Luis Obispo	San...	...ta	Santa Clara	Santa Cruz	Shasta	Sierra	Siskiyou
Population, 1950	556,808	775,357	200,750	51,		20,547		66,534	36,413	2,410	30,733
LOCAL GOVERNMENTS, JANUARY 1957											
Total (including county government)	117	8	138					52	72	13	74
Municipalities	10	1	5					3	1	1	8
Townships	...	...	...					...	...	...	...
School districts	52	1						19	43	1	42
Special districts	54	6						29	27	10	23
Exhibit: Other public school systems[1]	...	...						...	...	...	...
Exhibit: Intercounty units:											
Municipalities	...	...						...	...	...	...
Special districts	2							2	...	...	...
LOCAL GOVERNMENT EMPLOYMENT, APRIL 1957											
Employees, total	20,379									156	1,357
Full-time employees	17,955									115	1,051
Full-time teachers only	6,070									37	372
April payrolls	7,935.3									41.0	329.2
For full-time employees	7,414.7									38.2	313.2
For full-time teachers only	3,057.5									19.9	141.9
ASSESSED VALUE OF TAXABLE PROPERTY, 1956											
Subject to local general property tax, total	978,089								5,221		53,429
State-assessed	118,518								1,186		15,885
Locally assessed	859,571								,035		37,544
Real property	726,260	90							167		28,659
Personal property	133,311	25							868		8,885
Locally assessed values exempt from tax:											
Real property	42,903	20,							102		1,300
Personal property	7,876	5,7							27		403
REVENUE, FISCAL 1957 (Net of interlocal)											
Total	183,423	230,870									9,153
General revenue	165,644	176,851									8,960
Taxes	76,173	106,011									3,189
Property tax	63,954	92,958									3,110
County government	20,731	...									1,459
Municipalities	12,664	67,390									242
Townships	...	...									...
School districts	27,564	25,400									1,268
Special districts	2,994	168	2,								140
Other taxes	12,218	13,053	3,								79
Intergovernmental revenue	62,364	47,989	19,9								4,981
From State only	54,024	46,429	19,6								4,980
Charges and miscellaneous general revenue	27,106	22,850	9,92								789
Utility revenue	14,290	36,243	1,289								193
Water supply systems	13,867	15,933	444								193
Other utilities	422	20,310	845								...
Employee-retirement revenue	3,488	17,776	807								...
EXPENDITURE, FISCAL 1957 (Net of interlocal)											
Total	186,539	208,444	70,965								8,907
By character:											
Intergovernmental to State	176	...	88								9
Direct expenditure	186,362	208,444	70,876	15							8,897
Interest	3,995	6,342	1,806								50
Other current expenditure	139,347	175,710	47,207								7,692
Capital outlay	43,019	26,390	21,862								1,154
Exhibit: Expenditure for personal services	87,874	110,445	27,417								3,838
By function:											
General expenditure	169,221	164,039	69,738								8,676
Education	71,031	46,160	21,907								3,421
Highways	12,152	7,838	3,787								1,901
Public welfare	18,509	25,423	8,281								1,102
Hospitals	6,510	8,866	4,359								755
Health	1,539	3,519	873	210							9
Police	7,514	12,977	1,949	469							261
Fire protection	14,206	12,886	1,660	257	2,						53
Natural resources	5,214	...	10,076	381							194
Sewers and sewage disposal	4,269	3,516	1,381	307	1,4						42
Other sanitation	2,136	1,891	415	15	57						24
Parks and recreation	5,775	9,944	963	388	1,318						36
General control	7,764	7,681	1,947	806	3,518						397
Interest on general debt	2,535	3,977	1,803	165	1,452						32
Other general expenditure	20,060	19,360	10,330	1,214	4,922						443
Utility expenditure	15,078	30,500	833	695	3,070						231
Water supply systems	14,784	9,914	401	695	3,070						228
Other utilities	293	20,586	431	...	...						2
Employee-retirement expenditure	3,239	13,904	393	...	299						...
CAPITAL OUTLAY, FISCAL 1957											
Total[2]	43,019	26,390	21,862	2,127	17,730						1,154
Education	15,993	4,660	6,027	413	11,272	2,					732
Highways	7,131	3,035	1,477	414	2,127	30					69
Hospitals	138	727	113	19	637	55					144
Sewers and sewage disposal	2,425	1,779	1,027	195	801	774					7
Natural resources	3,338	...	8,052	158	106	26					20
Water supply systems	5,512	3,551	186	333	618	685					92
Other utilities	46	510	...	...	...	1,1					...
INDEBTEDNESS AND FINANCIAL ASSETS, END OF FISCAL 1957											
Debt outstanding	158,470	251,624	67,701	7,750	68,314	19,826	109,058				4,198
Long-term	158,048	247,071	63,830	7,699	68,073	19,699	109,058	10			4,181
Full-faith and credit	149,243	184,355	33,465	6,638	62,778	17,499	101,321	9,			4,113
Nonguaranteed	8,805	62,716	30,365	1,061	5,295	2,200	7,737	824			67
Short-term	421	4,553	3,870	51	241	127	...				16
Cash and security holdings	117,566	308,677	70,617	5,595	47,456	20,935	50,410	10,348			3,925

[1]School systems not classed as separate school districts.   [2]Including amounts for functional categories not shown separately.

FIGURE 2-13

municipal government. Since these volumes are likely to be encyclopedic, use them as you would use an encyclopedia: to find out what you need to know. With a little practice you can become skillful in the use of the index, the table of contents, the bibliographies, tables of statistics, and other parts of such volumes.

It pays to have a standard textbook on hand for reference. You will find that it will give you a brief and useful explanation of many points you need to understand; often the footnotes will guide you to other sources of information.

A textbook is likely to be indispensable to an understanding of the legal basis of local government. What is a municipal corporation? What is the source of the legal powers of the city? Look up chapters on the legislative control of cities, home rule, the municipal corporations, charters, etc. This material is basic to your survey.

Nowhere are you likely to find so useful a statement about the various forms of local government as in a textbook. Any good textbook will include brief explanations of the weak mayor, commission, strong mayor, and city manager forms of city government. You need to examine these summaries before you can classify the government of your own city.

Some useful texts are: Anderson and Weidner, *American City Government* (12), Phillips, *State and Local Government in America* (13), and Pate, *Local Government and Administration* (14).

Earlier textbooks, some recently revised, are by A. W. Bromage, J. E. McLean, L. W. Lancaster, C. M. Kneier, C. F. Snider, S. A. McCorkle, A. F. Macdonald, E. B. Schulz, R. H. Wells, and H. Zink.

INTERGOVERNMENTAL RELATIONS IN METROPOLITAN AREAS

Nine percent of the counties of the United States and approximately 20 percent of the municipalities in 1957 were included in 174 standard metropolitan areas. However, since more than 60 percent of the country's population lives in metropolitan areas, the chances are that your survey will cover part of a metropolitan area. Furthermore, even small independent cities must deal with fringe populations living outside their jurisdictions. At the least, every city has relations with its county and frequently with neighboring villages, cities, and special districts. See Jones, "Local Government Organization in Metropolitan Areas" in *The Future of Cities and Urban Redevelopment* (15).

More than 7,500 books, pamphlets, articles, and official reports are listed in *Metropolitan Communities: A Bibliography* and in the 1955-1957 Supplement. In addition to the material on

major functions of urban governments listed in Chapter I and on Politics in metropolitan communities in Chapter III, items on governmental organization and relationships are classified in Chapter II under the following headings: "General," "Strengthening Existing Local Governments," "Annexation," "Urban Counties and Townships," "City-County Consolidation and Separation," "Special Districts and Authorities," "Federation," "Incorporation," "Intergovernmental Cooperation," "Extra-Territorial Jurisdiction," "Intergovernmental Relations" (federal and local as well as interstate), "Home Rule," "State Supervision of Localities and Other State-Local Relations."

Metropolitan surveys are frequently an excellent source of information, not only about the relationship of local governments in a metropolitan area, but also about the organization and operation of specific units of government within the metropolitan area. Over a hundred such surveys were published between 1923 and 1957. Each of these surveys has been digested in Government Affairs Foundation, *Metropolitan Surveys: A Digest* (16). Read the introductory analysis by Daniel R. Grant. The digest also contains information about the organization of the survey, background events, survey staff and procedure, financial support, scope of report, summary of recommendations, action following recommendations, and a bibliography. This digest is an excellent source of names of community leaders whom you may wish to interview. The digest is kept current through supplements to the *Metropolitan Area Problems* bulletin.

The general discussion in the census of governments and in textbooks should be supplemented by material on local governments in the particular state under study. It is necessary to do this because it is easy to make generalizations too sweeping to fit your own community. You may find that the exception in your own community is more significant than the nationwide generalization. For instance, the inclusion by the Bureau of the Census of New England towns in the category of local government containing New York and Wisconsin towns is misleading. In most respects, New England towns are more like municipalities than they are like "towns" or townships elsewhere.

In many states, university bureaus of public administration have issued bulletins on local government in the state. For instance, the Institute of Public Service at the University of Connecticut has published bulletins on the county, units of local government, forms of town government, and forms of city government in Connecticut.

Even the information secured from local sources should be checked against the opinion of informed people at the city hall, county courthouse, local municipal research bureau, etc.

California ranks 13th among the States in number of local governments, with 3,878 as of January 1957.

COUNTIES (57)

In addition to the county governments in California, there is one consolidated city-county government—San Francisco. Because San Francisco operates primarily as a city, it is counted, for Census purposes, as a municipality rather than as a county. The governing body in other counties is the board of county supervisors. Counties are legally classified according to population for the purpose of regulating the compensation of officers.

MUNICIPALITIES (331)

Municipal governments in California are designated cities or towns. For the purpose of special legislation they are divided into eleven classes according to population size. However, all municipalities currently function either as charter cities or as fifth- or sixth-class cities.

TOWNSHIPS

California has no organized township governments. However, each of the counties is divided into "township" areas for the election of certain county government officers.

SCHOOL DISTRICTS (1,840)

California law provides for the following types of school districts that are included in the Census count of separate units of government:

Elementary districts
  City district—embracing a city other than one of the sixth class, or such a city plus adjacent territory
  Regular district—single elementary district other than a city district
  Union district—district formed by union of two or more regular districts
  Joint district—intercounty
  Joint union districts—intercounty union district

High school districts
  City district—superimposed on city elementary district
  Union district—superimposed on two or more separate elementary districts
  Joint union district—intercounty union high school district
  County district—district whose boundaries coincide with those of a county

Unified school district—a district, usually urban, providing both elementary and high school education and, in some cases, junior college facilities.

Junior college district—when superimposed on two or more high school districts (see below).

California school districts in general are governed by elected boards of education or trustees, although the districts serving charter cities may have appointed boards if the charter so specifies. Only two school districts, however, have appointed boards: The school district serving the city of Sacramento is administered by a board of education appointed by the city council, and the school district serving the city and county of San Francisco is administered by a board of education appointed by the mayor and ratified by the voters. The law also provides that a high school district board may be composed of the same personnel as the board of the elementary district it overlies. However, the two districts operate as separate entities. The school boards are authorized to determine their own fiscal requirements, and the counties levy and collect taxes found to be required. Bond issues for school district purposes are subject to the approval of the electors.

The following "districts" in California are not classified for Census purposes as independent units of government: Junior college districts that are coterminous with particular high school districts, being governed and maintained by the high school district boards, are treated as components of such high school districts; union high school library districts, which are governed by the union high school boards, are classified as dependent activities of the union high school districts.

SPECIAL DISTRICTS (1,650)[1]

California statutes authorize the creation of a variety of special districts or authorities that are included in the Census count of governmental units. These are discussed in detail below. The figure shown after the name of each kind of special district indicates the number of such units found to be in existence as of January 1957. (A zero entry appears for any authorized class of which no units appeared operative.)

It should be noted, that many of the classes listed below have the same name and functions as classes which are listed under the "Subordinate agencies and areas" list. For these classes, the enabling legislation provides for alternative methods of governing the districts. Where these districts have separate governing bodies, they are included in the count of independent governments; when they are governed by county or municipal officials in an ex officio capacity, they are treated, for Census purposes, as subordinate agencies of the governments they serve.

Airport districts (1)

Airport districts may be created by resolution of the county board of supervisors after public hearing and local referendum. Each such district is to be governed by an elected board of directors authorized to levy taxes, fix charges, and to issue bonds with the approval of the electors. Similar provisions are applicable to the Monterey Peninsula Airport District, which was established by a special act.

Automobile parking districts—2nd law of 1941 (0)

These districts may be established by the municipal or county governing body on petition of landowners after public hearing. The law provides for an elected board of commissioners with authority to issue bonds with the approval of the voters and to levy taxes and fix charges.

Bay Area Air Pollution Control District

This district, established by special act, is administered by a board of directors consisting of one member from and appointed by the board of supervisors of each county in the district area, plus one member appointed by a "City Selection Committee" which is composed of the major or council president of each city in the district area. Revenue is derived from the levy of ad valorem taxes and the district may accept county government loans.

Community service districts (31)

Districts to provide water, sewer, garbage collection, mosquito abatement, street lighting, fire protection, and park and recreational services, or any combinations thereof, are established by the county board of supervisors on petition of residents after hearing and referendum. Each district is governed by an elected board of directors empowered to levy taxes, issue bonds with the approval of the electors, fix rates and charges, and accept contributions.

---

[1]This number agrees with the figures shown in the Census of Governments report, Governments in the United States. However, the Transit Authority of the city of Sacramento (a dependent city agency) was erroneously counted in arriving at the figure.

U. S. Bureau of the Census. *U. S. Census of Governments: 1957*
Vol. VI, No. 4, Government in California
U. S. Government Printing Office, Washington, D. C., 1959

FIGURE 2-14

THE FUNCTIONS OF LOCAL GOVERNMENT

The people of a community are often divided by proposals that governments either undertake or give up some activity. This is why politics and government are inseparable in a democracy. The organization of a community for political agitation and decision is discussed elsewhere in this text. Here we merely want to emphasize the idea that a government exists to do certain things, or to get people to do or to refrain from doing certain things. What these functions are is in part a matter of history and in part a matter of contemporary debate, political maneuvering and decision.

Again it is necessary to remember that the federal and state governments function within the local community. Even the activity of the Secretary of State at a conference of foreign ministers or that of the Secretary of Defense in developing a budget will affect people and events in local communities. But there are also many other activities of the state and federal governments that are executed within the boundaries of local communities.

Turn the pages of the latest edition of the *United States Government Organization Manual* and note which activities of the various agencies are (a) likely to be carried out within local communities or (b) require federal-local or federal-state-local collaboration. As an example of the first type of activity, the Interstate Commerce Commission may "prescribe by order the rates, changes, regulations and practices to be observed by" railroads providing interstate commutation service. The activities of the Housing and Home Finance Agency under the Housing Act of 1949 in slum clearance and community development and redevelopment are examples of the second type of federal activity.

Make a similar list of state activities, using a recent copy of the state Register or Manual, or recent departmental administrative reports.

The list of federal and state activities prepared in this way should be checked and revised by reference to special reports that are probably available upon request to the proper agency. Be sure to examine state budgets or annual financial reports to discover which local activities are financed in part by grants-in-aid. See Figure 2-15 for an illustration of federal financing in New York State. The reports of the U.S. Commission on Intergovernmental Relations (Kestnbaum Commission) and of similar commissions in some twenty states are excellent sources of data and interpretation. See also two publications of the Council of State Governments: *Federal Grants-in-Aid* (Chicago, 1949) and *State-Local Relations* (Chicago, 1946).

Look in the telephone directory under the headings "U.S. Government," "State," and the name of your state to see which federal and state agencies are located in or near your community. If desirable, these agencies may be visited or written to for published information or for answers to specific questions. Such inquiries should be delayed, however, until you are well along in the study of the local governments of your community.

The previously enumerated principal functions of each of the local governments in your community should be identified and listed. One way of summarizing these data is suggested by Table 10 of the publication of the U.S. Bureau of the Census entitled *Governmental Units overlying City Areas* (1947). A sample page of this Table is reproduced as Figure 2-16. Another way is suggested by Chatters and Hoover, *Inventory of Governmental Activities in the United States* (17). Both of these bulletins also provide a check list of governmental activities to guide you in preparing a list of the activities of local governments in your community.

You will not have time to prepare a list of activities arranged in the chronological order of the year in which they were first undertaken. There are a few such lists already prepared, however, that you can use to see whether similar activities were simultaneously undertaken by local governments in your community. Try to account for the time lag in your community or in one or all of the reported communities.

The most famous of these studies is that of Detroit by Upson entitled *The Growth of a City Government* (18). The basic list is reprinted in Anderson and Weidner, pp. 71-84; see their discussion of municipal functions, beginning on page 58. A similar study of the growth between 1900 and 1948 of municipal services in Madison, Wisconsin, will be found in American Federation of State, County and Municipal Employees, *What Your Taxes Buy!* (Madison, 1948). For the growth of a metropolitan county, see Los Angeles County Bureau of Efficiency, *Growth of County Functions, 1852-1934* (Los Angeles, 1936).

None of these studies gives an adequate account of the political conflict leading to the decision that certain functions would be assumed by local governments. Nor is there a list of activities urged upon local governments but rejected by them. One of the most potentially illuminating studies yet to be made is a political, social, technological, and economic history of the growth of local governments.

A student making a local community survey will not be expected to write such a historical study. He will be expected, however, to see and understand the forces at work today and to re-

1. FEDERAL GRANTS IN AID TO THE STATE AND LOCAL GOVERNMENTS TO HELP THEM WITH *THEIR* PROGRAMS:

The Amount Invested Year Ending June 30, 1951

For workers:
Administration of unemployment insurance and State employment offices .... $ 27,496,136
Vocational rehabilitation for the disabled.......... 977,812
For farmers:
Agricultural experiment stations.......... 351,066
Agricultural extension services.......... 774,676
Better marketing facilities.......... 44,975
For veterans:
Institutions for the disabled.......... 2,452
Administration of unemployment and self employment allowances.......... 32,458
Supervision of on-the-job training.......... 79,144
For our needy population:
Aid to the needy aged.......... 40,353,288
Aid to the permanently disabled.......... 5,240,500
Aid to dependent children.......... 31,285,250
Aid to the blind.......... 1,501,485
Child welfare services: foster care, prevention of delinquency, etc... 163,918
Donation of perishable surplus foods to welfare agencies, public institutions, and schools:
Department of Agriculture program.......... 1,647,619
Commodity Credit Corp. program.......... 2,273,343
For our health:
To fight cancer:
Cancer detection and control.......... 231,006
Research laboratories and other facilities.......... 190,000
To fight heart disease:
Heart disease detection and control.......... 74,471
Research laboratories and other facilities..........
To fight T.B... 448,374
To fight V.D... 255,260
To fight water pollution.......... 34,800
To build hospitals.......... 5,778,135
To promote mental health.......... 258,921

Federal Spending in New York

FIGURE 2-15

FROM THE NEW YORK STORY, PREPARED BY RESEARCH DIVISION DEMOCRATIC NATIONAL COMMITTEE, 1952.

The Facts on Federal Spending in New York

(Continued from page 7)

The Programs and Benefits — *The Amount Invested Year Ending June 30, 1951*

To promote basic health services.......... 866,3__
For maternal and child health.......... 43__,16__
For services for crippled children.......... 30__,__40
For housing:
Low-rent public housing.......... 1,780,660
Conversion of re-use housing for veterans (e.g. Quonset huts, barracks).......... 2,643
For education:
Free books for the blind.......... 8,750
Vocational training for future workers for the farm, home, and industry.......... 1,848,929
Construction of schools in Federally-affected areas (includes survey of school facilities).......... 26,484
Maintenance and operation of schools in Federally-affected areas.......... __,019
Instruction in the land-grant colleges.......... 223,837
School lunch programs.......... 4,430,99__
Schools (and roads) from a sharing of revenue earned by:
Federal forests..........
Sub-marginal lands..........
Flood control lands.......... 1,758
Federal minerals..........
For transportation and communication:
Airports.......... 2,__3,560
Roads and highways:
Emergency grants.......... 46,053
Regular grants.......... 23,692,992
Training sailors for the Merchant Marine (includes some maintenance and repair of vessels).......... 79,394
For natural resources:
Establishment of migratory bird refuges.......... 112
Protection of non-Federal forests.......... 280,396
Wildlife conservation.......... 235,158
For general programs:
Payments to general treasury fund of the State from fees for use of Federal lands for power..........
Payments in lieu of taxes to general treasury funds of counties from proceeds of Federal timber and grazing land..........
TOTAL, grants-in-aid.......... 156,171,464

DEFENSE WORK: Value of prime contracts awarded for military procurement and construction, July '50 through December '51. (This includes only *prime* contracts and

The Programs and Benefits — *The Amount Invested Year Ending June 30, 1951*

therefore does not reflect the sub-contracting on military contracts being done in the State).......... 7,872,486,000
3. ATOMIC ENERGY COMMISSION.......... 4,800,000
4. FOREST HIGHWAYS: Payments to contractors for construction of highways in and adjacent to Federal forests..........
5. SOME OF THE PAYMENTS MADE TO FARMERS, including:
Payments to help defray cost of soil conservation practices.......... 6,731,160
Payments to sugar producers to insure adequate wages and a fair selling price for American sugar..........
Grants to needy farmers for minor but essential repairs on farm housing.......... 447
6. VETERANS BENEFITS administered by the VA, including:
Autos for disabled veterans.
Compensation and pension benefits.
Construction of hospitals and other facilities.
Life insurance benefits.
Pay adjustments for World War I veterans.
Readjustment benefits, including G.I. Bill, unemployment and self-employment allowances, and G.I. loans.
Vocational rehabilitation.......... 484,407,842
7. INTEREST ON GOVERNMENT BONDS HELD BY INDIVIDUALS, INCLUDING NON-PROFIT INSTITUTIONS (1950).......... 322,300,000
8. RIVERS AND HARBORS AND FLOOD CONTROL PROJECTS OF THE CORPS OF ENGINEERS.......... 26,430,000
9. FEDERAL PAYROLLS, 1950:
Civilian employee payrolls.......... 580,800,000
Civilian employee pensions.......... 25,782,000
Military pay and allowances, including dependents allowances and retirement pay.......... 205,948,000
10. SOCIAL SECURITY PAYMENTS FROM SOCIAL INSURANCE FUNDS, 1950: (Although these are technically not Federal "expenditures," they do represent insurance payments that are being made because of Federal programs.)
To unemployed workers.......... 296,729,000
To retired workers.......... 132,888,000
To unemployed railroad workers.......... 5,669,000
To retired railroad workers.......... 25,217,000

FIGURE 2-16

U. S. Bureau of the Census, Governmental Units Overlying City Areas (1947).

GOVERNMENTAL ORGANIZATION

Table 10.—GOVERNMENTS OTHER THAN THE CITY CORPORATION RESPONSIBLE FOR

[St = State; Co = County; T = Township; Sch = ...; City = ... Special District = ... small expenditure for the function. Overlying ...]

Pop. rank	CITY	PUBLIC SAFETY		Other	HIGHWAYS		Sanitation	Health	Hospitals
		Police	Fire		Roadways	Bridges and tunnels			
	MISSISSIPPI								
159	Jackson								
	MISSOURI								
125	St. Joseph								
163	Springfield								
	NEBRASKA								
111	Lincoln								
	NEW HAMPSHIRE								
122	Manchester								
	NEW JERSEY								
152	Atlantic City								
115	Bayonne								
136	East Orange								
197	Hoboken								
182	Irvington								
161	Passaic								
179	Union City								
	NEW YORK								
119	Binghamton								
142	Mount Vernon								
174	New Rochelle								
121	Niagara Falls								
102	Schenectady								
131	Troy								
	NORTH CAROLINA								
193	Asheville								
168	Durham								
169	Greensboro								
114	Winston-Salem								
	OHIO								
183	Cleveland Heights								
196	Hamilton								
135	Lakewood								
130	Springfield								
	PENNSYLVANIA								
97	Allentown								
113	Altoona								
173	Port ...								
171	Chester								
144	Harrisburg								
162	Johnstown								
181	Lancaster								
103	McKeesport								
178	York								
	RHODE ISLAND								
124	Pawtucket								
	SOUTH CAROLINA								
129	Charleston								
156	Columbia								
	TEXAS								
192	Amarillo								

GROUP V.—CITIES HAVING POPULATIONS

GOVERNMENTAL UNITS OVERLYING CITY AREAS

SELECTED LOCAL FUNCTIONS WITHIN THE 397 CITIES, BY CITY—Continued

[... city has no part in administration or financing of the function. ... shown in ( ).]

OF 25,000 TO 50,000—Continued

Pop. rank	City	Poll tax	PUBLIC WELFARE					Correction	Schools	Libraries	Recreation	Pop. rank
			Institutional care	General relief	Old-age assistance	Aid to dependent children	Aid to the blind					
	MICHIGAN											
340	Ann Arbor		*Co	*Co	*St	*St	*St	*Co	*Sch	*Sch	SD	340
227	Battle Creek		*Co	*Co	*St	*St	*St	*Co	*Sch	*Sch		227
207	Bay City		*Co	*Co	*St	*St	*St	*Co	*Sch			207
198	Hamtramck		*Co	(Co)	*St	*St	*St	*Co	*Sch			198
201	Jackson		*Co	(Co)	*St	*St	*St	*Co	*Sch			201
209	Muskegon		*Co	*Co	*St	*St	*St	*Co	*Sch	*Sch		209
309	Port Huron		*Co	*Co	*St	*St	*St	*Co	*Sch	[*28]		309
397	Royal Oak		*Co	*Co	*St	*St	*St	*Co	*Sch		SD	397
327	Wyandotte		*Co	*Co	*St	*St	*St	*Co	*Sch	*Sch		327
	MINNESOTA											
378	Rochester		*Co	*Co	*St	*St	*Co	*Co	*Sch			378
	MISSISSIPPI											
282	Meridian		*Co	(Co)	*St	*St	*St	(Co)	*Sch			282
	MISSOURI											
269	Joplin		*St	*St	*St	*St	*St	*Co	*Sch			269
306	University City		*St	*St	*St	*St	*St	*Co	*Sch			306
	MONTANA											
270	Butte		*Co		*St	*St	*St	*Co	*Sch			270
337	Great Falls		*Co		*St	*St	*St	*Co	*Sch			337
	NEW HAMPSHIRE											
365	Concord		*St Co		*St	*St	*St	*Co	*Sch			365
307	Nashua		*St Co		*St	*St	*St	*Co	*Sch			307
	NEW JERSEY											

Here is another — Census that takes a look at — population. 25,29

Public Health

Developments in 1952

By IRA V. HISCOCK

Chairman, Department of Public Health, Yale University, and Commissioner, Board of Health of New Haven

GENERALLY favorable mortality rates from total causes continued in the United States in 1952, with high birth rates and a large proportion of the babies being born in hospitals. Poliomyelitis raised its ugly head more frequently, and tuberculosis cases continued at a high level in spite of reduced rates of mortality. The leading cause of death for age group 1-14 is accidents, and for every fatal accident there are 90 to 150 severe injuries, with no real improvement for 10 years, according to an impressive statement in "Pediatrics" which concluded that there needs to be an evaluation of the methods used for parent-and-patient education. Of importance in community planning if representative of conditions

Sources of Information: Health

Sources of Statistics: Health

U. S. National Office of Vital Statistics. Washington, D. C. Weekly Mortality Index. Total deaths (excluding stillbirths) and deaths under one year for cities. Last number for each year gives annual figures.

--Vital Statistics — Special Reports, National Summaries and Selected Studies. The reports contain tables giving number of deaths in institutions and from motor vehicle accidents in cities over 100,000; number of deaths from certain rare causes in cities over 10,000; number of births and deaths classified by race and residence; number and rate of infant deaths for counties and cities over 10,000; delayed birth registration.

--Current Mortality Analysis. (Monthly). Data based on returns of a 10 per cent sample of death certificates received in vital statistics offices. Monthly discussion of returns from the mortality sample.

U. S. Public Health Service. Public Health Reports (Monthly). Government Printing Office, Washington, D. C. For 140 cities, cases of communicable diseases: diphtheria, influenza (cases and deaths), measles, pneumonia (deaths), scarlet fever, smallpox, tuberculosis (deaths), typhoid fever, whooping cough.

--Health Service Areas: Estimate of Future Physician Requirements. Government Printing Office, Washington 25, D. C. 1949.

--Health Service Areas: Requirements for General Hospitals and Health Centers. Government Printing Office, Washington 25, D. C. 1945. 25 cents. Contains figures on existing facilities and an evaluation of needs.

Selected Standard References: Health

ADMINISTRATIVE MEDICINE. By Haven Emerson. Thomas Nelson & Sons, 385 Madison Avenue, New York 17. 1951. 1007pp. $10.

AMERICA'S HEALTH: A REPORT TO THE NATION. National Health Assembly. Harper & Brothers, 49 East 33 Street, New York 16. 1949. 299pp. $4.00.

BASIC PRINCIPLES OF HEALTHFUL HOUSING. American Public Health Association, 1790 Broadway, New York 19. Second edition, 1950. 30 cents.

COMMUNITY HEALTH EDUCATION IN ACTION. By Ruth Patterson and Beryl Roberts. C. V. Mosby Company, 3207 Washington Boulevard, St. Louis 3, 1951. 356pp. $4.55.

COMMUNITY HEALTH ORGANIZATION. By Ira V. Hiscock. Harvard Univ....

THE LOCAL HEALTH DEPARTMENT — SERVICES AND RESPONSIBILITIES. In official statement of the American Public Health Association, 1790 Broadway, New York 19. 1950. 8pp. $10.

LOCAL HEALTH UNITS FOR THE NATION. By Haven Emerson and Martha Luginbuhl. The Commonwealth Fund, 41 East 57 Street, New York 22. 1945. 333pp. $1.25.

MANUAL OF RECOMMENDED WATER SANITATION PRACTICE. United States Public Health Service. Government Printing Office, Washington 25, D. C. 1947. 40pp. 15 cents.

MEDICAL SERVICES BY GOVERNMENT — LOCAL, STATE, AND FEDERAL. By Bernhard J. Stern. Commonwealth Fund, 41 East 57 Street, New York 22. 1946. 208pp. $1.50.

MENTAL HYGIENE IN PUBLIC HEALTH....

New Books and Pamphlets: Health

AMERICAN PUBLIC HEALTH ASSOCIATION YEAR BOOK, 1951-52. The Association, 1790 Broadway, New York 19. 1952. 151pp.

CHARTS ON INFANT, CHILDHOOD AND MATERNAL MORTALITY, 1949. United States Children's Bureau, Washington 25, D. C. 1951. 64pp.

DIRECTORY OF FULL-TIME LOCAL HEALTH...

INDEPENDENT PLANS PROVIDING MEDICAL CARE AND HOSPITALIZATION INSURANCE IN 1949, IN THE UNITED STATES, 1950 SURVEY. By Agnes W. Brewster. Social Security Administration, Government Printing Office, Washington 25, D. C. 1952. 122pp. 65 cents.

INTERGOVERNMENTAL RELATIONS IN PUB-...

Selected Periodicals: Health

AMERICAN JOURNAL OF PUBLIC HEALTH. American Public Health Association, 1790 Broadway, New York 19. $10.

HOSPITAL MANAGEMENT. 200 East Illinois Street, Chicago 11, Illinois. $2.

HOSPITALS. American Hospital Association, 18 East Division Street, Chicago. $2 to members; $3 to others.

JOURNAL OF MILK AND FOOD TECHNOLOGY. International Association of Milk and Food Technologists, Rich Bldg., Shelbyville, Ind.

JOURNAL OF SOCIAL HYGIENE. Monthly except July-September.) American Social Hygiene Association, 1790 Broadway, New York 19. $3.

LOCAL HEALTH UNITS FOR THE NATION. National Advisory Committee on Local Health Units. National Health Council, 1790 Broadway, New York 19.

MENTAL HYGIENE. (Quarterly). National Committee for Mental Hygiene, 1790 Broadway, New York 19. $5.

MILK DEALER. Olsen Publishing Company, 1441 North 5 Street, Milwaukee. $2.

MODERN HOSPITAL. 919 North Michigan Avenue, Chicago. $3.

MODERN SANITATION. Modern Sanitation, 205 Avenue of the Americas, New York 1, N. Y. $2.

MONTHLY VITAL STATISTICS REPORT. U. S. National Office of Vital Statistics, Washington 25, D. C.

PROGRESS IN HEALTH SERVICES. Health Information Foundation, 420 Lexington Avenue, New York 17.

PUBLIC HEALTH ENGINEERING ABSTRACTS. U. S. Public Health Service, Washington 14, D. C.

PUBLIC HEALTH NURSING. National Organization for Public Health Nursing, 2 Park Avenue, New York 16. $3 to members, $4 to nonmembers.

PUBLIC HEALTH REPORTS. U. S. Public Health Service, Government Printing Office, Washington 25, D. C. $4.25.

FIGURE 2-17 International City Managers' Association, The Municipal Year Book, 1953.

cord some of the pressures continually exerted on local, state,,and federal governments. Do not forget that governmental officials often exert counterpressures.

SOURCES OF DATA

The articles in the *Municipal Year Book* on municipal activities are important sources of data and of clues and suggestions for the analysis of the functions of local government in a community. As examples, parts of the articles on public health and fire administration are reproduced as Figures 2-17 and 2-18. Figure 2-18 also illustrates the tables showing data for cities over a certain size that accompany articles on major municipal activities. Before using the tables, be sure to read the summary and analysis preceding each table and the article on "How to Use the Year Book."

Statistical data for one community will probably be meaningless unless compared with similar data for other cities similarly situated, or for other time periods in the same city. Be sure that you are comparing the same things under similar conditions. You will recall from your study of Figure 2-16, for example, that local functions are often handled by a variety of governmental units. It is therefore misleading to compare the cost of government in one city with that in another without ascertaining whether or not they are engaged in the same activities.

Read the "Highlights" article at the beginning of the *Year Book* and the articles on each function you are interested in. Do you find that the same forces, decisions, and trends discussed in these articles are present in your community? If not, the reasons for their absence should be determined. Read the same articles in the *Year Book* for the five preceding years. Identify the trends that are developing and determine whether your community conforms to the typical behavior of other communities. Explain any differences and try to decide how desirable they are.

Other sources of data about the functions of local government are the annual reports of department heads or of the chief executive. If the reports consist only of financial or of other kinds of quantitative data, you will have to supplement them by talking with the officials responsible for the activities. Many quantitative data are not relevant to the interests of the student of local government and politics.

Good interpretative municipal reports that are available for a number of years can, however, prove invaluable. Not many municipalities or other units of local government issue annual reports as well written or as informative as that of the town of Greenwich, Connecticut. Two pages of the report for 1951, entitled *Proof of the Pud-*

ding, are reproduced as Figure 2-19. An outline history of the development of a full-fledged suburban government can be written from a series of these annual reports.

Local politics revolves to a great extent about what the city government does. In the course of performing its regular activities, the city government naturally produces conflict and public controversy. (If there is no conflict, you ought to be suspicious of the whole organization.) The best way to "break open" the subject of local politics is to see what the city is doing. A good way to begin is to read the chapter or chapters in a standard textbook on the functions of city governments. Next examine the chapters in the *Municipal Year Book* on municipal activities, as illustrated in Figures 2-17 and 2-18. These chapters will tell you much about what is being done in cities throughout the country.

The chapter on public health in the *Year Book* includes a summary of developments in this field during the year; it contains an invaluable discussion of standards of local public health service (you should be able to use this material), tabulates statistical data, and provides a classified bibliography and a list of sources of information about public health administration. Obviously, you would not talk to a member of the Board of Health in your community until you read this chapter.

Another source of information about what your city is doing is the local budget. Everything the city does costs money. The budget is the working program of the city. It ought to tell you something about the order of importance of government activities and provide you with a great number of toe holds for further exploration. A budget hearing is the most important occasion for a review of the whole program of the city. Do not give up easily if the budget is difficult to understand. Ask questions and keep on asking questions until you understand it. If you master the budget of your city, you will be one of the few to have done so, and professional politicians will respect you for your achievement.

Read what your textbook has to say about city charters and read the "model" city charter issued by the National Municipal League (Fig. 2-20). In what sense of the word is it a "model"? Then read the charter of your city. (Ask the mayor's office for a copy.) There are a number of questions to ask yourself when reading it:

1. Who made the charter? Is it a special act adopted by the state legislature? Was it drawn up in accordance with a general statute governing the incorporation of cities? How can the charter be amended?
2. Who controls the purse strings? Who levies taxes, borrows money, appropriates money, makes the budget? How are the accounts of the city audited?
3. Who has the power of appointment and removal?
4. What kind of personnel system does your city have?

Fire Administration

Developments in 1952

By Percy Bugbee

General Manager, National Fire Protection Association, Boston

THE fire loss experience of 1952 does not provide any grounds for complacency. There were 12,535 deaths caused by fire in the United States and Canada in 1952. There are no accurate estimates as to the number of people who suffered serious burns and other injuries in fires, but there is no question that the total is very much larger than the total for deaths, probably in a ratio of at least 10 to 1.

The preliminary estimates for property damage in the United States from fires for last year were $896,800,000. Included in this estimate is $792,000,000 ...

Fire Department Statistics

THE chief municipal activity measured by general fund expenditures and payroll is public safety—work of the city's police and fire departments. Detailed statistics on police and fire departments in cities over 10,000 population have been compiled to assist city officials in analyzing administrative problems. Table XIV shows individual city data for cities over 25,000 population on the number of fire department employees, hours of work, salaries of fire fighters and fire chiefs, outside fire service, number of public fire alarm boxes, fire inspection activities, expenditures, fire losses, and insurance classifications. The same data, except for fire losses, are shown in Table XV for cities between 10,000 and 25,000 population.

These data are analyzed and summarized in this article to enable city officials to make comparisons as to costs, performance, and accomplishments of municipal fire departments. The fire insurance classifications give an indication of the fire hazard, while the classification of the fire department ...

TABLE XIV—FIRE DEPARTMENT DATA FOR CITIES OVER 25,000—Continued

100,000 to 250,000—continued

City	Number of Full-time Paid Employees	Salary of Full-time Firemen—Entrance, Maximum	Fire Chief Salary, How Appointed	Work Hours Per Week, Hours on Day Shift	Fire Inspection	Mutual Aid; Outside Charge	No. Public Fire Alarm Boxes	Salaries and Wages	By-grade Required	Total for Dept.	Avg. Per Capita 1950-52	Bldg. Loss per $1,000	Per Bldg. Fire 1952	Total Fire Insurance Class and Deficiency Points; Fire Dept. Def. Pts., Year
Chattanooga, Tenn.	187	$3,000-3,720	$6,000S	72-24	3-Y	Y-N	130	$ 709		823	$3.36	5.3	$1,623	4-1784 497 48
Corpus Christi, Tex.	123†	3,042-3,284	6,540A	72-24	4-N	Y-F	123-48-22	412		478	1.71	3.5	382	6-2509 663 47
Dayton, Ohio	360	3,635-4,087	7,680A	63-24	7-Y	N-C	590-90-81	1,290	0	1,465	5.00	4.2	1,899	4-1301 462 41
Des Moines, Iowa	223	3,192-3,840	6,600A	72-24	4-Y	N-N	None	808	0	878			41	4-1795 645 46
Duluth, Minn.	163	3,444-3,840	6,060B	56-..	1-N	Y-N	184	642	27	709	3.54	2.3		4-1751 540 40
Elizabeth, N.J.	225	3,504-4,104	6,360B	72-24	3-Y	Y-F	286							2-938 265 44
El Paso, Tex.	144	3,247-4,019	7,794C	60-10	1-Y	Y-F	195-40-20	473	45	542		4.1	143†	4-1709 624 49
Erie, Pa.	200	3,420-3,720	5,400C	72-24	4-N	N-N	223-40-39	703	0	781	6.67	16.6	518	4-1752 696 41
Evansville, Ind.	193	3,801-3,999	5,500B†	72-24	2-Y	..-N	268-34-20	667	0	792		6.8	362	3-1343 422 33
Fall River, Mass.	293	3,100-3,100	6,300B	48-10	6-Y	Y-F	349	867†	0†	968†		3.9	594	2-A-note 3
Flint, Mich.	229	3,639-4,048	8,077A	63-24	4-Y	Y-N	323	945	14	1,087	2.81	4.7	420	4-1652 539 50
Fort Wayne, Ind.	178	3,060-3,600†	5,320M	72-24	3-Y	Y-N	299				5.37	7.1	420	3-1445 448 34
Gary, Ind.	260	3,393-3,848	5,760M†	72-24	4-Y	Y-F	144	633†	107	1,197		19.8	140	4-1570 381 41
Grand Rapids, Mich.	436	3,328-3,796	7,904A	72-24	8-Y	Y-N	454-108-115	965	10	1,739	2.70	2.0	1,428	3-1294 277 36
Hartford, Conn.	322	3,033-3,800	8,491A	56-10	4-Y	Y-F	631-73-30	1,564	56	1,396	2.52	5.0	929	2-A-note 3
Jacksonville, Fla.	173	3,240-3,420†	6,905C	72-24	4-N	Y-F	325	1,153	0†	663†	4.37	5.0	929	4-1564 539 51
Kansas City, Kan.	180	2,820-3,180†	5,540M†	72-10	5-N	Y-C	None	629†	71†	656†	2.87	5.1	396	4-1929 559 41
Knoxville, Tenn.	134	2,970-3,300	5,400S†	72-24	3-Y	Y-C	70-70-0	518†	34	492	1.16	7.4†	140†	3-1378 382 48
Little Rock, Ark.	451	3,036-4,020	4,980M	72-24	11-Y	N-F	None	432	20	1,958		7.1	654†	4-1988 589 47
Miami, Fla.	128	2,604-2,988	8,360M	72-24	1-Y	..-F	306-164-16	1,701	0	472	2.30	2.4	1,070	3-1444 273 51
Mobile, Ala.	151	2,460-2,880	5,856C	84-24	6-Y	Y-C	245	393	137	638	3.37	4.5	379†	5-2439 957 50
Montgomery, Ala.	355	3,000-3,600	5,760C	84-24	4-N	N-F	165	449	0	1,214		4.1	779	4-1671 552 47
Nashville, Tenn.	278	3,050-3,250	6,600..	60-12	2-Y	N-F	386-50-50	1,155		878	1.94	6.0	949†	3-1249 349 46
New Bedford, Mass.	354	3,138-3,503†	5,050M	48-10	2-Y	Y-C	233	842			3.02	3.0	656	2-A-note 3
New Haven, Conn.			7,320M	56-10	7-N	N-N	406					5.4	648	3-B-note 3

FIGURE 2-18   International City Managers' Association, *The Municipal Year Book*, 1953.

FIGURE 2-19

SEWERS

80 buried manholes were raised in 1951. Over the years, many manholes became buried through changes of grade or other pavement improvements, and this condition is now being corrected.

Rain was largely responsible for increasing flows 16.5% at the 4 treatment plants. Satisfactory sedimentation and sludge digestion were obtained at all plants. Sludge from 3 plants is used for fertilizer by the Park Division, but at Old Greenwich industrial wastes make it unusable. Disposal of this sludge has become a problem. Nearly 600,000 gallons of waste were cleaned from private sewage systems and taken to the Grass Island Plant. Chlorination was practiced at all plants from March 15 to November 15, to sterilize the effluent.

Sewage Treatment Plants	Byram	Grass Island	Cos Cob	Old Greenwich
Year built	1917	1918	1930	1926
Cost of land and plant to 1951	$61,241	$398,085	$197,850	$191,954
Connected population (est.)	3,680	13,640	5,300	6,740
Sewage flow (million gallons)	109	840	391	423
Total cost of operation				1951—$55,350

Six petitions for new sewers were presented in 1951. One petition went through the steps provided in the Sewer Act and has been advertised for bid; the others are "in the works." These petitions, plus the 171 new connections to sewer lines (1941 1950) show the continued growth of the Town. The increased flows at the plants will soon make it necessary either to enlarge the trunk lines or to cut down infiltration and illegal discharge of ground water into the system.

About 1.4 miles of new sewers were added to the system last year, 2/3 of it in Havemeyer Park and the rest in Byram and at Greenwich Point. Under the new Sewer Act, when trunk lines are laid, they can be made big enough to take care of future growth in an area. Under the old act this was not possible. A new pumping station was built in Bruce Park to abate the pollution of Davis Harbor and a by-pass was constructed at the Old Greenwich plant to prevent flooding of West End Avenue with raw sewage during heavy storms.

Results of the Dutch Elm control program are remarkable, with a minimum of new infections: 30 Town trees and 24 private elm trees were removed last year. Spraying is now done at night when there is less interference from traffic and pedestrians, and the air is quieter. Spraying is also more efficient at night, because with strong floodlights, the operator makes sure of covering the entire tree with protective spray. A Town-wide check is made to find and remove other dead or badly weakened trees, and this has greatly reduced emergency calls to the Division. In addition to trees killed by Dutch Elm disease, 515 dead or dangerous trees on streets and on other public property were removed. Many were maple trees which have been hard hit by diseases. Maples, crabapples and dogwoods constituted most of the 157 trees planted.

WASTE COLLECTION AND DISPOSAL

New homes and apartments mean more waste for the Incinerator. Nearly 17,500 tons were brought in in 1951, or 697 tons more than the year before. In 1939 when the Incinerator was first put in service tonnage was 10,465. It has increased steadily since then except for a drop during the war. Though pushed beyond capacity for an 8-hour day, the plant is kept in good condition.

The dump has been infested with water bugs, a kind of roach. Chemicals will be applied to keep the infestation from spreading. The dump is filling rapidly, mostly due to stumps brought in by private contractors from new developments.

SUMMARY OF ANNUAL REPORT, GREENWICH, CONNECTICUT, 1951

Article II
THE COUNCIL

Article III
THE CITY MANAGER

Article IX
NOMINATIONS AND ELECTIONS[1]

Section 153. Municipal elections

TABLE OF CONTENTS

v

MODEL CITY CHARTER

PREPARED BY

COMMITTEE ON REVISION OF THE
MODEL CITY CHARTER

FIGURE 2-20

FIFTH EDITION—1941
(COMPLETE REVISION)
SECOND PRINTING—1944
THIRD PRINTING—1947
FOURTH PRINTING—1948
FIFTH PRINTING—1951
SIXTH PRINTING—1955
SEVENTH PRINTING—1957
EIGHTH PRINTING—1960

NATIONAL MUNICIPAL LEAGUE
CARL F. PFORZHEIMER BUILDING
47 EAST 68TH STREET
NEW YORK 21, N.Y.

Section 4. Number, selection, term
5. Qualific...
6. Salary
7. Presidi...
8. Powers
9. Appoint...
10. Remova...
11. Council...
12. Vacanc...
13. Creation...
   duties...
14. City cle...
15. Inductio...
16. Council...
17. Rules o...
18. Ordinat...
19. Procedu...
20. Second...
21. Further...
22. Publica...
   sive r...
23. Indepen...

INTRODUCTORY Nor...
recognition of the ge...
council, the more effic...
fact that election at...
election by wards or...
tive bodies are ineffe...
of the minds around...
legislative body must...
before it and the v...
Election at large is pr...
of reasons chief amo...
to log-rolling and a c...
capable leaders distri...
it is difficult to pers...
representative.
   All the legislative...
it will be observed th...
form, which involves...
power, no administra...
the employment and...
ment of an independe...
the administration fo...
mining body.

...tion
...harter Committee are
...ovided in this article,
...t electing councilmen
...more voters than any
...uality so as to secure
...en may be modified
...t all with the major
...d by some authorities
...oice of members
...in odd (even)
...any reason, the non-
...the next best alter-
...results, it is, in the
...ward system and has
...here spoils politicians
...es which have adopt-
...ave provided for this
...adopted, subdivisions
...section 163 should be
...tuted for sections 157
...of the council shall
...ote for as many can-
...uncil. All candidates,
...ity vote shall be de-
...d receive a majority
...ted. A majority vote

Make an organization chart of your city government and ask city hall officials to criticize it. No organization chart can describe a city government satisfactorily, but you will find out a great deal about its structure when you attempt to make one.

Ask the controller, budget director, or finance commissioner two questions:

1. How much of the city budget is controlled by the city and how much is mandatory (made so by requirements imposed on the city by state laws), or is paid to other authorities over whose expenditures the city has no control?
2. How much money does the city receive from the federal and state governments?

City charters are products of politics. You should therefore read the report of the charter commission that drafted the charter (see Fig. 2-21 for an example) as well as newspaper clippings and other documents in the campaign for its adoption.

A survey of the government of your community, along with an examination of its other aspects, should enable you to answer the question with which Sayre and Kaufman end their study of politics in the New York metropolis:

The most lasting impressions created by a systematic analysis of New York City's political and governmental system as a whole are of its democratic virtues: its qualities of openness, its commitments to bargaining and accommodation among participants, its receptivity to new participants, its opportunities for the exercise of leadership by an unmatched variety and number of the city's residents new and old. Defects accompany these virtues, and in some situations overshadow them, but the City of New York can confidently ask: What other large (or small) American city is as democratically and as well governed? (p. 738)

THE ORGANIZATION OF LOCAL GOVERNMENTS

A local government is a social institution in the same way that the family, the church, the business firm, or the theatre are social institutions. They consist of groups of people who are operating through regularized sets of social rules and social structures. Government has characteristics that distinguish it from other institutions; we shall pay considerable attention to these characteristics.

One might expect sociologists to have studied the relationships of governmental and political structures to other institutions. Yet the student will not find any good sociological analysis of local government in the works of urban sociologists and ecologists. If they give any attention to local government, their treatment is purely descriptive. The student can get a better description of local government from the standard texts of political scientists.

The organization of every institution has both formal and informal aspects. Government is no exception. In this chapter we are concerned with what is called formal organization. Simon, Smithburg, and Thompson define these two types of organization as follows:

By *formal organization* is meant the pattern of behaviors and relationships that is deliberately and legitimately planned for the members of an organization....By *informal organization* is meant the whole pattern of actual behaviors—the way members of the organization really do behave—insofar as these actual behaviors do not coincide with the formal plan. (19)

There are two mistakes to avoid in studying the organization of a local government. The first is contained in the frequently quoted couplet from Pope's *Essay on Man*: "For forms of government let fools contest; Whate'er is best administer'd is best." This quotation is freely quoted by those who are opposed to changes in the form of government. The very fact that they are opposed testifies to the importance of the decision to change or not to change the form of government.

The other mistake is a common one among students, professors, and zealous advocates of a particular form of government. It holds that a change in organization will in itself change the behavior of the members of the organization.

It is essential that a student of a local community appreciate that state constitutions and statutes, local charters, ordinances, and administrative regulations do facilitate or impede the achievement of certain objectives. At the same time, he must understand that none of these can provide much more than a formal way to carry on the business of government. Nor can there be perfect assurance that the people who make up the government will behave as the formal organization specifies.

It is especially important to be aware of the factors of informal organization; they are likely to be the party organizations, influential individuals, and pressure groups that are discussed in the next chapter.

Be careful not to read too much into an organization chart. It is relatively easy to indicate on a chart a formal line of authority, of appointment, and of responsibility for a limited number of activities. Not even a three-dimensional organization chart, however, can show the lines of actual influence in a complicated and vital organization such as a government operating in the more complicated organization that we call a community.

Simon, Smithburg, and Thompson say that two words in their definition of a formal organization need explanation: "deliberately" and "legitimately." You can decide for yourself how deliberately the structures of your local governments have been created and modified.

The concept of legitimacy is important in any

4. Elections on Non-Partisan Basis.

The *Charter Commission* favors the retention of non-partisan municipal elections for Newark. Approximately seventy per cent. of all American cities now elect their local officials on this basis. Of 23 cities between 300,000 and 600,000 in population, eighteen have non-partisan elections and five use the regular political parties to nominate and elect their city officers.

It is the *Commission's* belief that Newark's poor election history has been the result of the commission form of government, rather than a failure of the non-partisan method of elections. The very nature of commission government has prevented the building of active citizens groups to support candidates under a non-partisan banner. Non-partisan elections are in accord with the best thinking on municipal government for the following reasons:

1. There is little or no relationship between national and state issues, on the one hand, and purely local questions on the other. Local problems inevitably are submerged when city officials are elected on a partisan basis in conjunction with state and national elections. While national and state issues commonly involve basic questions of policy, local questions generally are more concerned with the quality and cost of accepted local services. Thus, there is no Democratic way of cleaning the streets or Republican method of operating the public baths.

2. Partisan elections narrow the opportunities for a united effort for civic betterment by all elements in the community, regardless of political affiliations, thereby impeding the realization of the full benefits of home rule. There are deterrents to crossing party lines for party "regulars", and a hesitancy on the part of independent voters and non-political organizations to join in party-sponsored or supported municipal activities.

3. Party nominations for municipal office under partisan elections are determined by the primary elections. Large numbers of inde-

pendent voters do not vote in the primaries, leaving the field clear for party "regulars", endorsed by political leaders. Should one political party be dominant in the city, the primary elections of that party in effect would select the mayor and councilmen. Partisan elections, therefore, do not develop on the municipal level a broad participation in the selection of city officials.

4. Partisan elections inevitably result in an emphasis on the patronage needs of the successful political party, at the expense of efficiency and economy in municipal services.

5. Partisan elections leave the city with little influence with the county, state and Federal governments, should they be controlled by administrations of the opposite political faith from the city administration. On the other hand, a strong mayor elected on a non-partisan basis is likely to have substantial influence with other governmental bodies, regardless of which political party is in power.

It is clear, however, that the method of nominating and electing municipal officials on a non-partisan basis places a burden on civic-minded citizens and organizations to join together under a non-partisan banner to endorse and support candidates for municipal office. In the absence of a strong non-partisan movement such as that maintained for years in Cincinnati, political influence and control is likely to gravitate to the organized political parties or to personal political organizations of the mayor and those who aspire to be mayor.

An alert and active citizenry is required to maintain the spirit as well as the form of non-partisan elections.

**FINAL REPORT OF THE CHARTER COMMISSION
OF THE CITY OF NEWARK**

NEWARK, NEW JERSEY
September 3, 1953

FIGURE 2—21

formal organization; it is basic in government. This is one of the characteristics that distinguishes government from other social institutions. The formal organization of a local government can be traced back to an act of the state legislature, unless the state constitution authorizes local governments to act on their own initiative. See Anderson and Weidner, Chapters 6, 7, and 9, for a discussion of state legislative control of cities, municipal home rule, state administrative supervision, and the legal status of municipal corporations.

Find out whether the local governments in your community are organized under a special act of the legislature or under a general statute. Are they organized under a charter locally drafted in accordance with constitutional or statutory home rule? If the charter or enabling act is new, find out which groups in the community favored, opposed, or were indifferent to the changes. Do the same thing if a charter has recently been defeated. Relate your findings to the analysis of politics outlined in the next chapter.

A charter has the force of a statute. In many states, one has to go to the statutes, and to periodical supplements, to find the basic law under which a city operates. A charter then should be read in the manner suggested in Chapter 8 of Schattschneider, Jones, and Bailey, *A Guide to the Study of Public Affairs* (20).

Figure 2-22 is a reproduction of the first pages of two city charters: that of Gloucester, Massachusetts, is an act of the state legislature; that of Middletown, Ohio, was locally drafted and ratified in accordance with the home rule provisions of the state constitution.

In many communities, printed or mimeographed copies of the charter are available at the city hall. Sometimes the charter is published in a book that also contains the local ordinances and, at times, the administrative code. If a copy of the charter is not available for distribution, read a copy in the office of the city clerk or the corporation counsel. If necessary, use the bound volumes of the statutes; they may be found in the local law library or in the state library.

Outline the principal provisions of the charter and prepare a chart showing in outline the organization of the government. Any textbook in local government will contain very generalized charts showing the principal forms of local government. What type of government do you have in your community? How does it differ from other local governments of the same type?

Read the *Model City Charter*, prepared by a committee of the National Municipal League. You can decide for yourself whether the *Model City Charter* embodies "the best that practical experience can offer" and whether it is "a little in advance of general practice." It is a document that

was prepared after long discussion and debate among a large number of people with experience in studying and running municipal government. Were it revised today, it might undergo some radical changes.

Use the *Model City Charter* in two ways. Read it as a legal expression of the theories of municipal organization expressed in most textbooks. Remember that a theory must be legally expressed to be incorporated in a charter. Then compare it with the existing charter of your municipality or with proposed revisions of it.

This must be done critically. That is to say, you must be critical of both documents. Neither accept nor reject parts or the whole without considering alternative ways of accomplishing either your objectives or those of others in the community.

The *Model City Charter* is more than the handiwork of a legal draftsman. It contains numerous footnotes, some of them signed, in which the members of the committee take a position with respect to the desirable way of organizing a municipal government. Very few local charter commissions make their assumptions and objectives explicit or even undertake to discuss the alternative ways of organizing a local government. There are exceptions, however, that have been influencing the direction of American thought on the organization of local government. See, as examples, the *Final Report* of the Newark, N.J., Charter Commission (September, 1953) and *Four Steps to Better Government of New York City: A Plan for Action,* Report of the Temporary State Commission to Study the Organizational Structure of the Government of The City of New York (Parts 1 and 2, September, 1953 and February, 1954).

A great debate over the council-manager and strong mayor-administrator forms of government has been taking shape. See Sayre, "The General Manager Idea for Large Cities" in *Public Administration Review* (21).

You will find that a text like that of Anderson and Weidner has chapters that discuss most of the provisions of the Model Charter. Some of its features have been treated in excellent books and articles. Others, such as the city council, have been given very little consideration by scholars. This gap has been filled to some extent by the publications of Professor Arthur Bromage, a member of the city council of Ann Arbor, Michigan. See the bibliographies in the *National Municipal Review, Public Management, American City,* and the *Municipal Year Book.*

The literature on municipal government is filled with denunciations, praise and suggestions for changes in existing structures without any consideration of the role or function to be performed by the government. See the report of the

FIGURE 2-22

COMMONWEALTH OF MASSACHUSETTS

IN THE YEAR ONE THOUSAND EIGHT HUNDRED AND SEVENTY-THREE

AN ACT

To Establish the City of Gloucester

As changed by subsequent legislation. See footnotes at bottom of each page.

Be it enacted by the Senate and House of Representatives, in General Court assembled, and by the authority of the same, as follows;

SECTION 1. The inhabitants of the town of Gloucester shall continue to be a body politic and corporate under the name of the City of Gloucester, and as such shall have, exercise, and enjoy all the rights, immunities, powers and privileges, and shall be subject to all the duties and obligations now incumbent upon and pertaining to the said town as a municipal corporation.

*SECTION 2. The administration of all the fiscal, prudential and municipal affairs of the said city, with the government thereof, shall be vested in one officer, styled the mayor, one council of eight, to be called the board of aldermen, and one council of twenty-four, to be called the common council, which boards, in their joint capacity, shall be denominated the city council; and the members thereof shall be sworn to the faithful performance of their respective duties. A majority of each board shall constitute a quorum for the transaction of business. And no member of either board shall receive any compensation for his services.

†SECTION 3. The election of city and ward officers shall take place on the first ‡ Monday of December of each year; and the municipal year shall begin on the first Monday of January following.

SECTION 4. It shall be the duty of the selectmen of said town, as soon as may be after the passage of this act, and its acceptance as herein provided, to divide said town into

(margin notes) City of Gloucester established. — Government vested in mayor and city council. — Members to be sworn. — Quorum. — Annual election. — Municipal year.

* Superseded by Sect. 3 and 6 of the Amended Charter.
† Superseded by Sect. 1 of the Amended Charter.
‡ Changed by Chap. 54, Sect. 3 of the Revised Laws of the Commonwealth, now Chap. 11, Sect. 11, General Laws, and by Chap. 560, Sects. 2 and 4 of Acts of 1907, Sect. 2 of Amended Charter.

PREAMBLE

We, the people of the City of Middletown, State of Ohio, in order to secure for ourselves the benefits of local self government under the Constitution of the State of Ohio, do order and establish this charter for the government of said City of Middletown and its successors.

ARTICLE I

Section 1. Name and Boundaries. The municipal corporation now existing and known as "The City of Middletown" shall remain and continue to be a body politic and corporate under the same name and with the same boundaries, with power and authority to change its boundaries and annex other territory contiguous thereto in the manner authorized by the general laws of Ohio.

Section 2. Saving Clause. All general laws of the State of Ohio applicable to municipal corporations, now existing or hereafter enacted, not in conflict with the provisions of this charter, or with the ordinances enacted thereunder, shall apply to the government of the City of Middletown.

All ordinances, by-laws and resolutions now in force, or in force when this charter takes effect, not inconsistant or in conflict with the provisions of this charter, shall continue in full force and effect until repealed, altered or amended as provided by general laws and the provisions of this charter. All vested rights of the City of Middletown, and all property, real and personal, of the City, shall continue to be vested or belong to the city and not affected by the adoption of this charter; nor shall any right or liability, pending suit or prosecution, either on behalf of or against the City, be in any manner affected by the provisions hereof.

The enumeration of particular powers by this charter shall not be held or deemed exclusive, but in addition to the powers enumerated herein, or implied thereby, appropriate to the exercise thereof, the City shall have and may exercise all other powers granted to municipal corporations, unless such grant of general powers by the State of Ohio is in conflict with the provisions hereof.

Section 3. Officers—How Elected. All officers provided to be elected in this charter shall be elected upon one ballot, and without any party designation of any kind upon such ballot.

The names of all candidates shall be placed under a proper heading designating the title of the office to be selected, in the manner now provided for the election of members of the Board of Education.

Section 4. Nominations. The mode of nominations of all elective municipal officers shall be by petition. Before any name shall be placed

City Charter, Middletown, Ohio

City Charter, Gloucester, Mass.

Chicago Home Rule Commission, *Modernizing a City Government* (22) for an extensive discussion of the structure and procedures of the Chicago City Council.

All textbooks in municipal government have chapters on the weak mayor, strong mayor, commission, and council-manager forms of government. Each is likely to include simple organization charts to show the formal lines of authority between the major parts of the government. The caution given under each chart in Anderson and Weidner should never be forgotten: "Note that this chart represents formal methods of selection only. The actual methods of selection and the actual lines of authority may be different."

See Lancaster for typical governmental structures in counties, townships, New England towns, school districts, and other special districts. The student is also referred to:

Fairlie, J. A., and C. M. Kneier, *County Government and Administration*. New York: Appleton-Century-Crofts, Inc., 1930.
Tableman, B., *Governmental Organization in Metropolitan Areas*. Ann Arbor, Mich.: University of Michigan Press, 1951. (For a chart showing the organization of selected special districts.)
Wager, P. W., *et al.*, *County Government Across the Nation*. Chapel Hill, N.C.: University of North Carolina Press, 1950.

For data on the distribution of various structural features among cities of various sizes and with different forms of government, see the annual article in the *Municipal Year Book* entitled "Governmental Data for the 2,529 Cities Over 5,000 Population." The first two pages of the article in the 1953 *Year Book* are reproduced as Figure 2-23. In addition to Table 1, which is reproduced, showing the form of government by population groups, the article contains tables showing the method of selection and voting power of mayors, the veto power of mayors, the term of office of mayors, the number of councilmen, the type and method of councilmanic elections, the terms of office for city councils, the salaries of councilmen, the number of cities where city councilmen serve without salary, municipal elective officers other than the mayor and council, and the municipal ownership and operation of utilities. Most of these data are broken down by size of city and by form of government.

This article is followed by Tables 4 and 5 which present certain governmental and economic data for all cities over 10,000 and between 5,000 and 10,000 respectively. Look up your own city in one of these tables.

How does the structure of local governments in your community differ from the typical forms of their respective types? Why? How much difference does it make?

Remember that organization (even formal organization) is dynamic. The principal danger in studying the organization of a government is that it will be regarded and described as if it were static. This is why so many surveys appear unrealistic.

The formal and informal methods of selecting local officials are discussed in the next chapter. As the student reads, he should remember that these methods are an important part of the organization and structure of local government. This is well understood by those who urge that local elections be "nonpartisan."

One of the best statements of the argument in favor of nonpartisanship appears in the *Final Report* of the Newark Charter Commission (Fig. 2-21). Read this statement carefully and identify the assertions of fact and theory. For example: "There is little or no relationship between national and state issues, on the one hand, and purely local questions on the other .... Partisan elections inevitably result in an emphasis on the patronage needs of the successful political party, at the expense of efficiency and economy in municipal services."

Analyze these assertions for logical consistency and their relationship to the facts in your own and other communities. Compare them with the analysis of local politics in this book. Compare the assertions in the Report of the Newark Charter Commission with the discussion in Anderson and Weidner, pp. 277-281.

If elections in your city are nonpartisan, prepare a list of reasons that people in your community give for favoring or opposing the system. Analyze the list in the same manner you analyzed the Report of the Newark Charter Commission.

How have political parties adapted themselves to the nonpartisan ballot? What has been the effect on party organization and behavior? Who nominates candidates? Is there a local civic association that functions as a political party? If so, is the system nonpartisan? Would nonpartisan elections have a different meaning in a community with only one strong party organization (Cincinnati, Ohio, or Greenwich, Connecticut) than in one with two strong parties?

REFERENCES

1. Lancaster, L. W., *Government in Rural America*. rev. ed. Princeton, N.J.: D. Van Nostrand Company, Inc., 1952.

2. Vidich, A. J., and J. Bensman, *Small Town in a Mass Society*. Princeton, N.J.: Princeton University Press, 1958.

3. Wood, R. C., *Suburbia: Its People and Their Politics*. Boston: Houghton Mifflin Company, 1959.

4. Sayre, W. S., and H. Kaufman, *Governing New York City*. New York: Russell Sage Foundation, 1960.

5. Banfield, E. C., and M. Grodzins, *Government*

Governmental Data for the 2,529 Cities Over 5,000 Population

THIS summary of governmental data for 2,529 American cities includes all cities and other incorporated urban places (boroughs, villages and towns) over 5,000 population as shown in final figures of the 1950 census of population. In addition it includes 199 towns in the New England states and townships in Pennsylvania and New Jersey as "cities" even though the United States Bureau of the Census does not classify these political subdivisions as urban places.

Five cities have been added to the Year Book including the newly-created cities of Hampton and Warwick, Virginia, and Baldwin, Jefferson and Monroeville, Pennsylvania. Baldwin township, Pennsylvania, has been dropped because most of its population was taken by Baldwin borough; the former city of Hampton, Virginia, has been absorbed because it was absorbed by the new city of Hampton which also took in considerable surrounding area and population.

Governmental data are shown for 2,529 cities over 5,000 population in Tables IV and V and were obtained direct from city officials and state correspondents for the Year Book. The governmental information shown is summarized in this article and in Tables IV and V. Washington, D. C., although shown in Table IV, is omitted from the discussion because the city cannot be classified under any of the common forms of municipal government. Articles on the 1950 census of population, metropolitan areas, governmental units, municipal and economic classification of cities will be found elsewhere in the Year Book.

Selection of Towns and Townships. While the municipal corporation is by far the most common kind of American urban government, about one-half of the New England towns and Pennsylvania and New Jersey townships possess all or most of the social, economic and governmental characteristics of regularly incorporated cities. Such towns and townships have a high population density and carry on the commonly recognized functions of municipal government even though they do not have the same status in law as incorporated cities.

The New England states, Pennsylvania, and New Jersey have a total of 401 towns and townships over 5,000 population. As stated above, about one-half of these towns and townships are similar to cities in most characteristics. On the other hand, many of the towns and townships have low population densities and perform only a few of the usual functions of municipal government. Two primary standards were established to separate the more urban of these towns and townships as "cities." Each of the 199 towns and townships in the 1953 Year Book meets both of these standards:

1. The town or township does not contain any incorporated urban place within its boundaries.

2. The town or township has one-half or more of its inhabitants living in unincorporated urban places or in an urbanized area.[1] The assumption is made that the town or township is likely to be rendering at least some municipal government services when one-half or more of its citizens live in closely built-up areas.

The application of the first standard above reduced the 401 towns and townships to 365; the application of the second standard reduced the number from 365 to the 200 included in the 1952 Year Book; Baldwin township, Pennsylvania was dropped this year for Baldwin borough reducing the number to 199. These 199 towns and townships are divided among the various states as follows: 23 towns in Connecticut, one town in Vermont, 10 towns in Rhode Island, five towns in New Hampshire, 10 towns in Maine, 68 towns in Massachusetts, 39 townships in New Jersey, and 43 townships in Pennsylvania. Each of these towns and townships is designated with a "t" or "tp" in Tables IV and V and in other tables in the Year Book.

TABLE 1

FORM OF GOVERNMENT IN 2,528 CITIES OVER 5,000 POPULATION
BY POPULATION GROUPS

Population Group	Total Number of Cities	Mayor-Council		Commission		Council-Manager		Town Meeting		Rep. Town Meeting	
		No.	Per Cent	No.	Per Cent	No.	Per Cent	No.	Per Cent	No.	Per Cent
500,000...	17	15	88.2	1	5.9	1	5.9	0	0.0	0	0.0
250,000 to 500,000	23	7	30.4	7	30.4	9	39.2	0	0.0	0	0.0
100,000 to 250,000	65	30	46.2	15	23.1	20	30.7	0	0.0	0	0.0
50,000 to 100,000	129	49	38.0	28	21.7	51	39.5	0	0.0	1	0.8
25,000 to 50,000	276	115	41.7	50	18.1	101	36.6	4	1.4	6	2.2
10,000 to 25,000	836	389	46.5	144	17.2	257	30.7	27	3.2	19	2.4
5,000 to 10,000	1,182	765	64.7	138	11.7	242	20.5	36	3.0	1	0.1
All cities over 5,000	2,528	1,370	54.2	383	15.2	681	26.9	67	2.6	27	1.1

Form of Government. Table 1, which shows the form of government of cities over 5,000, indicates that 54 per cent of these cities operate under the mayor-council plan. "Mayor-council" is defined to include municipal organizations having a president and board, or a burgess and council, or a chairman and committee, if they are equivalent in powers and functions to a mayor and council in mayor-council cities. Included are "strong-mayor" cities in which the mayor has important duties as chief administrator, and "weak-mayor" cities in which the council (often through committees) has more direct control of administration. The

[1] Unincorporated urban places contain a definite nucleus of residences and include all surrounding closely settled area within their boundaries. Over 2,000 such places have been delineated for the first time in the 1950 census. Urbanized areas contain a central city or cities of 50,000 inhabitants or more plus all densely settled areas generally contiguous to the central city through commerce, industry, or transportation. The Bureau of the Census established 150 of these urbanized areas for the 1950 census. For concise definitions of unincorporated urban places, urbanized areas, and other census areas of the 1950 census, see the Bureau of the Census release, Geographic Reports (Series GEO. No. 1) issued August 21, 1951.

FIGURE 2-23   International City Managers' Association, The Municipal Year Book, 1953.

and Housing in Metropolitan Areas. New York: McGraw-Hill Book Company, Inc., 1958. p. 18.

6. Government Affairs Foundation, *Metropolitan Communities: A Bibliography with Special Emphasis on Government and Politics*. Chicago: Public Administration Service, 1956.

7. Jones, V., B. Hudson, and L. D. Johnston, eds., *Metropolitan Communities: Supplement for 1955-57*. Chicago: Public Administration Service, 1960.

8. U.S. Department of Commerce, Office of Domestic Commerce, *National Associations of the United States*. Washington, D.C.: U.S. Government Printing Office, 1949.

9. *Public Administration Organizations. A Directory*. Chicago: Public Administration Clearing House, 1954.

10. Bollens, J. C., *The States and the Metropolitan Problem*. Chicago: Council of State Governments, 1956.

11. Connery, R. H., and R. H. Leach, *The Federal Government and Metropolitan Areas*. Cambridge, Mass.: Harvard University Press, 1960.

12. Anderson, W., and E. W. Weidner, *American City Government*. rev. ed. New York: Holt, Rinehart and Winston, Inc., 1950.

13. Phillips, J. C., *State and Local Government in America*. New York: American Book Company, 1954.

14. Pate, J. E., *Local Government and Administration*. New York: American Book Company, 1954.

15. Jones, V. "Local Government Organization in Metropolitan Areas" in C. Woodbury, ed., *The Future of Cities and Urban Redevelopment*. Chicago: University of Chicago Press, 1953. pp. 497-605.

16. Government Affairs Foundation, *Metropolitan Surveys: A Digest*. Chicago: Public Administration Service, 1958.

17. Chatters, C. H., and M. L. Hoover, *Inventory of Governmental Activities in the United States*. Chicago: American Municipal Association, 1947.

18. Upson, L. D., *The Growth of a City Government*. Detroit: Bureau of Governmental Research, 1942.

19. Simon, H., D. Smithburg, and V. Thompson, *Public Administration*. New York: Alfred A. Knopf, Inc., 1950.

20. Schattschneider, E. E., V. Jones, and S. K. Bailey, *A Guide to the Study of Public Affairs*. New York: Holt, Rinehart and Winston, Inc., 1952.

21. Sayre, W. S., "The General Manager Idea for Large Cities," *Public Administration Review*, Vol. XIV, Autumn 1954. pp. 253-58.

22. Chicago Home Rule Commission, *Modernizing a City Government*. Chicago: University of Chicago Press, 1954.

23. Cottrell, E. A., W. W. Crouch, *et al.*, *Metropolitan Los Angeles: A Study in Integration*. 16 Vols. Los Angeles: The Haynes Foundation, 1952.

24. Studenski, P., *et al.*, *The Government of Metropolitan Areas in the United States*. New York: The National Municipal League, 1930.

Chapter *III*

LOCAL POLITICS

SOME ASSUMPTIONS ABOUT POLITICS

All political research is based on certain assumptions about the nature of public affairs. It is important to make these assumptions explicit at the outset.

All politics deals with power. Power may be defined in a number of different ways: as control of the legislative process, the administrative establishment, the police, the financial resources, the organizing capacity, the expertise and leadership of the government. There are many other definitions. Because government in any modern community is actually a complex of authorities, power presumably transcends any single governmental unit or office. Power exists within governments, but it is to be found outside of governments. Power may overflow the jurisdictional limits of any one of the complexes of governments because it is based on the social structure, exists in organizations more extensive than the scope of any one legal authority, or is based on public opinion that is able to influence people inside and outside of the governmental structures. Government operates within the social structure and is itself a part of the social structure. We are interested in the use of the public power of formal legal governmental organizations but want to avoid the illusion that government operates in a vacuum, or that governmental power is the only kind of power. In this sense, politics is the process of relating governmental power to all other kinds of power. Power is defined comprehensively to help you avoid narrow or technical or formal concepts of politics. If power is defined broadly, it follows that politics must be defined broadly also, for where there is power there is also politics. The moral of this discussion is: look for politics everywhere.

Sayre and Kaufman, *Governing New York City* (1) is a magnificent case study of the "local" politics of a very large metropolitan area. No student of local politics can afford to neglect this work.

Power is almost never an end in itself. Like money, it is a means toward a multitude of ends. To understand the struggle for power, it is necessary therefore to understand what people want to accomplish. The first rule in studying the politics of any community is accordingly to try to find out what the struggle is about. What do people want?

Politics makes sense only in terms of the objectives and purposes of people. One good way to open up this field for examination is to take a look at the functions of the various governments with which you are concerned. If you make a list of these functions, you have a good working base from which to begin.

You need have no illusions about your ability to find easy answers to the questions raised here. On the other hand, you are likely to find out a great deal about politics in your town if you keep on asking people what politics is about. This is apt to be a fruitful inquiry.

The political objectives of people are not always obvious. The conflicts in your community may be disguised, for example, as discussions of home rule, local self-government, economy, corruption, law, contract rights, and local pride—when they really are about tax assessments, zoning, new residential construction, public works contracts, control of schools, control of the police force, or the attempts of newcomers in the town to take control away from the old timers. Be prepared to interpret this kind of double talk when you hear it so that you can penetrate the semantic curtain. What do people really want?

It is not necessary to take a cynical view of politics and people to understand that people often have great difficulty in understanding their own political motivations. The best evidence of the involvement of people in politics is the fact that they tend to rationalize their attitudes. It is well to assume at the outset, therefore, that nearly everyone engages in a certain amount of self-deception when politics is discussed, no matter how honest he may be.

Considering everything you know about your community—what the local governments are doing, how people make a living, what kind of people live in the community, how they are divided, how they differ in status, income, and origin, what they need—try to make up your own mind about what they might reasonably be expected to want. Do your ideas of what politics ought to be about correspond with what seems to be happening? If not, try to find out why.

Test your hypotheses by asking people what they think politics is about; ask the question often and persistently, and follow up all the leads you get.

In a society in which "politics" is frequently regarded as a disreputable kind of business and the word "politician" is used as a term of opprobrium, the student should realize that not all politicians are easily identified. Thus, in addition to the recognized politicians in the community, there are apt to be a number of influential persons who play important roles in the political system without being stigmatized as politicians. This is a logical consequence of the proposition that politics deals with all kinds of power. There are usually a number of businessmen, bankers, labor leaders, lawyers, newspaper publishers, and even members of the clergy who seem to be able to engage in political activity while maintaining the fiction that they are above politics or outside of the political system. A little reflection is likely to suggest that immunity from criticism is itself evidence of power, and that people who are able to participate in politics without the political taint may be more important than those who suffer the penalties of identification. An understanding of this situation is essential to the study of all local politics. A safe rule is to take it for granted that all important people in the community are involved in politics in one way or another. This is an inclusive concept of politics.

Implicit in this survey is the assumption that there are likely to be conflicts within the community. To get you started on your analysis, we list a number of possible points of conflict. Can you find evidence of the presence of these conflicts in your community?

Some Potential Conflicts

1. Taxation: economy vs. the desire for better schools, streets, public works, and social services. Taxation is a perpetual source of conflict. Is there a conflict about who and what is to be taxed and how much? About how much money is spent? Is this a sore point in the community?
2. Zoning and City Planning: land use and the fight for space, quiet, light, air, and privacy. Attend some public hearings on zoning questions. These questions are involved in all discussions of housing, urban redevelopment, highway construction, parks and playgrounds, segregation, zoning, etc.
3. Housing: public vs. private. This source of conflict appears at all levels of American government. Ask real estate dealers and labor leaders for their views.
4. Segregation: who is able to live where? All segregation reflects division in the community and is a form of conflict, even when it is unavowed.
5. Friction between the old settlers and the newer immigrant population elements; between partly assimilated nationality groups; between ethnic groups.
6. Antagonism (in growing communities) between the old timers and invading newcomers. How does the community try to prevent invasion by undesirable newcomers?
7. Social and economic status: all stratification is a form of conflict.
8. Employment: labor vs. business.

9. Religion: especially in its secondary forms concerning education, patronage, "recognition," etc.
10. Intraparty discussion: organization vs. antiorganization interests.
11. Party struggles: open and unavowed.

These conflicts are especially important in one-party communities or in communities in which changes in political alignments are taking place. Watch primary elections and nominating conventions.

As you proceed with your survey you will become aware that the local community is a focus of conflicts. These conflicts are greatly magnified by the growth of the urban population, the rise of great metropolitan concentrations of population, and by a multitude of problems resulting from urbanization. As a matter of fact, it is likely that the politics of the future will concern itself largely with the frustrations of urban life, the struggle for light, space, quiet, air, and privacy in the new urbanized areas. You ought to consider the political implications of all the new problems of the modern urban complex.

Treat this list as a way of opening up the larger questions of conflict, power, and politics in your community. When you interview people ask them about these conflicts.

When businessmen, labor leaders, Republicans, Democrats, politicians, professional men, and others give you different answers about these conflicts, try to understand the reasons for the differences in their attitudes. Try to get people to cite specific instances to illustrate their answers.

Behind the struggles over taxation, land use, status, employment, and political organization, there exists some kind of struggle over the management of the community as a whole: the way people live, where they live, and the kind of a world they want. This struggle reveals itself in discussions of budgets, zoning, segregation, education, housing, and religion. Every time you try to understand a particular issue, try to relate it to the larger question. This is what gives politics its meaning.

When you think that you are able to make a good guess at what the politics in your locality is about, you can begin to understand why people act as they do. If the politics in your town does not make sense, try again. It is dangerous to conclude that people generally are so stupid that they do not know what they want.

The foregoing discussion should not be taken to mean that no genuine agreement exists in the local community. On the contrary, the very existence of a community implies a great body of agreement. Democracy involves a constant process of resolution of conflict, a movement from conflict to agreement, to new conflicts and new agreements. On the other hand, the absence of conflict may also indicate the absence of anything like a genuine body of agreement. All change involves conflict because conflict results from the attempt to revise or extend or amend the old basis of agreement. Do not be surprised if people tell you that there is no conflict in the community. If you persist, you are likely to penetrate the pretense that perfect harmony prevails. It is a good rule to assume that where there is life there is conflict.

Once you have identified a conflict, try to find out what people do about it. How does the community handle a conflict? Does it attempt to suppress it or does it try to get a full hearing of all arguments, followed by an attempt to work out a resolution that provides a new basis of agreement? What people do about conflicts is apt to shed a great deal of light on the nature of the community, its power structure, its significance.

If there seems to be no conflict in your community, what does the seeming absence of conflict mean? Who is most likely to run the city if there is no organized exploitation of political conflicts? If there is no opposition? Who is most likely to benefit when a nonpartisan government is kept permanently in power, when no major cleavage in the community is allowed to develop openly? Who has an interest in minimizing political conflict or in restricting the scope of politics? How is conflict suppressed? Make a list of potential conflicts that do not seem to have come to a head in your community. Ask local leaders for an explanation of the submergence of these issues. Conflict is the price of change: nothing is likely to be accomplished without controversy. You have reason to be extremely skeptical about any unusual quiescence in your community. This is a wonderful entering wedge for political research. You can discover a great deal about your community by questioning people about their attitudes toward a variety of conflicts, or about their reasons for feeling that certain conflicts ought to be depreciated or given more attention.

The tightest systems of political control strangle conflict so completely that it is impossible for the opposition to develop alternative public policies or to raise issues to the level of public discussion. Moreover, the tightest systems of control are very apt to be local. If there is no significant controversy, or if politics does not seem concerned with any real issue, or if there are no visible conflicts, you have reason to suspect the existence of a tight little local political monopoly. See if you can identify it. Test this proposition in your interviews with local politicians, with the leaders of minority groups, with newspaper reporters and social workers, and do not be surprised if it is difficult to penetrate the wall of silence. Do people get angry or irritated when they are questioned about this subject?

Political parties are often the most important instruments of conflict in a community, but they do not monopolize conflict. There are often differences of opinion about the role that the parties should be allowed to play in local politics. This should not surprise you because all conflict tends to become a conflict over the political organization of the community—the way in which the antagonists are permitted to mobilize their support, the forms of organization that are socially approved. No argument about strategy or the scope and nature of political organization is ever neutral. Partisanship and nonpartisanship can be understood most easily, therefore, as competing strategies of politics put forward by people who want to win their objectives in their own special way. The struggle is never one between nonpartisan saints and partisan sinners. If anyone tries to sell you that idea, bear down hard to find out who the saints and sinners are and what they are really fighting about.

NONPARTISANSHIP AS A WAY OF MANAGING CONFLICT

Nonpartisan local election systems should be examined with caution because the theory and practice of nonpartisan politics may differ widely. How nonpartisan are the nonpartisan elections in your town? A nonpartisan system may be designed to enable a minority party to divide or confuse the majority party. An organization of the "good" citizens to control the city and presumably to keep the "bad" citizens out of power is partisan in its assumptions; indeed, it is difficult to imagine anything more partisan than an alignment of "good" people against "bad" people. Nonpartisanship may, itself, therefore, be a form of politics designed to confuse familiar partisan patterns of politics and achieve political ends that could not be achieved by more frankly partisan means.

Do you think that people can be made nonpartisan by law?

An article in the *Hartford Courant* of October 30, 1955 concerning the nonpartisan council elected in Hartford illustrates the complexities of the question. Hartford has nonpartisan city council elections. A nonpartisan Citizens Charter Committee nominates slates of candidates and often wins council elections. In 1953, however, the Democratic Party picked its own slate and elected a council majority. Two years later, the Citizens Charter Committee and the Democratic Party openly endorsed slates of candidates while the Republican Party (a) refused to endorse any candidates, but (b) raised money to support those charter committee candidates who were registered Republicans. The slate of the Citizens Charter Committee included three registered Democrats who were ostensibly supported by the

Democratic Party but with a visible lack of enthusiasm. Excerpts from the article in the *Hartford Courant* follow:

So many cross currents are flowing in the city election campaign that the picture is beginning to look like a jigsaw puzzle.

There are more slates and combinations of candidates for the City Council than have appeared since council-manager elections began in 1947. There are wheels within wheels within wheels to such an extent that any analysis of the situation is in danger of foundering almost before it can be floated....

The reason for the confusion and bewilderment is because of the nature of the non-partisan election. It is every man for himself, for the nine who get the most votes among the 18 running will be elected. Thus it is vital that each candidate do all he can for himself. Each is seeking help from whatever source he can....

The Hartford case suggests the possibility that nonpartisan election systems may be used to promote partisan ends. Nonpartisan ballots have long been used in partisan elections in many parts of the world. No party labels appear on the ballots in British parliamentary elections. These elections are nonpartisan in about the same way that some local elections in the United States are nonpartisan. The point of this discussion is that it is necessary to look beyond the formal requirements of the election laws to find out what is actually going on.

It should always be possible to find out what the party affiliations of nonpartisan local candidates are. While the law can rule party labels off the local ballot, it does not forbid partisan activity at other levels of politics. Usually, a little research will show that some of the nonpartisans are nonpartisan Republicans, others, nonpartisan Democrats. You will find out something about the meaning of the system by learning who likes nonpartisan elections and who is unhappy about them. Do you think that there is a conflict between the idea of nonpartisan local elections and the idea of local self-government?

Behind all of the discussion of politics in this chapter is a question concerning the political attitudes of people in your town. What is the attitude of the community toward politics in general? Do people think that politics is a necessary evil, something they would like to get rid of if they could? Or do they see politics as an opportunity for many people to get together to work out democratic solutions of their common problems? Is the attitude of the community toward politicians and political parties largely negative or does it look to the parties for leadership? Nothing could be more important than the answers to these questions.

PARTY ORGANIZATION

Compared with nonpartisan politics, party politics is relatively visible and relatively easily understood; the antagonists were identified, the sides chosen, and the alignments formed many years ago, and nearly everyone knows where he belongs in the conflict. Party politics and nonpartisan politics reflect different strategies of politics, and the results of these strategies are apt to differ greatly.

Conflict is assumed in this analysis of politics, and conflict implies organization. Important conflicts do not simply happen; they become important when they are exploited, when people are persuaded to take sides and organize for a struggle. Organization is a basic ingredient of politics.

Political parties play an important role in your community even if local elections are nonpartisan. A local political survey is concerned with all politics in the community, including the local manifestations of national and state politics. No matter what the formal, theoretical, or legal relations of the parties to municipal elections may be, you should try to understand party organization and party politics at all levels of government in your community. Even if the parties are really excluded from local politics, they can have an impact on local government through their control of the state and national governments.

FORMAL PARTY ORGANIZATION

You can begin your study of the parties by identifying their formal structures. It is probably worth while to draw some kind of organization chart to help you make this kind of study, provided you do not take such a chart too seriously. You will then be able to locate political personnel in the formal structure. On the other hand, you may find that there are some very important politicians who hold no party office, or you may discover some politicians whom you might not have found otherwise. At any rate, the condition of the visible party organizations will tell you something about the status of the system. Do the party committees actually meet or are they paper organizations? Are there any long standing vacancies on the committees? Are decisions made by the committees or do the committees merely ratify decisions made elsewhere? Does the party structure rest on a legal base? Is it set up in the statutes or is it based on party rules? Can you get a copy of the party rules? Can you find any extralegal party committees? How are people appointed or elected to the committees? By the time you have found the answers to these questions, you will know something about the system. Get a copy of the election laws of your state by writing to the secretary of state at your state capitol and see what the laws say about parties, party primaries, and party committees.

Party organization traditionally takes the form of a hierarchy of committees having jurisdiction over geographical divisions and subdivisions of the country, ranging from the largest to the smallest units: a national committee, state committees, county committees, city and town committees, legislative district committees, ward and precinct committees. These committees always have chairmen and sometimes act through executive committees. Sometimes a chairman acts on behalf of the committee with a minimum of consultation, and the full committee rarely meets. It is always necessary to remember that the formal organization and the actual functioning structure may not be identical. In other words, the party may actually be run by a group functioning outside of the formal committee structure.

ELECTION LAWS

The formal structure of the parties is frequently described in the election laws of the state. Usually, the legal party structure is described in the direct primary laws, which establish a procedure for electing the party committees. You should consult your state election laws for this purpose.

See Figures 3-1, 3-2, 3-3, 3-4, and 3-5 for the sections of the New Jersey Election laws describing the legal pattern of party organization in that state. Do the election laws of your state contain similar provisions?

See the standard textbooks dealing with political parties for chapters on party organization. The textbooks will give you some ideas for the evaluation of the party structure you find in your town. The following are a few of many excellent textbooks in the field: Key, *Politics, Parties, and Pressure Groups* (2); Bone, *American Politics and the Party System* (3); and Penniman, *Sait's American Parties and Elections* (4). For another interpretation see Schattschneider, *Party Government* (5).

PARTY RULES

Next, try to find out what the party rules have to say about party organization. In spite of nearly two generations of direct primary legislation regulating the internal processes of the parties, much latitude is left to the parties in making their own rules. Party rules may be as important as, or even more important than, primary legislation in determining the structure of party organization, though the facts differ greatly from state to state.

Search your election laws for references to party rules. See, for example, the references to party rules in the New York Election Laws, reproduced as Figures 3-6 and 3-7, and note the

provisions for filing copies of the state and county party rules with the secretary of state. Do the election laws of your state include similar requirements? These statutory provisions tell you where to find copies of the rules. Sometimes the parties publish their rules; sometimes mimeographed copies are available. More often, however, it is difficult to get copies of the rules, especially local party rules. It may be necessary to pursue your quest through a variety of channels: influential political friends and public officials, among others. Do not give up if you do not succeed the first time.

Remember always that it is profoundly characteristic of American parties that much work is done outside of the legal and formal structures. See Sorauf, "Extralegal Political Parties in Wisconsin," *American Political Science Review* (6).

The parties themselves publish many organization charts, several of which are reproduced in Figures 3-8, 3-9, 3-10 and 3-11. Visit party headquarters to see if you can obtain copies, or write to the offices of the national committees in Washington, D.C. The parties publish also extensive literature about the structure and functions of party organizations. This material is likely to be helpful to you because it is used by the parties to instruct their own workers. See Figures 3-12, 3-13, 3-14, 3-15, 3-16, and 3-17 for examples of this kind of material.

You can find out something about the differences between the parties by talking to party leaders, newspapermen, businessmen, labor leaders. Do not be surprised if what people tell you is confusing. Party leaders are not in the habit of defining party issues with care and restraint; each is apt to claim everything for his own side and to give little credit to the other side. Discounting all exaggerations, try to find the real differences between the parties. One clue to these differences may be found in the makeup of the two parties.

A good way to begin examining differences in the composition of the parties is to see who are the leaders and workers in the two parties. Where do they live? What are their business and other associations? How do they make a living? What kinds of houses do they live in? What are their national origins or religious affiliations? As you look up data of this sort, you may find that two different party patterns emerge.

Next, compare strong Republican and Democratic precincts as to housing, living conditions, occupations of voters, number of families per dwelling, owner occupancy, and so forth. Do characteristic party patterns begin to appear in your data? If you find that Republicans and Democrats tend to be different kinds of people, you have a clue to the meaning of party politics.

The two major parties in the United States are

Chapter 5. PARTY ORGANIZATIONS.

Article 1. GENERAL PROVISIONS.

19:5-1. Powers of and restrictions upon political parties; party columns on official ballot. A political party may nominate candidates for public office at primary elections provided for in this Title, elect committees for the party within the State, county or municipality, as the case may be, and in every other respect may exercise the rights and shall be subject to the restrictions herein provided for political parties; except that no political party which fails to poll at any primary election for a general election at least ten per centum (10%) of the votes cast in the State for members of the General Assembly at the next preceding general election, held for the election of all of the members of the General Assembly, shall be entitled to have a party column on the official ballot at the general election for which the primary election has been held. In such case the names of the candidates so nominated at the primary election shall be printed in the column or columns designated "Nomination by Petition" on the official ballot under the respective titles of office for which the nominations have been made, followed by the designation of the political party of which the candidates are members.

Amended P. L. 1948, chapter 438.

Article 2. MUNICIPAL, COUNTY AND STATE COMMITTEES.

19:5-2. Membership and organization of municipal committees. The members of the municipal committees of political parties shall consist of the elected members of the county committee resident in the respective municipalities. The members of the municipal committee shall take office on the first Saturday following their election as members of the county committee, on which day the terms of all members of such committees theretofore elected shall terminate. The annual meeting of each municipal committee shall be held on the first Monday following the primary election for the general election, at an hour and place to be designated in a notice

local Committees

The New Jersey Election laws describe the formal organization of the parties in great detail. Note that the statutes describe the powers of the parties and the composition of the party committees.

FIGURE 3–1

to be given by the chairman of the outgoing municipal committee to each member-elect, at which annual meeting the members of each committee shall elect some suitable person as chairman to hold office for one year or until his successor is elected. The municipal committee shall have power to adopt a constitution and by-laws for its proper government. The chairman shall preside at all meetings of the committee, and shall perform all duties required of him by law and the constitution and by-laws of such committee.

A member of a municipal committee of any political party may resign his office to the committee of which he is a member, and upon acceptance thereof by the committee a vacancy shall exist. A vacancy in the office of a member of a municipal committee of any political party, howsoever caused, shall be filled for the unexpired term by the remaining members of the committee in the municipality in which the vacancy occurs.

19:5-3. Membership and organization of county committees; vacancies; certification of unit of representation and number of election districts. The members of the county committees of political parties shall be elected annually at the primary for the general election in the manner provided in this title for the selection of party candidates to be voted for at the general election by voters of a municipality. The county committee shall consist of one male and one female member from each unit of representation in the county. The male receiving the highest number of votes among the male candidates and the female receiving the highest number of votes among the female candidates shall be declared elected. Members of the county committee shall actually reside in the districts or units which they respectively represent. The county committee shall determine by its by-laws the units into which the county shall be divided for purpose of representation in the county committee.

The members of the county committee of each of the political parties shall take office on the first Saturday following their election, on which day the terms of all members of such committees theretofore elected shall terminate. The annual meeting of each county committee shall be held on the first Tuesday following the primary election, except that when such meeting day falls on a legal holiday then the said meeting shall be held on the day following, at an hour and place to be designated in a notice in writing to be mailed by the chairman of the outgoing county committee to each member-elect, at which annual meeting the members of such committee shall elect some suitable person as chairman, to hold office for one year, or until his successor is elected. Such committee shall have power to adopt a constitution and by-laws for its proper government. The chairman shall preside at all meetings of the committee and shall perform all duties required of him by law and the constitution and by-laws of such committee.

A member of a county committee of any political party may resign his office to the committee of which he is a member, and upon acceptance thereof by the committee a vacancy shall exist. A vacancy in the office of a member of the county committee of any political party, caused by death, resignation, failure to elect or otherwise, shall be filled for the unexpired term by the municipal committee of the municipality wherein the vacancy occurs, if there is such committee, and if not, by the remaining members of

Membership
Officers
By-laws
Annual meetings

County Committees
Composition
Chairman
By-laws

FIGURE 3—2

New Jersey Election Laws, 1954.

the county committee of such political party representing the territory in the county in which such vacancy occurs.

The chairman of the county committee of the several political parties shall before the first day of March, certify to the clerk of each municipality in the county the unit of representation in such municipality, together with the enumeration of the election district or districts embraced within such unit.

Amended P. L. 1948, chapter 2.

19:5–4. Membership and organization of state committees; vacancies; national committee members. At the primary for the general election of the year in which a governor is to be elected, one male and one female member of the state committee of each of the political parties shall be elected in each county. The male receiving the highest number of votes among the male candidates and the female receiving the highest number of votes among the female candidates shall be declared elected.

The members of the state committee of each of the political parties shall take office on the first Tuesday following their election, on which day the terms of all members of such committees theretofore elected shall terminate. The annual meeting of the state committee shall be held on the first Tuesday after such primary election at the hour and place to be designated in a notice in writing to be mailed by the chairman of the outgoing state committee to each member-elect, at which annual meeting the members of the committee in the year in which a governor is to be elected, shall elect some suitable person as chairman to hold office for four years, or until his successor is elected. The committee shall have power to adopt a constitution and by-laws for its proper government. The chairman shall preside at all meetings of the committee and shall perform all duties required of him by law and the constitution and by-laws of such committee.

A member of a state committee of any political party may resign his office to the committee of which he is a member, and upon acceptance thereof by the committee a vacancy shall exist. A vacancy in the office of a member of the state committee of any political party, howsoever caused, shall be filled for the unexpired term by the members of the county committee of such political party in the county in which the vacancy occurs.

Members of the state committee shall serve for four years or until their successors are elected. The state committee shall choose its chairman and the member or members of the national committee of its political party.

Amended P. L. 1948, chapter 216.
Chapter 216, P. L. 1948, Par. 3, reads as follows:
3. This act shall take effect immediately, but shall not affect the present terms of the Chairman or members of the State Committee.

19:5–5. Maintenance of party organization. Any state committee, county committee or municipal committee of any political party may receive and disburse moneys for the general purposes of maintaining such organization during the whole or any part of the year. The expenses for maintenance of organization shall be confined to the hiring of suitable rooms for meetings of such committee, for stationery, for hiring of necessary clerks, for the expenses of notices of the meetings of such committee, for giving publicity to the policies and candidates of their respective party organiza-

Bases of representation.

State committee

Annual meeting

By-laws

Chairman

Term of office

Party finances

FIGURE 3—3

New Jersey Election Laws, 1954.

tions, and other expenses incidental to the maintenance of such organization.

Within twenty days after the day of the general election, the person who has had the custody of the moneys contributed to or on account of any state, county or municipal committee during the previous year shall file with the secretary of state in the case of the state committee, and with the county clerk in the case of the county or municipal committee, a statement of the amount of money received by or on behalf of such committee during the previous year, together with the names and addresses of the persons from whom the money was received, and also a statement of the purposes for which it was expended, itemized as to all items in excess of five dollars, and with a general statement as to the purposes for which the items less than five dollars were expended. The person making such statement shall make affidavit that the same is true.

Article 3. STATE CONVENTIONS.

19:5–6. **Annual convention; membership; time and place of holding; platforms; resolutions committee; adjournments.** There shall be held in each year a state convention of each of the political parties.

Such state convention of each party shall consist of the following members:

(1) The party candidates for the following offices:

(a) Members of the senate or house of representatives of the United States from this state, nominated at the party primaries held for the nomination of candidates for any of said offices immediately preceding the convention.

(b) State senator nominated, in each county, at the party primaries, held for the nomination of a candidate for said office, immediately preceding the convention, and

(c) Members of the general assembly, nominated in each county, at the party primaries immediately preceding the convention, if the convention is to be held in a year in which all of the members of the general assembly are to be elected; or all of the party candidates for said offices, in each county, who were voted upon and were not elected at the general election held in the year immediately preceding the convention, if the convention is to be held in a year other than one in which all of the members of the general assembly are to be elected, except that any candidates nominated for the filling of vacancies, in said offices, at the party primaries held in the year in which the convention is held, shall replace, to an equal number, the candidates so voted upon and not elected at the general election held in the preceding year, who received the least number of votes in said general election;

(2) the candidate of the party for governor nominated at the primaries in the year in which a governor is elected, and in each year in which no governor is elected the governor of the state shall be a member of the convention of the political party to which he belongs;

(3) members of the state senate and of the general assembly belonging to the party who are holding office at the time of the state convention and whose successors are not to be chosen at the ensuing general election;

FIGURE 3—4

New Jersey Election Laws, 1954.

(4) members of the state committee chosen as herein provided; and

(5) members of the senate and house of representatives of the United States from this state, belonging to such party, who are holding office at the time of the holding of the state convention and whose successors are not to be chosen at the ensuing general election.

The convention of each party shall be held at the city of Trenton on the second Thursday after the primary election for the general election in each year. When the day prescribed by law for holding state conventions of political parties, or any adjournment thereof, falls on a legal holiday, the convention or adjournment thereof, as the case may be, shall be held on the day preceding such legal holiday. The place and the hour at which the convention shall meet shall be fixed by call of the existing state committee to be issued at least five days prior to the date of meeting. If no call is issued by the state committee, any person qualified to sit in the convention may issue a call.

The convention of each party shall have power to adopt and promulgate a party platform for its party, and to transact such other business as may properly come before it. The convention of each political party, in this title authorized, upon convening, shall appoint a committee on resolutions consisting of five members. The convention shall then be open for the reception of all proposed planks for the party platform, which planks shall be referred to the committee on resolutions, whose duty it shall be to prepare a tentative party platform and furnish to each member of the convention within one week thereafter a copy of the same and of all other planks submitted to it which have not been incorporated in the tentative party platform, together with the names and addresses of the delegates proposing the same. After the introduction of all proposed planks and the reference thereof to the committee on resolutions, the convention shall adjourn to meet again two weeks later at its originally set meeting place. At the adjourned meeting the respective conventions shall consider and may adopt the draft of the platform so prepared by the committee on resolutions with such amendments as shall be suggested and adopted in the conventions as a whole. The voting on the adoption of the party platform shall be on the entire platform as reported by the committee on resolutions, unless there be an objection to any separate plank or planks or to any amendment thereto, in which case the voting on such plank or planks or amendment shall be by the "ayes" and "nays" of the members of the convention present and voting.

Amended P. L. 1950, chapter 35.

FIGURE 3—5

New Jersey Election Laws, 1954

Note that the state convention makes no nominations; it is restricted to the adoption of a party platform.

shall be made directly by enrolled party voters at unofficial primaries.

5. Party nominations of candidates for town and village offices, in any county, shall be made in the manner prescribed by the rules of the county committee, heretofore or hereafter adopted, except that in any town in a county having a population of over seven hundred fifty thousand inhabitants party nominations of candidates for town offices shall be made at the fall primary preceding the election, and except that, in any other town, the members of the county committee of a political party elected to such county committee from such town may meet and adopt, by a two-thirds vote, a rule providing that its party candidates for town offices shall be nominated at the fall primary preceding the election and except that in any village of the first class, wherein personal registration is

75

required in accordance with section fifty-one-a of the village law, the village board may, by resolution, subject to a permissive referendum as defined in the village law, provide that party nominations of candidates for elective village offices shall be made at the same time as designated for the registration of voters in accordance with the provisions of section fifty-one-a of the village law and except that party nominations for village offices, or for town offices to be filled at a time other than that of a general election, shall not be made at the primary elections. In the absence or until the adoption of such a rule, nominations for such offices may be made in accordance with the existing practice in the county. If a rule of the county committee or of the members of the county committee of a political party elected to such county committee from a town, adopted as herein prescribed, provide that party candidates for town offices, in any town or towns of the county, to be filled at the time of general election, shall be nominated at the fall primary preceding the election, such rule shall not apply to nor affect a fall primary occurring less than sixty days after a certified copy of the rule shall have been filed with the board of elections. After the filing of such a copy of a rule heretofore or hereafter adopted, the rule shall continue in force until a certified copy of a rule revoking the same shall have been filed with such board at least sixty days before a subsequent fall primary preceding an election for filling such offices.

[Amended by chap. 218, Laws of 1949.]

FIGURE 3—6

New York Election Laws, 1954.

Note the extent to which New York nominations are governed by party rules.

board of elections of the county a certificate stating the names and postoffice addresses of such officers. Such officers shall be enrolled voters of the party but need not be members of such committees.

2. Each committee may prepare rules for the government of the party within its political subdivision, which may include provisions for the payment of dues, and that failure to pay them shall be cause for removal by the committee. Within three days after the adoption of such rules a certified copy thereof shall be filed by the state committee in the office of the secretary of state and by the county committee in the office of the secretary of state and in the office of the board of elections of the county. Such rules shall continue to be the rules for the committee until they are amended or new rules adopted. Such rules may be amended from time to time by a majority of the members of the committee present at a meeting at which there is a quorum, provided a copy of the proposed amendment shall be sent with the notice of the meeting at which such amendment is to be proposed, such notice to be not less than five days before such meeting, and to be mailed to the postoffice address of each member of the committee. Until the adoption of such rules, the rules of the existing committee, so far as consistent with this chapter, shall continue to be the rules of the party for that political unit.

3. If the rules of the county committee shall so provide, one district leader and one associate district leader shall be elected at primary elections as herein provided, for each assembly district or part of an assembly district within any county within the city of New York as may be designated in such rules for the purpose. The district leader or associate district leader shall be of opposite sexes, shall be enrolled voters of the party residing within the district and shall be elected at the same primary election and for the same term as members of the county committee. Each shall perform such duties, powers and functions as the rules of the county committee may prescribe. Vacancies in such positions shall be filled by the members of the county committee within the assembly district or part thereof as the case may be. District leaders and associate district leaders shall not be members or vote in meetings of the county committee or any sub-committee thereof unless also duly elected to membership thereon.

[Amended by chap. 746, Laws of 1954.]

Note that the law requires the parties to file copies of their rules with public authorities.

RULES AND REGULATIONS
(With amendments through April 17, 1948)
of the

DEMOCRATIC PARTY OF THE STATE OF NEW YORK

- - - - - -

The Democratic State Committee of the State of New York hereby adopts the following rules and regulations for the government of the Democratic Party of the State of New York:

RULES

of the Republican State Committee

Adopted September 5, 1950

FIGURE 3–7   New York Election Laws, 1954.

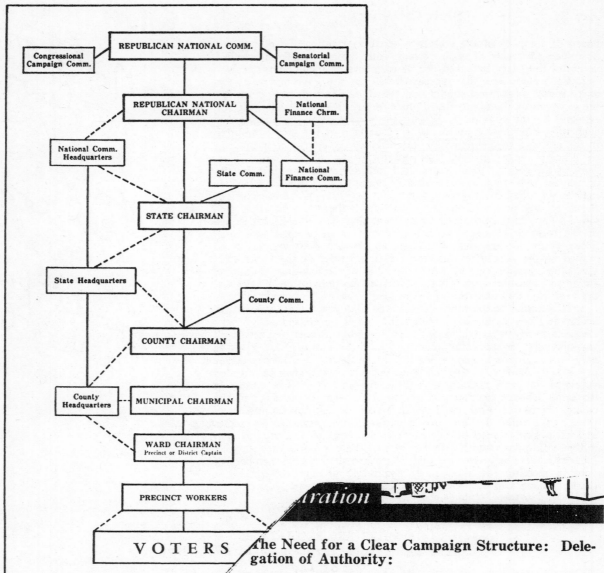

FIGURE 3—8

From Republican Campaign Manual

The Need for a Clear Campaign Structure: Delegation of Authority:

Many campaigns are run with the loosest and most haphazard campaign structure imaginable, without either clear lines of authority or clear understandings of responsibility. But such haphazard organization and structure bring only haphazard results.

The first job of every Campaign Manager is to set up a campaign organization with a clear structure. This simply means, as a practical matter, that every function should be delegated clearly and specifically to someone, preferably in writing, with a clear line of authority and a perfectly clear understanding of responsibility on the part of the person who is to carry out the particular program. Nothing causes so much trouble as a misunderstanding, and because of the fluid and dynamic character of a political campaign, especial care must be taken to prevent misunderstandings in this fast-moving field. And, the need for clarity increases with the scope of the campaign.

This Campaign Manual is intended to provide much of the written material to serve as a basis for delegation, and may, of course, be supplemented by written memoranda.

Where possible, the Campaign Manager should reserve no administrative or operational responsibilities for himself, but should delegate them all. When a new and workable idea appears on the horizon, he should put somebody in charge of it as a new program immediately, reserving for himself the basic

Organize FOR WORK
Work TO WIN

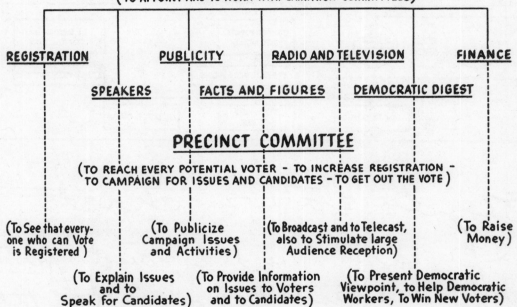

NATIONAL COMMITTEE
(TO ADVISE AND TO HELP)

STATE COMMITTEE
(TO PLAN AND TO DIRECT)

COUNTY COMMITTEE
(TO APPOINT AND TO WORK WITH CAMPAIGN COMMITTEES)

REGISTRATION   **PUBLICITY**   **RADIO AND TELEVISION**   **FINANCE**

SPEAKERS   **FACTS AND FIGURES**   **DEMOCRATIC DIGEST**

PRECINCT COMMITTEE

(TO REACH EVERY POTENTIAL VOTER – TO INCREASE REGISTRATION –
TO CAMPAIGN FOR ISSUES AND CANDIDATES – TO GET OUT THE VOTE)

(To See that every-
one who can Vote
is Registered)

(To Publicize
Campaign Issues
and Activities)

(To Broadcast and to Telecast,
also to Stimulate large
Audience Reception)

(To Raise
Money)

(To Explain Issues
and to
Speak for Candidates)

(To Provide Information
on Issues to Voters
and to Candidates)

(To Present Democratic
Viewpoint, to Help Democratic
Workers, To Win New Voters)

ELECTIONS ARE <u>WON</u>
in the <u>PRECINCTS</u>

㉘

FIGURE 3—9

From The Key to Democratic victory

(See figure 3-11)

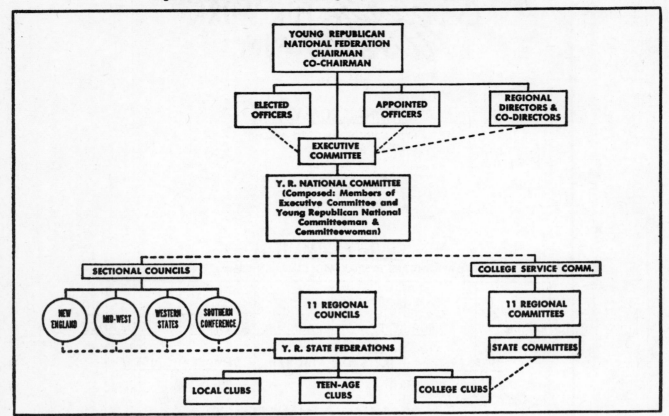

Organization charts
help you understand formal
party structure but they
may not show what the
real functioning relations
are.

FIGURE 3—10

(For source see figure 3-12)

PARTY ORGANIZATION

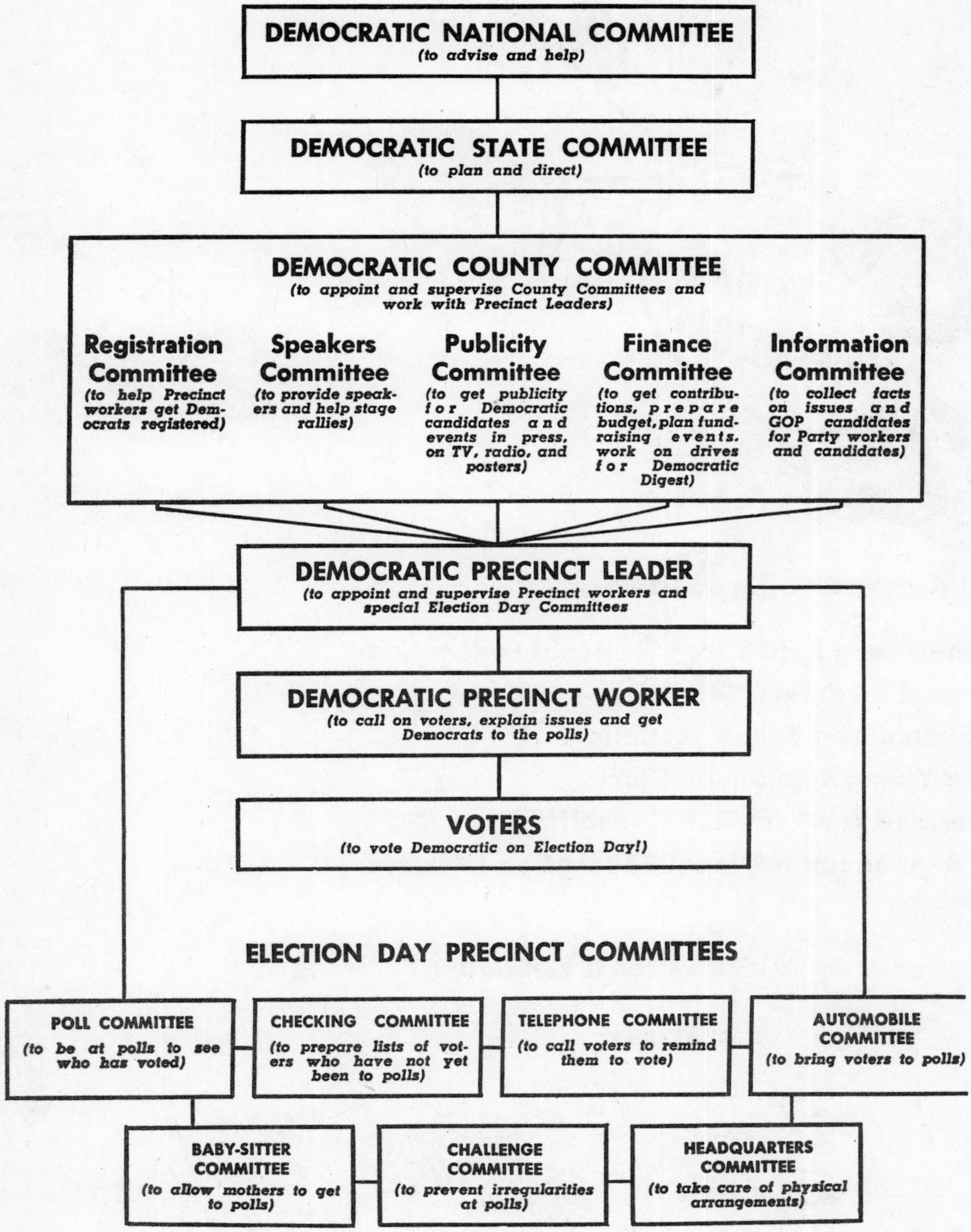

DEMOCRATIC NATIONAL COMMITTEE
(to advise and help)

DEMOCRATIC STATE COMMITTEE
(to plan and direct)

DEMOCRATIC COUNTY COMMITTEE
(to appoint and supervise County Committees and work with Precinct Leaders)

Registration Committee
(to help Precinct workers get Democrats registered)

Speakers Committee
(to provide speakers and help stage rallies)

Publicity Committee
(to get publicity for Democratic candidates and events in press, on TV, radio, and posters)

Finance Committee
(to get contributions, prepare budget, plan fundraising events. work on drives for Democratic Digest)

Information Committee
(to collect facts on issues and GOP candidates for Party workers and candidates)

DEMOCRATIC PRECINCT LEADER
(to appoint and supervise Precinct workers and special Election Day Committees

DEMOCRATIC PRECINCT WORKER
(to call on voters, explain issues and get Democrats to the polls)

VOTERS
(to vote Democratic on Election Day!)

ELECTION DAY PRECINCT COMMITTEES

POLL COMMITTEE
(to be at polls to see who has voted)

CHECKING COMMITTEE
(to prepare lists of voters who have not yet been to polls)

TELEPHONE COMMITTEE
(to call voters to remind them to vote)

AUTOMOBILE COMMITTEE
(to bring voters to polls)

BABY-SITTER COMMITTEE
(to allow mothers to get to polls)

CHALLENGE COMMITTEE
(to prevent irregularities at polls)

HEADQUARTERS COMMITTEE
(to take care of physical arrangements)

FIGURE 3—11

From The Key to Democratic Victory,
a handbook for County and Precinct workers
Women's Division, Democratic National Committee

ORGANIZATION MANUAL

note - this section

History of the Young Republican National Federation
Organizational Structure
Why You Should Be a Young Republican
Starting a Young Republican Club
Functions and Work of Club Committees
Young Republican National Federation Officers

ISSUED BY YOUNG REPUBLICAN NATIONAL FEDERATION

FIGURE 3—12

The parties issue many
publications of this kind
concerning party organization

THE ORGANIZATION OF THE PARTY

Organization in the political field has a single purpose—to SELL the Party's leaders and principles to the public. A political organization lacking in the ability to sell has little value. Organization is the first requirement for victory, for without effective political organization, it is difficult to sell the Party. The art of successful campaign management demands a thorough understanding of the principles of political organization.

The primary purpose of this Manual is to describe the workings of a campaign organization. Behind the campaign organization is the regular Republican organization which functions on a year round basis.

The smallest yet most active and important political subdivision is called a "precinct", "ward", or "election district", but for the purposes of this Manual the term "precinct" will be used. The precinct worker is the Party's official representative and contact at the local level; with the individual voter.

The duties and powers of the Republican PRECINCT CAUCUS vary in different states. They are open to all voters who legally qualify as Republican Party members. The members elect a precinct committeeman and committeewoman as their official representatives in the Party's organization. Precincts are usually units within larger political subdivisions such as assembly, senatorial, congressional and judicial districts.

The Precinct Committeemen and women constitute the COUNTY CENTRAL COMMITTEE and it is the key organizational unit. The County Central Committee elects a Chairman, and a Vice Chairman who is usually a woman. They are the official leaders of the Party in the county.

THE STATE CENTRAL COMMITTEE is the governing body of the Party in the state and its members are usually chosen by the county conventions or in primary elections. The State Committee elects its Chairman, and a Vice Chairman, usually a woman. The State Chairmen and Vice Chairmen are the Party spokesmen at the state level.

Nationally, the Party organization is headed by the REPUBLICAN NATIONAL COMMITTEE with a membership of one man and one woman from each state and territory. It is governed by the rules adopted at the National Convention.

7

From Republican Campaign Manual

FIGURE 3—13

ORGANIZING THE PRECINCT FOR THE CAMPAIGN

A. *The Mechanical Needs*

B. *Auxiliary Workers*

C. *Your Organization Meeting*

D. *Booth Officials*

The **first step** before calling an organization meeting of the precinct is to meet with the county chairman and vice-chairman to discuss the over-all plans for the year, and particularly the campaign, be it local or state and national. **Cooperation** is the **keynote** to victory. The work of each precinct **must dovetail** and become a single county unit of organization.

A. The Mechanical Needs

1. Calling cards for your workers. (See Page 2, Item A.)
2. A large map of the precinct.
3. List of registered or prospective voters marked "Republican"—"Democratic"—"Independent"—"Doubtful." This list can be prepared from your poll of the precinct.
4. Election statistics for the precinct for the preceding presidential and Congressional elections, showing the vote for major candidates. Set a winning goal for the campaign.
5. List of Party nominees (chosen at Primary or Nominating Convention). Biographical and background material should be available.

B. Auxiliary Workers

Depending on the size of the prec~~...~~ sity of the population and the ~~...~~

'From Republican workers' Manual

FIGURE 3—14

COMMITTEES TO BE ORGANIZED FOR THE ELECTION

1. *Checkers*
2. *Transportation*
3. *Sitters*
4. *Headquarters*
5. *Telephone*

EVERY VOTE COUNTS. DON'T MISS ONE!

1. Checkers Committee

This Committee functions on Election Day (both Primary and General). Its duty is to make **sure** that every **eligible** voter in the Precinct casts his vote. The Chairman of the Checkers Committee must be supplied with a **list** of all persons who will vote the Republican ticket. Telephone numbers are **absolutely necessary**. The Committee will be divided into teams—the number to be

The Precinct Leader and Election Day

It's sunup on Election Day! Now is the time for all good Democrats to come to the aid of the Party.

Now is the time for you, the Precinct Leader, to enlist all the help you can in order to get out the vote.

Remember, you *have had weeks and months* to work on registration, to conduct the campaign based on issues and candidates. You *have only one day* to convert all that effort into Democratic victory at the polls. Nothing short of a streamlined organization, with details thoroughly planned and workers carefully assigned, will enable you to do the job.

Assign your workers—augmenting your registration-drive assistants with as many volunteers as possible—to special Election Day committees, and do it in advance, to avoid last-minute confusion and delay. You should have functioning on Election Day the seven committees whose duties are outlined on pages 24-27.

Before Election Day, however, you, the Precinct Leader, have three specific duties to perform which are necessary to the work of two of your committees:

1. Reorganize your card file, removing all cards except those of registered Democrats. Index the file of registered Democrats "Has Voted" and "Has Not Voted" (all cards, of course, will be under "Has Not Voted" at this stage), and turn it over to the Checking Committee.

2. Collect the looseleaf notebooks from the Precinct Workers, remove all sheets except those of registered Democrats. Combine sheets of registered Democrats, in alphabetical order, into one looseleaf notebook, and turn it over to the Poll Committee.

3. Prepare a list of registered Democrats, compiling it from the card file or the master looseleaf notebook above mentioned. The list should be in alphabetical order, typewritten, single-spaced, on legal-sized

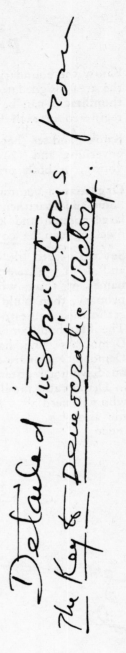

Detailed instructions from ... The Key to Democratic victory.

The Precinct Worker and Registration

The Precinct Leader and the Precinct Workers are the solid foundation on which the Party organization is built, and upon whom victory at the polls depends, for Elections Are Won in the Precincts.

Most of us like to do things together. Something that may seem like a chore if done individually is fun if done in company. There is no work in a political organization that is more interesting, brings greater satisfaction, or is more important than that of the Precinct Worker.

Women are particularly well qualified to perform the duties of a Precinct Worker. Women are neighborly, like to meet new

FIGURE 3—15

Duties of
Precinct Leader

1. **Know** the boundaries of your Precinct and have a map showing the area assigned to each Precinct Worker. Different colored thumbtacks can be used to show increasing number of voters registered in each Precinct Worker's area.

2. **Know,** and see that your Precinct Workers know, (1) the laws governing and (2) the dates and places for registration and voting, in both primary and general elections.

3. **Organize** a committee of Precinct Workers to call at every home and apartment in the Precinct. Keep the list of workers large enough and keep the areas small enough so that every dwelling can be covered effectively.

4. **Set up** a card file of persons of voting age in your Precinct and do it well in advance of the primary. Start with the names of those who registered Democratic in the previous primary, then build it up with information Precinct Workers get in their house-to-house canvass.
The file should include names of Democrats who have registered, Democrats who are eligible to vote but have not registered, first in Democratic families who will need absentee file also should be indexed.

maps

a card file

Duties of
County Leader

A strong County organization with roots extending into every Precinct is the responsibility of the County Leader.

It is the County Leader who must stimulate activity in the Precincts, for *Elections Are Won in the Precincts.* Campaigns are won not by a few generals at the top but by thousands of County Leaders, and thousands and thousands of Precinct Leaders and Precinct Workers all over the country, each doing her bit.

You, the County Leader, hold the key to victory. First, call a general meeting, to re-enlist former workers and to attract new ones. Meet with your Precinct Leaders (if election laws or Party rules do not provide for these officials, appoint them) and special campaign aides (see page 6), stir them into action, and instruct them on their duties. Know, and see that your workers know, the laws governing registering and voting, for both primary and general elections. Equip workers with facts about the key issues of the campaign. Campaign schools should be on a County-wide scale, open to all Democratic workers, and organized by the County Leader early in an election year. Start Precinct Leaders on a systematic plan for the door-to-door canvass by Precinct Workers. Hold regular meetings of Precinct Leaders to hear reports of their progress, once or twice a month until October, then weekly until Election Day. See that each campaign aide attends at least one meeting in each

Campaign Schools

More the Key to Democratic Victory

FIGURE 3—16

VII. Campaign Organization Chart:

Following are the Chairmen of Divisions, and key officers, responsible to the Campaign Manager, who may be appointed in a large-scale, all-out campaign. Any others should be responsible to these Chairmen and officers. Even a small-scale campaign operation may be of striking effectiveness with the activation of only a few of the functions mentioned:

1. Chairman of the Research Committee.
2. Chairman of the Canvassing Division.
3. Chairman of the Telephone Canvass.
4. Chairman of the Speakers Bureau.
5. Chairman of Literature Distribution Division.
6. Chairman of the First Voters Program.
7. Chairman of Rallies and Meetings.
8. Chairman of the Special Services Division.
9. Chairman of the Publicity Division.
10. Chairman of the Poll Watching Program.
11. Coordinator of the Candidate's Personal Program.
12. Headquarters Secretary.
13. Liaison Representative to the Regular Party Organization.

From Republican Campaign Manual

MODEL BY-LAWS FOR CLUBS IN THE FEDERATION

(The following model by-laws for a local or county club are suggested to make somewhat uniform and consistent the procedure of clubs within the National Federation. Necessary changes and additions can be made to fit the local needs.)

From Handbook for Women who Win, issued by Nat. Fed. of Women's Republican Clubs

BY-LAWS

ARTICLE I—*Name*

The name of this organization shall be ....

ARTICLE II—*Objects*

The objects of this organization shall be:

To foster and encourage loyalty to the Republican Party and to promote its ideals;

To cooperate with official Republican Party committees;

To collect, analyze, report upon and disseminate information concerning governmental and political affairs;

To cooperate in the election of Republican Party's nominees;

To promote the principles of freedom, equality and justice on which the government of this country is founded.

—Adapted from the constitution of the National Federation of Women's Republican Clubs.

ARTICLE III—*Membership*

Section I. Any woman believing in the principles of the Republican Party and intending generally to support its candidates is eligible to membership.

FIGURE 3—17

historical structures. Both are more than a hundred years old. Each has an old tradition and each is supported by traditional affiliations. Moreover, the major parties are now the largest competitive organizations in the country. Most Americans know where they belong in the party conflict with a minimum of overt mobilization. The problem of party organization is very different from that of many smaller, newer associations.

Party organizations tend to be loose, lacking in discipline; they have only the vaguest tests of loyalty, and they use their resources inefficiently (judging by the standards of many other organizations). In recent decades, there has been a revival of interest in attempts to develop new types of party organization, due, in part, to a great increase in the number of people who want to do party work. The following questions may give you some clues to the evaluation of the party organizations in your town.

Tests of the Adequacy of Party Organizations

1. How large are party registrations? Are they increasing in relation to nonparty registration? If the registration of either party is very low it is probably evidence of a weak organization.
2. Do parties nominate full slates of candidates? If not, they probably are not as active and effective as they ought to be.
3. Are there any vacancies on party committees? How long have the vacancies existed? Vacancies are evidence of indifference.
4. Do party committees actually meet? How often? The committees cannot do much if they do not meet.
5. What does the party organization do in the intervals between elections? Does it maintain a permanent headquarters?
6. Is the party situation in your town actually competitive? Is it a one-party town? How many overturns in party power have there been in the past generation?
7. How large is the party vote cast in primay elections? Is it high or low? Is there evidence of interest?
8. Are there any evidences that the minority party has entered into bipartisan agreements with the majority party? Is the competition real?

Urban party organization in many parts of the United States is in a state of transition from the old-fashioned, boss-dominated machines made famous in the literature of politics, to modern organizations largely based on a new kind of public involvement in politics. Can you find any evidence of this kind of transition in your community? What kind of motivation do party leaders and workers seem to have? What do they say they want to get out of the party work they do? What do they say about themselves? Why do they want their parties to win?

A critical datum about party politics in your town is the competitiveness of the system. Do the parties actually compete, or is the party ratio so one-sided that the second major party has very little chance of winning? Even if the party balance in the local community is extremely unequal, the parties may compete strenuously at the state level. If this is true (if statewide elections are close), every vote polled by the second major party in every town and city in the state may be important in statewide contests.

On the other hand, if the parties are really noncompetitive, be on the lookout for bipartisan local arrangements in which the secondary party begins to accept favors from the dominant party in return for its willingness to conduct a sham opposition.

Finally, you cannot afford to forget that national, state, and local politics are apt to be so closely connected that it is usually impossible to separate them. Your town is not a political island surrounded by a political vacuum. The local party organizations are inevitably the local branches of the national parties. They have a dual function: (a) in the politics of the local governments, towns, cities, counties, and other units; (b) as integral parts of the national party organizations. Citizens and politicians are likely to be unable to distinguish clearly between local and national party issues. This is true even when local elections are legally nonpartisan. Almost inevitably, people who are Democrats or Republicans in national politics will tend to be Democrats or Republicans in local politics. The result is that you cannot understand the party preferences of people in your community exclusively on the basis of the issues of local politics. For many reasons, national and local party alignments are not always identical, but the tendency to maintain party alignments at all levels of government can never be ignored.

THE POWER STRUCTURE OF THE COMMUNITY

It is well known that public officials, whether elected or appointed, are not the only people who make public policy. Many policies affecting the community are made by business firms or associations, labor unions, churches, and other organizations, as well as by government officials, political parties, and the electorate. The "leaders" among these various groups use the government, either negatively or positively, to achieve their objectives or to further their interests. Such interests, whether organized or unorganized, are the basic stuff of politics.

In many communities, the "management of conflict" is a private affair; that is, the leaders in the power structure attempt to exclude the public from participating in the conflict or in resolving it. At times this exclusion of the public has been formalized. One of the devices used to reduce the widespread participation of the mass of inhabitants of the community is nonpartisan elections. See Schattschneider, *The Semisovereign People* (7) for a discussion of the political nature of conflict and of recent changes in the formal and informal management and resolution of conflict in the United States.

As you are now probably convinced that you should study poweful and influential persons out-side of the government as well as inside the government, an immediate difficulty arises: How do you define powerful and influential in nontautological terms? See Kaufman and Jones, "The Mystery of Power," *Public Administration Review* (8), and Hunter, *Community Power Structure: A Study of Decision Makers* (9). Hunter defines a power structure as the network of "acts of men going about the business of moving other men to act in relation to themselves or in relation to organic or inorganic things."

Many other studies of community power structure have been made since Hunter's study of the top leaders in Atlanta. In many of these studies, sociologists have assumed that formal government and political parties function only to ratify decisions already reached by "real" leaders. Others have been led by such assumptions to overlook the exercise of influence and power at many points and through many people and institutions. See Sayre and Kaufman, Chapter XIII, "Nongovernmental Groups and Governmental Action," for an analysis of the interlocking roles of governmental, party, and nongovernmental leaders.

Political scientists such as R. A. Dahl, V. Ostrom, N. Long, R. E. Aggar, G. Belknap, and F. Cleaveland are now refining the methodology of studying decision-making in local communities. Some of their publications are listed in Bell, Hill and Wright, *Public Leadership in the United States* (10). Not only does this book provide a bibliography of 572 items, but it classifies them by the method used to identify public leaders. It also draws together material on sex, age, social class, ethnic and religious background of public leaders. The literature on attitudes toward public leaders and on the motivation of political behavior is also classified and analyzed.

The following books and articles, in addition to those already mentioned, will be helpful and suggestive:

Agger, R. E., "Power Attributions in the Local Community: Theoretical and Research Considerations," *Social Forces*, Vol. 34, May 1956. pp. 322-31.

Agger, E., and D. Goldrich, "Community Power Structures and Partisanship," *American Sociological Review*, Vol. 23, August, 1958. pp. 383-92.

Bailey, S. K., "Leadership in Local Government," *Yale Review*, Series 2, Vol. 45, June 1956. pp. 563-73.

Belknap, G. M., and R. H. Smuckler, "Political Power Relations in a Mid-West City," *Public Opinion Quarterly*, Vol. 20, Spring 1956. pp. 73-81.

Birch, A. H., *Small-Town Politics*. New York: Oxford University Press, 1959.

Dahl, R. A., "Hierarchy, Democracy and Bargaining in Politics and Economics," in *Research Frontiers in Politics and Government*. Washington, D.C.: The Brookings Institution, 1955. pp. 45-69.

Dollard, J., *Caste and Class in a Southern Town*. New York: Harper & Brothers, 1949.

Foskett, J. M., and R. Hohle, "The Measurement of Influence in Community Affairs," *Research Studies of the State College of Washington*, Vol. 25, June 1957. pp. 148-54.

Haer, J. L., "Social Stratification in Relation to Attitude toward Sources of Power in a Community," *Social Forces*, Vol. 35, December, 1956. pp. 137-42.

Hunter, F., R. C. Schaffer, and C. Sheps, *Community Organization: Action and Inaction*. Chapel Hill, N.C.: University of North Carolina Press, 1956.

Janes, R. W., "A Technique for Describing Community Structure through Newspaper Analysis," *Social Forces*, Vol. 37, December 1958. pp. 102-109.

Kimball, S. T., and M. Pearsall, "Event Analysis as an Approach to Community Study," *Social Forces*, Vol. 34, October 1955. pp. 58-63.

Long, N. E., "The Corporation, Its Satellites, and the Local Community" in E. S. Mason, ed., *The Corporation in Modern Society*. Cambridge, Mass.: Harvard University Press, 1960.

Miller, D. C., "Decision-Making Cliques in Community Power Structures: A Comparative Study of an American and an English City," *American Journal of Sociology*, Vol. 64, November 1958. pp. 299-310.

_____, "Industry and Community Power Structure: A Comparative Study of an American and an English City," *American Sociological Review*, Vol. 23, February 1958. p. 9-15.

Pellegrin, R. J., and C. H. Coates, "Absentee-Owned Corporations and Community Power Structure," *American Journal of Sociology*, Vol. 61, March 1956 pp. 413-19.

Polsby, N. W., "Three Problems in the Analysis of Community Power," *American Sociological Review*, Vol. 24, December 1959. pp. 796-803.

_____, "The Sociology of Community Power: A Reassessment," *Social Forces*, Vol. 37, March 1959. pp. 232-36.

Reid, I. deA, and E. Ehle, "Leadership Selection in an Urban Locality Area," *Public Opinion Quarterly*, Vol. 14, Summer, 1950. pp. 262-84.

Rossi, P. H., "Community Decision Making," *Administrative Science Quarterly*, Vol. 1, March 1957. pp. 415-43.

Schulze, R. O., "The Role of Economic Dominants in Community Power Structure," *American Sociological Review*, Vol. 23, February 1958. pp. 3-9.

Schulze, R. O., and L. U. Blumberg, "The Determination of Local Power Elites," *American Journal of Sociology*, Vol. 63, November 1957. pp. 290-96.

Smuckler, R. H., and G. M. Belknap, *Leadership and Participation in Urban Political Affairs*. East Lansing, Mich.: Michigan State University, Bureau of Government Research, 1956.

Wolfinger, R. E., "Reputation and Reality in the Study of 'Community Power'", *American Sociological Review*, Vol. 25, October 1960. pp. 636-44.

Both parties now run schools of politics for the training of party workers. If you can attend one or more of these schools you are likely to learn very much about the functioning of the party system. See the plans for a registration drive in Figure 3-18 and an instruction sheet issued by the Massachusetts Republican party for use in setting up a school of politics, Figure 3-19.

It is necessary to know something about election administration to understand the party sys-

AN EXAMPLE OF COMPLETED PRECINCT MAP

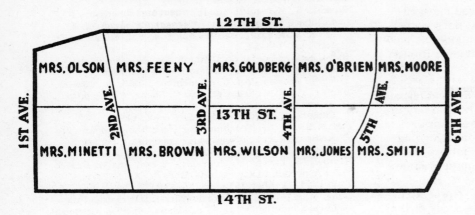

On the map, shown above, use different colored thumbtacks to indicate each worker's progress on registration; for example, green up to 25 percent, yellow for 25 to 50 percent, red for 50 to 75 percent, blue over 75 percent.

Blackboard is suggested for the tabulation shown below. Figures posted should remain from one meeting to the next, then brought up to date.

AN EXAMPLE OF A TABULATION

Precinct Worker	Area	Democrats in Area	Registered	Not Registered	Percent Registered
Mrs. Olson	1	100	53	47	53%
Mrs. Feeny	2	100	25	75	25%
Mrs. Goldberg	3	137	48	89	35%
Mrs. Smith	4	72	55	17	76.4%

Being a Precinct Worker is a hard job but it has its own reward. You're helping people to understand the issues that affect us all. You're making the machinery of government work. You're doing your job as a citizen in a working democracy. You're working to keep America free through the ballot box. You're proud to be a Precinct Worker. You're stepping up as a Party leader.

> *Get the Facts to the Voters and the Voters to the Polls*

FIGURE 3—18

FOR   VICTORY----------WORK   YOUR   PRECINCT

SCHOOL OF POLITICS FOR PRECINCT WORKERS

Based On The Workers' Manual

Instructions to the County Vice-Chairman:

Before you open the School of Politics for the Precinct Committeewomen and volunteer workers, ask your County Chairman to outline with you the general organization plans. Make arrangements with him for a Women's Division in Headquarters and suggest that your volunteer women will be available to help wherever needed. Tell him about the School and ask if he desires his precinct committeemen to attend.

In the School please stress the election of Republican Congressmen in 1954. STREAMLINE the SESSIONS -- Have a time schedule, and keep it. Instill "PEP" and ENTHUSIASM. Impress the number of Republican votes you must have in each precinct to WIN.

1. As well as ALL precinct or district committeewomen, invite the following volunteers (at least one from each precinct or district):

Republican Women's Club members   Labor groups
Young Republicans   Minority groups
Non-partisan club members   Farm groups
Nationality groups   Young Housewives
Church groups   Business and Professional women

2. Each Precinct Committeewoman should be supplied with the following:

   (a) A poll book for the after-primary poll, or poll cards. (Depending on your preference.)
   (b) A precinct map and calling cards. (A sufficient number.)
   (c) Printed or mimeographed instructions on registration, absentee voting; sick and disabled voting; election laws; voting booth locations.
   (d) List of county and state officials; assemblymen; Congressmen and Senators; List of Republican nominees.

3. Election statistics for each precinct for 1950 and 1952 for major offices. (Ask your County Chairman or Republican Board of Elections member to help work out a quota of votes for each precinct based on the 1950-1952 returns). GIVE EACH PRECINCT COMMITTEEWOMAN THE NUMBER OF VOTES NECESSARY TO WIN. THIS GOAL IS HER CHALLENGE.

4. Have each woman bring a box lunch. Ask the Republican Women's Clubs to prepare and provide a simple dessert and coffee.

5. Set up Class in schoolroom atmosphere. Have a blackboard. Select assistant teachers who are well qualified. New faces stimulate interest and attendance.

6. Ask each woman to bring a notebook and pencils.

7. Have literature for distribution after School (National, State and local). Obtain supply of data on candidates.

8. Publicize the School well in advance.

FIGURE 3-19

Both of the major parties now run schools of politics.

Subtitle 7.   ENFORCEMENT OF ELECTION LAW.
Chapter 32.   SUPERINTENDENT OF ELECTIONS.

19:32–1. Appointed by governor; term; salary; vacancy.   The office of superintendent of elections in counties of the first class is established. The offices shall be filled by some suitable persons who shall be nominated by the governor with the advice and consent of the senate and who shall hold office for the term of five years from the date of appointment and until their successors are appointed and have qualified.   Each superintendent shall receive a salary of five thousand dollars ($5,000.00) per annum to be paid by the county treasurer.   The person so appointed shall have their offices in the counties for which they are appointed.   Vacancies shall be filled in the same manner as original appointments, but shall be for the unexpired term only.

Amended P. L. 1944, chapter 45.

19:32–2. Deputy, clerk, secretary and other assistants.   Each superintendent may appoint a chief deputy, a clerk, a secretary, such personnel as is authorized under section 19:48–6 of this title, and any other assistants he considers necessary to carry out the provisions of this title, and may remove the same whenever he deems it necessary. Those so appointed shall not be subject to any of the provisions of Title 11, Civil Service, but shall be in the unclassified service.   Each superintendent shall fix the salaries of the persons so appointed and such salaries certified to and approved under his hand shall be paid semimonthly by the county treasurer of the county in which such persons are so engaged.   All other necessary expenses incurred in carrying out the provisions of this title when certified to and approved by the superintendent shall be paid by the county treasurer of the county in which the superintendent shall maintain his office;   provided, however, that all expenses of every nature in the office of the superintendent of elections shall not exceed the sum of three hundred twenty thousand dollars ($320,000.00) per annum commencing with the year one thousand nine hundred and forty-six and annually thereafter, of which the sum of one hundred twenty thousand dollars ($120,000.00) per annum shall be used exclusively for expenses arising out of his duties in connection with the use of voting machines;   and the unexpended balance which remains of the amount or amounts appropriated to the county board of elections in each county of the first class by the board of chosen freeholders thereof for the year one thousand nine hundred and forty-five for the purpose of paying all salaries in connection with and defraying the cost of storing, delivering to and from polling places, repairing, servicing, and maintaining voting machines, shall be transferred forthwith to the account of the superintendent of elections and shall be used by him solely for such purpose, and no other.

Amended P. L. 1945, chapter 304.

FIGURE 3—20

New Jersey Election Laws, 1954.

Election law administration. Note the powers of the county superintendent of elections. In many states the Secretary of State has certain supervisory powers.

Powers and Duties of the Secretary of the Commonwealth

The "Pennsylvania Election Code" of 1937, P. L. 1333 and its amendments provide as follows:

Section 201. The Secretary of the Commonwealth shall exercise in the manner provided by this act all power granted to him by this act and shall perform all the duties imposed upon him by this act, which shall include the following:

(a) To determine, in accordance with the provisions of this act, the forms of nomination petitions and papers, expense accounts and all other forms and records, the form of which he is required to determine under the provisions of this act.

(b) To examine and reexamine voting machines, and to approve or disapprove them for use in this State, in accordance with the provisions of this act.

(c) To certify to county boards of elections for primaries and elections the names of the candidates for President and Vice-President of the United States, presidential electors, United States senators, representatives in Congress and all State offices, including senators, representatives, and judges of all courts of record, and delegates and alternate delegates to National Conventions, and members of State committees, and the form and wording of constitutional amendments or other questions to be submitted to the electors of the State at large.

(d) To receive and determine, as hereinafter provided, the sufficiency of nomination petitions, certificates and papers of candidates for President of the United States, presidential electors, United States senators, representatives in Congress and all State offices, including senators, representatives and judges of all courts of record, and delegates and alternate delegates to National Conventions and members of State committees.

1

From Pennsylvania. Election guide.

The Secretary of State often has extensive administrative functions in the conduct of elections.

FIGURE 3—21

tem in your city. You should see first the election laws of your state to identify election officials and get some conception of their duties. See Figure 3-20 for an excerpt from the New Jersey Election laws dealing with the duties of the county superintendents of elections. Very often the secretary of state has some general administrative supervision of elections. See, for example, the statement concerning the duties of the Secretary of the Commonwealth of Pennsylvania in Figure 3-21.

You will find the instructions for polling officials issued by election authorities useful. These instructions cover such subjects as registration, the operation of voting machines, counting the vote, the form of election returns, challenges, who may vote, election calendars. See Figures 3-22, 3-23, 3-24, 3-25, 3-26, 3-27, 3-28, and 3-29.

See Figure 3-30 for excerpts from two political calendars. Every state publishes a calendar of this sort. Consult the political calendar for your state to see what is going on while you are making your survey. In this way you can anticipate political events and sometimes you may be able to attend them. Figure 3-31 shows the kind of election day instructions issued by the parties. See Schubert, *The Michigan State Director of Elections*, (11).

You can find out about the informal (real) party structure only by talking to experienced political reporters and local politicians who are thoroughly familiar with the operations of the party. The inference of this statement is not that the informal organization is secret or corrupt, but merely that in party politics as in business, church work, the management of colleges and labor unions, much

HOW TO TAKE REGISTRATIONS

A WHITE AND YELLOW REGISTRATION CARD MUST BE FILLED OUT IN EACH CASE

ADMINISTER OATH TO EACH APPLICANT.

PRINT, DO NOT WRITE, NAME AND ADDRESS ON REGISTRATION CARDS!
(Married women must give their own first name, and not husband's first name.)
(Example—Clara Jones—Not Mrs. John Jones.)

American Born Citizen:

1. Must give State (not city) where born.
2. The period of time that he has resided in the State of Illinois, in the County of Cook and in the precinct from which he is registering.

   The "term of residence" column on the registration card means term of residence in the State of Illinois and the County of Cook. (Term of residence must be a definite period of time—do not accept answer of "over 21" or "21 years plus.")

All persons, in addition to being citizens of the United States, must:

1—Be 21 years of age or over
2—Reside in the State of Illinois one year
3—Reside in the County ninety days, and
4—Reside in the precinct thirty days

} on or before election in order to qualify to vote.

Foreign Born Citizens:

Insert the name of the country in which applicant was born.

Insert the period of time he has resided in the State of Illinois, County of Cook and in the precinct from which he is registering in column "Term of Residence."

Ask each foreign born applicant "HOW DID YOU BECOME A CITIZEN OF THE UNITED STATES?" Citizenship may be accomplished in one of three ways:

1—Through own papers   2—Through Parent   3—Through Marriage

After this is ascertained, refer to explicit instructions in this booklet concerning the specific case, and obtain the complete information as per the example.

A person is Not required to give his age.

The answer "Yes" to the question: "Age 21 or over?" is sufficient to qualify a person as to age— (DO NOT ASK AGE—DO NOT INSERT FIGURES IN COLUMN: "Age 21 or over")

[1]

Chicago, Instructions to Election Officials

FIGURE 3—22

Pennsylvania Election Guide published by the Secretary of State instructs election officials in their duties.

Election Officers

The election board in every district consists of a judge of election and two (2) inspectors of election. They are elected at every Municipal election and serve for a term of two years, beginning the first Monday of January following their election. In paper ballot districts each inspector shall appoint one clerk to serve at the election. In voting-machine districts one clerk shall be appointed by the minority inspector to serve at the election. In addition thereto, in each district in which more than one voting machine is used, the county board of election shall appoint a voting machine inspector for each additional machine to be used in such district.

Each elector may vote for one inspector and the majority inspector in any district is the one who received the highest number of votes at the election. The minority inspector is the one who received the second highest number of votes at the election.

Preliminary Duties

All election officers are required to be at the polling place at least thirty (30) minutes before 7 o'clock A. M., Eastern Standard Time, so that the board may organize and take care of the preliminary details. The election officers shall thereupon in the presence of each other take and subscribe in duplicate to the respective oaths of office as required by law. The minority inspector or a magistrate, alderman or justice of the peace shall administer the oath of office to the judge of election, who then shall administer the oath to the inspectors, clerks and machine inspectors. The oaths must be signed in duplicate by the persons so sworn at the time the board is being organized and before the electors are permitted to vote and must be attested by the officer who administered the oath. Any election officer who shall act as such without first being duly sworn, or any judge or minority inspector who refuses or fails to administer an oath in the manner required, shall be guilty of a misdemeanor and subject to a fine and imprisonment.

50

by operating the separate straight political party lever if the machine has such lever.

To vote for any person whose name does not appear upon the voting machine as a candidate, the elector should ask an election officer for instructions.

As soon as the elector has adjusted the voting machine so that it will record his vote for candidates and on the various questions submitted, he shall operate the recording mechanism and forthwith leave the booth.

AT PRIMARIES NO PERSON IS ENTITLED TO VOTE AS A MEMBER OF ANY PARTY UNLESS HE IS REGISTERED AND ENROLLED IN THE DISTRICT REGISTER AS A MEMBER OF SUCH PARTY. THIS ENROLLMENT IS CONCLUSIVE AS TO HIS PARTY MEMBERSHIP AND IS NOT SUBJECT TO CHALLENGE.

Challenge of Voters

A challenge is the test of a person's right to vote. A person is not entitled to vote at any primary or election unless his registration card appears in the district register. However, even though his registration card is in the district register, any person may be challenged by any qualified elector, election officer, overseer or watcher, as to his identity, as to his continued residence in the election district, as to any alleged violation of the law pertaining to the signing of the voter's certificate, or as to any alleged violation of the law prohibiting bribery at elections. If an elector is challenged as to identity or residence, he must produce at least one qualified elector of the election district as a witness who shall make affidavit of the elector's identity or continued residence in the election district. If challenged as to any violation of the law pertaining to the signing of a voter's certificate, or the law prohibiting bribery at elections, the elector shall not be permitted to vote until he shall

58

FIGURE 3—23

DATES GOVERNING STATE AND
COUNTY PRIMARY

———

For Primary To Be Held April 13, 1954

———

Polls Open 6:00 A.M. to 5:00 P.M.

1954

Jan. 4   First day absent electors in mili-
          tary or naval service may make ap-
          plication for official ballot. (Chap.
          46, Par. 20-2.)

Jan. 18   First day for candidates to file peti-
          tions in the office of the Secretary
          of State or in the office of the
          County Clerk. (Chap. 46, Pars.
          7-12, 8-9.)

Jan. 25   Last day for candidates to file peti-
          tions in the office of the Secretary
          of State or in the office of the
          County Clerk. (Chap. 46, Pars.
          7-12, 8-9.)

Jan. 30   Last day for candidates to file
          withdrawal of nominating petitions
          in the office of the Secretary of
          State or in the office of the County
          Clerk. (Chap. 46, Pars. 7-12, 8-9.)

Feb. 2   Last day for Senatorial Committee
          to meet and by resolution, fix and
          determine the number of candi-
          dates to be nominated for Repre-
          sentatives in the General Assem-
          bly. (Chap. 46, Par. 8-13.)

[13]

NATIONAL, STATE AND COUNTY
OFFICIALS TO BE ELECTED

———

Election, November 2, 1954

———

State officers as follows:
    United States Senator.
    State Treasurer.
    Superintendent of Public Instruction.
    Trustees of the University of Illinois
        (three to be elected.)

Congressional officers as follows:
    One Representative in Congress from
        each district.

Senatorial officers as follows:
    One State Senator in each odd numbered
        senatorial district.
    Three Representatives in the General
        Assembly in each district.

County officers as follows:
    County Judge.
    County Clerk.
    Probate Judge. } In counties of 70,000 or
    Probate Clerk. } more population.
    County Treasurer.
    Sheriff.
    County Superintendent of Schools.
    One County Commissioner in counties
        not under township organization.

[17]

MINIMUM NUMBER OF SIGNATURES
REQUIRED FOR NOMINATING
PETITIONS

For

REPRESENTATIVES IN CONGRESS

	Republican		Democratic
Dist.	Number	Dist.	Number
1	172	1	488
2	514	2	504
3	540	3	467
4	666	4	557
5	346	5	520
6	359	6	586
7	259	7	571
8	352	8	458
9	453	9	429
10	721	10	427
11	555	11	404
12	628	12	497
13	1,214	13	637
14	715	14	317
15	527	15	355
16	574	16	328
17	555	17	346
18	471	18	366
19	492	19	346
20	434	20	338
21	516	21	473
22	470	22	363
23	480	23	377
24	380	24	578
25	405	25	393

[9]

From Illinois Primary and Election
Calendar, 1954

FIGURE 3—24

SPECIAL ENROLLMENT

Voters

Jan. 2 to Aug. 14......Absent in service of army or navy, or who became of age after preceding general election or became naturalized subsequent to ninety days prior to preceding general election, or who did not have the necessary residential qualifications of a voter at the preceding general election; or who have changed to another election district in same county, city or village. If incapacitated by illness on days of enrollment in previous year. Sub. 1 and 2. § 187.

PRIMARY PETITIONS

To designate candidates, petitions must be signed by not less than 5% of the enrolled voters of party in political subdivision, but the number of signatures need not exceed the number mentioned below, namely:

5,000 signatures for any office voted for by all the voters of the city of New York. § 136.

2,500 signatures for any office to be filled by all the voters of any county or borough within the city of New York.

1,000 signatures for any office to be filled by all the voters of any other city of the first class or of any other county or borough containing more than two hundred and fifty thousand inhabitants. § 136.

750 signatures for any office to be filled in the city of New York by all the voters of any municipal court district, or of any congressional or senatorial district. § 136.

500 signatures for any office to be filled by all the voters of any other county or borough containing more than twenty-five thousand and not more than two hundred and fifty thousand inhabitants or any city of the second class or any other congressional or senatorial district. § 136.

350 signatures for any office to be filled in the city of New York by all the voters of any assembly district. § 136.

250 signatures for any office to be filled by all voters of any other county or any city of the third class or any other assembly district. § 136.

Form of petition in section 135, Election Law; last amended by Chapter 745, Laws of 1954. Chapter 351, Laws of 1951, provides that a subscribing witness must be an enrolled voter of the same political party and a resident of the same political subdivision as the voters qualified to sign the petition; however, in the case of a petition for members of the county committee, residence of the subscribing witness in the same assembly district is sufficient.

Section 135 also provides that sheets must be numbered consecutively, beginning with number one, and Section 136 provides that petitions must be signed in ink and bound together when offered for filing.

June 1............Last day for County Chairman to notify Board of Elections of party positions to be filled. § 18.

JULY 6
June 20............First day for signing petitions. Sub. 4. § 136.

Aug. 3 to Aug. 10....Dates for filing designating petitions. Sub. 1. § 143.

Aug. 13............Last day to accept or decline designations. Sub. 2. § 143.

Aug. 17............Last day to fill vacancy after declination. Sub. 3. § 143.

Aug. 26............Certification by Secretary of State, to Boards of Election, designations filed in his office. § 69.

Sept. 14............FALL PRIMARY. Sub. 5. § 314.
Hours for voting in New York City, 3 p.m. to 10 p.m. Sub. 2. § 191.
Hours for voting outside New York City, 12 noon to 9 p.m. Sub. 2. § 191.

Sept. 22............Last day to accept or decline when person nominated without designation at a primary election. Sub. 14. § 314.

Sept. 24............Last day to fill vacancy after such declination. Sub. 14. § 314.

CONVENTIONS

Sept. 21 to Sept. 23..Dates for holding State Conventions Sub. 6. § 314.

Sept. 23 to Sept. 25..Dates for holding Judicial District Conventions. Sub. 7. § 314.

Sept. 27............Last day for filing party nominations. Sub. 8. § 314.

Sept. 30............Last day for filing certificate of acceptance or declination of party nominations. Sub. 9. § 314.

Oct. 1............Last day to fill vacancy after such declination. Sub. 10. § 314.

INDEPENDENT NOMINATIONS

To nominate independently signatures must be obtained to the number of

12,000 for State-wide offices, with at least 50 from each county (Fulton and Hamilton considered as one). Sub. 5. § 138.

5% of total vote for governor, excluding blank and void votes in any political subdivision, except that:

7,500 may nominate a city-wide candidate in city of New York. Sub. 5. § 138.

5,000 may nominate a candidate for a borough or county office in the city of New York. Sub. 5. § 138.

3,000 may nominate a candidate in municipal court, congressional or senatorial district in the city of New York. Sub. 5. § 138.

1,500 may nominate a candidate in any assembly district in the city of New York. Sub. 5. § 138.

1,500 may nominate a candidate for any office to be filled in any county, or portion thereof, outside of the city of New York. Sub. 5. § 138.

Form of independent petition in Section 138, Election Law; last amended by Chapter 745, Laws of 1954.

Section 138 also provides that sheets must be numbered consecutively, beginning with number one, and provides that petitions must be signed in ink and bound together when offered for filing.

Aug. 16............First day for signing petitions. Sub. 7. § 138.

Sept. 22 to Sept. 27..Dates for filing nominations. Sub. 11. § 314.

Sept. 30............Last day to accept or decline nominations. Sub. 12. § 314.

Oct 1............Last day to fill vacancy after declination. Sub. 13. § 314.

Oct. 9............Last day for Secretary of State to certify nominations. Sub. 20. § 314.

VOTING BY ABSENTEE BALLOT

Personal registration required to vote absentee. Sec. 117.

(Exceptions. Inmate of Veterans' Bureau Hospital and the spouse, parent or child of such inmate. In non-personal registration district, person whose name is registered therein who is in federal service or in military service or student matriculated, or superintendent or teacher employed at institution of learning outside county where applicant resides, or accompanying spouse, parent or child of an absentee voter, may mail or deliver application for absentee ballot from May 1 to Oct. 23, incl.) Sub. 4. § 314.

In all election districts, a person whose name is registered therein, and whose duties, business or occupation require him to be outside the county of his residence, or his accompanying spouse, parent or child, may mail or deliver application for absentee ballot from Oct. 4 to Oct. 23, inclusive. Sub. 6. § 117.

FIGURE 3—25

New York Political Calendar 1954.
Issued by the office of the Secretary
of State.

1954

Voter's Guide

TED W. BROWN, Secretary of State

QUALIFICATIONS FOR VOTING

YOU ARE QUALIFIED TO VOTE IF:

- You are a citizen of the U. S.
- You are at least 21 years of age or will be on the day of the next General Election (Nov. 2, 1954)
- You have by Nov. 2, 1954 been a resident of:
  the state for one year;
  the county for 40 days;
  the voting precinct for 40 days.

  (If you have moved from one county to another county within Ohio, or from one precinct to another in the same county within 40 days before the election (from September 22 to November 2, 1954), you may vote in the precinct from which you moved.)

- You must be registered to be eligible to vote if you reside in registration territory. (See section on REGISTRATION below.)

REGISTRATION

YOU MUST BE REGISTERED TO VOTE IF:

You reside in registration territory (Any city having a population of 16,000 or over, or any area which has adopted registration. Contact your County Board of Elections to determine your registration status.)

Registration in Ohio is permanent, and need not be renewed unless:

- You have not voted at least once in the past two calendar years.
- You moved since you registered.
- You have changed your name. (A woman must re-register if she has married since she registered.
  If married after September 22, she may vote on November 2, but not thereafter, under her former name.)

If you have not voted in the past two calendar years, or have changed your name, you must appear in person in order to re-register. If you have moved, you may register your change of address by mail on a form obtained from your County Board of Elections.

Page 1

FIGURE 3–26

To Preserve Freedom's Score — Register and Vote in '54

The population of Ohio in 1952 was estimated by the Bureau of the Census to be 8,273,000. Of this number 5,460,180 were estimated to be twenty-one years of age or older, and hence were potential voters. At the November 2, 1952 election, 3,749,828 persons voted. Thus, 68.7% of Ohio's potential voters went to the polls in November 1952.

In 1950 less than 57% of the eligible voters went to the polls in November to cast their ballots.

The most recent population figure for Ohio as published by the Bureau of Census in July of 1953 is 8,482,000. Of this number 5,598,120 are potential voters.

In order to surpass the record of 68.7%, over 3,846,000 voters must cast their ballots this year.

IMPORTANT DATES IN 1954

Sept. 3 — Boards of Elections begin mailing Absent Voter Ballots to members of the armed services from whom applications have been received.
Also first day for Boards of Elections to receive applications for Absent Voter Ballots by civilians outside the United States, and to begin mailing Absent Voter Ballots to civilians outside the United States.

Sept. 22 — Last day to register.

Oct. 3 — First day for Boards of Elections to receive applications for disabled and civilian absent voter ballots for persons located within the United States.
Also first day of period during which votes may be cast at Boards of Elections by voters who expect to be absent from their counties and precincts on Election Day.

Oct. 28 — Last day (ending at 4 P.M.) for voting at Boards of Elections by voters who will be absent from their counties and precincts on Election Day.

Oct. 29 — By 12:00 noon of this date civilian absent, sick or disabled voter ballots must be delivered to clerks of Boards of Elections.

Oct. 30 — By 12:00 noon of this date applications for Armed Service Absent Voter Ballots must be received by clerks of Boards of Elections.

Nov. 2. — Election Day. Polls open at 6:30 A.M. (E.S.T.) and close at 6:30 P.M. (E.S.T.). By 12:00 noon of Election Day, Armed Service Absent Voter Ballots must be delivered to clerks of Boards of Elections.
All Election times are Eastern Standard Time.

This information has been compiled to acquaint the voters with the provisions of Ohio law pertaining to elections. It is intended as an easy-to-read, pocket-sized leaflet—a service manual for voters.

TED W. BROWN, Secretary of State.

Page 8

County	Population, 1950	Number of Electors Voting Nov. 1952	Registration	Voting Machines
Adams	20,499	9,946		
Allen	88,183	40,905	PR	
Ashland	33,040	17,807		
Ashtabula	78,695	38,105	PR	
Athens	45,839	18,221		
Auglaize	30,637	15,912	PR	
Belmont	87,740	42,970		
Brown	22,221	10,658	CR	
Butler	147,203	67,164	PR	
Carroll	19,039	8,913		
Champaign	26,793	13,592		VM
Clark	111,661	49,139	CR	VM
Clermont	42,182	23,205		
Clinton	25,572	12,080	PR	
Columbiana	98,392	46,090		
Coshocton	31,141	15,822		
Crawford	38,738	20,474	CR	
Cuyahoga	1,389,532	661,570		
Darke	41,799	21,039		
Defiance	25,925	13,051		
Delaware	30,278	15,037		
Erie	52,565	22,581	PR	VM
Fairfield	52,130	24,277	PR	
Fayette	22,554	10,831		
Franklin	503,410	233,362	CR	VM
Fulton	25,580	11,853		
Gallia	24,910	10,307		
Geauga	26,646	13,314	CR	
Greene	58,892	22,225	CR	
Guernsey	38,452	16,633	PR	
Hamilton	723,952	352,336	PR	VM
Hancock	44,280	20,672		
Hardin	28,673	14,486		
Harrison	19,054	9,127		
Henry	22,423	11,173		
Highland	28,188	14,106		
Hocking	19,520	8,869		
Holmes	18,760	6,329		
Huron	39,353	17,762		VM
Jackson	27,167	12,436	PR	
Jefferson	96,495	47,536	PR	VM
Knox	35,287	18,565		
Lake	75,979	39,961	CR	VM
Lawrence	49,115	21,408	CR	
Licking	70,645	32,347	CR	
Logan	31,329	15,985	CR	
Lorain	148,162	65,811	CR	
Lucas	395,551	190,173	CR	VM
Madison	22,300	9,624	CR	
Mahoning	257,629	124,532	CR	VM
Marion	49,959	20,659		
Medina	40,417	20,195		
Meigs	23,227	10,992		
Mercer	28,311	13,992		
Miami	61,309	30,155	PR	VM
Monroe	15,362	6,871		
Montgomery	398,441	176,305	CR	VM
Morgan	12,836	6,077		
Morrow	17,168	8,574		
Muskingum	74,535	33,925		
Noble	11,750	6,259		
Ottawa	29,469	14,650		
Paulding	15,047	7,310		
Perry	28,999	12,876		
Pickaway	29,352	12,280		
Pike	14,607	7,032		
Portage	63,954	31,083	CR	
Preble	27,081	13,346		
Putnam	25,248	12,344		
Richland	91,305	41,022	CR	VM
Ross	54,424	22,302	CR	
Sandusky	46,114	21,111	CR	
Scioto	82,910	39,091	PR	
Seneca	52,978	25,049		
Shelby	28,488	14,414		
Stark	283,194	131,192	CR	
Summit	410,032	190,492	CR	
Trumbull	158,915	77,846	CR	
Tuscarawas	70,320	35,273		
Union	20,687	10,708		
Van Wert	26,971	14,648		
Vinton	10,759	5,101		
Warren	38,505	18,733	PR	
Washington	44,407	21,475		
Wayne	58,716	26,928		
Williams	26,202	13,317		
Wood	59,605	26,615	CR	
Wyandot	19,785	9,904		

CR indicates the county has registration throughout the county.
PR indicates the county has registration in part of the county.
VM indicates voting machines are used in the county.

1954

Election Guide

TED W. BROWN, Secretary of State

GENERAL PROVISIONS FOR 1954 CANDIDATES

In reading the following provisions, it will be helpful to bear in mind that party candidates file Declaration of Candidacy forms which contain petitions, and non-partisan or independent candidates file Nominating Petitions. Therefore, whenever "Declarations of Candidacy" are mentioned, party candidates are being referred to; and when the term "Nominating Petition" is used, the reference is to non-partisan types of candidates only. If the word "petition" alone is used, both types of candidates are indicated.

TIME OF FILING:

All candidates for office to be elected at the General Election, November 2, 1954, must file their petitions before 4 p.m., February 3, 1954. (R.C. 3513.05, 3513.256, 3513.237, 3513.258.)

WHERE TO FILE:

State candidates—file in the office of the Secretary of State. District candidates—file in the office of the Board of Elections of the most populous county of the district. County candidates—file in the office of the county Board of Elections.

FILING FEE:

At the time of filing, each candidate shall pay a fee of one-half of one percent of the annual salary of such office; but in no case shall the fee be more than $50 nor less than $1. (R. C. 3513.10, 3513.261.)

IMPORTANT:

Each petition paper shall contain signatures of qualified electors of one county only. If you are running for office in a district which extends into two or more counties, separate petition papers shall be circulated in each county.

There is no provision in Ohio law allowing one person to affix the signature of another person to a petition. Each signature must be the actual signature of the person whose signature it purports to be.

SIGNATURES:

All signatures on petitions affirm that they have not signed the nominating petitions of more candidates for said office than the number to be elected to said office. It should be pointed out that this applies only to nominating petitions and is not applicable to declarations of candidacy. For instance, if there is but one county auditor to be elected—"A" is a Republican candidate, and "B" and "C" are independent candidates, the same person could sign "A's" declaration of candidacy petition form, and "B's" nominating petition form. Such person could not, however, sign both "B's" and "C's" nominating petition.

If a person signs the nominating petitions of more independent candidates than there are to be elected, his signature is valid on the first one he signed. It is therefore important that the "Date of Signing" be filled in for each signature on nominating petitions.

(Continued inside)

This information has been compiled to acquaint the 1954 candidates with the provisions of Ohio law pertaining to filing for office. It is intended as an easy-to-read, pocket-sized leaflet—a service manual for candidates for state, district and county office.

TED W. BROWN
Secretary of State.

1954 CANDIDATES' CALENDAR

Jan. 1. Applications for armed service absent voters ballot may be received on or after this date.

Feb. 3. ALL CANDIDATES FOR OFFICE SHALL FILE BEFORE 4 P.M. OF THIS DATE.

Feb. 8. Declaration of Candidacy Petitions open to public inspection until 4 p.m. of this date.

Feb. 9. On or before this date Boards of Elections shall examine Declaration of Candidacy Petitions and determine the validity or invalidity of signatures thereon.

Feb. 9. On or before this date all Declaration of Candidacy Petitions sent to Boards shall be returned to Secretary of State or Board of most populous county with certification as to validity or invalidity of signatures thereon.

Feb. 13. By 4 p.m. of this date protests against candidacy of any party candidate shall be filed with the election officials with whom the Declaration of Candidacy and Petitions were filed.

Feb. 18. Secretary of State shall certify forms of official primary ballots to each Board of Elections.

Mar. 5. Applications for absent voter Primary ballots may be made by civilians outside the U. S. from this date and until 4 p.m. of April 29.

Mar. 5. Clerk of Board shall mail or deliver armed service absent voter Primary ballots from this date and until 12 noon of May 1.

Mar. 5. Clerk of Board shall mail absent voter Primary ballots to civilians outside the U. S. from this date.

Mar. 24. Registration closes.

Apr. 4. Applications for disabled and civilian absent voter Primary ballots, for persons in U. S., not valid if delivered to Clerk prior to this date.

Apr. 4. Clerk of Board shall mail or deliver ballots to disabled and civilian absent voters in U. S., from this date.

Apr. 24. Name of candidate for State or District office shall not appear on Primary ballot if candidate dies prior to this date.

Apr. 29. Name of candidate for County office shall not appear on Primary ballot if candidate dies prior to this date.

Apr. 29. On or before this date committees on questions or issues shall have filed petition to be recognized as committee for appointment of challengers and witnesses.

Apr. 29. 4 p.m. of this date closes time for receiving applications for absent voter ballots by civilian and disabled voters.

Apr. 30. By 12 noon of this date civilian absent voter ballots shall be returned to Clerk.

May 1. Applications for armed service absent voter Primary ballots not valid if dated, postmarked or received by Clerk later than 12 noon of this date.

May 4. PRIMARY ELECTION DAY.

May 4. Armed service absent voter ballots received by Clerk prior to 12 noon shall be delivered to proper precinct.

May 5. Not later than 12 noon Board shall certify unofficial results to Secretary of State and Board of most populous county.

May 14. Before 4 p.m. of this date all candidates and committees shall file statements of receipts and expenditures.

May 15. Registration resumes.

1954 CANDIDATES' CALENDAR—(Continued)

June 15. Nominating Petitions filed with Secretary of State or most populous county, to be forwarded to other Boards.

June 15. Nominating Petitions open to public inspection from this date until 4 p.m. of June 30.

July 15. Nominating Petitions returned to office where filed, with certification as to validity or invalidity of signatures thereon.

July 30. By 4 p.m. of this date protests against Nominating Petitions shall be filed.

Aug. 13. Last day for withdrawal of candidates.

Aug. 18. Vacancies caused by withdrawals of candidates nominated at Primary, shall be filled.

Aug. 19. Secretary of State shall certify forms of official ballots to each Board of Elections.

Sept. 3. Applications for absent voter ballots may be made by civilians outside the U. S. from this date and until 4 p.m. of October 28.

Sept. 3. Clerk of Board shall mail or deliver armed service absent voter ballots from this date and until 12 noon of October 30.

Sept. 3. Clerk of Board shall mail absent voter ballots to civilians outside the U. S. from this date.

Sept. 22. Registration closes.

Oct. 3. Applications for disabled and civilian absent voter ballots, for persons in U. S., not valid if delivered to Clerk prior to this date.

Oct. 23. Certificate to fill vacancy on ballot caused by death of State or District candidate nominated at Primary shall be filed not later than 4 p.m. of this date.

Oct. 28. Certificate to fill vacancy on ballot caused by death of independent candidate shall be filed not later than 4 p.m. of this date.

Oct. 23. Certificate to fill vacancy on ballot caused by death of County candidate nominated at Primary shall be filed not later than 4 p.m. of this date.

Oct. 28. On or before this date committees on questions or issues shall have filed petition to be recognized as committee for appointment of challengers and witnesses.

Oct. 28. 4 p.m. of this date closes time for receiving applications for absent voter ballots by civilians and disabled voters.

Oct. 29. By 12 noon of this date civilian absent voter ballots shall be returned to Clerk.

Oct. 30. Applications for armed service absent voter ballots not valid if dated, postmarked or received by Clerk later than 12 noon of this date.

Nov. 2. GENERAL ELECTION DAY.

Nov. 2. Armed service absent voter ballots received by Clerk prior to 12 noon shall be delivered to proper precinct.

Nov. 3. Not later than 12 noon Board shall certify unofficial results to Secretary of State and Board of most populous county.

Nov. 12. Before 4 p.m. of this date all candidates and committees shall file statement of receipts and expenditures.

Nov. 13. Registration resumes.

FIGURE 3—27

FIGURE 3—28

3. Where the voter erases a mark he had previously made and then places a mark before the name of another candidate, it is to be counted as a vote for the last candidate. Erasures do not invalidate the ballot, if the intent of the voter is clear. (Notice: Tampering with ballots is a felony, punishable by imprisonment.)

4. Where the voter, instead of erasing an "X" mark, marks or scratches out the "X" he had previously made before the name of a candidate and then places an "X" before the name of another candidate, it is to be counted as a vote for the last candidate.

5. Where lines are drawn through the name of a candidate, the ballot is not to be considered as a defaced, invalid or disputed ballot. It is not, however, to be counted as a vote for the candidate through whose name the lines are drawn, even though that name is marked with an "X".

6. Where parts of the lines forming an "X" extend into more than one of the rectangular spaces in which are printed the names of candidates, it shall be counted as a vote for that candidate in whose space the lines of the "X" intersect or cross.

If a ballot contains any marks which would identify the voter, the entire ballot is invalid.

DISPUTED BALLOTS

A disputed ballot is one on which there is doubt as to how to count the marks—if there is doubt as to a voter's qualifications, this should have been determined before he is handed a ballot. After the ballot has been marked by the voter, it is counted along with the others.

If there is any disagreement as to how a ballot should be counted, it shall be submitted to all of the judges. That part of the ballot upon which three of the judges agree, shall be counted. That part upon which three judges do not agree, shall not be counted, and a notation shall be made on the back of the ballot indicating which part has not been counted; and the ballot shall be placed in the envelope marked for disputed ballots.

FRAUDULENT BALLOTS

If two or more ballots are found folded together among the ballots removed from the ballot box, they shall be deemed to be fraudulent. Such ballots shall not be counted. They shall be marked "Fraudulent", placed in the envelope so designated, and returned to the Board of Elections with other uncounted ballots.

CHECK LIST — BEFORE OPENING POLLS

- ☐ Vacancies filled
- ☐ Oath signed by each official
- ☐ Supplies examined and distributed
- ☐ Duties assigned
- ☐ Cards of Instructions posted
- ☐ Pencils in each booth and lighting checked
- ☐ Flags displayed
- ☐ Ballot boxes inspected and locked
- ☐ Ballots examined and counted, totals in poll books
- ☐ Names of challengers and witnesses entered in poll books

VOTING MACHINES

Preparation of Machines:

In precincts using voting machines, it is most important that each precinct official be familiar with the machine and the preparation for voting. The voting machine corresponds to the ballot box and should be checked thoroughly before the polls are opened. You will be provided with a book explaining in detail the steps to be followed in checking the machine — each step is vital and should be taken with care.

The voting machine keys will be sealed in an envelope on which is written the number of the voting machine, the number of the seal, the number on the protective counter, and the precinct. This envelope shall not be opened until at least one judge from each political party has examined it and found it sealed.

The following steps shall then be taken:

Sample ballots and instruction cards posted in conspicuous places;
Keys examined to insure they are the proper keys for each machine;
Public Counter inspected — this should show Zero;
Protective Counter examined — this should show the same number as appears on the key envelope;
Ballot labels on machine checked — the offices, candidates, and issues should be in the same order as that on the return sheets;
Individual Counters for each candidate and issue inspected — each should show Zero;
Counter Compartment locked;
Number on metal seal checked — this should correspond with number on key envelope.

If any discrepancy or variation appears on a machine, call your Board of Elections immediately and report it. When all of the preparatory steps have been taken, remove the seal.

Do not expose the counters under any circumstances until the last voter has voted. Once these are exposed, the machine automatically locks itself against further voting.

Casting the Vote:

After each person has qualified to vote, ask if he has operated a voting machine before. You will save much time if each voter is instructed in the operation before he approaches the machine.

Each voter is handed an "Authority to Vote" slip after he has qualified to vote (see preceding sections on "Voter's Qualifications" and "Establishing Right to Receive Ballot"). This slip is then presented to the Judge in charge of the voting machine. As each voter leaves the machine, it should be examined by the Judge to see that the ballot labels have not been disturbed, and that no campaign literature has been left in the machine.

If there is a line of voters in the polling place, keep the line in back of the table, not between the table and the machines.

If a person is physically unable to operate the machine, he may be assisted in the manner prescribed by law (see section on "Assisting Voters"), but in no other instance shall the curtains be opened while a voter is inside. If the voter asks for instructions after he has entered, they can be heard through the curtains.

Write-Ins:

Ohio law provides that no "write-in" votes may be cast at a General Election unless there is an office for which there is no candidate, or unless there are not as many candidates' names printed on the ballot as there are to be elected. The "write-in" spaces on the voting machine will therefore be locked off for all offices for which no "write-in" votes are allowed. If "write-ins" are allowed for some offices in your precinct, advise the voters which slots may be used by them for such offices.

In counting "write-in" votes cast after the polls close, the same rules apply as those set forth for paper ballots — if the intent of the voter can be ascertained, the vote shall be so counted.

After the Polls Close:

As soon as the last voter has cast his vote, lock the machine against further voting. Check the number on the Public Counter — this number should equal the number of voters shown on the poll books. If there is any variance, write a report to the Board of Elections explaining the reasons for the variance. Open the Counter Compartment in the presence of all persons lawfully within the polling place and expose the results.

The Presiding Judge shall then read aloud and distinctly the result as shown on each counter, in the following manner: "Three-two-four", not "Three hundred and twenty-four". As the Presiding Judge reads, a Judge of opposite politics shall stand beside him and ascertain that the figures are properly read. The results for each candidate and issue shall be read in the order that they appear on the return sheets. As each vote is read and announced, it shall be recorded on the return sheets by the two clerks. It is suggested that the clerks then read off the figures from the machine and the Judges verify the results on the return sheets.

If found to be correct, the return sheets shall be signed by the precinct officials. Examine the return sheets to be sure they contain all of the information requested. One copy of the return sheets shall be posted on the outside of the polling place and two copies returned to the Board of Elections.

After the return sheets have been certified, the Counter Compartment shall be locked. The keys should then be sealed in the envelope provided, the information on the envelope filled in, and the envelope returned to the Board of Elections.

IMPORTANT — ALL PRECINCTS

Your work as a Precinct Official is not complete until the returns are reported to the Board of Elections. Do not sacrifice accuracy for the sake of speed — but as soon as your results are determined, they should be reported. The Board of Elections is required to report to the Secretary of State's office by telephone as the results come in, and one tardy precinct can cause undue delay. You, the Precinct Official, are the focal point and upon you depends the efficiency of this election.

AS A PRECINCT OFFICIAL, you are one of the vast army of election workers who are the very "heart" of an efficient, honest election system in Ohio. Your responsibility is one of great proportions and your service to your state and nation is one to be gratefully admired and respected.

TED W. BROWN
Secretary of State

1954

STATE OF OHIO

Precinct Officials Guide

TED W. BROWN, Secretary of State

APPOINTMENT

Precinct officials are appointed on September 15 each year by the County Board of Elections, to serve a one-year term. Ohio law requires that a precinct official be a qualified elector, resident of the county in which the precinct is located.

No person who has been convicted of a felony, or any violation of the election laws, or who is unable to read and write English, or who is a candidate for an office to be voted for by the voters of the precinct in which he is to serve, shall act as a precinct official. If you have been appointed as a precinct official and do not possess the qualifications, advise the Board of Elections so that a replacement can be appointed. The law provides a penalty for acting without being properly qualified. The Board of Elections may remove precinct officials for good and sufficient reasons, or their compensation may be withheld for failure to comply with the law or with instructions issued by the Board of Elections.

The Presiding Judge in each precinct is appointed from the political party which is "dominant" in the precinct, meaning the party whose candidate for Governor in the next preceding General Election (November 1952) received the most votes. There are at least four judges (including the Presiding Judge) and two clerks in each precinct at a General Election. In some counties there are two crews of officials, one serving during the day, and another after the close of polls to count ballots.

PREPARATION OF THE POLLING PLACE

All precinct officials are to report to the polling place by 6:00 in the morning, in order to have the voting supplies prepared by the time voting commences at 6:30 a. m. If any precinct officials are absent, the Presiding Judge, with the concurrence of a majority of the precinct officials present, shall appoint qualified electors who are members of the same political party as the absent officials. The persons appointed then fill the vacancy until the County Board of Elections sends a replacement. The Presiding Judge shall promptly notify the County Board of the vacancy, by telephone or otherwise.

Each precinct official shall take the oath of office which is printed on the first page of the poll book, and subscribe to the oath by signing at the space provided in the poll book.

A kit of supplies is furnished for each precinct, which will include ballots, cards of instruction, one poll list (or signature book), two poll books, tally sheets, pencils, etc. This kit should be checked first to be sure that all of the supplies are on hand. In case anything is missing, call the Board of Elections and they will send out the needed supplies by messenger.

In appointing you to serve as a Precinct Official, the Board of Elections has placed upon you the responsibility of conducting the elections in your precinct in accordance with Ohio law. This guide is not intended as a full course of instruction, but is compiled to acquaint you with some of the important provisions of the law. Your Board of Elections will give you more detailed instructions, and you are urged to study the material supplied you in advance of Election Day.

INSTRUCTIONS
on
ELECTION
PROCEDURE

Issued by
THE BOARD
of
ELECTION COMMISSIONERS
of
THE CITY OF CHICAGO
1954

FIGURE 3—29

ELECTION GUIDE
(Revised January 1, 1954)

•

COMMONWEALTH OF PENNSYLVANIA
DEPARTMENT OF STATE

•

JOHN S. FINE
Governor

GENE D. SMITH
Secretary of the Commonwealth

E4-6m-4-54-912114

The Commonwealth of Massachusetts
EDWARD J. CRONIN
Secretary of the Commonwealth

POLITICAL CALENDAR
RELATING TO
STATE PRIMARIES and ELECTION
1954

NOMINATION PAPERS

JUNE 29, JULY 6, 13, 20,	Registrars of Voters and Election Commissioners are required to hold meetings for certifying names on all nomination papers on the four Tuesdays preceding July 27.
JULY 20,	5 P.M., last day and hour for filing all nomination papers, with Registrars of Voters and Election Commissioners for certification of signatures.
JULY 26,	Last day for holding convention of nonpolitical parties for the nomination of candidates.
JULY 27,	5 P.M., last day and hour for filing all nomination papers and certificates of nomination for the State Election with the Secretary of the Commonwealth.
JULY 27,	5 P.M., last day and hour for filing certicates of enrolment of candidates to the State Primaries.
JULY 30,	5 P.M., last day and hour for filing withdrawals of or objections to all nomination papers and certificates of nomination for the State Election with the Secretary of the Commonwealth.
AUG. 3,	5 P.M., last day and hour for filling vacancies caused by withdrawals.
AUG. 13,	Last day to register voters for the State Primaries.
AUG. 27,	Last day for filing public policy applications with Registrars of Voters and Election Commissioners for certification of signatures.
SEPT. 3,	Last day for filing with the Secretary of the Commonwealth applications for submission to voters at the State Election of questions of public policy.
SEPT. 14,	STATE PRIMARIES.

FIGURE 3—30

New Jersey Political Calendar. See N. J. Election Laws.

Chronological Index for Filing Petitions, Duties of Election Officers, Etc.

February 1, 1954—
On or before this date the chairman of the State committee, each political party, shall notify the Secretary of State of the number of delegates-at-large and alternate delegates-at-large to be elected to the next convention. *Sec. 19:24-1.*

February 1, 1954—
On or before this date the chairman of the State committee shall notify the chairman of each county committee that a member of the State committee is to be elected from said county at the ensuing general election. *Sec. 19:23-1.*

February (Month), 1954—
During this month it shall be the duty of the chairman of State committee of parties qualifying to participate in primary election to nominate two persons in each county for county board. *Sec. 19:6-18.*

February 9 to March 9, 1954—
County boards in counties of the first class shall cause a notice to be published twice during this period of time in each municipality in their respective counties. *Sec. 19:12-7, (B). (1).*

BALLOTS OF ABSENTEE VOTERS and MILITARY VOTERS

The Board of Election will send all absentee and military voters' envelopes received. After the closing of the polls, proceed as to these ballots pursuant to provisions of Sections 204, 309 and 310.

You should be thoroughly familiar with the provisions of these sections.

If any voter has voted in person, an absentee ballot or military ballot from such voter should not be counted (Sections 204, 309).

Objections to military ballots may be sustained only by a *majority vote* of the board of inspectors. A tie vote renders the ballot valid and it must be canvassed. The Chairman of the board of inspectors, or if he refuses, any inspector may indorse "not sustained" on any ballot to which objection is made and not sustained by a majority of the board (Sec. 309).

If the board should refuse to open any envelope or should reject any military or absentee voter's ballot which you believe to be a Democratic vote, insist that the envelope or ballot *is marked in accordance with the provisions of Sections 213 and 309, and so recorded on the official returns.*

INSTRUCTIONS FOR WATCHERS (Sec. 223)

The Watcher should be all that the name signifies. He should be present in the polling place from 5:30 A. M., and should remain there all day. It is *most* important that he be present and diligently active from the time the polls are closed until the canvass is completed.

The Watcher's job is to observe that the Inspectors fully and properly perform their duties. He should familiarize himself with their duties. Any failure to comply with the Election Law should be immediately reported to the local Democratic Headquarters. Especially note the following:

Procure a copy of the registry list from your leader. Check off each Democratic vote as it is cast. At *one o'clock*, make a list of all the registered Democrats who have not yet voted and see that they are sent for. *Do the same again at five in the evening.*

Make sure every registered Democrat entitled to vote is permitted to do so.

A voter is permitted to remain within the booth three minutes. (Sec. 258.)

As soon as the polls are closed see that the canvass is properly made. Be familiar with Sec. 261.

The Watcher should be present behind the machine as the numbers on the counters are read off. He should be very careful to see that the correct count is taken off.

The absentee voters and military voter's ballots should be separately counted and entered.

The number of votes cast for each candidate on each row on which his name appears on the machine and by Absentee and Military Voters' ballots should be recorded on the statement of canvass.

INSTRUCTIONS FOR CHALLENGERS (Sec. 223)

A reasonable number of challengers (who are qualified voters of the city or county in which they serve) representing the Democratic Party should be present at each polling place where they can see what is done within the guard rail from the opening to the close of the polls.

Challengers should challenge the right to vote of any person whose qualifications have been found lacking.

If legal assistance is needed, call your local Democratic headquarters and get in touch with the local members of the Democratic State Law Committee.

129

1952

Instructions for ELECTION DAY

REMINDER: This year the polls are to remain open from 6 A. M. to 9 P. M.

To reach the Democratic State Headquarters on Election Day, communicate with

DEMOCRATIC STATE COMMITTEE
Hotel Biltmore, New York, N. Y.
Tel. MUrray HIll 6-9090

DEMOCRATIC STATE COMMITTEE
PAUL E. FITZPATRICK, Chairman

WILLIAM J. O'SHEA,
Chairman, State Law Committee,
102 Maiden Lane, New York 5, N. Y.

GENERAL INFORMATION

Inspectors must be at the polls at 5:15 A. M. Watchers and challengers should be present at 5:30 A. M. The County Chairmen will assign the members of the Law Committee.

The Chairman of the board of inspectors, appointed on the first day of registration, continues to act on election day. Vacancies are filled pursuant to Section 46 of the Election Law. The Board of Inspectors are in charge of the election and under the law are supreme and *no one else should be permitted to interfere.* THE ATTORNEY GENERAL OR HIS DEPUTIES DO NOT AT ANY TIME SUPERSEDE THE BOARD OF INSPECTORS. The Attorney General and his deputies have the powers of a watcher plus the powers of a peace officer (Executive Law, Section 69).

All qualified voters in line at the hour fixed for closing the polls should be permitted to vote. (Election Law, Sec. 201[4]).

FIGURE 3–31

business is often transacted outside of regular channels because it is much more convenient to do so. You will not really understand the party system in your community unless you understand how these informal arrangements work. The formal party apparatus may do little more than to ratify and register decisions already made elsewhere. For the best reasons in the world, no good party organization is likely to take public action on any important matter that has not been carefully considered in advance.

To get behind the formal facade of politics it is useful to get politicians to identify party leaders who are likely to attend private meetings at which tentative plans are made. Who is invited? In a showdown, whose point of view prevails? Is there an inner circle within the party leadership? Are there identifiable patterns of cleavage within the group? How are differences resolved?

The student should realize that a substantial change has taken place in the nature of American party organization at the local level in recent years in many urban areas. One of the most remarkable of these changes has been the decline of the power of the old-fashioned local party bosses who dominated the system a generation ago. Consequently, traditional descriptions of local bosses and machines may no longer fit the facts in your community. (If they do fit, your community is probably backward in its political development and its backwardness should be explained.) The decline of the local boss is due to a variety of causes: (a) government has become too important to be managed by old political methods; (b) there has been a revolution in public administration; (c) for many reasons, politics is more competitive now than it was a generation ago; (d) politics is dealing with a new set of policies; and (e) there has been a change in public attitudes toward politics.

TESTS OF THE DECLINE OF THE BOSS SYSTEM (or of the status of the boss system, since the transition from the older to the newer patterns of party organization goes on at variable rates)

The problem is made difficult by the fact that change is largely accomplished through substantial and informal arrangements and understandings within the parties rather than through a modification of their formal structure. If the form remains the same while the substance changes, it is likely that such changes will not be easily visible. Therefore, do not trust appearances.

1. What is the status of the patronage system in your community today, rated: not only by appointments to public office but also by procedures for letting contracts, purchases, tax assessment? See Merriam and Gosnell, *The American Party System* (12) for an account of the various kinds of spoils and patronage available to the old-time political bosses. Make a list of the kinds of spoils described and try it out on public officials who are well informed about conditions in your city now. Be careful not to accept accounts of practices remembered from a more or less remote past. You are interested in current practices. Patronage may be abolished or reduced in scope by the establishment of a merit system; it may also be restricted by city ordinances or union contracts giving city employees tenure, or by practices and understandings that remove some offices from politics. Do state agencies prescribe the qualifications for any city employees? The patronage system is valuable to the boss only when there is a relatively high rate of turnover in city employment. When employees acquire tenure, they resist demands made on them by the boss. New accounting and auditing systems, modern purchasing procedures, and competitive bidding on contracts tend similarly to dry up a variety of the older sources of spoils. What is the reputation of the local police for integrity in law enforcement? Can traffic tickets be "fixed"? What is the reputation of the tax assessor for fairness in the assessment of property in the city? Do gamblers, contractors, or suppliers seem to have undue influence in city hall?

2. Usually, the old-fashioned political machines were bipartisan. That is, the minority party was a captive of the dominant organization. Is there any evidence that the dominant party in your city controls the minority party? Is the system genuinely competitive? Do minority party leaders receive patronage from the dominant organization? Does the minority party lend a hand to the leaders of the majority party when they are in difficulties?

3. Is the organization exclusive or does it attempt to broaden the base of participation in the work and decisions of the party? Is an attempt being made to assimilate new elements into active party membership? Old-fashioned local party bosses, interested primarily in patronage and spoils, tended to restrict their organizations narrowly to discourage unwanted claims for patronage. Since the machines were bipartisan, it was unnecessary to develop a large organization in order to win elections. Is the organization hospitable to the extensive use of volunteers or are volunteers forced to form their own special organizations outside of the regular organization? Is it easy or difficult to get into politics?

4. How interested does the organization seem to be in winning elections? What steps are taken to build up party registration between elections? Is there a continuing registration drive? Does the party maintain a permanent organization continuously at work? What kinds of activities are carried on between elections?

5. How are party decisions made? What kinds of consultations take place? Who is consulted? Do decisions represent a wide consensus of party opinions? Do party workers feel that they have participated in decisions? Do party members have confidence in their party leaders?

6. What seems to be the motivation of party leaders? Are they interested in issues, public affairs, public policy—or are they interested chiefly in patronage? What do political leaders talk about? Do they seem to be well informed about questions of public policy?

Do they talk well about public business? What do they read? Have there been changes in the types of party leaders who have risen to positions of prominence in recent years? Can the leaders talk intelligently about the differences between the parties? How do party leaders make a living? Is there a high rate of turnover among party leaders?

7. Are party leaders conscious of the need for research in public affairs? Do they consult experts and specialists? Are there any study groups in the party? Do candidates use research assistants as speech writers? Does the party maintain files of newspaper clippings? Do the parties use opinion surveys? What do they think of your attempt to make a political survey of the community?

8. What is the status of elected office holders in the party organization? Do elected officials make policy, or is there evidence that they are told what to do by the party organization? Do party leaders try to get the ablest men available to become candidates for public office or do they seem to value chiefly reliability and availability? Does the organization have unusual difficulties in getting along with public officials? How are party candidates recruited? Is there a high rate of turnover among elected officials?

9. What is the relation of local party leaders to the state party organizations? What role do they play in the statewide organization? Do local delegates to state conventions vote as a block? There is no such thing as a purely local political organization or a purely local political alignment. The objectives of local politics (housing, health, education, highways, taxation, and finance) involve cooperation with the state and national governments. Control of the state and national governments is therefore always a consideration in local politics. Modern local political leaders must be able to play a role in state and national politics. Do party leaders in your city have the interest and aptitude for this kind of role? Moreover, the same party organizations used to fight local election campaigns are used also to wage state and national campaigns. This is nearly inevitable because party organizations are too difficult to create and too difficult to maintain to make the idea of duplicate organization tolerable. Once a party organization is formed there is every reason to use it at all levels of politics. State-local party relations are a significant factor in the status of the party system. The relations among the older type of local political bosses were often characteristically bad because the local bosses were likely to compete for state patronage so vigorously that it was difficult to get them to work together to win statewide elections. As a matter of fact, local bosses often used their power to refuse to support the state ticket as leverage to extort state patronage. These questions should be raised so that you can get some conception of the extent to which political leaders in your community have adapted themselves to the new conditions.

10. What is the impact of statewide party competition on local party politics? If the parties compete on equal terms in state elections, the state party organization may have a strong interest in local party organization—even in areas where the party is in the minority—because every vote counts, no matter where it comes from. What evidence is there that state party leaders have fostered local party organizations?

THE MEANING OF PARTY CLEAVAGES AT THE LOCAL LEVEL

While there has been a great increase in the number of states having competitive two-party systems, party competition at the local level tends strongly to produce one-party neighborhoods, districts, and areas. Everything that has been said about the local patterns of distribution of people according to income, social status, housing, rentals, nationality, and race creates the expectation that a competitive party system will produce strongly marked differences in the geographical distribution of the party vote at the local level. If this kind of distribution does not appear in your community, it may be due to the fact that (a) the community is unusually homogeneous or is a homogeneous segment of a larger community (you may be working on too restricted a definition of your community); or (b) the party system is not competitive; or (c) your city lies in a section of the state with a strong sectional bias against another section of the state, (i.e., upstate New York versus downstate New York). Local party cleavages are likely, therefore, to reflect the same kind of social cleavages that appear in national politics, but two-party competition may produce one-party areas in restricted localities.

Contrary to popular opinion, the old political machines were not efficient in the sense of getting out a large vote. They won power by eliminating competition. The basic assumption of the older type of political organization was that the public was profoundly indifferent to politics.

In a transitional period, you may find local party organizations which have lost the old motivation and interests and have not yet discovered how to use interest in public affairs as motivation for party work. See Berelson, Lazarsfeld, and McPhee, *Voting* (13), for a description of one party organization in this condition. How do you rate party organizations in your city?

The problems of the minority party, especially a minority that has won its independence from the dominant party only recently, are very different from those of the old majority party. It is necessary to get some historical perspective on the development of the parties. How does the condition of the minority party today compare with its status ten or fifteen years ago? Party leadership, experience, prestige, and morale are not likely to be built up overnight.

Modern party organization, motivated by a widespread interest in public policy, is likely to give rise to new patterns of relations between the local and state and national leaders.

It is impossible to develop a good party system without public cooperation. You might expect to find that the decline of the local party boss in your community has tended to temper the hostility of the public toward the parties. As is the case with all change, people do not necessarily perceive or understand equally rapidly what is happening to them. You should beware, therefore, of observers whose sense of time is imperfect, i.e., people who attribute old data to the present. When you interview politicians, try to get them to date their experiences as accurately as possible. How aware is the public of the nature of changes in the party system? What kind of reputation do the parties have?

A ready-made test of the efficiency of local party organizations is to be found in the manuals of organization issued by the parties. Test your local parties by the standards set up in the *Republican Campaign Manual* (Republican National Committee) or *The Key to Democratic Victory* (Democratic National Committee). How many of the activities described in these manuals do your parties actually carry on?

LOCAL IMPACT OF STATE AND NATIONAL POLITICS

It is well for the student to remember that the neat division of governmental functions into national, state, and local categories is not true to life. In reality, governmental functions are remarkably well scrambled. Many functions are performed at all levels of American government. This is true of governmental activities dealing with health, education, housing, urban redevelopment, highways, traffic police, and welfare, for example. In these areas of action, the national, state, and local authorities cooperate: they supplement each other's efforts, exchange information and personnel, establish uniform standards, share costs, and assume joint contractual obligations. It is impossible, therefore, to make a purely local survey. As a matter of fact, local government is so largely a creature of state policy and state legislation that it is impossible to understand any local government apart from the policies of its parent state government. Moreover, nearly all programs of local government necessitate some kind of action by the state. Relatively few major objectives of local politics can be achieved unless the local community can make its political weight felt in the state capitol and in Washington. On the other hand, local governmental activity is often stimulated by national and state policy.

It is well to be aware of the role of the state throughout your survey. What is the local government policy of the state? How is state policy concerning local governments made? The state legislature plays a crucial role in defining the task of local governments. What kind of interest does the state legislature have in the cities? (Take a look at the apportionment of representation in the legislature as an introduction to this question.) Does the governor furnish leadership in the formation of state policy in this area of state concern? What state agencies are active in this field?

Because action in many fields of public policy takes place at all levels of American government, it is often possible to get results by moving at one governmental level when an impasse has been reached at other levels. Thus, the state may intervene in an area where local authorities are unable to act because they find it difficult to cooperate with other local authorities or because they are inadequately financed. On the other hand, the national government may offer financial incentives to local authorities when the state fails to take necessary action. Often the impact of national policy in some local areas is so great that local authorities are unable to cope with it promptly and effectively, as, for example, in the case of the development of new war industries. (See Fig. 2-15 for one compilation of federal expenditures in the state of New York as an example of this type of federal-state-local relation.) In metropolitan areas, cooperative action at all levels of government is made necessary by concentrations of population which swamp all local governments and all local and special authorities in the area.

If local government and politics are looked upon as ways of getting things done, it is obvious that a mixed system of national, state, and local government is more flexible and resourceful than a system in which the functions of the various levels of government are rigidly separated. The student has a legitimate interest in rotten borough systems of representation in state legislatures, in the development of strongly marked, one-party systems of local politics, in conflicts between local and state administrations, and in the representation of satellite and central cities in the state legislature because all these factors influence the capacity of the various levels of American government to function. There are a variety of forms of local power monopolies, sometimes disguised as nonpartisan local governments, sometimes written into state constitutions, sometimes assuming the protective coloration of local self-government, home rule, or appointive metropolitan authorities. One of the best ways to test the power system in a local governmental complex is to find out how to get things done. One of the purposes of a survey is to discover how the resources of the whole governmental apparatus can be used to deal with the problems of the area.

REFERENCES

1. Sayre, W. S., and H. Kaufman, *Governing New York City*. New York: Russell Sage Foundation, 1960.

2. Key, V. O., Jr., *Politics, Parties, and Pressure Groups*. 2d ed. New York: Thomas Y. Crowell Company, 1947.

3. Bone, H. A., *American Politics and the Party System*. New York: McGraw-Hill Book Company, Inc., 1949.

4. Penniman, H. R., *Sait's American Parties and Elections*. 4th ed. New York: Appleton-Century-Crofts, Inc., 1948.

5. Schattschneider, E. E., *Party Government*. New York: Holt, Rinehart and Winston, Inc., 1942.

6. Sorauf, F. J., "Extra-Legal Political Parties in Wisconsin," *American Political Science Review*, XLVIII, No. 3, September 1954, pp. 692-704.

7. Schattschneider, E. E., *The Semisovereign People*. New York: Holt, Rinehart and Winston, Inc., 1960.

8. Kaufman, H., and V. Jones, "The Mystery of Power," *Public Administration Review*, Vol. XIV, Summer 1954, pp. 205-12.

9. Hunter, F., *Community Power Structure: A Study of Decision Makers*. Chapel Hill, N.C.: University of North Carolina Press, 1953.

10. Bell, W., R. J. Hill, and C. R. Wright, *Public Leadership in the United States*. San Francisco: Chandler Publishing Co., 1961.

11. Schubert, G. A., Jr., *The Michigan State Director of Elections*. Alabama: The University of Alabama Press, 1954.

12. Merriam, C. E., and H. F. Gosnell, *The American Party System*. 3d ed. New York: The Macmillan Company, 1940. Chaps. 8-12.

13. Berelson, B. R., P. F. Lazarsfeld, and W. N. McPhee, *Voting: A Study of Opinion Formation in a Presidential Campaign*. Chicago: University of Chicago Press, 1954. Chap. 8.

14. Hawley, A., *The Changing State of Metropolitan America*. New York: The Free Press of Glencoe, Inc., 1956.

15. Simon, H. A., *Fiscal Aspects of Metropolitan Consolidation*. Berkeley, Calif.: Bureau of Public Administration, 1943.

16. Keats, J. C., *The Crack in the Picture Window*. Boston: Houghton Mifflin Company, 1957.

17. Spectorsky, A. C., *The Exurbanites*. Philadelphia: J. B. Lippincott Company, 1955.

18. Wilson, S., *The Man in the Gray Flannel Suit*. New York: Simon and Schuster, Inc., 1955.

19. Coleman, J. S., *Community Conflict*. New York: The Free Press of Glencoe, Inc., 1957.

20. The Editors of *Fortune, The Exploding Metropolis*. New York: Doubleday & Company, Inc., 1958.

21. Sweeney, S. B., and G. S. Blair, eds., *Metropolitan Analysis: Important Elements of Study and Action*. Philadelphia: University of Pennsylvania, 1958.

22. *The Path of Progress for Metropolitan St. Louis*. Metropolitan St. Louis Survey. University City, Mo., 1957.

23. Handlin, O., *The Newcomers: Negroes and Puerto Ricans in a Changing Metropolis*. Cambridge, Mass.: Harvard University Press, 1959.

24. Matthews, D. R., *The Social Background of Political Decision Makers*. New York: Doubleday & Company, Inc., 1954.

Chapter IV

ELECTION STATISTICS

In any study of the relation between social conditions and politics, election statistics constitute something like half of the equation because elections are a major source of information about the political half of the formula. Nearly everybody agrees that economic and social status has some connection with the way people vote. The question is, how much? One way to try to find out is to examine the relations between election statistics and demographic data. This is a good way to try to find out what politics in your community is about.

So many elections are held in the United States that the quantity and diversity of election statistics make up to some extent for their deficiencies in other respects. Elections are an integral part of the conduct of the business of the 155,000 governmental units in the country. According to the Bureau of the Census, 130,931 elections were held in the United States in a recent year. It is estimated that Americans elect 800,000 local, state, and national officials. These elections, held at various times, at a variety of levels of interest and attention, and in a great variety of jurisdictions, can be used to investigate many facets of American politics. This is especially true because the functions of the officials elected, the public business involved, and the nature of the constituencies vary tremendously. Moreover, related data concerning the registration of voters, party registrations, and direct primary elections provide other dimensions of information about politics. For an excellent statement of statistical concepts and techniques, illustrated by election data, see Key, *A Primer of Statistics for Political Scientists* (1). National elections constitute the largest collective activity of the American people. Because of their historic continuity and their scope, range and variety, election statistics are one of the principal sources of information about American politics.

The study of American politics has suffered greatly from the fact that scholars have often been preoccupied with the study of presidential election statistics to the exclusion of all other kinds of election data. This concentration on a single kind of election has given their research a one-dimensional quality which fails to take into consideration

tendencies that can be discovered only by a study of the whole political system. Presidential elections are so important that they must be considered even in a local political survey, but it is necessary to consider the political system as a whole if we want to understand it. An examination of a representative cross-section of all election statistics (local, state, congressional, presidential), is required to give research a dimension of depth. Indeed, scholars ignore nonpresidential data at the risk of developing serious misconceptions of the situation because political trends are not necessarily identical at all levels of American politics. The "spread" in the vote cast for national, state, and local candidates of the same party is apt to be so great that no single election can be taken as an adequate measure of party strength. This creates a problem. If you want to get a reliable index of the party vote you will need to sample a variety of kinds of election returns before you can decide which set of election statistics is the best measure of party strength in your town. Use a combination of several different kinds of election data taken from several levels of the political system, bearing in mind the proposition that the vote is likely to be important only if the office is important.

It is usually necessary to consider mayoralty, congressional, gubernatorial, and presidential election statistics as the minimum of data needed to estimate the strength of the parties in any community and to establish the patterns of distribution of the party vote within the community. The intensity of partisan feeling is not necessarily equal at all levels of politics. It is never safe to rely exclusively on local elections in any survey of local politics because local elections may be nonpartisan or the turnout may be very low, or the local party alignment may be atypical. You are trying to measure party strength throughout your study because party alignment is the basic political datum. The end result of your analysis may well be a series of graphs and maps showing the distribution of the party vote in a number of different kinds of elections.

Since it may be impossible to examine all election data, it is important to find out which elections are most apt to reveal political trends at the various levels of politics. You are interested in the party vote. Examine the statistics, then get local expert opinion on this subject.*

You gain significant leverage for the understanding of politics in your community as soon as you attempt to explain the discrepancies that appear in elections at the various levels of government in your area. If there is a discrepancy between the party vote cast in your community in national, state, and local elections, you can try out a number of hypotheses. Is the total vote cast in these elections significantly different? Is the basis of representation in city council, state legislature, and Congress so different as to affect the result? Do the offices at stake in the election seem important enough to arouse public interest? Was the total vote affected by a lack of competition at any one level of politics? Did the public have valuable alternatives in all of the elections? Do bipartisan agreements hold down popular participation in certain elections? Did both parties nominate the same candidates in some instances, depriving voters of a choice? Is politics at the various levels of government about important questions of policy? Are some of the elections legally nonpartisan? How does the total vote cast in primary elections compare with the total vote cast in general elections? Do election laws, the makeup of the ballot, or the setup of voting machines make it easy or difficult to split tickets? One thing you are likely to discover as soon as you begin to work with the data: all election statistics call for interpretation.**

The public uses elections in a variety of ways to express a variety of attitudes. In a way, even the people who do not vote pass a kind of judgment on the government: indifference, boredom, satisfaction, contempt, or confusion. Sometimes the voters have merely a choice of evils, or the issues are so badly defined that it is difficult to vote intelligently. Does the system make excessive demands on the voter? When there are too many elections, the public response is likely to be poor.

When local elections are nonpartisan, it is necessary to look at state and national election statistics to discover the party complexion of the community. Even if the elections are not really

nonpartisan, the statistics may be, if the vote is not tabulated according to party.

The second important characteristic of voting statistics is the size of the total vote cast in the election. The total vote may actually be as important as the percentage of the vote polled by each of the parties because the total vote measures the public attitude toward the system as a whole. The total turnout indicates what the public thinks it can accomplish in the elections. Do people think that the election is likely to make a difference? Are the parties competitive? Are they able to define and exploit the alternatives? Do the officers elected have enough power to do anything important? Does the election make a difference? If politics in your community bores the public, you ought to try to find out why this is so, because a dull government is apt to be a bad government. It is always necessary, therefore, to compare the total vote (the Democratic vote plus the Republican vote) with the total number of citizens twenty-one years of age or over residing in the community. See, for example, Senate Document No. 150, *Comparison of Potential Voters and Actual Votes Cast by Counties in Each State, 1948-1950* (2). (Note that the "total number of citizens twenty-one years of age or over" is not the same as the total number of registered voters.) Moreover, a change in the total vote cast nearly always alters the party ratio, i.e., the vote polled by the two parties does not rise or decline equally with a rise or decline of the total vote. Off-year elections, special elections, or elections held at unusual times rarely arouse as much interest as do general elections, and the consequent decline in the total vote may itself be sufficient to change the political landscape. On the other hand, the vote cast for minor offices on long ballots is influenced by the ease or difficulty of splitting tickets, by the form of the ballot, and the setup of voting machines.

Examine closely the impact of the total vote on each of the major parties. Which of the parties seems to profit by a large turnout or, conversely, by a small turnout? How do local political experts explain the facts? Consult local experts about the reputation of the various elections for attracting a large vote. Do they think that the prospects of the parties vary from one level of politics to another?

Election statistics have one important advantage over all other political statistics: they are the most confidential, the most extensive and the most accurate statistics available. A great effort has been made in the United States to guarantee the secrecy of the ballot, and in most jurisdictions, the count is now apt to be accurate and reliable. On the other hand, election statistics suffer from the fact that the aggregates are so large that it is often difficult to relate election statistics to other data.

---

*In any given election you can make an index number showing the extent of ticket splitting by dividing the total vote cast for the candidate who led the ticket by the total vote cast for the candidate who polled the smallest vote. This is one kind of index number. You may devise other indices to suit yourself.

**It is possible to produce an index number showing the representative character of legislative bodies, i.e., the population of the largest district divided by that of the smallest district. Use the total vote cast in legislative elections if population figures are not available. Compare the index number for your state with those for several other states. Here again, you can devise other kinds of index numbers if you want to.

HOW TO FIND ELECTION STATISTICS

The federal government, unfortunately, collects and publishes election statistics only on a very restricted basis. For certain kinds of elections, the states assemble and publish election returns. The secretary of state in each of the states is the returning officer for many elections and, according to the general practice, publishes some of the returns of these elections. He also publishes state election laws and state manuals or registers which include election statistics, rosters of successful candidates, data concerning the expiration of the terms of elected officials, and political calendars. The secretary of state often has some general administrative supervision over the conduct of elections by local officials. The staff of the secretary of state's office is likely, therefore, to include experts on election laws, election statistics, and election procedures. This is worth remembering if you have difficulty in interpreting election laws or if you need advice about election data.

Figure 4-1 is a part of the bibliography of sources used by the U.S. Bureau of the Census in its compilation of presidential and congressional election statistics published in 1946.

As we have observed, the secretary of state's office is usually responsible for the publication of election statistics. Find out if this is true in your state. The most important private compilation of election statistics is *American Votes, A Handbook of Contemporary American Election Statistics* (3), a series beginning in 1956. These volumes include election returns for presidential, gubernatorial, and congressional elections for all of the states.

Many states do not require central reporting of local election returns. A variety of local officials are responsible for the custody of these returns: town clerks, county clerks, boards of elections. Search the election laws of your state for statutory provisions for the custody of election returns. To whom are the returns made? Do the laws require the returning officers to preserve these records indefinitely? Figure 4-2 is an excerpt from Illinois election laws concerning local election returns. Look for corresponding provisions in the laws of your state.

Where local election statistics are not preserved indefinitely by local officials (sometimes the statutes require that these records be preserved for no more than five years), you can get some figures by consulting the files of your local newspapers. Newspaper statistics are unofficial and may be incomplete and inaccurate, but they are sometimes the only figures available. Sometimes the state library or state archives is given authority to preserve local records. When necessary, consult the state librarian or state archivist to find out what kinds of election records he collects.

Do the parties maintain their own files of election statistics? Figure 4-3 is a form used by Democratic election officials to make returns to Democratic party headquarters in Pittsburgh. For an example of a statistical study made by a political party, see *1952 Congressional Vote Statistics*, published by the Republican Congressional Campaign Committee, Washington, D.C. Both national committees make compilations of this kind. Have your state and local party committees made compilations of election returns or have they made analyses of election statistics?

CORRELATING ELECTION STATISTICS WITH OTHER DATA

It is important to observe the geographical areas for which election returns are broken down. In some states the returns for state elections are broken down only by counties. In these states it may be necessary to consult county officials to get more detailed breakdowns. Whenever possible get returns by precincts. As is the case with all statistics, the figures become more valuable as they are broken down for smaller areas. The smaller the area, the more apt it is to be socially homogeneous and the more useful a comparison of election statistics and demographic data may be.

Note Figure 4-4 showing that Illinois election reports, published by the secretary of state, break down statistics only as far as the county totals. On the other hand, New York figures are broken down by districts, and Massachusetts figures by wards and precincts. (See Fig. 4-5 and Fig. 4-6.)

Unfortunately for you, election precincts are not used as the basis for reporting census data. It follows that the areas used for reporting social and economic data are usually not identical with those used for reporting political data. With ingenuity it is possible, however, to fit the two kinds of data together sufficiently well to make possible some useful comparisons. Sometimes census tracts follow ward lines, or do not cross ward lines. The wards, in turn, are made up of precincts. A careful comparison of ward, tract, precinct, enumeration district, and block lines will show what kinds of comparable data are available. Often it is possible to select sample precincts within wards or census tracts, or to add the figures for a number of precincts wholly within certain census tracts for comparison with other precincts wholly within other tracts. This method is useful when you are able to make a physical inspection of the area to see to it that you are really using data for representative areas.

If a physical inspection of an area (noting housing, nationality, race, etc.) shows that it is reasonably homogeneous, you can afford to take liberties with the statistics. That is, you can treat

From Vote Cast in Presidential and Congressional Elections, 1928-1944.

BIBLIOGRAPHY

Alabama

Department of Archives and History. Alabama Official and Statistical Register. 1943.

Secretary of State. [Vote in the General Election]. (photostated) November 7, 1944.

Arizona

Secretary of State. Official Canvass; General Election Returns. (mimeographed) November 5, 1940; November 7, 1944.

Arkansas

Compilation by Census Bureau representatives from official records.

California

Secretary of State. Statement of Vote; General Election; Party Registration, Voting Precincts, Total Vote Cast. November 5, 1940; November 7, 1944.

Colorado

Secretary of State. Abstract of Votes Cast at the Primary Election...and at the General Election.. 1940; 1942; 1944.

Connecticut

Secretary of State. Register and Manual. 1941.

Secretary of State. Statement of Vote; General Election; Tabulated from Returns in the Office of the Secretary. November 7, 1944.

Delaware

Secretary of State. State Manual Containing Official List of Officers, Boards, Commissions and County Officers. 1941; 1943; 1945.

Florida

Secretary of State. Official vote—State of Florida, General Election, Tabulated by Counties. 1940; 1944.

Georgia

Department of Archives and History. Georgia's Official Register. 1939-1941-1943.

Secretary of State. Returns of General Election. (typewritten) November 7, 1944.

Idaho

Secretary of State. Biennial Report. 1939-40; 1941-42.

Secretary of State. Abstract of Votes in the Several Counties of the State of Idaho. November 7, 1944.

Illinois

Secretary of State. Official Vote Cast at the General Election, Judicial Elections, Primary Election. 1940; 1942; 1944.

Indiana

Secretary of State. Annual Report. 1940; 1944.

Iowa

Secretary of State. Canvass of the Vote; General Election. November 5, 1940; November 3, 1942; November 7, 1944.

Kansas

Secretary of State. Biennial Report. 1939-40; 1941-42; 1943-44.

Kentucky

Secretary of State. Official Statement Issued by ...of "Tabulated Vote" of the General Election... November 5, 1940; November 3, 1942; November 7, 1944.

Louisiana

Secretary of State. Election Returns for El tors for President and Vice-President of the U States (Clipping from Baton Rouge, Louisiana *Times*, November 30, 1944). November 7, 194

Secretary of State. Report. 1939-40

Maine

Department of State. General E Senator. (typewritten) 1940.

Department of State. [Votes C dential Election]. (typewritten

Governor and Council. [Re for U. S. Senator]. Septembe

Maryland

Secretary of State. G (mimeographed) November 7

Secretary of State.

Massachusetts

Clerk of the Sena Manual for the Use of

Secretary of the tics...; Together wi Elections. Public

Michigan

Secretary of General Primary 1944.

Minnesota

Canvassing November 5, 1

Mississippi

Secretar 1940-41; 194

Secreta tors. Nove

Missouri

Secret

Secret and County Cast for

Shows principal sources of election statistics in the United States

FIGURE 4—1

the result of the canvass of such ballots.

§ 18-14. The said judges of election shall make duplicate statements of the result of the canvass, which shall be written or partly written and partly printed. Each of the statements shall contain a caption stating the day on which, and the number of the election precinct and the ward, city and county, in relation to which such statements shall be made, and the time of opening and closing of the polls of such election precinct. It shall also contain a statement showing the whole number of votes given for each person, designating the office for which they were given, which statement shall be written, or partly written and partly printed, in words at length; and in case a proposition of any kind has been submitted to a vote at such election, such statements shall also show the whole number of votes cast for or against such proposition, written out or partly written and partly printed, in words at length. And at the end thereof a certificate that such statement is correct in all respects; which certificate, and each sheet of paper forming part of the statement, shall be subscribed by the said judges and election clerks. If any judge or election clerk shall decline to sign such return, he shall state his reason therefor in writing, and a copy thereof, signed by himself, shall be enclosed with each return. Each of the statements shall be enclosed in an envelope, which shall then be securely sealed with sealing wax or other adhesive material; and each of the judges and each of the election clerks shall write his name across every fold at which the envelope, if unfastened, could be opened. One of the envelopes shall be directed to the county clerk and one to the comptroller of the city, or to the officer of such city whose duties correspond with those of comptroller. Each set of tallies shall also be signed by the election clerks and judges of the election. And each shall be enclosed in an envelope, securely sealed and signed in like manner; and one of the envelopes shall be directed on the outside to the election commissioners and the other to the city, village or town clerk. On the outside of every envelope shall be endorsed whether it contains the statements of the votes cast or the tallies, and for what precinct and ward, village or town.

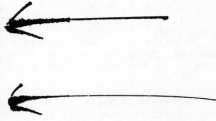

Illinois election laws show that returns are sent to county clerks, city comptrollers, election commissioners, and village or town clerks. That is where to look for the detailed statistics.

FIGURE 4—2

ELECTION — TUESDAY, NOVEMBER 3, 1953

_____DISTRICT _____WARD

CITY
BOROUGH
_____TOWNSHIP

JUDGE OF SUPERIOR COURT

J. Colvin Wright	Rep. _____
Harold L. Ervin	Rep. _____
John Inghram Hook	Dem._____
W. C. Sheely	Dem._____

JUDGE OF COMMON PLEAS COURT

Ralph T. Bell	Rep. _____
John Drew	Rep. _____
Anne X. Alpern	Rep. _____
	Dem._____
	Total_____
Lois Mary McBride	Rep. _____
Walter P. Smart	Dem._____
Loran L. Lewis	Dem._____
P. J. Columbus	Dem._____

JUDGE OF ORPHANS' COURT

Hugh C. Boyle	Rep. _____
	Dem._____
	Total_____

JUDGE OF COUNTY COURT

Benjamin Lencher	Rep. _____
	Dem._____
	Total_____

JUDGE OF JUVENILE COURT

Gustav L. Schramm	Rep. _____
	Dem._____
	Total_____

SHERIFF

Thomas E. Whitten	Rep. _____
William H. Davis	Dem._____

CORONER

Jay A. McCaffery	Rep. _____
William D. McClelland	Dem._____

CLERK OF COURTS

Leonard J. Parsons	Rep. _____
Thomas E. Barrett	Dem._____

MEMBER OF COMMISSION FOR SELECTION OF JURORS

Ralph E. Ord	Rep. _____
Alex P. Meanor	Dem._____

COUNTY SURVEYOR

Webster Hinnau	Rep. _____
Hiram Milton	Dem._____

MAYOR

Leonard P. Kane	Rep. _____
David L. Lawrence	Dem._____

MEMBER OF COUNCIL

Joseph N. Mackrell, Jr.	Rep. _____
William P. Young	Rep. _____
Robert A. Doyle	Rep. _____
Harry E. Richter	Rep. _____
Samuel L. Sherman	Rep. _____
Thomas J. Gallagher	Dem._____
Frederic G. Weir	Dem._____
Patrick T. Fagan	Dem._____
A. L. Wolk	Dem._____
Bennett Rodgers	Dem._____

Tally sheet for use by Democratic workers in Pittsburgh, Pa.

FIGURE 4—3

IMPORTANT--Please call Grant 1-8784 as soon as Election Board has finished the

JOHN J. KANE, Campaign Chairm

RETURN MADE BY_____

ADDRESS_____

8

VOTE FOR PRESIDENT—NOVEMBER 4, 1952

Counties	Plurality		Democratic — Adlai E. Stevenson and John J. Sparkman	Republican — Dwight D. Eisenhower and Richard M. Nixon	Socialist Labor — Eric Hass and Stephen Emery	Write-ins
Adams	R	6,351	13,301	19,652	21	
Alexander	R	914	4,305	5,219	29	
Bond	R	1,789	2,776	4,565	15	3
Boone	R	4,341	2,287	6,628	17	
Brown	R	580	1,557	2,137	5	
Bureau	R	8,127	6,173	14,300	25	
Calhoun	R	461	1,454	1,915	2	
Carroll	R	4,394	2,584	6,978	14	
Cass	R	747	3,405	4,152	8	
Champaign	R	13,237	13,951	27,188	105	7
Christian	R	62	9,844	9,906	17	
Clark	R	2,079	3,621	5,700	5	1
Clay	R	1,822	3,432	5,254	14	
Clinton	R	1,907	4,853	6,760	7	
Coles	R	4,784	7,876	12,660	20	
Cook (see below)						
Crawford	R	2,821	3,947	6,768	9	
Cumberland	R	1,102	2,200	3,302	11	1
DeKalb	R	9,697	5,110	14,807	28	2
DeWitt	R	1,991	3,221	5,212	3	
Douglas	R	2,824	2,706	5,530	5	
DuPage	R	48,645	22,489	71,134	194	23
Edgar	R	3,765	4,558	8,323	10	
Edwards	R	2,340	1,162	3,502	5	
Effingham	R	1,785	4,745	6,530	25	
Fayette	R	1,729	5,299	7,028	12	
Ford	R	4,095	2,121	6,216	6	2
Franklin	D	258	11,981	11,723	62	
Fulton	R	4,888	8,414	13,302	44	
Gallatin	R	147	2,153	2,300	8	
Greene	R	913	4,106	5,019	7	
Grundy	R	4,229	3,118	7,347	13	
Hamilton	R	1,385	2,662	4,047	8	
Hancock	R	4,500	4,681	9,181	18	1
Hardin	R	421	1,563	1,984	6	
Henderson	R	1,381	1,458	2,839	6	
Henry	R	7,743	8,558	16,301	33	6
Iroquois	R	7,822	4,634	12,456	11	
Jackson	R	2,736	7,457	10,193	24	
Jasper	R	1,025	2,728	3,753	9	1
Jefferson	R	1,143	8,698	9,841	19	
Jersey	R	607	3,424	4,031	6	
JoDaviess	R	4,274	2,858	7,132	13	
Johnson	R	1,713	1,614	3,327	6	
Kane	R	26,743	24,058	50,801	96	
Kankakee	R	7,643	12,636	20,279	90	
Kendall	R	3,506	1,476	4,982	3	
Knox	R	8,215	10,354	18,569	17	
Lake	R	22,576	32,353	54,929	145	
LaSalle	R	11,536	21,321	32,857	98	1
Lawrence	R	2,332	3,875	6,207	4	
Lee	R	7,241	4,700	11,941	9	1
Livingston	R	8,483	5,612	14,095	20	
Logan	R	4,114	5,048	9,162	19	
Macon	R	3,467	22,277	25,744	45	

FIGURE 4—4

[handwritten note:] Illinois election returns published by the Secretary of State. Note that returns are broken down for counties only. It is necessary to go to the individual counties for break downs by precincts.

CANVASS BY THE COUNTY BOARD OF CANVASSERS OF THE
COUNTY OF WESTCHESTER OF THE VOTES CAST BY ALL
PARTIES IN SAID COUNTY AT A GENERAL ELECTION HELD
THEREIN ON NOVEMBER 6, 1951, FOR TOWN OFFICES,
TOWN OF GREENBURGH

| Election District | Number of Ballots Canvassed | Supervisor | | Town Clerk |
		William C. Duell Republican	Frederick J. Waters Democratic	Wm. H. Van Dorn Republican
1	395	244	151	269
2	293	174	119	181
3	518	335	183	374
4	683	466	217	552
5	581	383	198	449
6	164	91	73	116
7	154	82	72	100
8	416	234	182	279
9	290	187	103	239
10	497	319	178	381
11	309	216	93	245
12	414	224	190	268
13	387	227	160	261
14	437	286	151	321
15	353	211	142	274
16	506	301	205	371
17	298	190	108	264
18	366	212	154	238
19	413	273	140	324
20	533	333	200	401
21	583	380	203	485
22	284	186	98	232
23	358	213	145	285
24	308	163	145	230
25	283	168	115	196
26	193	128	65	146
27	303	199	104	220
28	275	180	95	200
29	430	342	88	361
30	349	236	113	262
31	557	310	247	444
32	427	218	209	299
33	355	210	145	269
34	198	119	79	150
35	471	302	169	399
36	472	240	232	345
37	359	217	142	268
38	257	161	96	205
Town Total	14,469	8,960	5,509	10,903

FIGURE 4—5

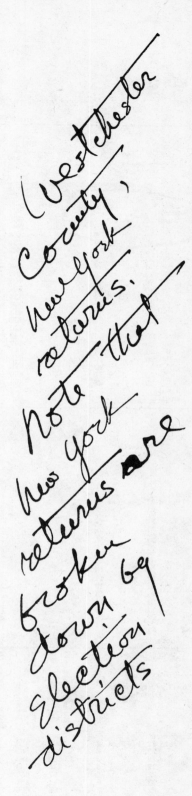

Westchester County, New York returns. Note that New York returns are broken down by Election districts

Representatives in the General Court — Continued.

County of Suffolk—Continued.

Nineteenth District.	Edmond J. Donlan of Boston, Democratic.	Frederick W. Bunker of Boston, Republican.	Charles Robert Doyle of Boston, Democratic.	Eric A. Nelson of Boston, Republican.	Joseph M. O'Loughlin of Boston, Democratic.	George J. Shagoury of Boston, Republican.	*Walter D. Bryan of Boston.
BOSTON:							
Ward 20, Precinct 1	389	316	353	279	430	260	254
" 20, " 2	380	295	308	282	375	286	188
" 20, " 3	430	206	365	177	356	173	262
" 20, " 4	434	286	361	289	393	256	242
" 20, " 5	385	313	361	294	439	265	111
" 20, " 6	811	362	770	337	727	316	362
" 20, " 7	448	204	384	192	400	159	208
" 20, " 8	486	225	435	198	418	158	234
" 20, " 9	493	254	441	279	404	247	177
" 20, " 10	501	297	528	326	388	410	387
" 20, " 11	424	309	352	351	281	317	282
" 20, " 12	403	344	349	360	335	317	294
" 20, " 13	411	324	421	325	391	287	176
" 20, " 14	533	250	608	252	413	280	351
" 20, " 15	451	314	451	315	387	479	379
" 20, " 16	642	438	616	356	567	340	445
" 20, " 17	567	366	567	361	604	325	364
" 20, " 18	354	302	356	322	370	275	273
" 20, " 19	517	315	533	342	529	268	228
" 20, " 20	519	554	488	489	547	469	341
" 20, " 21	490	395	465	253	399	248	270
" 20, " 22	404	264	335	277	308	249	233
Totals	10472	6933	9847	6656	9461	6384	6061

*Sticker candidate.

Twentieth District.	Richard R. Caples of Boston, Democratic.	Edmund V. Lane of Boston, Democratic.	Helen G. Holmes of Boston, Republican.	Charles A. Hubbard of Boston, Republican.	Leonard Sheinfeld of Boston, Republican.	Norman S. Weinberg of Boston, Democratic.
BOSTON:						
Ward 21, Precinct 1	605	664	758	751	749	613
" 21, " 2	487	571	547	539	490	455
" 21, " 3	547	533	434	371	421	491
" 21, " 4	539	507	360	321	320	448
" 21, " 5	465	448	295	286	315	472
" 21, " 6	693	619	357	344	445	538
" 21, " 7	733	722	407	359	466	759
" 21, " 8	709	715	396	384	533	740
" 21, " 9	502	484	334	319	312	454
" 21, " 10	402	381	244	254	229	292
" 21, " 11	1453	1375	436	484	532	1322
" 21, " 12	733	807	317	294	493	908
" 21, " 13	550	596	487	485	678	660
" 21, " 14	638	747	519	472	672	828
" 21, " 15	535	649	549	501	577	631
" 21, " 16	478	553	232	173	405	576
" 21, " 17	556	528	191	159	328	564
" 21, " 18	670	773	297	293	479	883
Totals	11295	11672	7160	6789	8444	11634

Twenty-First District.	Charles J. Artesani of Boston, Democratic.	Joseph P. Graham of Boston, Democratic.	Edgar F. Noble, Jr. of Boston, Republican.	Twenty-First District—Concluded.	Charles J. Artesani of Boston, Democratic.	Joseph P. Graham of Boston, Democratic.	Edgar F. Noble, Jr. of Boston, Republican.
BOSTON:							
Ward 22, Precinct 1	594	463	169	Ward 22, Precinct 10	800	838	299
" 22, " 2	645	553	218	" 22, " 11	678	655	256
" 22, " 3	562	483	236	" 22, " 12	611	624	254
" 22, " 4	616	533	175	" 22, " 13	664	637	201
" 22, " 5	707	653	174	" 22, " 14	608	628	271
" 22, " 6	644	661	144	" 22, " 15	648	665	207
" 22, " 7	596	608	186	" 22, " 16	668	802	254
" 22, " 8	585	541	146	" 22, " 17	993	974	270
" 22, " 9	803	917	491	Totals	11422	11235	3951

FIGURE 4—6

precinct election returns as fair samples of the political tendency of a census tract, a ward, or an assembly district. Or you may be able to make up a combination of precincts that corresponds approximately to some larger area for which you have economic or social data. This procedure may produce valid results provided that (a) it is used only for small areas, (b) it is carefully checked by a physical inspection of the area, and (c) your report shows the reader exactly how you derived your figures. Remember that although you cannot discover accurately the political tendency of an area by walking through it, you <u>can find out a great deal about the social and economic characteristics of an area by this kind of personal observation</u>. You can always check social and economic data for any area by visiting it, walking around it, and by observing conditions for yourself, but it is difficult to find a substitute for election statistics.

For purposes of observing the relation between election statistics and social data you may wish to make an intensive study of two contrasting areas. For example, you may want to compare a relatively poor ward or a group of precincts in which social and economic conditions are clearly below the average with another ward or group of precincts in which the economic and social level is clearly above the average for the community. You can establish the economic level of these areas by what you can observe about housing, congestion, upkeep of houses, size and condition of building lots, among other physical features, even if you can get no census data for the area. A camera is a very useful research tool in this connection because a few pictures will show a great deal about the character of a neighborhood. Note the number of mailboxes at the front doors as evidence of the number of families in each house. Street lists in your city directory will show who owns his own house.

With a little practice you can become skillful at rating the standard of living of a neighborhood. Once you have learned what to look for, your personal observations are the best kind of evidence— even better than census data. You can get a good grasp of the essential facts of the social and economic life of a neighborhood by using your own eyes and ears, by talking to people and getting acquainted with them. Census data are at best only a somewhat stilted and artificial substitute for this kind of first-hand observation. In selecting areas for comparison, choose election precincts or wards; election statistics are compiled by precincts and wards and you can then compare the voting habits of the contrasting areas.

This kind of comparative analysis of political and social data is useful if you do not push it too far. About all it can reveal is that a tendency of the voting habits of people is related to their so-cial and economic status. Such an analysis will, however, give you an entering wedge for making a further analysis. It goes without saying that your data are equally important even if you can find no relation between social status and voting.

USE OF THE FRANCHISE

<u>Is the right to vote valuable in your community</u>? The most significant statistics concerning voter turnout are not those showing the ratio between total vote cast and total registration, but those showing the ratio of the total vote to the <u>total potential vote</u>, i.e., the total number of citizens twenty-one years of age and over. You can find statistics concerning the total potential vote in the *Census of Population* or the *Statistical Abstract*. (See Fig. 4-7 and 4-8 for some Democratic party studies of total potential vote and total registration statistics.) The ratio of the potential vote to the total vote cast is a kind of measure of the efficiency of the party system. The amount of light shed on political conditions in your community by this ratio is so great that you should make this analysis with great care. You should be able to interpret the statistics for your city better if you make similar calculations for a number of other cities of approximately the same size.

In attempting to interpret election statistics, it is necessary to consider the conditions under which the right to vote is likely to be valuable to the voters. The value of the vote is likely to be great in elections in which the parties compete strongly, i.e., are well matched in a contest for valuable stakes, an election in which the alternatives are well defined. Conversely, in noncompetitive, one-party situations in which the voters have no real alternatives and in which the outcome of the election is known in advance, the vote is relatively valueless. How do you think that nonpartisan local elections affect the value of the vote? The situation is complicated by the fact that the parties may be competitive on one level of government and noncompetitive at another level. In strongly one-party states, elections at all levels of government may be so one-sided that there is little point in voting at all. In some southern states, the only valuable alternative enjoyed by the voter may be developed in the Democratic primaries. On the other hand, <u>in states in which the parties compete strongly on the state level, the vote in statewide contests is valuable even in one-party cities or towns</u>. Thus, in Connecticut where gubernatorial elections are closely contested by the major parties, a Democratic vote is valuable even if it is cast in Greenwich, which is overwhelmingly Republican, and a Republican vote is valuable even if it is cast in Hartford, which is strongly Democratic, because these votes contribute to the statewide totals of the parties. This is usually true

FIGURE 4-7

DEMOCRATIC NATIONAL COMMITTEE
Research Division
1200 Eighteenth Street, N.W.
Washington 6, D. C.

POTENTIAL VOTERS AND REGISTRANTS

Registration figures below were obtained from official State records and from election officials in the most populous counties of various States through a mail and telegraphic survey. The 1952 data are the most recent available to this office as of October 28, 1952.

NOTE: P   indicates a late preliminary report or estimate.
        F   indicates a final report or estimate.
       NLFA indicates no late figures available.

State and County or City	1952 Potential Voters (000)	Current Report		1948 Registrants as per cent of 1948 Potential
		Number of Registrants (000)	Per cent of 1952 Potential	
ARIZONA				
Maricopa County (Phoenix)	220	F 164	75	58
Pima County (Tucson)	97	P 65	67	58
Pinal County (Coolidge)	24	P 13	54	41
CALIFORNIA				
Alameda County (Oakland)	531	F 443	83	82
Contra Costa County (Richmond)	205	F 159	78	68
Los Angeles County (Los Angeles)	3,116	F 2,511	81	77
Sacramento County (Sacramento)	200	F 155	78	65
San Diego County (San Diego)	400	F 328	82	79
San Francisco County (San Francisco)	603	F 431	71	82
CONNECTICUT				
Fairfield County (Bridgeport)	363	P 288	79	76
Hartford County (Hartford)	387	P 309	80	76
New Haven County (New Haven)	387	P 354	91	80
New London County (Norwich)	99	P 78	79	73
ILLINOIS				
Cook County (Chicago)	3,247	P 2,768	85	NA
Peoria County (Peoria)	120	P 100	83	NA
Rock Island County (Rock Island)	92	P 75	82	NA
St. Clair County (East St. Louis)	141	F 131	93	NA
Will County (Joliet)	94	F 85	90	NA
Winnebago County (Rockford)	106	F 81	76	NA
INDIANA				
Allen County (Fort Wayne)	126	F 87	69	76
Lake County (Gary)	248	F 200	81	75
Marion County (Indianapolis)	385	F 322	84	74
St. Joseph County (South Bend)	141	NLFA		88
Vanderburgh County (Evansville)	110	F 90	82	83

State and County or City	1952 Potential Voters (000)	Current Report		Per cent of 1952 Potential	1948 Registrants as per cent of 1948 Potential
		Number of Registrants (000)			
OHIO					
Cuyahoga County (Cleveland)	998	F	768	77	68
Franklin County (Columbus)	360	P	279	78	NA
Hamilton County (Cincinnati)	510	LFA			76
Lucas County (Toledo)	276	F	210	76	59
Mahoning County (Youngstown)	179	NLFA			76
Montgomery County (Dayton)	279	P	205	73	72
Summit County (Akron)	283	P?	212	75	62
OREGON					
Lane County (Eugene)	86	F	61	71	71
Multnomah County (Portland)	348	F	284	82	73
PENNSYLVANIA					
Allegheny County (Pittsburgh)	1,052	F	890	85	72
Berks County (Reading)	181	F	114	63	54
Delaware County (Chester)	290	F	245	84	69
Lackawanna County (Scranton)	173	P	149	86	83
Luzerne County (Wilkes-Barre)	261	F	198	76	67
Philadelphia County (Philadelphia)	1,471	F	1,070	73	70
Westmoreland County (New Kensington)	208	F	156	75	63
WASHINGTON					
Snohomish County (Everett)	75	F	70	93	94
Pierce County (Tacoma)	187	P	145	78	77
Spokane County (Spokane)	156	F	125	80	83
WISCONSIN					
Milwaukee County (Milwaukee)	615	P	438	71	NA

The Research Division of the Democratic National Committee does not at present have figures available for other states.

Sources: It should be emphasized that in preparing this report the Research Division has relied upon statements about registration supplied by county election officials. In some cases, county election rolls are not cleared - one state, for instance, reported registration at least three per cent greater than the total number of adults in that state, because many counties in that state have continued to list as registered voters people who have died or moved. In some cases, the pressure of business during October upon over-worked election boards is so great that their estimates may vary substantially from the actual figures.

FIGURE 4-7 (Continued)

FROM: Research Division
Democratic State Committee
Hotel Biltmore
New York 17, New York
Mu 6-9090

September 1952

FIGURE 4-8

COMPARISON OF POTENTIAL AND ACTUAL VOTE IN NEW YORK STATE
1948 and 1950

It is a shocking fact that forty-five million or 48% of the eligible voters in the United States did not choose to vote in 1948. In our own state of New York 39.5% of the electorate failed to go to the polls the same year. New York will have over 10,000,000 eligible voters in 1952. As a candidate you will be vitally interested in stimulating increased voter interest and in leading the fight against apathy and indifference in your county. The following chart will help arm you with the statistics needed to awaken the electorate:

County (Number of counties 62)	Total Population, 21 years and over	Total 1948 Vote For President	Total 1950 Vote For Governor
Albany...............	167,583	142,118	139,345
Allegany.............	27,041	17,867	15,241
Bronx................	1,021,133	632,652	537,408
Broome...............	124,638	71,876	65,970
Cattaraugus..........	50,081	30,741	27,102
Cayuga...............	47,059	34,206	29,291
Chautauqua...........	91,451	52,809	44,530
Chemung..............	57,725	37,263	33,600
Chenango.............	25,291	17,076	15,501
Clinton..............	33,086	20,079	19,899
Columbia.............	29,746	21,079	19,882
Cortland.............	23,846	15,283	13,692
Delaware.............	28,584	19,719	17,638
Dutchess.............	97,435	53,039	49,955
Erie.................	612,485	388,083	338,082

The best measure of the total potential vote is total population over 21 years of age.

39. Voting. Any person offering to vote at a primary shall at the time of announcing his name also announce the name of the party to which he belongs. If his name is found upon the check-list, and if his party membership has not been before registered, it shall then be registered, and he shall be allowed to vote the ballot of his party. If his party membership has been before registered he shall be allowed to vote only the ballot of the party with which he is registered, unless he desires to vote the ballot of a party not having official existence at the time that his party membership was previously registered. 1909, 153:11. 1913, 179:5. 1913, 192:1.

New Hampshire closed Primary

19:23–46. Determination of right to vote. Each voter offering to vote shall announce his name and the party primary in which he wishes to vote. The district board shall thereupon ascertain by reference to the signature copy register or the primary election registry book required by this title, and, in municipalities not having permanent registration, if necessary by reference to the primary party poll books of the preceding primary election, that such voter is registered as required by this title and also that he is not ineligible or otherwise disqualified by the provisions of section 19:23–45 of this title; in which event he shall be allowed to vote.

New Jersey provision for the closed primary

Sec. 2. Persons Entitled to Vote.—At any primary election, any person possessing the qualifications of a voter, under sections one and two, article two of this chapter, who shall have been registered as a voter of a particular political party, and whose political affiliations are disclosed by the list of registered voters of the precinct; and also any person, registered in the voting precinct as a voter and as a member of a political party, who shall be entitled to vote at the general election

West virginia closed primary clause.

next to be held after the date of the primary election, by reason of arriving at the age of twenty-one years at and before the date of such general election, or by that time having resided within the State for one year and within the county in which the person offers to vote for a period of sixty days next preceding the date of the general election, shall be entitled to vote the primary party ballot of the political party to which he belongs.

Any person, registered as a voter in any election precinct in the county, who presents a certificate of transfer entitling him to vote in another election precinct, which certificate discloses the political party to which the voter belongs, shall be entitled to vote at the primary election in the election precinct to which the voter is by such certificate transferred. No person shall be permitted to vote at any primary election whose political affiliations are not disclosed by the registration list of voters or a transfer certificate.

The closed primary. Note requirements for voting in primary elections in these states.

FIGURE 4-9

It will be noted that there is a difference in the towns between the total number enrolled and the total number registered. This is due to the fact that there is non-personal registration in towns and the names of the voters are copied in the registration books from year to year instead of having them appear in person to register each year, as in cities. The few who do appear in person to register in towns enroll at that time, and the rest are entitled to enroll when they appear to vote on election day.

Many persons whose names appear in the registration books do not appear to vote on election day, some refuse to accept enrollment blanks; and the inspectors neglect to offer blanks to others. The number of names appearing in the registration books and included in the registration figures is, therefore, greater than the number of names accounted for by enrollment blanks and appearing in the enrollment figures.

The following table shows this difference for the last 38 years:

	1911	1912	1913	1914	1915	1916	1917	1918
Registration	10,364	10,166	10,658	10,831	11,207	10,933	10,764	19,351
Enrollment	5,442	7,401	7,631	8,249	8,015	8,002	7,034	10,782
Difference	4,922	2,765	3,027	2,582	3,192	2,931	3,730	8,569

	1919	1920	1921	1922	1923	1924	1925	1926
Registration	19,829	20,143	20,410	21,044	21,793	22,821	24,162	24,523
Enrollment	11,257	12,310	11,397	12,838	13,247	15,158	14,365	14,306
Difference	8,572	7,833	9,013	8,206	8,546	7,663	9,797	10,217

	1927	1928	1929	1930	1931	1932	1933	1934
Registration	25,699	27,356	28,017	28,747	30,098	30,832	31,438	31,586
Enrollment	15,352	18,212	15,359	16,053	18,029	20,926	20,031	19,697
Difference	10,347	9,144	12,658	12,694	12,069	9,906	11,407	11,889

	1935	1936	1937	1938	1939	1940	1941	1942
Registration	32,155	33,095	33,909	34,571	35,263	36,655	37,585	38,713
Enrollment	21,372	23,022	21,052	23,690	21,653	25,806	21,657	23,828
Difference	10,783	10,073	12,857	10,881	13,610	10,849	15,928	14,885

	1943	1944	1945	1946	1947	1948
Registration	39,483	40,359	40,785	41,532	42,803	44,712
Enrollment	22,291	25,212	20,099	25,359	25,177	30,347
Difference	17,192	15,147	20,686	16,173	17,626	14,365

FIGURE 4-10

[Handwritten note, right margin] Albany County, New York 1948-1949 enrollment and registration statistics. Note that "registration" refers to qualification for voting in elections. "Enrollment" is required for voting in party primaries.

[Handwritten note, bottom] This explanatory note sheds much light on the meaning of registration and enrollment statistics.

FIGURE 4-11

ENROLLMENT — COUNTY OF ALBANY, 1948-1949
CITY OF ALBANY
First Ward

District	Dem.	Rep.	Amer. L.	Liberal	Void	Blank	Total
1............	371	78	3	2	1	233	688
2............	350	79	3	0	0	339	771
3............	450	64	0	2	0	277	793
4............	338	89	5	3	3	274	712
5............	560	109	2	2	2	279	954
6............	392	85	4	2	0	214	697
7............	410	118	4	0			

Sixth Ward

District	Dem.	Rep.	Amer. L.	Liberal	Void	Blank	Total
1............	293	110	6	0	3	209	621
2............	281	14	6	3	1	31	336
3............	411	33	5	2	4	59	514
4............	355	48	10	2	0	218	633
Total......	1,340	205	27	7	8	517	2,104

Fourth Ward

District	Dem.	Rep.	Amer. L.	Liberal	Void	Blank	Total
1............	422	19	13	8	8	167	637
2............	435	40	5	1	0	258	739
3............	336	43	5	1	0	202	587
4............	372	35	12	2	1	200	622
Total......	1,565	137	35	12	9	827	2,585

[3]

Party enrollment in Albany County, new York. In the term "enrollment" is used to describe voters who have qualified to vote in the primaries of their parties.

what does the Republican enrollment in the 2nd district of the 6th ward and the 1st district of the 4th ward suggest about the character of the Republican organization in these areas?

COUNTIES	REPUBLICAN			DEMOCRATIC			NON-PARTISAN			OTHER
	Men	Women	Total	Men	Women	Total	Men	Women	Total	Men
Adams,	5,776	4,842	10,618	4,158	3,275	7,433	145	121	266	4
Allegheny,	166,583	172,011	338,594	230,173	220,760	450,933	–	–	–	2,760
Armstrong,	11,439	10,262	21,701	7,112	5,700	12,812	42	14	56	44
Beaver,	23,355	20,854	44,209	17,406	14,894	32,300	399	308	707	–
Bedford,	6,660	5,559	12,219	4,195	3,152	7,347	25	15	40	10
Berks,	21,596	20,673	42,269	36,317	28,620	64,937	1,173	911	2,084	75
Blair,	20,444	18,444	38,888	8,476	7,359	15,835	123	94	217	
Bradford,	8,435	8,489	16,924	2,671	2,371	5,042	77	46	123	
Bucks,	27,750	26,010	53,760	11,692	10,522	22,214	1,412	1,153	2,565	
Butler,	15,022	14,838	29,860	7,908	7,189	15,097	–	–	–	
Cambria,	23,422	21,473	44,895	27,575	25,192	52,767	102	62	164	
Cameron,	1,493	1,464	2,957	485	440	925	28	17	45	
Carbon,	8,043	6,693	14,736	6,198	5,149	11,347	–	–	–	
Centre,	7,887	7,336	15,223	4,784	4,347	9,131	274	230	504	
Chester,	29,145	23,838	52,983	7,713	6,310	14,023	541	443	984	
Clarion,	4,487	4,278	8,765	3,706	3,317	7,023	36	23	59	
Clearfield,										
Clinton,			10,309			5,480				
Columbia,	6,514	5,036	11,550	7,686	5,680	13,366	103	76		
Crawford,	10,579	10,731	21,310	5,354	4,749	10,103	–	–		
Cumberland,	15,272	15,211	30,483	7,075	6,409	13,484	305	241		
Dauphin,	41,527	42,381	83,908	8,333	8,519	16,852	784	623		
Delaware,	102,431	101,528	203,959	13,677	15,399	29,076	2,393	2,163		
Elk,	3,878	3,270	7,148	4,394	3,629	8,023	85	66		
Erie,	27,778	25,436	53,214	22,885	18,127	41,012	465	276		
Fayette,	15,377	14,173	29,550	29,263	23,724	52,987	65	3		
Forest,	868	776	1,644	400	327	727	8			
Franklin,	9,077	8,123	17,200	5,898	4,364	10,262	324			
Fulton,	1,124	916	2,040	1,249	957	2,206	15			
Greene,	2,754	2,579	5,333	7,628	6,466	14,094	10			
Huntingdon,	6,329	5,815	12,144	2,256	1,854	4,110	37			
Indiana,			20,045			11,174				
Jefferson,	7,074	6,854	13,928	3,583	3,011	6,594	48			
Juniata,	2,229	1,951	4,180	1,914	1,675	3,589	2			
Lackawanna,	32,877	34,944	67,821	42,520	44,593	87,113				
Lancaster,	39,036	34,105	73,141	12,341	11,503	23,844				
Lawrence,	16,581	16,008	32,589	8,256	7,523	15,779				
Lebanon,	12,948	12,012	24,960	5,221	4,167	9				
Lehigh,	23,476	21,629	45,105	21,773	18,782					
Luzerne,	73,450	69,117	142,567	23,050	21,056					
Lycoming,	14,311	14,204	28,515	8,636	7					
McKean,	8,604	8,623	17,227	2,500						
Mercer,	14,683	14,661	29,344	12,102						
Mifflin,	4,947	4,274	9,221							
Monroe,	3,530	3,744	7,274							
Montgomery,	79,166	74,854	154,0..							
Montour,	1,877	1,931								
Northampton,	17,361	17,170								
Northumberland,	19,059	17..								
Perry,	4,049									
Philadelphia,	319,661									
Pike,	2..									
Potter,										
Schuylkill,										
Snyder,										
Somerset										
Sulli..										
S..										

Pennsylvania party registration in 1954. Note that statistics for men and women are given separately. Compare party registration in Pennsylvania with the party vote.

FIGURE 4-12

NUMBER OF REGISTERED VOTERS AND PERSONS WHO VOTED AT ELECTIONS

CITIES, WARDS AND VOTING PRECINCTS.	STATE ELECTIONS, Nov. 4, 1952.		CITY ELECTIONS, 1952.		
	Registered Voters.	Persons who Voted.	Date of Election.	Registered Voters.	Persons who Voted.
Attleboro	**12,875**	**12,067**	–	–	–
Ward 1	2,404	2,227	–	–	–
" 2	2,021	1,935	–	–	–
" 3	2,103	1,963	–	–	–
" 4	2,041	1,935	–	–	–
" 5	2,080	1,915	–	–	–
" 6, Precinct A	983	914	–	–	–
" 6, " B	1,243	1,178	–	–	–
Beverly	**17,336**	**16,161**	Dec. 9	**17,450**	**11,085**
Ward 1, Precinct 1	1,096	1,024	9	1,102	765
" 1, " 2	728	681	9	732	486
" 1, " 3	1,051	989	9	1,059	670
" 2, " 1	1,443	1,270	9	1,458	915
" 2, " 2	1,877	1,809	9	1,895	1,213
" 3, "	1,853	1,704	9	1,870	1,250
" 4, " 1	1,034	981	9	1,035	710
" 4, " 2	1,643	1,536	9	1,647	1,006
" 4, " 3	1,029	962	9	1,031	715
" 5, " 1	1,969	1,791	9	1,997	1,121
" 5, " 2	2,204	2,096	9	2,212	1,328
" 6, " 1	1,086	1,018	9	1,089	
" 6, " 2	323	300	9	323	
Boston	**412,838**	**363,356**	–		
Ward 1	24,325	20,557	–		
" 1, Precinct 1	2,260	1,909			
" 1, " 2	2,147	1,802			
" 1, " 3	1,947	1,623			
" 1, " 4	2,075	1,7••			
" 1, " 5	1,953				
" 1, " 6	2,061				
" 1, " 7	2,1•				
" 1, " 8					
" 1, " 9					
" 1, " 10					
" 1, " 11					
" 1, " 12					
Ward 2					
" 2, Pre•••					

FIGURE 4-13

Massachusetts publishes data concerning the number of registered voters. Compare statistics for the total vote cast.

Returns for Massachusetts Democratic presidential primary.

Cities and Towns.	Edward A. Pecce of Waltham.	J. Henry Goguen of Leominster.	Peter J. Levanti of Fitchburg.	James Leo O'Connor of Franklin.	Stanislaus G. Wondolowski of Worcester.	Edward F. Doolan of Fall River.	Salvatore Camelio of Cambridge.	Paul T. Smith of Boston.	Charles Collatos of Boston.	Elizabeth A. Stanton of Fitchburg.	Louis H. Glaser of Malden.	Helen J. Fay of Westwood.	Silas F. Taylor of Boston.	Francis H. Murray, Jr. of Woburn.	Thomas F. Graham of Great Barrington.	Edith T. Wilcox of Woburn.	Blanks.	Total Votes Cast.
Adams	50	52	51	52	61	52	50	50	50	50	50	49	50	49	52	50	958	1776
Alford	2	2	2	3	2	2	2	2	2	2	4	2	2	2	3	2	140	176
Ashfield	2	2	2	2	2	2	2	2	2	2	2	2	2	2	2	2	–	32
Athol	36	38	44	35	38	37	38	35	33	39	37	38	35	34	33	35	503	1088
Becket	17	15	15	16	17	16	15	16	15	15	16	16	16	15	17	17	178	432
Belchertown	14	15	15	15	17	14	15	14	15	15	15	14	14	15	15	15	179	416
Bernardston	2	2	2	2	2	2	2	–	2	2	2	2	2	2	2	2	48	80
Blandford	–	–	–	–	–	–	–	–	–	–	–	–	–	–	–	–	16	16
Buckland	7	7	7	7	7	7	8	7	7	7	7	7	7	7	7	7	127	240
Charlemont	5	5	5	5	5	5	5	5	5	5	5	5	5	5	5	5	128	208
Cheshire	25	24	24	25	26	24	24	25	24	25	25	25	24	25	24	24	167	560
Chester	–	–	–	–	–	–	–	–	–	1	–	–	–	1	–	–	62	64
Chesterfield	2	2	2	2	2	2	2	2	2	2	2	2	2	2	2	2	–	32
Clarksburg	5	4	5	6	5	3	3	5	3	3	3	3	3	4	3	4	145	208
⸱⸱lrain	9	9	10	9	9	9	9	9	9	9	10	10	9	9	9	9	61	208
⸱⸱way	5	5	5	5	5	5	5	5	5	5	5	5	5	5	5	5	64	144
⸱⸱nmington	1	1	1	1	1	1	1	1	1	1	1	1	1	1	1	1	–	16
Dalton	44	40	40	41	16	44	16	40	40	17	40	16	16	40	41	41	812	1344
Deerfield	43	42	42	44	42	43	42	42	40	40	43	42	42	42	43	42	286	960
Egremont	7	7	7	7	7	7	7	7	6	7	6	7	7	7	10	7	143	256
Erving	10	11	11	11	11	8	10	11	8	10	9	8	9	10	9	9	325	480
Florida	4	4	4	4	4	4	4	4	4	4	4	4	4	4	4	4	–	64
Gill	8	8	8	8	8	8	8	8	8	8	8	8	8	8	8	8	112	240
Goshen	–	–	–	–	–	–	–	–	–	–	–	–	–	–	–	–	32	32
Granville																	32	32
Great Barrington	58	56	60	59	58	58	58	57	57	58	57	56	58	58	72	61	979	1920
Greenfield	180	175	174	175	174	179	170	173	169	175	177	168	169	175	171	167	2045	4816
Hancock	3	3	3	4	3	3	3	3	3	3	3	3	3	3	3	3	15	64
Hawley	1	1	1	1	1	1	1	1	1	1	1	1	1	1	1	1		

DEMOCRATIC.
Alternate Delegates at Large.*
District 1.

VOTE FOR UNITED STATES SENATOR—ALL PARTIES—APRIL 13, 1954

Counties	Republican										Democratic
	John B. Crane	Lar (America First) Daly	Edgar M. Elbert	Herbert F. Geisler	Edward A. Hayes	Julius Klein	Park Livingston	Joseph T. Meek	Deneen A. Watson	Austin L. Wyman	Paul H. Douglas
Adams	252	47	296	51	545	924	209	1,093	57	354	3,716
Alexander	108	39	80	24	212	115	439	1,587	87	224	1,671
Bond	79	59	32	28	803	102	230	919	55	93	875
Boone	368	112	155	92	418	255	1,265	1,637	147	192	225
Brown	39	8	19	7	116	68	32	313	18	100	1,223
Bureau	396	110	37	68	1,701	350	797	2,858	89	191	1,660
Calhoun	37	26	25	36	264	101	91	215	43	171	976
Carroll	84	106	43	66	240	98	166	989	46	95	753
Cass	31	8	76	6	258	49	37	759	13	94	1,645
Champaign	899	61	378	379	1,602	440	2,889	3,387	104	843	3,123
Christian	232	50	97	44	1,326	236	150	964	69	322	5,800
Clark	102	24	31	148	483	143	104	1,101	40	96	1,093
Clay	118	113	37	25	885	96	238	1,055	58	152	739
Clinton	129	111	111	42	671	136	154	1,349	40	68	1,515
Coles	382	66	108	207	1,466	238	855	1,608	67	155	1,588
Cook	14,100	7,732	12,539	13,978	70,872	16,623	22,154	81,661	6,440	56,229	338,636
Crawford	71	24	13	22	180	53	284	1,279	59	153	561
Cumberland	124	33	25	26	561	54	276	2,339	27	143	796
DeKalb	502	174	153	343	2,361	589	869	2,333	235	1,038	581
DeWitt	348	35	28	59	967	190	402	767	127	155	980
Douglas	253	31	102	140	873	104					

This is what senatorial primary returns look like in Illinois. Note that Senator Douglas was unopposed in the Democratic primary.

FIGURE 4-14

of the votes cast in presidential elections, outside of the solid South.

It is impossible to fix the precise statistical point at which parties may be said to become competitive. The history and stability of the party ratio is an important consideration in estimating the value of the vote. A stable two-to-one supremacy of one party at the state level is probably sufficient to disintegrate the opposition. On the other hand, a local party may be kept alive even if it is outnumbered ten to one in local elections provided the parties compete actively at the state level. It is necessary to consider all the evidence before deciding that party competition at any level has ceased to exist. Consult local experts. What do they think about this question?

Wherever possible, you should get election statistics covering a sufficient period of time to enable you to discover long-range political trends in your community. See Key, Chapters 2 and 3, for a discussion of time series. In view of the general reorganization of American politics since 1932, it is usually desirable to go back to pre-1932 elections to get an adequate historical base.

REGISTRATION AND ENROLLMENT STATISTICS

Whenever possible, get party registration statistics. Party membership in nearly all states is regulated by law. See your election laws under the heading, "direct primary elections," to find out whether or not your state has a "closed" or "open" primary, i.e., whether or not it is necessary to belong to a party in order to vote in its primaries. This requirement (in the closed primary states) makes a great difference in the value of party membership and may give special significance to party registration statistics and the party primary vote. In states having an "open" primary (states in which it is possible for anyone to vote in any of the party primaries regardless of party membership), party registration tends to become meaningless, and party primary vote totals do not prove very much about party strength. (See Fig. 4-9 for closed primary provisions in the election laws of New Hampshire, New Jersey, and West Virginia.)

On the other hand, in one-party states, the right to vote in primary elections may be much more valuable than the right to vote in general elections. In states such as Connecticut with permanent registration, the party registration of new voters gives some indication of political trends. In New York party registration is called "enrollment." See Figures 4-10 and 4-11 for a discussion of party enrollment statistics in Albany County, New York. As a test of your ability to interpret election statistics, explain the significance of the extremely low Republican enrollment in some precincts of Albany? Note in Figure 4-12 that Pennsylvania figures on party registration show separate totals for men and women. If you are working with Pennsylvania statistics, this kind of information ought to be very valuable to you. You should always compare party registration statistics with (a) party votes in primary elections; (b) party votes in elections; (c) the total vote cast in the election; and (d) the total potential vote.

In closed primary states the ratio of the party primary vote to the party vote in the election may be significant. A marked discrepancy between the ratios for the two parties in the primary vote and in the general election vote may indicate that voters who are registered as members of one party are tending to switch their allegiance to the other party or are under some sort of pressure not to reveal their party preferences. Voting tendencies of this sort covering a period of years may show a change in the party complexion of the community. In open primary states, on the other hand, voters tend to vote in the most hotly contested primaries, regardless of party affiliations. The significance of the vote in open and closed primaries is therefore apt to differ radically.

Note that Massachusetts publishes statistics showing total registration and total vote cast by precincts, (Fig. 4-13). These figures may enable you to find out where one or the other of the parties may have lost ground in the election when there is a small turnout. It may also enable you to test the efficiency of the party organization in any locality. See Figure 4-14 for primary election returns in Illinois.

REFERENCES

1. Key, V. O., Jr., *A Primer of Statistics for Political Scientists.* New York: Thomas Y. Crowell Company, 1954.

2. 82d Congress, 2d Session, Senate Document No. 150, *Comparison of Potential Voters and Actual Votes Cast by Counties in Each State, 1948-50.* Washington, D.C.: U.S. Government Printing Office, 1952.

3. Scammon, R. M., ed., *America Votes, A Handbook of Contemporary American Election Statistics.* New York: The Macmillan Company, 1956.

Chapter V

THE POLITICAL SIGNIFICANCE OF DEMOGRAPHIC, SOCIAL, AND ECONOMIC DATA

The political significance of demographic, social, and economic data is well illustrated by the way students of public opinion make use of these materials in the construction of their polling samples. Pollsters assume that these data are sufficiently closely related to political behavior to make it necessary to take account of them in the makeup of the samples of the electorate that they use. Students of public opinion became interested in the political significance of social data a generation ago. It will be instructive to examine the conclusions of these technicians. For a good introduction to this material, see Powell, *Anatomy of Public Opinion* (1).

The question is: What social criteria are significant in the construction of the samples used by pollsters? What is the relative influence of social and economic factors? Although the problem of the pollsters in finding variables that have predictive values is not precisely your problem, you need what Professor Powell calls "an initial theory of determinants of voting behavior." It is not enough simply to compile the data for your community unless you can formulate some theory for testing the relevance of economic and social statistics to your study of politics.

We may assume at the outset that all of the data we can get have some political significance. On the other hand, we are bound to admit that we do not know as much as we would like to know about the relative significance of the data. Your survey should, therefore, be looked upon as a way of testing a number of propositions.

DATA USED IN POLLS

Since polls often report on the political attitudes of people classified according to age, sex, residence, occupation, race, religion, national origins, economic status, they are a source of information concerning the political significance of social and economic data.

What kinds of factors are considered by pollsters in making samples? Campbell, Gurin, and Miller, in *The Voter Decides*, (2) relate voting to the following data:

1. Type of community (size of community in which voters live.)

2. Socio-economic groups to which voters belong (social and economic status)
3. Ethnic origins of voters
4. Religious affiliation
5. Age
6. Sex
7. Education
8. Occupation
9. Trade-union affiliation
10. Income

Lazarsfeld, Berelson, and Gaudet in *The People's Choice* (3) use an index of political predisposition (IPP) based on (a) ratings of the socio-economic status; (b) religious affiliation; and (c) urban-rural residence.

Campbell and Kahn in *The People Elect a President* (4) use: (a) type of community; (b) occupation; (c) labor union membership; (d) income; (e) education; (f) age; (g) sex; (h) race; and (i) religion.

Elmo Roper takes into consideration data concerning the size of place of residence, economic level, sex, age, color, male factory labor, and employed women in constructing his samples. See Mosteller, *Pre-Election Polls of 1948* (5). A vast compendium of public opinion polls, including many polls of demographic groups, is to be found in Cantril, *Public Opinion, 1935-1946* (6). This volume contains nearly all published polls taken by well-established and recognized polling organizations in the world during the 12 years covered.

RELATING THE DATA

You will find the discussion in Berelson, Lazarsfeld, and McPhee, *Voting* (7) a helpful introduction to the political meaning of social and economic data. In Chapter 4, "Social Differentiation," Berelson and his associates take the position that voting is related to socio-economic status (occupation, education, plus interviewer's rating of the social status of the respondent), class consciousness, class identification, political generation (age), minority religious and ethnic status, and size of the community. (See pp. 75-76 for fifteen propositions concerning the political significance of social data.)

A useful summary of the findings of a number of studies may be found in Appendix A, pp. 333ff. of *Voting,* including twenty-nine findings concerning the relation of socio-economic status, religious affiliation, residence, region, age, education, membership in organizations, and family and personal associations to voting behavior. These assumptions should be examined before you attempt to evaluate the meaning of your own data. They will give you some idea of the way in which a number of students of politics have attacked the problem.

You will find it instructive to see what all of the works cited above have to say about the construction of their samples. Equally informing are the questionnaires used (8).

A general theory of the relation of social data to politics has been formulated by Lazarsfeld in *The People's Choice* (pp. 27, 138, 148): "Social characteristics determine political preferences." He subsequently notes: "Different social characteristics, different votes." Lazarsfeld describes voting as a social experience; the social characteristics of people influence their political attitudes: "People tend to associate with others of their own age rather than with people considerably older or younger than themselves.... Common experiences, as well as precise studies, show that an individual chooses his friends and finds his neighbors on about his own SES (socioeconomic status) level.... People who have similar ratings according to the index of political predispositions (IPP) are also likely to live in closer contact with each other....People who live together under similar conditions are likely to develop similar needs and interests....Politically, formal associations have a class character. They facilitate the transformation of social characteristics into political affiliations."

Sociologists use the word "segregation" to describe the tendency of people of similar status and interests to live in the same area. Essentially this tendency is about what was meant by the proverb that birds of a feather flock together. See Hawley, *Human Ecology* (9). Segregation is really an aspect of the "spatial patterning" of urban life that has been discussed elsewhere in this book. The assumption is that these patterns (i.e., where people live) have something to do with the way people vote—enough to make it worth looking into.

Berelson, Lazarsfeld, and McPhee (p. 74), make an attempt to distinguish between politically significant and politically unimportant social and economic data as follows:

1. Social relations produce political differences if there is an economic division of labor, a physical separation, and a social differentiation sufficient to produce people with unlike characteristics who are affected in different ways by the same political policy. "Differentiation is a condition for disagreement."

2. Political differences must be transmitted from one generation to another. "Transmission is a condition for persistence."

3. Members of the social groups must be substantially more in contact with each other than they are with other groups. "Contact is a condition for consensus."

Merton and Lazarsfeld are convinced that influence tends to be exerted in a horizontal direction within a social stratum. (See Powell, pp. 145-146.) You should remember, however, that everyone is talking about relative differences, differences of degree, not about absolute differences. Nearly everyone agrees that social and economic factors have some effect on voting. The question is how much.

Scholars like Lazarsfeld get information about the social basis of politics directly by interviewing a large number of people. Unfortunately, you may not be able to use this method because it is usually very expensive. (See the "Acknowledgments" in *The People's Choice* to get some idea of the size of the staff employed in making the Sandusky study.)

In spite of the fact that you may not be able to use the polling techniques outlined in the foregoing statement, the concepts and the rationale of sample construction ought to help you to interpret the data you have.

THE PHYSICAL UNITS OF INVESTIGATION

Since you rely largely on census data and election statistics (i.e., totals for given areas), it is necessary to work with the smallest units for which data are available. The larger the units, the more complex the composition of the population is likely to be and the less meaningful the statistics. The smaller the areas for which they are compiled, the more meaningful the statistics. Every census tract, enumeration district, ward, city, or county consists of a mixture of people; it is therefore rare to find data for districts that consist 100 percent of people of Italian extraction or 100 percent of manual laborers, or 100 percent of the poor. However, the smaller the units, the more likely the population characteristics are to be uniform in one respect or another. Moreover, if you supplement your statistics with personal observation of the area and with interviews, and test the validity of your conclusions by using related statistical data, you can find out a great deal about small areas in spite of the limitations of the data.

Your problem is further complicated by the fact that the areas for which census data are compiled are not usually identical with the election precincts or districts for which voting statistics are collected. Even if you can find census areas and voting areas that are identical, you can usually do no more than compare a complex of social and economic data with a political tendency; it is usually impossible to measure the political impact of any single social or economic factor. This may be changing, however, as election data, such as party registration, come to be recorded through electronic equipment by census tracts. Alameda County (Oakland), California, has installed such a system.

THE CORRELATION OF STATISTICAL DATA

It will help if you remember that many different kinds of statistics can be used to measure the same thing. Factors such as housing, rentals, owner-occupancy, crowding, years of schooling, occupation, segregation, employment, race, national origins, and religious affiliation are all more or less closely related to income and status. That is, statistics showing family income say explicitly what statistics about contract rentals, congestion, housing, occupation, employment say by implication, because people with low incomes have spending and living habits unlike those of people with high incomes. Do not suppose that the references in this book to many different kinds of statistical information are simply duplication. Demographic studies of politics present so many difficulties that it is always useful to know of a variety of ways of getting at the same problem. If one kind of data is unavailable, another kind may tell you substantially the same thing. If no statistical data are available, you can make your own personal inspection of living conditions, economic status, and the like. Statistics are, after all, only a poor substitute for the evidence you can see with your own eyes and hear with your own ears. See Chapter IV for a more extended discussion of this problem.

Many kinds of data are related to social and economic status. People who have large incomes spend more money on housing, rentals, space, education, and live in more exclusive sections of the city, than people who have less money. It is a fairly safe assumption that people buy all of the space, air, sunshine, and quiet (in the form of housing) that they can afford. Above all, they strive to get into the best neighborhoods they can afford because the neighborhood is a very large factor in the attractiveness of any residence. Land values affect land use; the price system is used to maintain the social pattern.

Since all opinion surveys are based on the assumption that social and economic status is related to politics, it is obvious that you can do something to get at the problem even if you are dealing with "aggregates" rather than with individuals.

INTERPRETING THE DATA

The foregoing discussion refers to political tendencies. Lazarsfeld's statement, "A person thinks politically, as he is socially," propounds a theory of social determinism that calls for critical examination. It is repeated here, not as a dogmatic assertion of a proposition that has been conclusively demonstrated, but as a hypothesis to be investigated. There are theoretical difficulties implicit in all determinist political propositions. The student should be careful, therefore, not to read too much into these formulations. It is probably enough for him to say that there is a relation between social status and political behavior without committing himself to more drastic formulations of the proposition, because there is a great deal of guesswork in all calculations concerning the political consequences of social data. His studies are more likely to show tendencies than they are likely to demonstrate anything like a complete identity of social and political factors. For example, only 75 percent of persons with the most strongly Republican index of political predisposition voted Republican, and only 83 percent of persons with the most strongly Democratic predispositions voted Democratic, according to Lazarsfeld's Sandusky study. A total of only 292 persons in a sample of 1,650 were included in the most strongly Republican and Democratic categories. The remaining 1,358 persons exhibited less sharply marked political characteristics.

The relative nature of demographic and other social data is indicated in every poll showing the political preferences of social groups. The statistics contained in Gallup's *Political Almanac* (10), will do as well as any other. Mr. Gallup shows that the following occupational groups favored the Republican candidate for President in 1948 in the percentages reported here:

Professional and business	58 percent
White Collar	51 percent
Manual workers	34 percent
All farmers	48 percent

These figures do not show anything remotely approaching a complete identity of occupational status and political attitude. Moreover, the net impact of the social groups referred to was not what it appears to be at first glance, because the net impact of any group which divides its allegiance equally between the parties is zero. That is, if the group divides equally between the parties it follows that the Republican and Democratic preferences cancel out. Thus, farmers and white-collar workers in the Gallup statistics shown were divided so equally that their net impact on the election seems to have been small, if we take these figures as they stand. Even the net impact of the two more extreme groups is much less than the percentages seem to show at first glance. If business and professional groups divide 58 to 42 percent, the net gain for the Republican party is only 16 percent of the total group. A 34 to 66 percent split of manual workers yields only a

32 percent net for the Democratic party. An examination of the data compiled by Cantril shows that it is not often that either of the parties gets the support of more than 70 percent of any social group. Since 50 percent equals a net gain of zero, and since parties rarely mobilize more than 70 percent of any social group, the range of potential political variations in any social group is relatively narrow.

When Lazarsfeld writes of the political homogeneity of social groups, therefore, he means only that social groups show political tendencies within relatively narrow limits, not that anything like 100 percent homogeneity has ever been found in any of the statistics developed from his own surveys or from surveys made by other students of public opinion.

What you may expect to find is a difference of degree in the political tendencies of social groups. When you translate your data for the whole community into votes, you are extremely likely to find that the correlations between political and social data are subject to a substantial discount. Imperfect as the correlations may be, however, they are important: they are important enough to explain why one kind of community tends to be Democratic and another kind of community tends to be Republican.

POLITICAL DATA GATHERING

It may be instructive to see what use the parties make of the kind of economic and social data discussed in this chapter. In a pamphlet of instructions for the making of precinct surveys, *Know Your Precinct* (11) Republican party workers are advised to get information about:

Election statistics
Employment and unemployment
Income, wealth, and poverty
Strikes and lockouts
Home ownership
Housing
Public utilities, social services, transportation
Construction
Living conditions
Tax rates on residential real estate
Schools
Teachers and teachers' organizations
Parent-teacher associations
Churches and religious leaders
Church work with children
Church welfare work
Church attendance
Women's organizations
Clubs, associations, organizations, and their activities
Ethnic groups
Magazines and newspapers circulating in precinct
New voters
Citizenship and civic education
Juvenile delinquency
Social services in the precinct
Organization and activities of the Republican party

No attempt is made in these instructions to establish the relative importance of the data listed, but it is clear that professional politicians do attach some significance to social data.

See Figure 5-1 for lists of data thought to be useful to workers in Republican party headquarters. Note references to maps, "voter analysis by precincts," lists of nonpartisan organizations, and special lists of voters. Figure 5-2, an excerpt from a Democratic party publication, describes the duties of a local "Information Chairman," i.e., a local research director. Note the emphasis placed on the use of files of newspaper clippings. Figures 5-3 and 5-4 describe a Republican plan for the organization of a local research committee. Observe the use of census data recommended in Figure 5-4. Local party research organizations may be helpful to you in a variety of ways if you can find them. They may also provide a good point of contact with the local party organization, because party research workers are likely to be interested in what you are doing in your own survey. Even if you cannot locate a party research organization in your community, you ought to talk to local party leaders about the uses and potentialities of research because you have a personal interest in demonstrating the value of your own survey. What kind of social data do the party experts value most highly?

Note that Figure 5-5 describes a kind of local political survey. Check your own survey against the items listed in Figure 5-6, the Table of Contents of the *Handbook for Political Candidates in Rhode Island*, issued by the Rhode Island Public Expenditure Council. Figures 5-7, 5-8, 5-9, and 5-10 are taken from the *Fact Sheets* issued by the Democratic National Committee for two counties. (Two county fact sheets are shown here to let you see the complete list of items covered in these surveys.) Make a note of the items of information used in these surveys and check them against the lists you are using.

Figures 5-11, 5-12, 5-13, 5-14, and 5-15 are taken from the Democratic National Committee's *Target Analysis Project*. The purpose of this project was to get significant local information for the use of the Committee in the campaign of 1952. The data called for in these surveys are significant in the opinion of the Committee's research organization. Finally, Figures 5-16 and 5-17 show what information is assembled by the Democratic National Committee for the use of congressional candidates.

Test some of the propositions made in this chapter by discussing them with political leaders in your community. All good politicians are aware of social differences in their communities and take them into account but they may not use the words you do in talking about them.

The payoff for your efforts comes when you try

to see if you can explain the political tendencies of a number of election precincts (party voting statistics) in terms of the social data you have assembled. Is it true that there is a difference between the voting tendencies of poor and well-to-do precincts? Begin by comparing the richest and the poorest precincts, then try comparing precincts that differ less sharply.

If you find precincts that do not fit the pattern (a well-to-do precinct that is Democratic, for example), you have a problem.

REFERENCES

1. Powell, N. J., *Anatomy of Public Opinion*. Englewood Cliffs, N.J.: Prentice-Hall, Inc., 1951.

2. Campbell, A., *et al.*, *The Voter Decides*. Evanston, Ill.: Row, Peterson & Company, 1954. Chap. 5, "The Demography of the Vote." pp. 70ff; Appendix F, "Sample Design," pp. 227ff.

3. Lazarsfeld, P. F., B. Berelson, and H. Gaudet, *The People's Choice*. New York: Columbia University Press, 1944. Chap. 3, "Social Differences Between Republicans and Democrats."

4. Campbell, A., and R. L. Kahn, *The People Elect a President*. University of Michigan, Social Survey Research Center. Ann Arbor, Mich.: University of Michigan Press, 1952. Chap. 3, "Demography of the Voters."

5. Mosteller, F., *et al.*, *Pre-Election Polls of 1948*. New York: Social Science Research Council Bulletin No. 60, 1949.

6. Cantril, H., ed., *Public Opinion, 1935-1946*. Princeton, N.J.: Princeton University Press, 1951.

7. Berelson, B. R., P. F. Lazarsfeld, and W. N. McPhee, *Voting: A Study of Opinion Formation in a Presidential Campaign*. Chicago: University of Chicago Press, 1954.

8. Janovitz, M., and W. E. Miller, "The Index of Political Predisposition in the 1948 Election," *Journal of Politics*, XIV, 1952. pp. 710-27.

   Kitt, A., and D. B. Gleicher, "Determinants of Voting Behavior," *Public Opinion Quarterly*, Vol. XIV, Autumn 1950. pp. 393-412.

9. Hawley, A. H., *Human Ecology: A Theory of Community Structure*. New York: The Ronald Press Company, 1950. pp. 264-87.

10. Gallup, G., *Political Almanac*. New York: B. C. Forbes and Sons Pub. Co., 1952. pp. 36-37.

11. *Know Your Precinct*, Washington, D.C.: National Federation of Women's Republican Clubs, 1950.

BASIC AND ELEMENTAL ARE THE LISTS WHICH EVERY COUNTY HEADQUARTERS SHOULD HAVE. THE FOLLOWING SHOULD BE COMPLETE AND UP-TO-DATE AT ALL TIMES:

1. Map of county marked by precincts and townships.
2. List of names, addresses and telephone numbers of all Party workers in county - precinct and county committees; state committee members; officers of state and national committees; National Committeeman and woman
3. List of candidates
4. List of Office-holders - local, county and state (Republicans in italics)
5. Voter analysis by precincts. (Survey of population shifts or other changing conditions which might have an effect on elections)
6. Contributors and potential contributors.
7. List of speakers
8. All Republican clubs in the county with names and addresses of officers
9. All non-partisan organizations in the county that support the basic philosophy of the Party
10. Special lists (teachers, ministers, doctors, etc.)
11. All newspapers in the county, classified according to political sympathies; their editors, owners and political correspondents
12. List of radio and television stations in county; owners, managers and commentators.

The County Committee Headquarters should be the source of all information, inspiration, assistance and direction for the precinct workers. Every County Chairman and woman must always keep in mind that carrying the county is not enough. The county must be carried by the largest possible majority. It might make the difference between victory and defeat in the state as a whole.

Successful county leaders set the standard of unremitting political activity.

D. Vital Voting Information

Each precinct committeeman and woman should be equipped with the following vital information:

1. Location of the voting place for the precinct.
2. A map of the precinct showing boundary lines.
3. What are the registration requirements?
4. Must persons changing their names re-register?
5. When may persons register? (Check Board of Elections.)
6. Date of Primary Election; General Election; Special Elections (if any).
7. Who may vote an absent voter's ballot? what is the procedure?
8. Who are the city, township, county and state Republican office-holders? Term of office?
9. Who are the Republicans for office for whom the electors in your precinct will vote at the next election? What offices are to be filled? What are qualifications of the candidates?

NOTE: If any questions regarding registration, election laws or Party stands arise which you cannot answer, consult your county chairman or vice-chairman.

Women's Division Rep. Nat. Com.

Republican Workers' Manual

FIGURE 5-1

5

Information Chairman

You and your committee are responsible for accumulating the information that will help other committees and Precinct Leaders and workers function. Write to the Democratic National Committee, 1001 Connecticut Avenue N.W., Washington, D. C., for materials on campaigning and on national and international issues.

Your duties are to:

1. Set up a file of information on issues. Include in it fact sheets and literature from the Democratic National Committee; speeches and statements by Democratic candidates and Party spokesmen; Democratic and Republican voting records on the issues. Include newspaper clippings and notes on radio and television debates.

2. Keep a file on all campaign literature, how much it costs, where it can be obtained.

3. Keep track of Democratic events and activities and suggest literature for distribution at these meetings, rallies, house-to-house canvassing campaigns, etc.

4. Make a file on **opposition** candidates—what they are doing, where they are speaking, what they are saying, how they are voting if they are members of Congress or a State Legislature.

5. Keep a complete file of back copies of the *Democratic Digest* for reference.

6. Keep a file of material on campaign techniques, fund-raising ideas, etc.

7. Be ready to supply Party workers and candidates with materials for speeches, pamphlets, news stories, etc.

BETWEEN CAMPAIGNS

Keep your files up to date. Watch newspapers and magazines for quotable articles. Be all ready to go at election time.

[10]

FIGURE 5—2

From Key to Democratic Victory

How do we produce the good ideas which are so essential to make a campaign come alive? There is a very simple answer. Good ideas, that is, those which are sound and which are adequately supported by facts, and which will stand up under counter-attack, can come only from *study and research*.

This is not as complicated a process, or as dull and dry an operation as the label "research" may sound. There are a number of people who are specially interested and qualified for this type of work, and who, with very meager facilities, can literally accomplish wonders. So, we come to the business of producing good ideas, that is, utilizing the available material and setting up a local Research Committee.

II. The Research Facilities of the Republican National Committee:

The Republican National Committee has a Research Division which prepares analyses and memoranda of current political

issues and problems, Campaign Area Studies, voting records of candidates, etc. Most of these are in mimeographed or printed form, and copies are obtainable by writing the Committee. Any Republican group or individual may be placed on the list for current research material by writing the committee.

III. Setting Up a Local Research Committee:

A. In General:

All research material received from the Republican National Committee should be kept in a central place, or at least one person or a group should be aware of what has been received, and where it can be located.

In addition, there is a vast amount of valuable current material which appears locally in newspapers, magazines and books, and which can be utilized directly at the local level. For this reason, in any organization, State Committee, Congressional District Campaign Organization, Ward, County, or independent group, it is best to make a real business out of research, and so to appoint a Committee, or at least one person, in charge of this activity. All the material from the Republican National Committee should go to that Committee or individual as the central clearing-house for facts and ideas.

It is of great value to set up a local Research Committee of several people. A Committee can act as a team, with the basic issues or subjects of the day being apportioned among them. Indeed, each member of the Committee may become a kind of walking-encyclopedia on one broad subject, such as (1) Taxes, the National Debt, and the Budget; (2) Communism in the United States; (3) Foreign Policy, etc., depending upon the events of the time.

B. Functions:

A local Research Committee's functions can be divided up as follows:

1. *Clipping:* Divide up the political field into its *basic* subjects, a suggested list of which will be found below. See Page 13. Then obtain the services of a group of people (the "Clippers"), each to clip from a certain newspaper or magazine all the material on every

Political parties have established research organizations of their own. Compare this statement with some of your own plans and projects.

FIGURE 5—3

from Republican Campaign Manual

b. *Census Publications:*

The Bureau of the Census in the Department of Commerce, Washington, D. C., puts out a number of interesting publications which are listed in the "Catalog of 16th Decennial Census Publications." These include such things as population figures, including those on "Characteristics of the Population", in which various states are grouped together, price $2.25-$2.75 per volume. Other volumes break the population down by "The Labor Force", and "Characteristics by Age", prices $1.50-$3.00. There are also "Population and Housing" bulletins and releases, costing less than $1.00.

c. *Election information* is also issued by an Election Division of the Bureau of Census.

d. *The Congressional Directory* lists members of Congress, departments of the Government, addresses, and key personnel.

e. *All Government Publications are listed in a Monthly Catalog*, obtainable from the Government Printing Office at 20c per copy, or $2.40 per year. It lists all publications of the Government, and contains a veritable gold mine of information on every controversial subject of current importance.

f. Information on any *specific topic* is obtainable by writing to the Campaign Bureau, Republican National Committee, 923 Fifteenth St., N. W., Washington, D. C.

g. *The Congressional Record* contains the proceedings of the Senate and House of Representatives, and a valuable Appendix of the remarks of Senators and Congressmen on a wide variety of topics of current interest which lead political thinking. Excerpts of particular remarks can often be obtained from the Senator or Congressman who inserted them in the Record.

D. Advantages of a Local Research Committee:
This system has several distinct values:

1. It divides up research work among a number of people, making it a group activity, so as not to provide a backbreaking load for any one person.

2. It provides a central place or clearing-house at the local level, where any Republican who is called upon to make a speech or to enter a radio debate or forum, etc., can become oriented on the subject matter in a minimum period of time. This, in turn, makes possible a considerably greater amount of speaking activity and publicity, and the development of leadership at the local level. It tends to develop more and better advocates, and that, in turn, tends to develop increasingly-favorable publicity and opinion at the local level.

3. It provides an effective, year-round activity for volunteers.

4. You will find that if only a small part of the research activities are attempted by any local campaign organization, the resulting wealth of facts and good ideas which will become available will stimulate a great deal of additional activity, enable you to interest new members, and generally to strengthen your campaign or local organization substantially, thereby giving it new life and vitality and more of a year-round program.

Use of census data

Note Uses of research.

FIGURE 5—4

From Republican Campaign Manual

one of the subjects, and send it on to the Central Editor.

2. *Classification:* The Central Editor, in turn, should finally classify, by subject matter, all the material pertaining to each category received from the "Clippers". That is, all the material coming from the various groups relating to a single subject such as the "National Debt, Taxes and the Budget" should be placed together in chronological or other order. All the material pertaining to "Communism in the United States" should be similarly classified, etc.

3. *Summarization:* The way is now clear for the third phase, which is the process of summarization of the material on each subject. Once this material has been organized as above described, a clear picture can be obtained in a remarkably short time by merely reading it.

C. **Subject Matter Coverable:**

The general scope of activity for a local Research Division may be roughly described as follows:

1. *Political Issues* (Samples):
    a. National debt, taxes and the budget.
    b. Foreign Policy.
    c. Communism in the United States.
    d. Excessive governmental regulation and control of business.
    e. Labor.
    f. Agriculture.
    g. Housing.
    h. National Health and Socialized Medicine.
    i. The Administration and Crime.

2. *Campaign Area Studies:*
    Each campaign area or district should be studied, and a written report thereof made, along the following lines:

    a. *Voting* groups and statistics, broken down into nationality, racial, ethnic, religious, income, Democratic, Republican, etc., groups.

    b. *Geographic* characteristics, urban, rural areas, etc., and their peculiarities.

    c. *Candidates'* voting records. These can be obtained from the Republican National Committee.

13

3. *Obtaining Government Publications:*

    There are valuable Government publications which are available:

    a. *U. S. Government Manual*, published annually by the Bureau of Budget for $1 a copy. It sets forth the costs, duties, personnel, etc., of every Government Agency and Bureau.

Newspaper clippings

These are local political surveys.

From Republican Campaign Manual

FIGURE 5—5

TABLE OF CONTENTS

FIGURE 5—6

Handbook for Political Candidates in Rhode Island, prepared by
Rhode Island Public Expenditure Council

FIGURE 5—7

Preliminary

THE PORTLAND (MULTNOMAH COUNTY) FACT SHEET
(A Supplement to The Oregon Story)

Population Facts

Total Population: 1950..	471,537	Potential Voters (Population 21 years
Males, 21 Years & Over.	161,706	Old and Over): 1952 Est.. 348,000
Females, 21 Years & Over.	171,814	
% Nonwhite.............	3.0	
Rural.................	45,569	
Children (14-17).......	19,520	
Young Voters (20-24)...	30,730	
Senior Citizens (65 & Over)	48,539	

SIZE OF SPECIAL GROUPS	RELIGIOUS*	FOREIGN BORN**
Largest.......	R. Cath.	Canada-Ot.
2nd Largest...	Jewish	U.S.S.R.
3rd Largest...	Presby.	Germany

*From 1936 Census Data (only available)   **From 1950 Census of Population.

For twenty years the people and their Government have been working for prosperity and progress. The results are clearly visible. Here is the story, briefly told in official Government statistics, for Multnomah County.

I. There are MORE JOBS, at HIGHER EARNINGS — and this stems in no small measure from Government programs for full employment, minimum wage laws, and support for free collective bargaining.

LABOR FORCE	1930	1950
Total Labor Force......	159,979	206,973
% Unemployed.........	23.6*	8.0
Civilian Employment:		
Nonagricultural......	xxx	186,288
Agricultural.........	xxx	3,673

EARNINGS	1932*	1951
Factory Hourly Earnings.	$ 0.45	$ 1.82
Factory Weekly Earnings.	$17.05	$70.89
		1949
Family & Individual Incomes over $2000 Yr. %	xxx	67.5

*(*1932 National Averages - Only available)*

II. MORE PEOPLE OWN BETTER HOUSES — aided by Government housing programs which have pushed down interest rates, insured and guaranteed mortgages, and helped provide low-rent public housing for those who cannot afford privately built housing.

MORE AND BETTER HOUSES	1930	1950
Total Occupied Units...	97,095	
% Owner Occupied.....	56.1	
Average Value......	$ 4,346	
	THRU JUNE '52	
Low-Rent Public Housing Units: Completed or Under Construction.	400	

BETTER FACILITIES	1930	1950
% of Dwellings With:		
Electricity.............	xxx	
Private Interior Toilets and Baths........	xxx	
Mechanical Refrigeration	xxx	
Radio or TV............	57.2	

FHA Home Mortgage Program: Year 1951 - Number of Units.. 3,158 - Amount ($000).. $ 23,513
Cumulative, through 1951 - Number of Units.. 22,217 - Amount ($000).. $127,131

DEMOCRATIC NATIONAL COMMITTEE
Research Division

1200 Eighteenth Street, N. W.
Washington 6, D. C.

III. FARMERS ARE BETTER OFF TODAY — and THEY ARE LIVING BETTER, TOO
— largely as a result of the soundly-built Federal programs to increase farm
income, to conserve soil and water, to make credit available at reasonable
rates for farm production, rural electrification, and farm ownership.

Farms Are More Efficient, And Farmers Are Earning More

FARMS AND OUTPUT	1930	1950	MECHANICAL EQUIPMENT	1930	1950
Number of Farms........	2,969	2,937	Tractors..............	1,430	3,940
Products Sold ($000)...	$7,423	$20,647	Motor Trucks..........	939	1,435
Crops................	$3,178	$9,932	Combines..............	xxx	1,259
Livestock & Products.	$4,240	$10,714	Farms With Milking		
Poultry & Products.	(Included)	$1,233	Machines............	xxx	952
Dairy Products.....	(Above)	$3,109			

More Farmers Own Their Land, And Farm Families Are Living Better, Too.

FARM OWNERS	1930	1950	MORE CONVENIENCES	1930	1950
Farms - % Owned........	51.1	61.7	Farms - % Electrified..	24.2	95.8
Average Value..........	$21,206	$31,080	Autos per 100 Farms....	99.5	113.0

IV. PRIVATE ENTERPRISE IS ON FIRMER GROUND THAN EVER BEFORE. There
are more businesses and they are growing and prosperous. They have bene-
fitted tremendously from the Government programs to increase the income
of workers and farmers — who are the customers of businessmen — and from
programs to prevent monopoly and stimulate the growth of new enterprises.

BUSINESS INDICATORS	1932	1951	MANUFACTURING	LATEST CENSUS DATA	
				1929	1947
Bank Deposits ($000)....	$10,440	$84,347	Establishments.........	151	163
Per Capita............	$ 94	$ 628	Total Payrolls ($000)..	$16,326	$43,383
Bldg. Const'n. ($000)...			Value Added by Manu-		
Saving & Loan Ass'n:			facture. ($000)......	$44,081	$101,449
Capital ($000)........					
First Mortgages ($000)					
Bank Failures...........	5	None			
Deposits Involved ($000)	$5,911	None			

Wholesale and Retail Trade and Services — Latest Census Data

	WHOLESALE TRADE		RETAIL TRADE		SERVICES	
	1933	1948	1933	1948	1933	1948
Establishments............	104	128	1,382	1,499	303	401
Sales, Year ($000).........	$10,489	$67,300	$18,795	$112,665	$1,843	$6,811

FIGURE 5—8
(Democratic National Committee, Research Division)

V. THERE ARE MORE AND BETTER HEALTH FACILITIES, and MORE PEOPLE ARE GETTING BETTER SCHOOLING — aided by Government programs of research, Federal aid for hospital construction and local public health activities, aid for vocational education, and other health and educational programs. But population changes have meant that grave health and education problems still remain. These require further cooperative efforts.

HEALTH ACTIVITIES	1940	1949
Doctors per 10,000 Population...........	18.7	18.6
Public Health Nurses	1932	1951
per 10,000 Pop.......	xxx	.8
Federally-Aided Hospital and Clinic Projects - Cumulative, Through JUNE 1952		
Number of Beds.............		475
Approved Federal Share($000)		$1,248

EDUCATIONAL ACTIVITIES	1930	1950
% of Persons, 7-19 Years Enrolled in Schools...	79.5	88.5
Median School Years Completed by Persons 25	1940	
Years Old and Over....	10.0	11.7

VI. There are FAR BETTER MEANS to help those who need SPECIAL ASSISTANCE and for WORKERS who reach RETIREMENT AGE — through the Federal-State programs of vocational rehabilitation and public assistance and Federal social insurance programs.

IN DECEMBER 1951	THE AGED	DEPENDENT CHILDREN	THE BLIND	THE DISABLED	THE NEEDY
Number of Cases........	9,168	3,259 (Children)	163	580	3,207
Average Payment........	$55.82	$109.33 (Per Family)	$69.95	$73.42	$61.30

Old-Age and Survivors Insurance - Coverage (Latest County Figures Available 1948) ... 149,241
- Number of Beneficiaries (1951).................. 23,403
- Average Monthly Payment: Old Age (1951)....... $ 43.22

VII. And the programs for VETERANS have helped to give them opportunities to return to an independent and self-supporting status in the community. They are given the SPECIAL ATTENTION they well deserve — towards readjustment and rehabilitation, health, education, security, and a chance for advancement.

ALL HOME, FARM AND BUSINESS LOANS GUARANTEED OR INSURED BY VETERANS ADMINISTRATION (CUMULATIVE, THROUGH FEBRUARY 25, 1952)
Number........................... 7,716
Principal Amount ($000)......... $41,684

VETERANS ENROLLED IN INSTITUTIONS OF HIGHER LEARNING: Fall of 1950 -- Number.. 2,042

NSTITUTION NAMES AND LOCATIONS:

University of Portland, Portland Extension Center, Lewis and Clark College, North Western College of Law, Reed College, Multnomah College, Vanport Extension Center, Cascade College and Portland School of Music.

VETERAN HOSPITAL CARE AND EXPENDITURES: JULY 1950-JUNE 1951
Number of Patients.............. 5,317
Expenditures - Total ($000)....... $3,451
Patient Care ($000)............. $3,169
Construction ($000)............. $ 282

KINDS AND LOCATIONS OF HOSPITALS:

GM&S Hospital at Portland.

FIGURE 5—9
(Democratic National Committee, Research Division)

THE JOLIET (WILL COUNTY) FACT SHEET

(Democratic National Committee, Research Division)

COUNTY VOTING RECORD

Presidential Elections

	1944				1948	
ROOSEVELT		*DEWEY		TRUMAN		*DEWEY
27,085		30,058		26,430		28,601

1896	1900	1904	1908	1912	1916	1920	1924	1928	1932	1936	194
R	R	R	R	P	R	R	R	R	D	D	R

Congressional Elections

	1944	1946	1948	1950
House	D 40,093	D 27,667	D 57,296	D 47,633
	*R 58,358	*R 49,895	*R 74,213	*R 82,155

Will is one of 6 counties in the 15th Congressional District.

NOTES:

FIGURE 5—10

April 18, 195

FIGURE 5—11   TARGET ANALYSIS PROJECT

I. The purpose of this project is to help select areas of Democratic National
Committee concentration in the 1952 Presidential campaign for:

-- registration and vote campaigns

-- allocation of campaign funds

-- TV and radio expenditures

-- campaign speeches by Presidential and Vice-Presidential candidates by the
President and by other campaign speakers

-- work of Women's Division and of the special group set-ups in or associated
with the national office

-- work with special nationality, racial and religious groups and other specia
groups

-- research on local issues   (Democratic National Committee, Research Division

II. To help achieve these purposes, the following materials are being supplied:

By A. An analysis of "pivotal" States (with full tabulations of political behavior
4/24 of all States in last three Presidential elections)

By B. An analysis of areas of greatest potential Democratic votes in pivotal States
5/12 with accompanying tables)1/

By C. Location in pivotal States of certain groups which deserve special attention,
5/19 with a separation between those areas referred to in B and those elsewhere
(with accompanying tables)

    1. Nationality and racial groups

        a. Negroes

        b. Italian-Americans

        c. German-Americans

        d. Polish-Americans

        e. Others

    2. Religious Groups

        a. Catholics

        b. Jews

    3. Farmers (by types)

    4. Union members

    5. People on Federally-aided public assistance programs

    6. Senior citizens (over 60 or 65)

    7. Unemployed

    8. Government workers

    9. Lower income groups

    10. Women

    11. Soldiers

    12. New voters

By D. Brief summary and analysis of location of Truman and Barkley 1948 campaign
5/26 speeches and Truman 1950 trip (with special emphasis on pivotal States and
special groups)

1/ This is not an analysis of "marginal" House Districts. Some areas of greatest
potential Democratic votes are found in "safe" House Districts.

FIGURE 5—12

(Democratic National Committee, Research Division)

TARGET AREA ANALYSIS

Table I — Areas of Greatest Potential Democratic Voters in the State of (_____)

Selected Area	Potential Voters 1/ 1952	Voting Participation Rate 2/	Democratic Strength Rate 3/	Democratic Voting Goal		1952 Actual Vote	Principal Population Characteristics
				Reasonable Optimum 4/			
				Number	% of Actual 1948 Vote		
1.							
2.							
3.							
4.							
5.							
6.							
7.							
8.							
All Others							
State Total							

1/ Estimated population 21 years of age and over.
2/ Highest percent of potential voters turning out in either the 1936 or the 1940 or 1948 Presidential elections. (Election in 1944 omitted because of war year.)
3/ Highest Democratic percent of the total vote in either the 1936 or the 1940 or 1943 Presidential elections. (Election in 1944 omitted because of war year.)
4/ Potential voters in 1952 x highest rate of voting participation x highest rate of Democratic strength.

FIGURE 5-13

(Democratic National Committee, Research Division)

TARGET AREA ANALYSIS

Table II - Selected Population Characteristics on Key Areas Deserving Special Attention
State of (_____)

Part I - Racial, Nationality, and Religious Characteristics

Selected Areas	Major Racial or Nationality Groups					Religion	
	Largest	2nd Largest	3rd Largest	4th Largest	5th Largest	Catholics	Jews
1. _____	____	____	____	____	____	____	____
2. _____	____	____	____	____	____	____	____
All Other Areas	____	____	____	____	____	____	____
State as a whole	____	____	____	____	____	____	____

Part II - Occupation, Unemployment, Income, and Congestion Characteristics

Selected Areas	Occupational Group			Federal Employees	Excessive Unemployment	Low Income Families	Acutely Crowded Needing:	
	Farmers						Housing Schools	Other Facil'
	A Type	B Type	C Type					
1. _____	____	____	____	____	____	____	____	____
2. _____	____	____	____	____	____	____	____	____
All Other Areas	____	____	____	____	____	____	____	____
State as a whole	____	____	____	____	____	____	____	____

Part III - Other Group Characteristics

Selected Areas	Major Industries	Public Assistance Recipients	Number or Percent of Group Consisting of:				
			Union Members	Soldiers	Women	Young Voters	Senior Citizens
1. _____	____	____	____	____	____	____	____
2. _____	____	____	____	____	____	____	____
All Other Areas	____	____	____	____	____	____	____
State as a whole	____	____	____	____	____	____	____

FIGURE 5-14
(Democratic National Committee, Research Division)

Speech By:	Pivotal State	Target Area	Principal Characteristic of Audience Importance		Principal Issues Discussed Importance		General Re-Action
			1st	2nd	1st	2nd	
Truman in 1948							
1. Date							
2.							
Etc.							
Etc.							
Barkley in 1948							
1. Date							
2.							
Etc.							
Etc.							
Other National Speeches in 1948							
1. Date							
2.							
Etc.							
Etc.							
Truman in 1950							
1. Date							
2.							
Etc.							
Etc.							
Other National Speeches in 1950							
1. Date							
2.							
Etc.							
Etc.							

TARGET AREA ANALYSIS

Table III - Speeches by Truman and Barkley, and Other Major Campaign Speeches Made in 1948 and 1950 in Pivotal States and Target Areas of 1952.

FIGURE 5—15
(Democratic National Committee, Research Division)

CONNECTICUT

SECOND CONGRESSIONAL DISTRICT

INCUMBENT -- HORACE SEELY-BROWN, JR. -- REPUBLICAN

Mr. Seely-Brown carried this district in 1952 with a majority of almost 18,000 votes and received 55.5% of the total vote cast. President Eisenhower and the two Republican candidates for Senate carried the district handily. The district has returned pluralities for Republican congressional candidates in each of the "off" year elections since 1934. It had turned in Democratic pluralities in Presidential years since 1936. Prior to 1936 it had been consistently Republican.

Following is an analysis of the vote in this district since 1940:

Year		Republican	Democrat	Other	Total	Plurality	Repub. % of Total
1952	Congress	90,827	72,868	.....	163,695	17,959 R	55.5
	President	91,750	72,056	347	164,153	19,694 R	55.9
	Senate(unexp)	85,929	77,726	199	163,854	8,203 R	52.4
	Senate (full)	86,529	73,360	3,963	163,852	13,169 R	52.8
1950	Congress	68,747	66,523	.....	135,270	2,224 R	50.8
	Governor	69,757	65,339	1,193	136,289	4,418 R	51.2
1948	Congress	64,916	69,339	.....	134,255	4,423 D	48.4
	President	66,239	67,437	1,937	135,613	1,198 D	48.8
1946	Congress	59,828	48,376	.....	108,204	11,452 R	55.3
1944	"	59,973	63,013	.....	122,986	3,040 D	48.8
1942	"	46,426	43,934	96	90,456	2,492 R	51.3
1940	"	56,825	63,021	374	120,220	6,196 D	47.3

Former Incumbents

Chase Going Woodhouse (D) of New London -- 1949 to 1950 and 1945 to 1946
Horace Seely-Brown, Jr. (R) of Pomfret Center -- 1947 to 1948
John D. McWilliams (R) of Norwich -- 1943 to 1944
William J. Fitzgerald (D) of Norwich -- 1941 to 1942 and 1937 to 1938
Thomas R. Ball (R) of Old Lyme -- 1939 to 1940
William L. Higgins (R) of South Coventry -- 1933 to 1936
Richard P. Freeman (R) of New London -- 1915 to 1932
Bryan F. Mahan (D) of New London -- 1913 to 1914
Edwin W. Higgins (R) of Norwich -- 1905 to 1912

Population Characteristics

The district is composed of four counties in the eastern half of the State and had a population of 318,621 in the 1950 Census. The principal cities are: New London, population 30,367; Middletown, population 29,665; and Norwich, population 23,382. The district has a land area of 1,978 square miles.

FIGURE 5—16

(Democratic National Committee, Research Division)

Population Characteristics - cont'd

According to the Bureau of the Census, the population is classified as 81.0% urban; 16.0% rural non-farm; and 3.0% rural farm. The population includes 85,028 foreign born of which 16,942 are aliens. The largest group of foreign born are of Italian origin -- 19,419. There are also 12,779 persons of Polish origin. The Negro population of the district was 16,242. The population over 21 years of age in 1950 was 350,152.

Economic Characteristics

The 1950 census reports 233,830 persons employed in the district. The largest employment group is manufacturing, accounting for 94,932 persons. The wholesale-retail trades and finance and insurance businesses employed 41,284 and 21,560 persons respectively.

Daily Newspapers

Bristol Press	- circulation	11,874	(evening)
Hartford Courant	"	74,847	(morning)
Hartford Times	"	102,372	(evening)
Manchester Herald	"	10,056	(evening)
New Britain Herald	"	25,465	(evening)

FIGURE 3—17

(Democratic National Committee, Research Division)

Chapter VI

AREAS AND BOUNDARIES

A community, as we use the term in this book, occupies a definite territory and consists of the people living within this territory. According to Pauline Young, people must, however, have certain characteristics other than geographical propinquity in order to constitute a community. They must: (a) have important common interests; (b) have enough of a common culture and of common patterns of social and economic relations to be able to work together; (c) be able to derive a sense of identification and solidarity from the fact that they live in the area and share in its life; (d) have a number of common social institutions. There must, in addition, be some degree of control by the community of its own affairs. See Young, *Scientific Social Surveys and Research* (1).

No matter what kind of a survey you make, geography and ecology will be a part of it. All people live in a dimension of space, and all social and political behavior is fitted into some kind of spatial pattern.

"The Urban Community as a Spatial Pattern and a Moral Order" is the title of an essay written by Robert E. Park in 1925 that was supposed to indicate, among other things, the basic difference in the concern of geographers and ecologists with the urban community:

Human ecology, as the sociologists would like to use the term, is ... not identical with geography, nor even with human geography. It is not man, but the community; not man's relation to the earth which he inhabits, but his relations to other men, that concerns us most. (2)

Whatever the difference in former days between urban geographers and urban sociologists, an inspection of the current issues of the professional journals of the two groups indicates that frequently only a formal distinction exists between their interests and their methods. For a discussion of their differences and similarities in purpose, orientation, and methods, see Duncan, Cuzzort, and Duncan, *Statistical Geography* (3). The purpose of this chapter is to call to your attention the frames of reference and methods of both for possible use in the political study of the local community.

All social phenomena are distributed in some kind of spatial pattern over the territory occupied by a community. All concepts of community organization, including those based on the notion of social distance, are related to some notion of the use of physical space. Political issues are frequently engendered controversies over the use of land. Segregation, for instance, involves the denial of the use of certain portions of land in the community to people with certain characteristics. In some instances zoning is a form of segregation. It is easy to see, therefore, why students of local politics and government must understand the spatial patterns according to which community activities are dispersed or concentrated.

SELECTED READINGS

See Hawley, *Human Ecology* (4) and Quinn, *Human Ecology* (5) for ecological theory. All urban sociology texts have chapters on the spatial patterns of the distribution of community activities. The discussion in Queen and Carpenter, *The American City* (6) dealing with the "localization of activity in the city," will give the student some concepts of the spatial patterning of the community. Also see Hawley, Chapters 11-14 and 18-20; Anderson and Lindeman, *Urban Sociology* (7), Chapters 1-4; Hallenbeck, *American Urban Communities* (8), Chapter 10; and Riemer, *The Modern City* (9).

Many articles on ecology and its use in studying the urban community may be found in such periodicals as the *American Sociological Review,* the *American Journal of Sociology,* and *Social Forces.* Quinn lists and discusses 347 titles in his article, "Topical Summary of Current Literature on Human Ecology," *American Journal of Sociology* (10). You can easily bring this list up to date. In addition to the *Public Affairs Information Service* and indexes to professional journals, ecological items are listed in the *Population Index* (Fig. 8-1).

There are two books of readings on urban sociology in which the student will find articles and sections of books reprinted along with the comments and occasional original essays of the editors: Hatt and Reiss, *Cities and Society* (11) with sixty-seven selections, and Dobriner, *The Suburban Community* (12) with twenty-five selections. The first edition of Hatt and Reiss, *Reader in Urban Sociology* (13) contained twenty-two excerpts omitted from the second edition.

The principal works of urban geographers that will be helpful in making a survey of local government and politics are Dickinson, *City, Region and Regionalism* (14) and Taylor, *Urban Geography* (15). See also James, "The Geographical Study of Population" in *American Geography: Inventory and Prospect* (16). American geographical journals containing articles on the urban community or on particular cities are *Economic Geography*, the *Annals of the Association of American Geographers*, and *The Geographical Review*. A useful British publication is *The Geographical Journal*.

The American Geographical Society publishes each month, except July and August, a list of new additions to its research catalog, *Current Geographical Publications* (Fig. 6-1). General items on city geography are listed under the heading, "Geography of Population." Local items are listed under Section 2 on "Regional Geography." In 1952, over 120 general items on city geography were listed in addition to many local items. Look up your city by name in every index of this kind that you can find. Do not overlook references to the county, region, or state in which your community is located. Frequently, information about the larger area will illuminate the community that you are studying.

The best bibliographical guide is Wright and Platt, *Aids to Geographical Research* (17). Read the introduction carefully, not only for information about how to find and use bibliographies, but for advice and suggestions on doing geographical research.

For a collection of fifty-four essays in urban geography see Mayer and Kohn, *Readings in Urban Geography* (18).

ECOLOGICAL THEORIES OF URBAN STRUCTURE

Urban sociologists and urban geographers are concerned with the spatial patterning of urban activities and institutions. There are four principal concepts of the spatial pattern of community activities: axiate, concentric zone, sector, and multiple nuclei. The student should understand the generalizations contained in these theories and the major criticisms of them. After he has collected and studied the distribution of social data relevant to the local political process, he should determine which, if any, of these theories best explains the spatial pattern of his community.

For a discussion of the axiate structure of the community, with illustrative maps, see Kinneman, *The Community in American Society* (19). See Hawley, (pp. 382 ff.), for a discussion of the axiate and concentric zone pattern. Dickinson (pp. 93-164) defends the concentric zone theory and says that, in general, the study of European cities substantiates it.

For a criticism of the concentric zone theory and for the development of the sector theory, see Hoyt's study published by the Federal Housing Administration under the title, *The Structure and Growth of Residential Neighborhoods in American Cities* (20).

Four important essays on the spatial pattern of cities are reprinted in Hatt and Reiss, *Cities and Society*; Harris and Ullman, "The Nature of Cities" (21); Ogburn, "Inventions of Local Transportation and the Patterns of Cities" (22); Dickinson, "The Regional Relations of the City" (23); Duncan and Duncan, "Residential Distribution and Occupational Stratification" (24). See Hatt and Reiss, *Reader in Urban Sociology* for Firey, "Sentiment and Symbolism as Ecological Variables" (25) and Davie, "The Pattern of Urban Growth" (26).

Ecologists and geographers have also been interested in the territorial expansion of the urban community. No one has yet gone far beyond the analysis made by McKenzie and his colleagues for President Hoover's Research Committee on Social Trends. See his *Metropolitan Community* (27). The story told there has been repeated many times. You will need to study in your own community the expansion of the urbanized area and the correlation therewith of the expansion of the jurisdiction of the political city.

There are maps showing the historical growth of several American urban communities in Federal Housing Administration, *The Structure and Growth of Residential Neighborhoods in American Cities* (28). A number of local and regional planning commissions have prepared similar maps. Check with your local agency to see if any are available.

If the U.S. Geological Survey has issued maps showing cultural features over a period of several decades for your community, you can prepare a rough map showing the expansion of the urbanized area in your locality. You can also prepare one from the data in your local city directory. A complete file of the city directory will probably be found in your local library.

For the first time in the history of the United States census, maps of "urbanized areas" were published in the 1950 Census volumes (see Figs. 6-2, 6-3, and 6-4). They were prepared by geographers after a field survey, and are useful in showing the extent of the urban street pattern in the unincorporated area of medium- and large-size urban communities. Unfortunately, the urban street pattern as of 1949 cannot be compared with that of earlier periods for which similar maps have not been published. Only rough comparisons can be made between the boundaries of urbanized areas in 1950 and in 1960. The urbanized areas for the 1960 Census were not drawn after field surveys as in 1950, but were con-

FIGURE 6-1

Selected Items from

CURRENT GEOGRAPHICAL PUBLICATIONS

Additions to the Research Catalogue of

THE AMERICAN GEOGRAPHICAL SOCIETY

Broadway at 156th Street, New York 32, N. Y.
Vol. XVIII, No. 1 (January, 1955)

This is an illustration of kind of bibliographical material published by the American Geographical Society

Urban Geography

Sorre, Max. The structure of cities. (Landscape. Vol. 4. No. 2. 1954-55. p. 5-15.) Translated from: Max. Sorre: Fondements de la géographie humaine. Vol. 3, Chap. X. 1952.

Murphey, Rhoads. The city as a center of change: Western Europe and China. (Annals of the Association of American Geographers. Vol. 44. No. 4. December, 1954. p. 349-362.)

Winz, Helmut. Die soziale Gliederung von Stadträumen; der "natural area" - Begriff der amerikanischen Sozialökologie. (Lehmann, Herbert, ed. Deutscher Geographentag Frankfurt a. M., 12.-18.5.1951. Tagungsbericht und wissenschaftliche Abhandlungen. 1952. p. 141-148.)

United States

Gross, Edward. The role of density as a factor in metropolitan growth in the United States of America. (Population studies. Vol. 8. No. 2. November, 1954. p. 113-120.)

House, J. W. Medium sized towns in the urban pattern of two industrial societies; England and Wales: U. S. A. (Planning outlook. Vol. 3. No. 2. 1953:4. p. 52-79.)

Harris, Chauncy D. The market as a factor in the localization of industry in the United States. (Annals of the Association of American Geographers. Vol. 44. No. 4. December, 1954. p. 315-348. Maps.)

Northeastern United States

Columbia University. Summer Engineering School. The town of Litchfield [Conn.]; a student survey of the community. [New York] 1948. 28 p. Maps.

Columbia University. Summer Engineering School. Naugatuck, Connecticut, 1952; a student survey of the community. New York [1954] 78 p. Maps.

Columbia University. Summer Engineering School. Terryville, in the town of Plymouth, Conn. [New York] 1949. 48 p. Maps.

Columbia University. Summer Engineering School. The town of Thomaston [Conn.]; a student survey of the community. [New York] 1948. 39 p. Maps.

(SOURCE: CENSUS OF POPULATION, 1950. VOLUME II CHARACTERISTICS
OF THE POPULATION. PART 38, PENNSYLVANIA p. 38—40)

FIGURE 6-2 MAP OF ALLENTOWN — BETHLEHEM URBANIZED AREA.

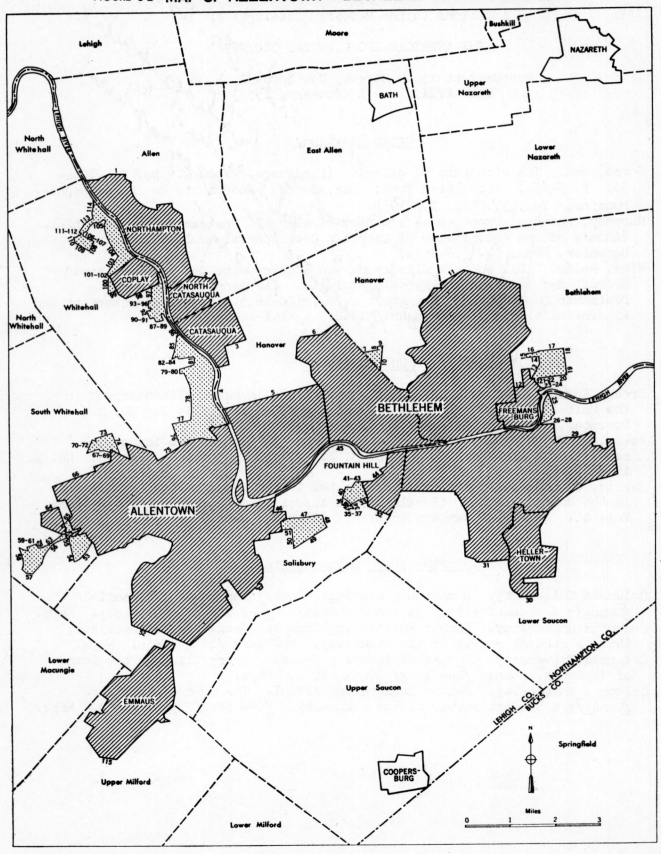

FIGURE 6-3   INDEX MAP OF THE NEW YORK — NORTHEASTERN NEW JERSEY URBANIZED AREA.

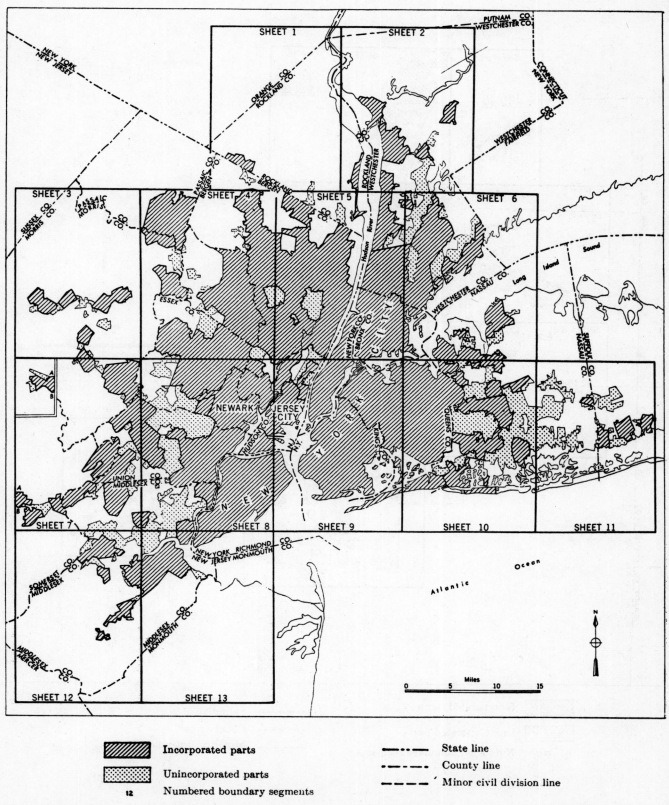

Incorporated parts

Unincorporated parts

12   Numbered boundary segments

—··— State line

—·— County line

——— Minor civil division line

The New Jersey portion of the New York-Northeastern New Jersey Urbanized Area appears on the following pages.

(SOURCE: CENSUS OF POPULATION, 1950. VOLUME II
CHARACTERISTICS OF THE POPULATION, PART 13 ILLINOIS P. 13—36.)

FIGURE 6-4   INDEX MAP OF THE CHICAGO URBANIZED AREA.

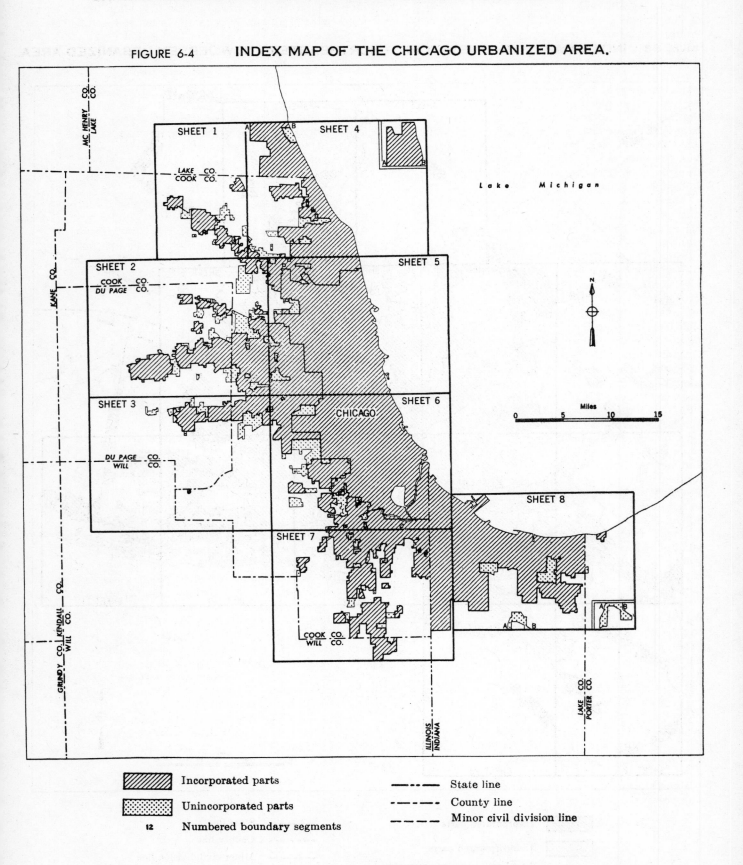

structed prior to the census from enumeration districts. Figure 6-5 is a map of the Atlanta urbanized area in 1960.

The census maps do not, moreover, present a complete picture of the area of a community with an urban street pattern. No attempt was made to draw the line bounding the "urbanized" part of incorporated municipalities. Consequently, large portions of some municipalities that are sparsely settled are included in the "urbanized area." Stamford, Connecticut, is a good example. The town had been recently consolidated with the city, and, therefore, the "estate" area north of the Merritt Parkway is indistinguishable on the 1950 Census maps from the thickly settled portion on Long Island Sound.

Annexation is the principle means of expanding city boundaries. There have been very few annexations in notheastern cities during the past twenty-five years. This does not mean, however, that the community has not been growing beyond the city limits. As a result of the failure of the political city to expand as rapidly as the community has grown, many acute problems have developed. Do not overlook these problems as a source of political conflict. See Jones, *Metropolitan Government* (29) and the article "Local Government Organization in Metropolitan Areas: Its Relation to Urban Redevelopment," in Woodbury, *The Future of Cities and Urban Redevelopment* (30). See also Esser, "Economic Aspects of Annexation," in *Public Management* (31). See, too, Scott and Keller, *Annexation? Incorporation? A Guide for Community Action* (32). This publication contains a bibliography on annexation, incorporation, and metropolitan problems, but a more complete bibliography can be found in Government Affairs Foundation, *Metropolitan Communities* (33), and in the supplement for 1955-1957 compiled by Jones, Hudson, and Johnston (34).

Check with your local planning commission for studies of the need for the areal expansion of your city. J. C. Bollens has an annual article on annexation in the *Municipal Year Book*. Read these articles for several years back to see what cities have been doing about annexation since World War II. Even if your city is not reported as having annexed territory, the articles will suggest questions for you to ask in your own community. The reproduction in Figure 6-6 of a summary table and of the main table from one of Bollen's articles will indicate the kind of data on current annexations available in the *Municipal Year Book*. The 1960 Census of Population shows population for that portion of cities annexed since 1950. See Table 9, Chapter A, "Number of Inhabitants" in Vol. I, *Characteristics of Population*.

Maps showing the original area of a city and dates of annexations may often be secured from the offices of the planning commission or city engineer, or may be consulted in these offices. A map of this kind, prepared by the City Plan Commission of Madison, Wisconsin, is reproduced as Figure 6-7.

MAPS: THEIR COLLECTION AND USE

A political survey of a local community involves the use of many existing maps and the construction of others. The making of maps to show the distribution and correlation of social, economic, and political phenomena will be discussed in a subsequent chapter. However, you should start immediately to ask wherever you go in the community if the agencies you visit (public or private) have maps available showing the location of their special problems or the distribution of their activities. Collect maps methodically. You will be surprised at the number you can secure for the asking. Maps are an indispensable part of the operations of many local agencies and organizations. Some possible public and semipublic sources of maps are:

Public works departments or city engineer's office
Municipal highway or street departments
City, county, or regional planning commission
Zoning boards
Housing authorities
Council of social agencies
Election authorities
Board of education
Chamber of commerce
Real estate dealers
Published reports of local government departments and reports made by special study commissions
Frequently local book stores or office supply dealers sell small street directories which include maps of the city

You will need a base map upon which you may indicate the distribution of data not shown by existing maps. These maps should show the principal legal boundaries and subdivisions of the city or metropolitan area. They should contain as little irrelevant data as possible. Such maps are frequently available at planning commission offices or at communitywide social agencies. Often they can be secured free or at nominal cost. If you cannot find a base map already prepared, it is not too difficult to make your own map by tracing the outline onto a mimeograph or other type of duplicating stencil and reproducing as many copies as you need. See Schmidt, *Handbook of Graphic Presentation* (35).

A map, like a graph, is no better than the data and the interpretations of data represented on it. A word of caution, therefore, from two geographers about the use and abuse of maps:

Students of the social sciences ... are often more prone than are geographers to take geographical documents at their face value and might profit by greater awareness

Georgia

ATLANTA URBANIZED AREA, 1960

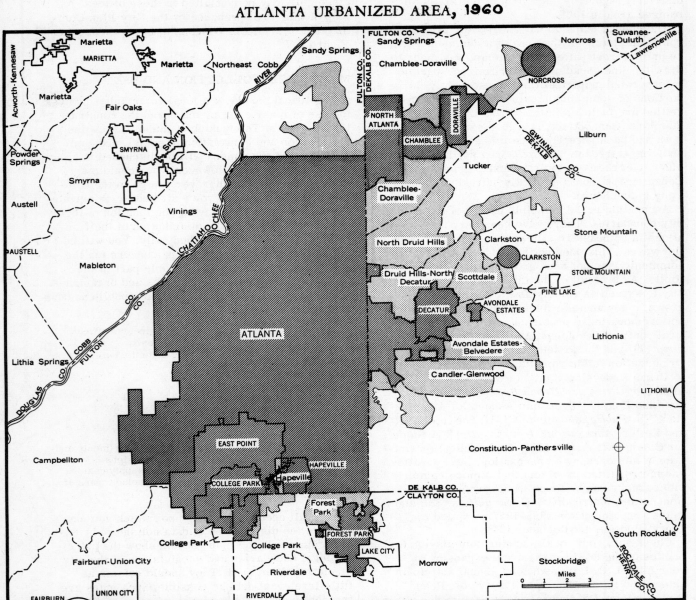

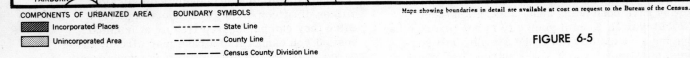

COMPONENTS OF URBANIZED AREA

▨ Incorporated Places

▒ Unincorporated Area

BOUNDARY SYMBOLS

–··–··–··– State Line

–·–·–·– County Line

–––––– Census County Division Line

Maps showing boundaries in detail are available at cost on request to the Bureau of the Census.

FIGURE 6-5

FIGURE 6-6

Metropolitan and Fringe Area Developments in 1952

By John C. Bollens

Department of Political Science, University of California, Los Angeles

PROMINENT among the metropolitan area
square-mile annexation made by Sa...
annexation in the current cen...
several factors important to...
ments include libera...
research and ...
chang...

METROPOLITAN AND FRINGE AREAS

ve to be finished in early 1954. For either proposal to go into opera-
it will have to receive separate majority vote approval in the city
n the county. Refuse disposal district was added to the list of
well-established its functions. Metropolitan District Commission in the Boston area.
try increased its functions of the Metropolitan cities and the amount of total area
horized sewerage, water, and park services in many years during last year. There
ovides their highest points in annexing cities and exceeds the attainment
Annexation. The number of annexing land acquisitions the attainment gai...
annexed reached their completed the preceding year and exceeds a 733 per cent was ut...
were 402 municipalities over the preceding year. It is more than annexation was ut...
of the previous record made in 1950. Furthermore, annexation
is a sizable increase of 48 cities. smaller municipalities.
over the 1935–39 average
lized more by both larger and

TABLE 1

ANNEXATION TRENDS, 1945–52

	All Cities Over 5,000		Cities of 5,000 to 10,000		
Year	Total No. of Annex- ing Cities	No. of Cities Annex- ½ Sq. Mi. or Over	Total No. of Annex- ing Cities	No. of Cities Annex- ½ Sq. Mi. or Over	
1952	402	75	155	17	
1951	382	55	159	10	
1950	309	60	98	12	
1949	301	56	113	11	
1948	288	59	95	7	
1947	298	68	128	15	
1946	259	43	105	13	
1945	152	25	63	3	

a...
ou...
wea...
ices ...
prop...
and we...

In th...
conclude...

'Since an...
sion about l...

...territory absorbed was similarly significant
...within the boundaries of 402 municip...
...miles in 1951 (including ...
...relative action in that y...
...the larger ci...
...mple...

39

...as th...
Carroll, Pa. Calif.
Border, Tex. Calif. ...
Bould...
Gr...
Generally, ...
lles not behind but ahead.

46

...continued to be widespread interest in area matters in California...
...of urban...
2—Continued

THE MUNICIPAL YEAR BOOK

City	No. of Annex- tions	No. of Mi. of Total City An...
10,000 to 25,000		
Anaheim, Calif.	5	.75

TABLE III

ANNEXATION OF ONE-FOURTH SQUARE MILE OR MORE BY CITIES OVER 5,000: 1952

Data in this table were obtained directly from city officials in January and February,
1953. The table contains information on annexations of one-fourth square mile or more
completed by 106 cities in 1952. Replies from three of these cities, however, were received too late for inclusion in the summary in the latter part of the preceding article;
these cities are indicated by a single dagger (†) after the name of the city. Seven other
cities which reported annexations of one-fourth square mile or more but did not furnish
additional information are listed at the end of the table. Under "Origin of Annexation
Movement," "C" indicates city government and "F" fringe area (including also real estate
subdivision developers). Under "Adequate Facilities in Area When Annexed," "D" means
drainage, "F" fire protection, "G" garbage collection, "P" police protection, "S" sewer
facilities, "St" streets, "W" water supply, and "Z" zoning; facilities not listed in columns
Needs Which Most Influenced Fringes to Annex" where they are supplemented by "Sc" for
schools and "Stm" for street maintenance.

TABLE III—ANNEXATION OF ONE-FOURTH SQUARE...

THE MUNICIPAL YEAR BOOK

48

City	No. of Annexa- tions	Total City Area An- nexed Sq. Miles	Total City Land Area Incl. 1952 Annexed Sq. Miles	Current City Pop. of An- nexed City Pop. (000 omitted)	Estimated Origin of An- Program Move- ment	Origin of Current City Annexation Move- ment Explain- ing Benefits Annexed	Adequate Service needs Facilities City More Than it in Area Will Return in When Revenues Annexed	Area Will Cost	Imme- diately	In Long Run
500,000 to 1,000,000										
Houston, Tex.	2	1.10	163.3	1,264	665	C	No	DSS	...	Yes	Yes
Milwaukee, Wis.	34	1.83	52.5	2,179	642	F	Yes	DGZ	SW	Yes	No
250,000 to 500,000										
Columbus, Ohio	1	1.46	41.4	0	376	F	No	W	...	Yes	No
Dallas, Tex.	20	27.64	170.3	35,000	535	CF	No	None	SW	Yes	Yes
Fort Worth, Tex.	10	1.98	98.0	0	325	F	No	None	FPSW	...	Yes
Indianapolis, Ind. ...	7	.28	55.8	300	440	F	No	DPSWZ	S	Yes	No
Long Beach, Calif. ...	11	.59	36.3	0	254	F	No	WZ	...	Yes	No
Omaha, Neb.	..	.25	41.4	1,000	258	CF	No	FZ	Sc	Yes	No

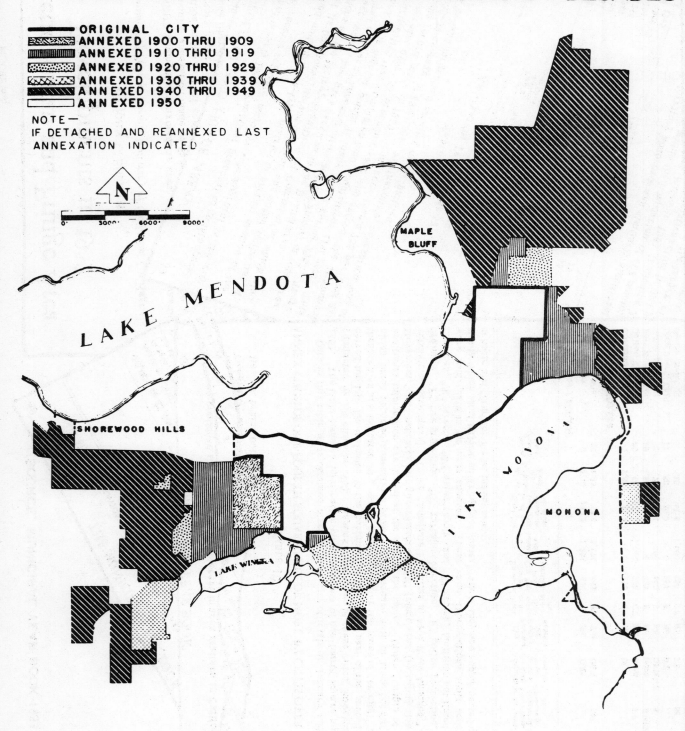

FIGURE 6-7

GROWTH OF MADISON-ANNEXATIONS BY DECADES

ORIGINAL CITY
ANNEXED 1900 THRU 1909
ANNEXED 1910 THRU 1919
ANNEXED 1920 THRU 1929
ANNEXED 1930 THRU 1939
ANNEXED 1940 THRU 1949
ANNEXED 1950

NOTE—
IF DETACHED AND REANNEXED LAST
ANNEXATION INDICATED

N

0'   3000'   6000'   9000'

LAKE MENDOTA

MAPLE BLUFF

SHOREWOOD HILLS

LAKE WINGRA

LAKE MONONA

MONONA

SOURCE:
CITY PLAN COMMISSION, MADISON, WISCONSIN.
MADISON'S PEOPLE (1952) PP16

of the possibilities of error in the evidence that such documents—maps especially—present.*

This warning is all the more relevant if you realize that many maps that you will acquire during a community survey will be the product of people untrained in map making or in social science research.

IMPORTANCE OF SELECTING THE CORRECT GEOGRAPHICAL AREA

In making a local community survey you should remember that the social and economic community is seldom identical with any of the legal areas known as towns, villages, cities, townships, or counties. Most metropolitan communities, as well as many other local communities, are larger than any local political unit except, in some instances, the county. Many metropolitan areas include dozens or hundreds of local governmental units. You must be able to see your own city or town as a fragment of a larger community, because the part and the whole help to explain each other. The "standard metropolitan statistical area," as the term is used by the U.S. Bureau of the Census, is one concept of a larger community including a number of lesser legal areas and subcommunities. You should, therefore, become acquainted immediately with the concept of the standard metropolitan statistical area. The distribution of these areas in the United States in 1960 is shown in Figure 6-8. (See how the Census Bureau defines a "standard metropolitan statistical area" in Fig. 6-12.)**

It may be necessary to study a metropolitan area (an extralegal concept of the community) in order to understand the politics of a suburban city (a legal entity). In many ways, the deepest political cleavage in the United States is between the central city and its suburban satellites in the metropolitan areas. In view of the suburban origins of a very large fraction of the American people, perhaps the most significant single political situation that any student of politics needs to understand is the fact that nearly every suburb is an area of political conflict. See Wood, *Suburbia, Its People and Their Politics* (36).

---

*J. K. Wright and E. T. Platt, *Aids to Geographical Research*. 2d ed. New York: Columbia University Press, 1947. p. 22. See also J. K. Wright, "Map Makers are Human: Comments on the Subjective in Maps," *Geographical Review*, Vol. 32, 1942, pp. 527-544.

**In the 1950 Census the term used was "standard metropolitan area" (SMA). Prior to 1950 various agencies of the federal government used such terms as "metropolitan district," "metropolitan county," "industrial area," "labor market area." See U.S. Bureau of the Budget, *Standard Metropolitan Statistical Areas*, Washington, D.C.: U.S. Government Printing Office, 1959.

It might be assumed that a constant attempt is being made in all communities to revise the legal boundaries of local governmental jurisdictions to conform with the scope of the social and economic community, but this is not the case. Do the people of your community want to rationalize their local governmental boundaries? That is, do they want to annex or to be annexed to the larger community within which they live, or do they resist attempts to bring them into a union with neighboring towns? Questions you cannot afford to ignore are: What is the best geographical base for the government of your community? "Best" for what? For whom? These questions underlie much of your survey, though you may never find satisfactory answers to them.

There are many reasons for relating smaller areas to larger ones. People living in any given area may belong to many different communities. It is extremely important, therefore, that you select the proper area for your study. It is also important that you know why you select an area and what the implications of your decision are likely to be to your survey.

POLITICAL SYMBOLISM OF AREAS AND BOUNDARIES

Frequently an area becomes a symbol around which intense loyalties develop. Such symbols are politically important. They have an organizing effect on the attitudes of many people and on many of their activities. Very often people identify themselves with the locality where they live instead of with the place where they work. This identification becomes most intense when proposals are made to consolidate or annex political units.

Areas, or institutions attached to areas, are also ingredients of many of our most common political concepts, such as states' rights, home rule, representation, federalism, *ad hoc* authorities, sectionalism, and regionalism. These symbols of area are manipulated by opponents and proponents of many public policies. Opposition to a public housing project, for example, may be expressed as an assertion of the "right" of a particular residential area in the city or metropolitan area to "local" self-determination, the "right" to determine the kind of people who are allowed to settle in the area. Such an argument may be made by the inhabitants of any area. Frequently the argument is devised by outside organized groups, and used when and where it appears necessary or desirable. See Schattschneider, Jones, and Bailey, *A Guide to the Study of Public Affairs* (37) for an example of this.

Likewise, the idea of home rule can be evoked in the disputes that develop out of the relationships between the state government and local units of government. In recent years, the principle of home

STANDARD METROPOLITAN STATISTICAL AREAS: 1960

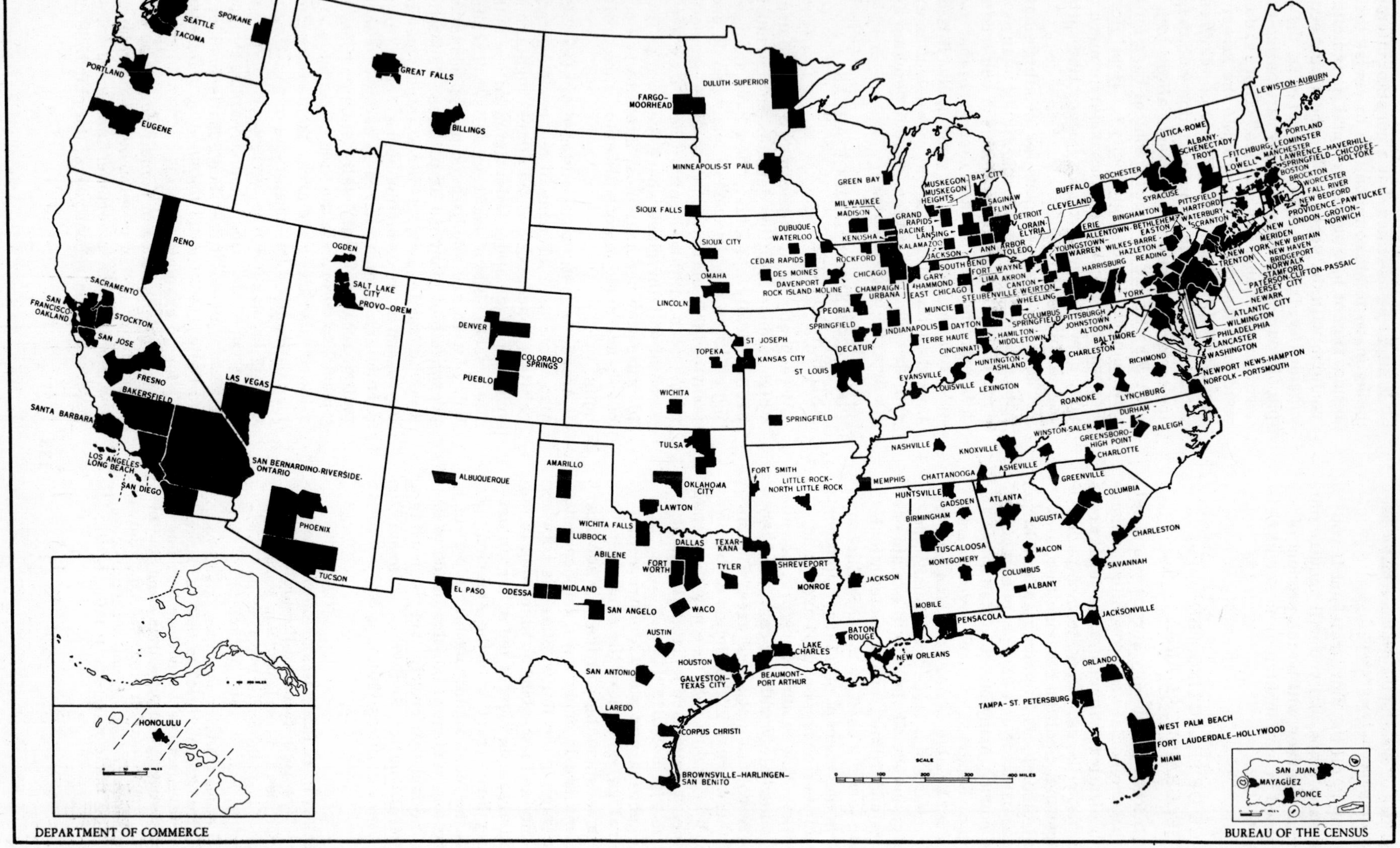

FIGURE 6-8

DEPARTMENT OF COMMERCE

BUREAU OF THE CENSUS

GSA WASH DC 61-10150

rule has sometimes been taken to mean that any unit of local government, however small a fragment of the total community it may be, is entitled to special constitutional protection against a reorganization of local governmental areas and powers by the state. For example, before any power vested in Ohio municipalities can be concurrently or exclusively exercised by the county, the state constitution requires a favorable vote (a) in the county as a whole; (b) in the largest municipality in the county; (c) in the county outside such municipality; and (d) in each of a majority of the municipalities and townships in the county. The village of North Randall, with a population in 1930 of 107, cast four votes for and six votes against the Cuyahoga County Charter of 1935. Its unit vote counted as much as the vote of the city of Lakewood (70,509 inhabitants), which opposed the charter by a vote of 8,787 to 8,136.

AREAS AND REPRESENTATION

See Key and Silverman, "Party and Separation of Powers: A Panorama of Practice in the States," *Public Policy* (38). Component geographical areas, except where election is at large, form the bases of the American system of legislative representation. The area is almost always divided into districts, each of which elects a single representative by a plurality vote, i.e., the candidate receiving the most votes is elected even if he does not receive a majority of all votes cast. Sometimes representation is apportioned among areas that are, or are supposed to be, approximately equal in population. Frequently, however, areas such as counties in California, or states in the United States Senate are given equal representation in their respective legislative bodies without regard to differences in population. In other states, such as Pennsylvania, a similar result is accomplished by limiting the number of representatives from any one county.

The term "rotten borough" is applied to the systems of gross overrepresentation and underrepresentation of the component areas. See Zeller, *American State Legislatures* (39). In Connecticut the town is the unit of representation in the lower house of the General Assembly. One hundred ten of the 169 towns have two representatives each, and each of the other 59 towns has one representative. Of the 279 members of the House of Representatives, Hartford, New Haven, Bridgeport, Waterbury, and New Britain, with a combined population of 677,644, elect a total of only ten members. The representatives of the five largest cities in the state can, therefore, be outvoted by the representatives of the nine smallest towns with a combined population of 4,734. Inevitably, systems of representation of this kind can be maintained only if they are supported by intense

local loyalties, which are in turn stimulated by the very existence of the rotten borough system. See the following discussions of this subject: Dauer and Kelsey, "Unrepresentative States," *National Municipal Review* (40); Merry, "Minority Rule: Challenge to Democracy," a series of articles in *The Christian Science Monitor* (41); another series of articles in *The Christian Science Monitor*, "How Minorities Help Shape Congress" by the same author (42); Strout, "The Next Election is Already Rigged," *Harper's Magazine* (43); and Baker, *Reapportionment and Redistricting of State Legislatures* (44).

Political areas are also used as units for counting and apportioning votes in general and primary elections. Two good illustrations are the county-unit system for nominating the Democratic candidate for governor of Georgia and the electoral college system for electing the President of the United States. Any candidate who receives a plurality of the votes cast in the Democratic primary in a Georgia county receives all of the unit votes of the county. When account is taken of the fact that the most populous counties in the state have been allocated a disproportionately small number of unit votes, it is easy to see that the successful candidate may not be the one who received the greatest popular vote in the primary. The political theory upon which these arrangements are based is that area or acreage is entitled to a representation sufficient to check the power of concentrated population. No matter what arguments are used to justify systems of unequal representation, the consequences of these arrangements may be so great that politics cannot be understood if we ignore them.

How is your community represented in the county, state, and national legislative bodies? How well represented is it in the formal governing organs of the two major political parties, the state conventions and state committees? How well are the various parts of your community represented in community councils? You can make a variety of calculations to measure the degree of overrepresentation or underrepresentation produced in your community by the way representation is apportioned. Is party control in your community related to the bias of the system of representation?

EMPHASIS BY ECOLOGISTS ON MARGINAL ZONES INSTEAD OF BOUNDARY LINES

The ecological approach to the study of the spatial distribution of communal activities is considered elsewhere in this book. (Human ecologists attempt to relate social phenomena to the geographical environment of communities.) At this point, however, you should become aware of the terms natural areas and cultural areas used by anthropologists, geographers, sociologists and human ecologists. See Hawley, Chapter 6, "Habitat and Population" for a discussion of these concepts and for references to works in which they are used. These concepts may provide you with some basis for evaluating the adequacy of the legal areas with which you deal.

The concept of a community larger than the central political city suggests that each of the activities carried on by an urban community covers an area with a common center and varying peripheries. This concept has led some urban sociologists and human ecologists to underrate the significance of legal boundary lines. As Hawley says:

community boundaries are zones rather than lines. They are formed where the territories of neighboring communities converge and overlap, where the integrating influences emanating from different centers meet in competition, and where in consequence, the communal attachments of the local residents are not only divided but in a state of flux. The dynamics of the modern community is, in fact, largely responsible for the diffuseness of its boundaries. Every relative change in the time and cost of transportation and every relative shift in market conditions has immediate repercussions in the expansion or contraction of the scope of the community. (p. 249)

One of the principal fruits of a community survey will be the realization that your city, town, or village is a dependent part of a larger community. You should realize, however, that precise boundary lines of political units are themselves important social data. They are part of the "cultural landscape." The way in which governmental boundary lines can be used to achieve social or economic objectives is illustrated in Nelson, "The Vernon Area, California—A Study of the Political Factor in Urban Geography," *Annals of the Association of American Geographers* (45).

It is naive to dismiss legal boundary lines as arbitrary, thus making an invidious comparison between legal boundaries and the flexible zones that bound natural or cultural areas. It is necessary to have a boundary that fixes the geographical limits within which government officials can legally exercise control over the lives, activities, and property of people. This is true, for example, of the power to levy taxes, the power to make an arrest, the power to compel school attendance. It must be possible to determine definitely in individual cases where the jurisdiction of public officials begins and where it ends; it would be impossible to run a government, as we understand the term, without boundary lines.

This is not to say that the boundaries of governmental units are drawn rationally. The metropolitan problem is largely that of providing for governmental programs covering the whole metropolitan community. This calls for extending some area of government to include a vastly enlarged

community. Any boundary line fixed by statute is likely to be arbitrary at any given time with respect to some of the activities carried on in the community; it is rarely possible to find a line that meets all situations equally well.

When you attempt to use census data in your survey, your first task is to learn the meaning of the various areas for which census data are compiled. If you have not mastered the precise definition of the census areas, you naturally will not be able to use the statistical materials intelligently. For this reason the census definitions are given here. It will pay you to study these statements carefully and to refer back to them whenever you are in doubt about them.

AREAS FOR WHICH CENSUS AND OTHER COMMUNITY DATA ARE AVAILABLE

The political area, as Hawley remarks, is important as a reporting unit for quantitative data about the activities of people.

As it has turned out, however, most of our knowledge about population is cast in territorial units that approximate the culture area conception more closely than the natural area conception. These, to be more specific, are the political or administrative areas into which the world has been subdivided. The political area, though bounded arbitrarily in many instances, is readily determined and therefore is the most convenient unit in which to observe population. Furthermore, the occupants of the political area are usually sufficiently organized to constitute a more or less distinct population. In fact, were it not for their political organization, it is unlikely that the people would be induced to take inventories of their numbers and characteristics. (p. 91)

Published social, economic, demographic, and political data are usually broken down by governmental units or officially recognized subdivisions of the units. Data are often published, moreover, for areas larger than states and local governmental units. For instance, census data are published for divisions and regions of the United States and for metropolitan and urbanized areas.

Census data are also published or are available for areas smaller than local governmental units. Examples of such areas are census tracts, blocks, and census enumeration districts. Some reporting units, such as the urbanized area, are smaller than some governmental units (the county) and larger than other units (the city).

The following governmental units are used by the Bureau of the Census in reporting data:

1. The United States. The reference is to the continental area except where it is indicated that the territories and possessions are included. Almost all census data are available for the United States. Many other data, such as that reported in the Current Survey of Business, are only available for the whole country.

2. States and Territories. Most subjects in the 1950 censuses of population and housing were reported by states. Volume I of the 1960 Census of Population, entitled "Characteristics of the Population," is published in fifty-seven parts. Part 1 is the summary for the United States; Part 2 is Alabama; Part 9 is the District of Columbia, and so on through Wyoming. Parts 54-57 for Guam, the Virgin Islands, American Samoa, and the Canal Zone are bound together.

3. Counties. Data are presented by counties for each state. The county, however, is not an important subdivision of the New England States. In Rhode Island it is not an organized governmental unit. In New York City there are five counties, each equivalent to one of the boroughs. You will notice that the county (except in New England) is the basic reporting unit around which standard metropolitan areas are constructed. The 1950 Census map of New Jersey showing counties is reproduced as Figure 6-9, and the 1960 Census map of Georgia as Figure 6-10. Certain population and housing characteristics of the urban, rural-nonfarm, and rural population are published for the United States, for each state, and for each county. See the definitions in the "Introduction" to the census reports. Notice that a basic change in the definition of urban population was made in the 1950 Census. This affects the comparability of 1950 and 1960 data with those of previous censuses.

4. Incorporated Places. The number of inhabitants is reported for every incorporated place regardless of its size. Data on the general and economic characteristics of the population are not reported for places of less than 1,000 inhabitants. Most data are not reported for places of less than 2,500.

5. Minor Civil Divisions of the County. Only the number of inhabitants is reported for these areas. The result is that for important sectors of some metropolitan areas, (particularly in Pennsylvania, New Jersey, New York and New England where the town and township is a basic unit of local government), there are no published data on the general and economic characteristics of the population in 1950. For the areas in which the central city and adjacent areas are "tracted," however, such data may be secured from the U.S. Bureau of the Census, U.S. Census of Population: 1950, Vol. III, "Census Tract Statistics" (Series P-D Bulletins). In the 1960 Census some of these towns and townships were recognized as unincorporated urban places.

The minor civil divisions in southeastern Pennsylvania are shown in the map reproduced as Figure 6-11. In Pennsylvania, each unit of local government —township, borough, or city—is a separate minor civil division of its county. In other states, such as Ohio, some cities and villages are separate civil divisions, but other cities and villages are subdivisions of a township. The population of the latter are listed as subtotals of the population of townships. In nontownship states, the civil divisions of a county may be designated as precincts, districts, beats, gores, grants, islands, purchases, surveyed townships, etc. For the usage in the state you are studying see the prefatory notes in Volume I, Chapter A, "Number of Inhabitants" of the U.S. Census of Population: 1960.

It has been increasingly recognized in each decennial census of the twentieth century that the area of the local community is not coterminous with the area of local governmental units. Even the largest cities contain only a portion of the total area and population of their respective local communities. The Bureau of the Census and other government and unofficial agencies, report data by several areas that are supposed to include most of the community. In the 1960 Census, areas of this kind were:

1. The Standard Metropolitan Statistical Areas. These reporting units are defined in the excerpt from a volume of the 1960 Census of Population reproduced as Figure 6-12. Note carefully the statement on the origin and purpose of the term. How many other varieties of published data can you discover for your standard metropolitan statistical area by adding up the data published by counties? Note that this can not be done for most data for New England standard metropolitan statistical areas.

Read the statements on page XV of the excerpts from the 1950 Census (Fig. 6-12) to compare standard metropolitan areas with urbanized areas in the 1950 Census and with the metropolitan districts of the 1940 Census.

For the meaning of the concept of the metropolitan community, see McKenzie, Hallenbeck, (Chaps. 12 and 13), Duffus, *Mastering a Metropolis* (46), and Queen and Carpenter (Chap. 7).

Figure 6-9 shows the standard metropolitan areas in 1950 in New Jersey; those for Georgia in 1960 are shown in Figure 6-10. Similar maps for each state will be found in the U.S. *Census of Population: 1950*, Vol. II. Notice that one New Jersey area extends into New York, two into Pennsylvania, and one into Delaware. Three of the seven standard metropolitan statistical areas of Georgia extend into adjacent states. Figure 6-8 shows the location of the 168 standard metropolitan statistical areas in the United States and Territories.

2. Standard Consolidated Areas. Each of the two largest metropolitan areas have been divided in the 1960 Census into two separate standard metropolitan statistical areas. The census recognizes the need for data on the older, more inclusive New York-Northeastern New Jersey and Chicago metropolitan areas. Consequently, consolidated data are reported for these two areas. You may wish to also add Fairfield County, Connecticut, or at least the Stamford SMSA, to the New York-Northeastern New Jersey standard consolidated area.

3. Urbanized Areas. These are smaller than the standard metropolitan areas. The 1960 Census definition of the area is reproduced in Figure 6-12. The same procedure was not followed in 1960 as was followed in 1950, when urbanized areas were mapped in the field by geographers from the Bureau of the Census. The maps represented the actual build-up fringe area with an urban street pattern. The street names bounding urbanized areas were also published in the census reports.

Maps of 1950 urbanized areas, all drawn to the same scale, will be found in the respective state volumes of the 1950 censuses of population and housing. Figure 6-2 is a map of the Allentown-Bethlehem Urbanized Area. Notice that while the map of this area takes up less than a page of the census reports, the complete map of the New York-Northeastern New Jersey Urbanized Area requires thirteen sheets and that of the Chicago Urbanized Area requires

FIGURE 6-9   MAP SHOWING COUNTIES AND STANDARD METROPOLITAN
AREAS IN NEW JERSEY.

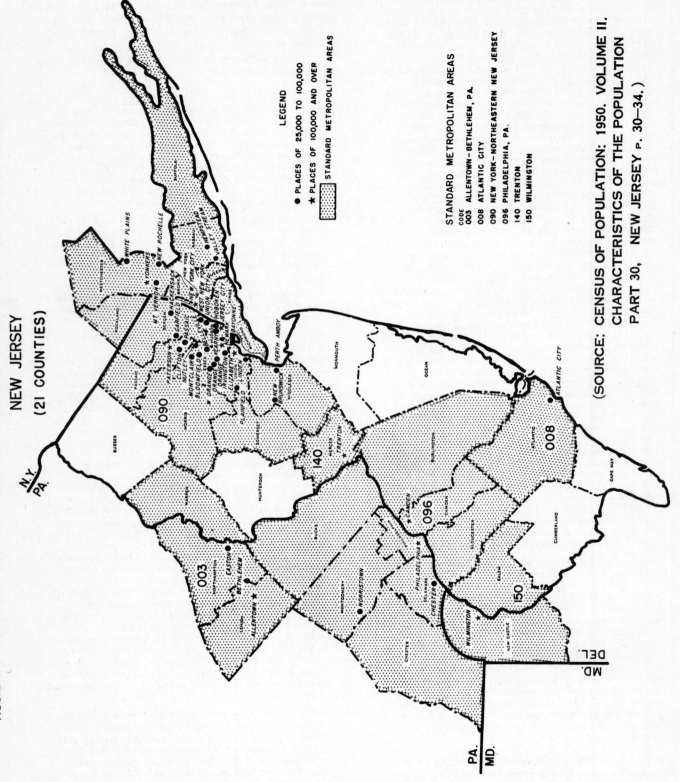

NEW JERSEY
(21 COUNTIES)

LEGEND

● PLACES OF 25,000 TO 100,000
★ PLACES OF 100,000 AND OVER
▦ STANDARD METROPOLITAN AREAS

STANDARD METROPOLITAN AREAS

CODE
003 ALLENTOWN-BETHLEHEM, PA.
008 ATLANTIC CITY
090 NEW YORK-NORTHEASTERN NEW JERSEY
096 PHILADELPHIA, PA.
140 TRENTON
150 WILMINGTON

(SOURCE: CENSUS OF POPULATION: 1950. VOLUME II.
CHARACTERISTICS OF THE POPULATION
PART 30, NEW JERSEY P. 30—34.)

FIGURE 6-10

GEORGIA— COUNTIES, PLACES OF 25,000 OR MORE, AND STANDARD METROPOLITAN STATISTICAL AREAS, 1960

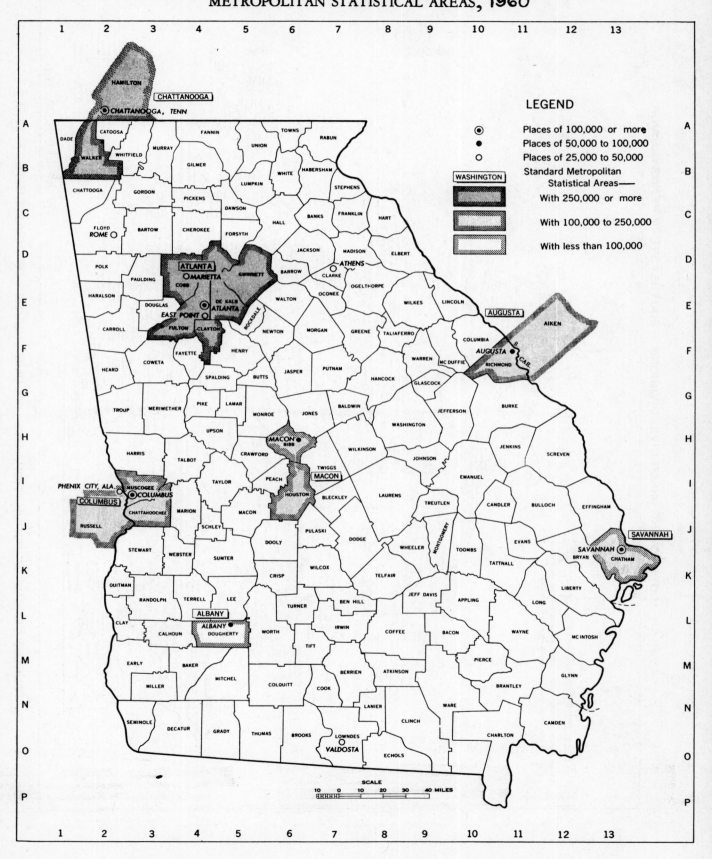

LEGEND

◉ Places of 100,000 or more
● Places of 50,000 to 100,000
○ Places of 25,000 to 50,000
Standard Metropolitan
   Statistical Areas——

With 250,000 or more

With 100,000 to 250,000

With less than 100,000

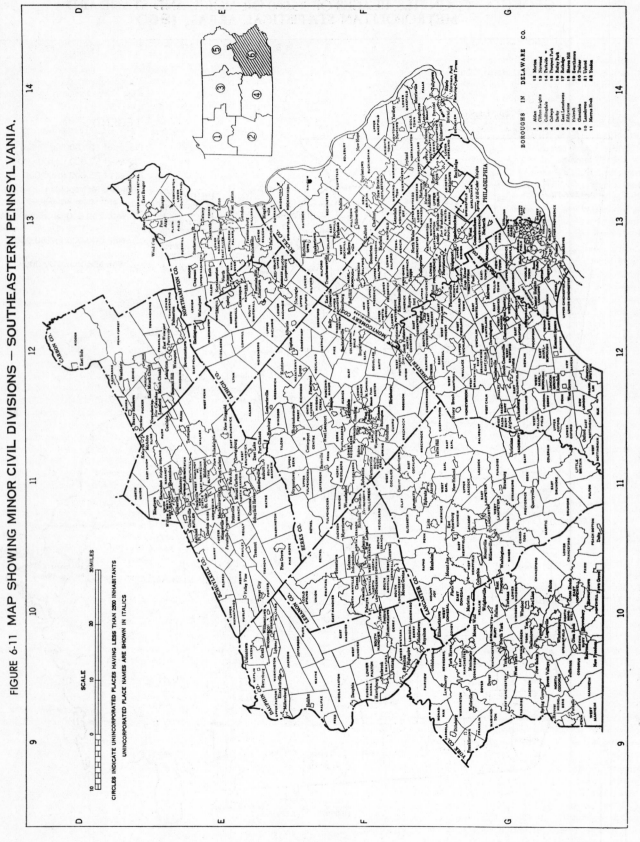

FIGURE 6-11 MAP SHOWING MINOR CIVIL DIVISIONS — SOUTHEASTERN PENNSYLVANIA.

CIRCLES INDICATE UNINCORPORATED PLACES HAVING LESS THAN 2500 INHABITANTS
UNINCORPORATED PLACE NAMES ARE SHOWN IN ITALICS

SCALE

10   0   10   20   30 MILES

BOROUGHS IN DELAWARE CO.

1 Aldan
2 Clifton Heights
3 Collingdale
4 Colwyn
5 Darby
6 Eddystone
7 Folcroft
8 Glenolden
9 Lansdowne
10 Marcus Hook

12 Morton
13 Norwood
14 Parkside
15 Prospect Park
16 Ridley Park
17 Rutledge
18 Sharon Hill
19 Swarthmore
20 Trainer
21 Upland
22 Yeadon

(SOURCE: CENSUS OF POPULATION, 1950. VOLUME I NUMBER OF INHABITANTS, P. 38–7.)

URBANIZED AREAS

As indicated above, one of the components of urban territory under the new definition of urban-rural residence is the urban fringe. Areas of this type in combination with the cities which they surround have been defined in the 1950 Census as urbanized areas.

Each urbanized area contains at least one city with 50,000 inhabitants or more in 1940 or according to a special census taken since 1940. Each urbanized area also includes the surrounding closely settled incorporated places and unincorporated areas that comprise its urban fringe. The boundaries of these fringe areas were established to conform as nearly as possible to the actual boundaries of thickly settled territory, usually characterized by a closely spaced street pattern. The territory of an urbanized area may be classified into incorporated parts and unincorporated parts. (See urbanized area maps which follow table 9 in Chapter A.)

An urbanized area also may be divided into central city or cities and urban fringe as defined below.

Central cities.—Although an urbanized area may contain more than one city of 50,000 or more, not all cities of this size are necessarily central cities. The largest city of an area is always a central city. In addition, the second and third most populous cities in the area may qualify as central cities provided they have a population of at least one-third of that of the largest city in the area and a minimum of 25,000 inhabitants. The names of the individual urbanized areas indicate the central cities of the areas. The sole exception to this rule is found in the New York–Northeastern New Jersey Urbanized Area, the central cities of which are New York City, Jersey City, and Newark.

Urban fringe.—The urban fringe includes that part of the urbanized area which is outside the central city or cities. The following types of areas are embraced if they are contiguous to the central city or cities or if they are contiguous to any area already included in the urban fringe:

1. Incorporated places with 2,500 inhabitants or more in 1940 or at a subsequent special census conducted prior to 1950.

2. Incorporated places with fewer than 2,500 inhabitants containing an area with a concentration of 100 dwelling units or more with a density in this concentration of 500 units or more per square mile. This density represents approximately 2,000 persons per square mile and normally is the minimum found associated with a closely spaced street pattern.

3. Unincorporated territory with at least 500 dwelling units per square mile.

4. Territory devoted to commercial, industrial, transportational, recreational, and other purposes functionally related to the central city.

Also included are outlying noncontiguous areas with the required dwelling unit density located within 1½ miles of the main contiguous urbanized part, measured along the shortest connecting highway, and other outlying areas within one-half mile of such noncontiguous areas which meet the minimum residential density rule.

TYPES OF PLACES

The term "place" refers to a concentration of population regardless of legally prescribed limits, powers, or functions. Thus, some areas having the legal powers and functions characteristic of incorporated places are not recognized as places.

Incorporated places.—In a majority of instances, however, the legally prescribed limits of incorporated places serve to define concentrations of population. Of the 18,548 places recognized in the 1950 Census, 17,118 are incorporated as cities, towns, villages, or boroughs. In New England, New York, and Wisconsin, however, towns, although they may be incorporated, are minor civil divisions of counties and are not considered as places. Similarly, in the States in which townships possess powers and functions identical with those of villages, the township is not classified as a place. Although areas of this type are not recognized

as places, their densely settled portions may be recognized as unincorporated places or as a part of an urban fringe.

Unincorporated places.—In addition to incorporated places, the 1950 Census recognizes 1,430 unincorporated places. These unincorporated places, which contain heavy concentrations of population, are recognized as places by virtue of their physical resemblance to incorporated places of similar size. To make this recognition possible, the Bureau of the Census has defined boundaries for all unincorporated places of 1,000 inhabitants or more which lie outside the urban fringes of cities of 50,000 inhabitants or more. Because local practice as to incorporation varies considerably from one part of the country to another, some States have very few if any such unincorporated places and others have a great many. Although there are also unincorporated places within the urban fringe, it was not feasible to establish boundaries for such places, and, therefore, they are not separately identified.

Urban places.—In the 1950 Census urban places comprise incorporated and unincorporated places of 2,500 inhabitants or more. Because incorporated places of fewer than 2,500 which lie in the urban fringe are not recognized as urban places and because unincorporated places of 2,500 or more are not identified in the urban fringe, the total population of urban places is somewhat less than the total urban population.

FARM POPULATION—RURAL AND URBAN

The farm population for 1950, as for 1940 and 1930, includes all persons living on farms without regard to occupation. In determining farm and nonfarm residence in the 1950 Census, however, certain special groups were classified otherwise than in earlier censuses. In 1950, persons living on what might have been considered farm land were classified as nonfarm if they paid cash rent for their homes and yards only. A few persons in institutions, summer camps, "motels," and tourist camps were classified as farm residents in 1940, whereas in 1950 all such persons were classified as nonfarm. For the United States as a whole, there is evidence from the Current Population Survey that the farm population in 1950 would have been about 9 percent larger had the 1940 procedure been used.

In most tables, data by farm residence are presented for the rural-farm population only, since virtually all of the farm population is located in rural areas. Only 1.2 percent of the farm population lived in urban areas in 1950. Figures on the urban-farm population are shown in tables 13, 34, 42, and 50.

RURAL-NONFARM POPULATION

The rural-nonfarm population includes all persons living outside urban areas who do not live on farms. In 1940 and earlier, persons living in the suburbs of cities constituted a large proportion of the rural-nonfarm population. The effect of the new urban-rural definition has been to change the classification of a considerable number of such persons to urban. The rural-nonfarm population is, therefore, somewhat more homogeneous than under the old definition. It still comprises, however, persons living in a variety of types of residences, such as isolated nonfarm homes in the open country, villages and hamlets of fewer than 2,500 inhabitants, and some of the fringe areas surrounding the smaller incorporated places.

FIGURE 6-12 (Continued)

of Employment Security. The usefulness of data published for any of these areas was limited by this lack of comparability.

Accordingly, the Bureau of the Census in cooperation with a number of other Federal agencies, under the leadership of the Bureau of the Budget, established the "standard metropolitan area" so that a wide variety of statistical data might be presented on a uniform basis. Since counties instead of minor civil divisions are used as the basic component of standard metropolitan areas except in the New England States, it was felt that many more kinds of statistics could be compiled for them than for metropolitan districts. These new areas supersede not only the metropolitan districts but also the industrial areas and certain other similar areas used by other Federal agencies.

Definitions

Except in New England, a standard metropolitan area is a county or group of contiguous counties which contains at least one city of 50,000 inhabitants or more. In addition to the county, or counties, containing such a city, or cities, contiguous counties are included in a standard metropolitan area if according to certain criteria they are essentially metropolitan in character and socially and economically integrated with the central city. For a description of the standard metropolitan areas in this State, if any, see p. xxx.

Criteria of metropolitan character.—These criteria relate primarily to the character of the county as a place of work or as a home for concentrations of nonagricultural workers and their dependents. Specifically, these criteria are:

1. The county must (a) contain 10,000 nonagricultural workers, or (b) contain 10 percent of the nonagricultural workers working in the standard metropolitan area, or (c) have at least one-half of its population residing in minor civil divisions with a population density of 150 or more per square mile and contiguous to the central city.

2. Nonagricultural workers must constitute at least two-thirds of the total number of employed persons of the county.

Criteria of integration.—The criteria of integration relate primarily to the extent of economic and social communication between the outlying counties and the central county as indicated by such items as the following:

1. Fifteen percent or more of the workers residing in the contiguous county work in the county containing the largest city in the standard metropolitan area, or

2. Twenty-five percent or more of the persons working in the contiguous county reside in the county containing the largest city in the standard metropolitan area, or

3. The number of telephone calls per month to the county containing the largest city of the standard metropolitan area from the contiguous county is four or more times the number of subscribers in the contiguous county.

Areas in New England.—In New England, the city and town are administratively more important than the county, and data are compiled locally for such minor civil divisions. Here towns and cities were the units used in defining standard metropolitan areas, and some of the criteria set forth above could not be applied. In their place, a population density criterion of 150 or more persons per square mile, or 100 or more persons per square mile where strong integration was evident, has been used.

Central cities.—Although there may be several cities of 50,000 or more in a standard metropolitan area, not all are necessarily central cities. The largest city in a standard metropolitan area is the principal central city. Any other city of 25,000 or more within a standard metropolitan area having a population amounting to one-third or more of the population of the principal city is also a central city. However, no more than three cities have been defined as central cities of any standard metropolitan area. The name of every central city is included in the name of the area, with the exception that in the case of the New York–Northeastern New Jersey Standard Metropolitan Area, "Jersey City" and "Newark"

are not part of the name. Data for standard metropolitan areas located in two or more States are presented in the report for the State containing the principal central city.

Difference Between Standard Metropolitan Areas and Metropolitan Districts

Since the metropolitan district was built up from minor civil divisions and since the standard metropolitan area is usually composed of whole counties, the standard metropolitan area ordinarily includes a larger territory than the corresponding metropolitan district. There are, however, cases in which parts of the metropolitan district, as defined in 1940, do not fall within any standard metropolitan area. It is also true that in a number of cases single metropolitan districts of 1940 have been split into two standard metropolitan areas. Many metropolitan districts would have been changed, of course, had they been brought up to date for 1950.

In general then, the two kinds of areas are not comparable. Since metropolitan districts were defined almost wholly in terms of density and standard metropolitan areas include whole counties selected on the basis of more complicated criteria, the population density of the standard metropolitan areas is considerably lower on the average and shows more variation from one area to another. Differences between the two types of areas are relatively small in New England, and would have been even less had the metropolitan districts been brought up to date.

Difference Between Standard Metropolitan Areas and Urbanized Areas

The standard metropolitan area can be characterized as the metropolitan community as distinguished from both the legal city and the physical city. Standard metropolitan areas are larger than urbanized areas and in most cases contain an entire urbanized area. However, in a few instances, the fact that the boundaries of standard metropolitan areas are determined by county lines, and those of urbanized areas by the pattern of urban growth, means that there are small segments of urbanized areas which lie outside standard metropolitan areas. In general then, urbanized areas represent the thickly settled urban core of the standard metropolitan areas, with the exceptions noted above. Because of discontinuities in land settlement, there are also some cases in which a single standard metropolitan area contains two urbanized areas. The lists of urbanized areas and of standard metropolitan areas also differ somewhat because the former had to be established for cities of 50,000 or more before 1950, whereas the latter were established for cities of 50,000 or more as determined in the 1950 Census.

QUALITY OF DATA FOR SMALL AREAS

Data for the smaller areas represent the work of only a few enumerators (often only one or two). The misinterpretation by an enumerator of the instructions for a particular item may, therefore, have an appreciable effect on the statistics for a very small community—e. g., places of less than 10,000 inhabitants and particularly places of less than 2,500 inhabitants—even though it would have a negligible effect upon the figures for a large area.

URBANIZED AREAS,
STANDARD METROPOLITAN AREAS,
AND CERTAIN OTHER TERMS.

(SOURCE: CENSUS OF POPULATION: 1950,
VOLUME II, CHARACTORISTICS
OF POPULATION. PP. XIV—XV.)

FIGURE 6-12 (Continued)   **Nevada**

(Source: U.S. Census of Population, 1960)

To improve its measure of the urban population, the Bureau of the Census adopted, in 1950, the concept of the urbanized area and delineated, in advance of enumeration, boundaries for unincorporated places. All the population residing in urban-fringe areas and in unincorporated places of 2,500 or more is classified as urban according to the "current" definition. The urban towns, townships, and counties as defined for the 1960 Census are somewhat similar in concept to the minor civil divisions classified as urban under special rules in 1940 and 1930.

For the convenience of those interested in the historical trend of the urban and rural population, the 1950 and 1960 population figures are shown on the basis of both the "current" definition and the "previous" definition. Although the Bureau of the Census has employed other definitions of "urban" in prior years, the urban and rural population figures published here as according to the "previous" definition have been revised to present a substantially consistent series.

Counties.—The primary divisions of the States are, in general, termed counties, but in Louisiana these divisions are known as parishes. There are no counties in Alaska; in this State, data are shown for election districts, which are the nearest equivalents of counties. In some States (Maryland, Missouri, and Virginia), there are also a number of cities which are independent of any county organization and thus constitute primary divisions of their States.

Minor civil divisions.—To the primary political divisions into which counties or comparable areas are divided, the Bureau of the Census applies the general term "minor civil divisions." Statistics on the population of each county or comparable area by minor civil divisions appear in table 7. Incorporated places which are not themselves minor civil divisions and unincorporated places are shown indented under the minor civil divisions in which they are located. When an incorporated or unincorporated place lies in more than one minor civil division, the population of the several parts is shown in table 7 under the appropriate minor civil division, and each part is designated as "part." The total population of such places appears in table 8. Unincorporated places are designated by "U" and urban towns and townships by "UT." Changes effected between 1950 and 1960 in boundaries of the areas are shown in the notes at the end of table 7. Boundary changes occurring between 1940 and 1950 are given in table 6 of State reports of the 1950 Census of Population.

Places.—The term "place" as used in reports of the decennial censuses refers to a concentration of population, regardless of the existence of legally prescribed limits, powers, or functions. Most of the places listed are incorporated as cities, towns, villages, or boroughs, however. In addition, the larger unincorporated places outside the urbanized areas were delineated and those with a population of 1,000 or more are presented in the same manner as incorporated places of equal size. Each unincorporated place possesses a definite nucleus of residences and has its boundaries drawn so as to include, if feasible, all the surrounding closely settled area. Furthermore, unincorporated places are shown within urbanized areas if they have 10,000 inhabitants or more and if there was an expression of local interest in their recognition. The towns in New England and townships in New Jersey and Pennsylvania recognized as urban are also counted as places.

Incorporated places.—Political units recognized as incorporated places in the reports of the decennial censuses are those which are incorporated as cities, boroughs, towns, and villages with the exception that towns are not recognized as incorporated places in the New England States, New York, and Wisconsin. The towns in these States are minor civil divisions similar to the townships found in other States and not necessarily thickly settled centers of population such as the cities, boroughs, towns, and villages in

other States. Similarly, in New Jersey and Pennsylvania, where some townships possess powers and functions similar to those of incorporated places, the townships are not classified as "incorporated places." Thus some minor civil divisions which are "incorporated" in one legal sense of the word are not regarded by the Census Bureau as "incorporated places." Without this restriction all of the towns in the New England States, New York, and Wisconsin and the townships in New Jersey and Pennsylvania would have to be counted as incorporated places without any consideration of the nature of population settlement. A number of towns and townships in these States do qualify, however, as urban towns or townships and in others the densely settled portions are recognized as unincorporated places or as parts of an urban fringe.

Unincorporated places.—As in the 1950 Census, the Bureau has delineated boundaries for densely settled population centers without corporate limits. All such places of 1,000 inhabitants or more are shown in tables 7 and 8. Population data for 1950 are shown only for those unincorporated places which had the same name in both 1950 and 1960. Of course, the boundaries of many such places have changed as the communities have grown.

Urban places.—The count of urban places in 1960 includes all incorporated and unincorporated places of 2,500 inhabitants or more, and the towns, townships, and counties classified as urban. Under the "previous" urban definition, places of 2,500 or more and the areas urban under special rules were urban places.

Annexations.—The population figure for an incorporated place at earlier censuses applies to the area of the place at the time of the given census. Hence, the indicated change in population over the decade reflects the effect of any annexations or detachments. In order to permit an analysis of the relative importance of population growth within the old boundaries and of population added in annexed territory, table 9 for incorporated places of 2,500 or more has been included in this report. There were a great many annexations to cities in the decade of the 1950's, and some of them involved large areas.

Urbanized areas.—The major objective of the Bureau of the Census in delineating urbanized areas was to provide a better separation of urban and rural population in the vicinity of the larger cities, but individual urbanized areas have proved to be useful statistical areas. They correspond to what are called "conurbations" in some other countries. An urbanized area contains at least one city of 50,000 inhabitants or more in 1960,[1] as well as the surrounding closely settled incorporated places and unincorporated areas that meet the criteria listed below. All persons residing in an urbanized area are included in the urban population.

It appeared desirable to delineate the urbanized areas in terms of the 1960 Census results rather than prior to the census as was done in 1950. For this purpose a peripheral zone around each 1950 urbanized area and around cities that were presumably approaching a population of 50,000 was recognized. Within the unincorporated parts of this zone small enumeration districts were planned,[2] usually including no more than one square mile of land area and no more than 75 housing units.

Arrangements were made to include within the urbanized area those enumeration districts meeting specified criteria of population density as well as adjacent incorporated places. Since the urbanized area outside of incorporated places was defined in terms of enumeration districts, the boundaries for the most part follow such features as roads, streets, railroads, streams, and other clearly defined lines which may be easily identified by census enumerators in the field and often do not conform to the boundaries of political units.

[1] There are a few urbanized areas where there are "twin central cities" that have a combined population of at least 50,000. See the section below on "Standard Metropolitan Statistical Areas" for further discussion of twin central cities, neither of which has a population of 50,000 or more.

[2] An enumeration district (ED) is a small area assigned to an enumerator which must be canvassed and reported separately. In most cases an ED contains approximately 250 housing units.

FIGURE 6-12 (Continued)   **Number of Inhabitants**

In addition to its central city or cities, an urbanized area also contains the following types of contiguous areas, which together constitute its urban fringe:

1. Incorporated places with 2,500 inhabitants or more
2. Incorporated places with less than 2,500 inhabitants, provided each has a closely settled area of 100 dwelling units or more
3. Towns in the New England States, townships in New Jersey and Pennsylvania, and counties elsewhere which are classified as urban
4. Enumeration districts in unincorporated territory with a population density of 1,000 inhabitants or more per square mile (The area of large nonresidential tracts devoted to such urban land uses as railroad yards, factories, and cemeteries, was excluded in computing the population density of an enumeration district.)
5. Other enumeration districts in unincorporated territory with lower population density provided that they served one of the following purposes:
   a. To eliminate enclaves
   b. To close indentations in the urbanized area of one mile or less across the open end
   c. To link outlying enumeration districts of qualifying density that were no more than 1½ miles from the main body of the urbanized area.

Contiguous urbanized areas with central cities in the same standard metropolitan statistical area are combined. Urbanized areas with central cities in different standard metropolitan statistical areas are not combined, except that a single urbanized area was established in the New York–Northeastern New Jersey Standard Consolidated Area, and in the Chicago–Northwestern Indiana Standard Consolidated Area.

The boundaries of the urbanized areas for 1960 will not conform to those for 1950, partly because of actual changes in land use and density of settlement, and partly because of relatively minor changes in the rules used to define the boundaries. The changes in the rules include the following:

1. The use of enumeration districts to construct the urbanized areas in 1960 resulted in a less precise definition than in 1950 when the limits were selected in the field using individual blocks as the unit of area added. On the other hand, the 1960 procedures produced an urbanized area based on the census results rather than an area defined about a year before the census, as in 1950.
2. Unincorporated territory was included in the 1950 urbanized area if it contained at least 500 dwelling units per square mile, which is somewhat different criterion than the 1,000 persons or more per square mile of the included 1960 unincorporated areas.
3. The 1960 areas include those entire towns in New England, townships in New Jersey and Pennsylvania, and counties that are classified as urban in accordance with the criteria listed in the section on urban-rural residence. The 1950 criteria permitted the exclusion of portions of these particular minor civil divisions.

In general, however, the urbanized areas of 1950 and 1960 are based on essentially the same concept, and the figures for a given urbanized area may be used to measure the population growth of that area.

An urbanized area may be thought of as divided into the central city, or cities, and the remainder of the area, or the urban fringe. Any city in an urbanized area which is a central city of a standard metropolitan statistical area (see the following section) is also a central city of the urbanized area. With but two exceptions, the names of the central cities appear in the titles of the areas. The central cities of the New York–Northeastern New Jersey Area are the central cities of the New York, Newark, Jersey City, and Paterson–Clifton–Passaic Standard Metropolitan Statistical Areas. Likewise, the central cities of the Chicago–Northwestern Indiana Area are the central cities of the Chicago and Gary–Hammond–East Chicago Standard Metropolitan Statistical Areas.

Data for the entire urbanized area are shown in this report in table 10 for each State in which a central city of the area is located. If that part of an urbanized area that extends into another State does not include a central city, data are shown only for that part within the State.

Standard metropolitan statistical areas.—It has been long recognized that for many types of social and economic analysis it is necessary to consider as a unit the entire population in and around the city whose activities form an integrated social and economic system. Prior to the 1950 Census, areas of this type had been defined in somewhat different ways for different purposes and by various agencies. Leading examples were the metropolitan districts of the Census of Population, the industrial areas of the Census of Manufactures, and the labor market areas of the Bureau of Employment Security. To permit all Federal statistical agencies to utilize the same areas for the publication of general-purpose statistics, the Bureau of the Budget has established standard metropolitan statistical areas (SMSA's).[3]

Except in New England, an SMSA is a county or group of contiguous counties which contains at least one city of 50,000 inhabitants or more or "twin cities" with a combined population of at least 50,000. In addition to the county, or counties, containing such a city or cities, contiguous counties are included in an SMSA if, according to certain criteria, they are essentially metropolitan in character and are socially and economically integrated with the central city. The criteria followed in the delineation of SMSA's relate to a city, or cities, of sufficient population size to constitute the central city and to the economic and social relationships with contiguous counties that are metropolitan in character.

1. Each SMSA must include at least:
   a. One city with 50,000 inhabitants or more, or
   b. Two cities having contiguous boundaries and constituting, for general economic and social purposes, a single community with a combined population of at least 50,000, the smaller of which must have a population of at least 15,000.
2. If two or more adjacent counties each have a city of 50,000 inhabitants or more and the cities are within 20 miles of each other (city limits to city limits), they will be included in the same area unless there is definite evidence that the two cities are not economically and socially integrated.

The criteria of metropolitan character relate primarily to the attributes of the outlying county as a place of work or as a home for a concentration of nonagricultural workers. Specifically, these criteria are:

3. At least 75 percent of the labor force of the county must be in the nonagricultural labor force.
4. In addition to criterion 3, the county must meet at least one of the following conditions:
   a. It must have 50 percent or more of its population living in contiguous minor civil divisions with a density of at least 150 persons per square mile, in an unbroken chain of minor civil divisions with such density radiating from a central city in the area.
   b. The number of nonagricultural workers employed in the county must equal at least 10 percent of the number of nonagricultural workers employed in the county containing the largest city in the area, or the outlying county must be the place of employment of at least 10,000 nonagricultural workers.
   c. The nonagricultural labor force living in the county must equal at least 10 percent of the nonagricultural labor force living in the county containing the largest city in the area, or the outlying county must be the place of residence of a nonagricultural labor force of at least 10,000.
5. In New England, the city and town are administratively more important than the county, and data are compiled locally for such minor civil divisions. Here, towns and cities are the units used in defining SMSA's. In New England, because smaller units are used and more restricted areas result, a population density of at least 100 persons per square mile is used as the measure of metropolitan character.

The criteria of integration relate primarily to the extent of economic and social communication between the outlying counties and the central county.

6. A county is regarded as integrated with the county or counties containing the central cities of the area if either of the following criteria is met:
   a. If 15 percent of the workers living in the given outlying county work in the county or counties containing the central city or cities of the area, or

[3] See also the Bureau of the Budget publication *Standard Metropolitan Statistical Areas*, U.S. Government Printing Office, Washington 25, D.C., 1959.

FIGURE 6-12 (Conclusion) Nevada

b. If 25 percent of those working in the given outlying county live in the county or counties containing the central city or cities of the area.

Only where data for criteria 6a and 6b are not conclusive are other related types of information used. This information includes such items as average telephone calls per subscriber per month from the county to the county containing central cities of the area; percent of the population in the county located in the central city telephone exchange area; newspaper circulation reports prepared by the Audit Bureau of Circulation; analysis of charge accounts in retail stores of central cities to determine the extent of their use by residents of the contiguous county; delivery service practices of retail stores in central cities; official traffic counts; the extent of public transportation facilities in operation between central cities and communities in the contiguous county; and the extent to which local planning groups and other civic organizations operate jointly.

7. Although there may be several cities of 50,000 or more in an SMSA, not all are necessarily central cities. The following criteria are used for determining central cities:

a. The largest city in an SMSA is always a central city.
b. In addition, one or two additional cities may be secondary central cities on the basis and in the order of the following criteria:
   (1) The additional city or cities have at least 250,000 inhabitants.
   (2) The additional city or cities have a population of one-third or more of that of the largest city and a minimum population of 25,000, except that both cities are central cities in those instances where cities qualify under criterion 1b. (A city which qualified as a secondary central city in 1950 but which does not

qualify in 1960 has been temporarily retained as a central city.)

8. The titles of the SMSA's consist of the names of the central cities followed by the names of the States in which the areas are located.

In this report, data for SMSA's which cross State lines are shown in full in table 11 for each State in which a central city is located. If that part of an SMSA that extends into another State does not include a central city, data are shown only for the part within the State. In table 12 only that part of the SMSA which is within the State is shown.

In the 1950 Census reports, data were presented for standard metropolitan areas (SMA's) and in several earlier censuses a somewhat similar type of area called the "metropolitan district" was used. In 1959, the criteria for delineating SMA's were revised by the Bureau of the Budget, and, at the same time, the areas were designated as standard metropolitan statistical areas. The comparative figures shown here for 1950 apply to the SMSA as defined in 1960.

Standard consolidated areas.—In view of the special importance of the metropolitan complexes around New York and Chicago, the Nation's largest cities, several contiguous SMSA's and additional counties that do not appear to meet the formal integration criteria but do have strong interrelationships of other kinds have been combined into the New York–Northeastern New Jersey and the Chicago–Northwestern Indiana Standard Consolidated Areas, respectively. The former is identical with the New York–Northeastern New Jersey SMA of 1950, and the latter corresponds roughly to the Chicago SMA (two more counties having been added).

---

eight sheets. Index maps for the latter areas are reproduced as Figures 6-3 and 6-4.

4. State Economic Areas. The 1950 Census of Agriculture and some data from the censuses of population and housing are presented for a new unit called state economic areas. These are groupings of counties "having similar agricultural, demographic, climatic physiographic, and cultural characteristics." See the Special Report of the 1950 Census, "State Economic Areas: A Description of the Procedure Used in Making a Functional Grouping of the Counties in the United States."

Some census data are also reported by areas smaller than the central city and its larger suburban municipalities and townships.

1. Unincorporated Places. For the first time, unincorporated concentrations of 1,000 or more people were listed and data reported for them in the 1950 censuses of population and housing. Unfortunately, unincorporated places within the urban fringe (urbanized areas) were not identified. For the 1960 Census, see the statement of the Bureau of the Census reproduced in Figure 6-12.

2. Census Tracts. "Census Tracts are small areas, having a population usually between 3,000 and 6,000, into which certain large cities (and sometimes their adjacent areas) have been subdivided for statistical and local administrative purposes." Separate bulletins were published for 62 cities in 1950. For 43 of these cities, adjacent areas had also been tracted. In 1960, the number of urban areas divided into census tracts was considerably larger. All of 135 standard metropolitan statistical areas and parts of

43 additional areas have been tracted. Tables showing the kinds of data published by census tracts are reproduced in Chapter VII of this book. One limitation of census tracts is that they are bounded by streets. The result is that opposite sides of a boundary street lie in different tracts. This may often make it unsafe to equate census tracts with a "natural area." Land uses, for instance, are more likely to change in the middle of a block than in the center of a street. See Foley, "Census Tracts and Urban Research" (47).

3. Census Enumeration Districts. Housing and population data have been tabulated but not published for each of the districts in which an enumerator took the census. The breakdown of data by these districts will be especially useful for communities that have not been divided into census tracts. In Middletown, Connecticut, for instance, the use of data tabulated by enumeration districts made it possible to subtract the population of three large institutions from the data published for the town. Age and sex distributions were quite different—and more like the normal pattern--after subtracting the population of the three enumeration districts that consisted for the most part of the inmates of a state school for girls, the patients of a state hospital for the mentally ill, and the students of Wesleyan University.

4. Blocks. Certain housing data are available by blocks. Data on dwelling units by occupancy, occupied dwelling units by color, condition, and plumbing facilities, persons per room, average contract rent, and average value are published in 1960 block bulletins. Other housing data are available from the Bureau of the Census at the cost of compilation or reproduction.

FIGURE 6-13

Catalog of United States Census Publications

JANUARY-JUNE 1953

United States Government Printing Office
Washington : 1953

or sale by the Superintendent of Documents, U. S. Government Printing Office, Washington 25, D. C.

Sinclair Weeks, *Secretary*

INDEX TO REPORTS BY SUBJECTS

indexing of large groups of commodities, general references
se instances where coverage is all-inclusive; reports are
commodities when they are limited to a specific item.

INDEX TO REPORTS BY GEOGRAPHIC AREAS

Census Regions
Census Divisions
Cities
Counties
Standard Metropolitan Areas
States
Territories and possessions
Urban and/or Rural Areas

To avoid the indexing of la
in those instances
ommoditi

Barley — special import reports.
3–10 (FT 550, FT 587)
5–2 (M75A)
es in dwelling units__ 6–12
plugs, starting, light-
equipment, special
3–10 (FT 3009)
ture, household.
5–2 (M54A)
5–2 (M15S)
cial import re-
3–10 (FT 546)
1–10 (Vol. II)
e of foreign
7–3
cial import
3–10 (FT 555)
6–11
6–20 (P-90)
belts
rt.
0 (FT 679)
–2 (M67H)
2 (M31E)
(M77E)
(M51N)
M25A)
26B)
15C)
–10
II)
–3

Page
73

Cities

Marital status — 6–11
Married couples — 6–12
Migration, special census — 6–11
Milan, Ind., special census — 6–11
Mortgage status of dwelling units — 6–11
Nativity and citizenship — 4–2
Nonwhite population — 6–12
Occupancy and tenure — 4–2
Occupation groups — 6–12
Oxnard, Calif., special census — 6–20 (P-28)
Payrolls, city — 6–11
Pelzer, S. C., special census — 6–12
Perris, Calif., special census — 4–2
Place of birth — 6–11
Plumbing facilities — 6–12
Race of population — 6–11

Standard Metropolitan Areas

Married couples — 6–12
Migration — 6–11
Mortgage status of dwelling units — 6–11
Nativity — 6–12
Nativity and citizenship — 6–11
Nonfarm dwelling units — 6–11
Nonwhite population, housing — 6–11
Nonwhite population — 6–12
Occupancy and tenure, housing — 6–11, 6
Occupation groups, employed persons — 6–12

San Clemente, Calif., special census — 6–20 (P-28)
San Diego, Calif., special census — 6–20 (P-28)
San Jose, Calif., special census — 6–20 (P-28)
Santa Ana, Calif., special census — 6–20 (P-28)
School:
Enrollment by age — 6–11
Years completed — 6–11
South Gate, Calif., special census — 6–20 (P-28)
Spanish surname — 4–2
Taxes, city — 4–2
Television — 6–11
Toilet facilities, dwelling units — 6–11
Unemployment — 6–11
Utilities, city, or city-operated — 6–20 (P-28)
Vacant dwelling units — 6–11
Vallejo, Calif., special census — 6–20 (P-28)
Value of dwelling units — 6–11
Warren, Ark., special census, Territory Annex
Water supply — 6–11

facilities in dwelling units — 6–20 (P-28)
ntry of
nativity
selected — 6–11
persons per, dwelling units
and/or unfilled orders, retail
special census — 6–20 (P-28)
townships, selected — 6–11
government: — 6–12
dence — 6–11
t systems, city — 2–21
trade — 4–2
 nt contract gross monthly
frigeration equipment — 6–11
adios — 6–12

mily — 4–2
Calif., special census — 6–20 (P-28)
stry — 6–12
surance trust revenue and expenditure — 6–11
tergovernmental revenue and expenditure — 6–11
S. C., special census — 6–20 (P-28)
ks in dwelling units — 6–20 (P-28)

with or without — 6–11
6–20 (P-28)
6–12

household population
nt of gross monthly
ulation — 6–11
farm properties
units — 6–12

household facilities
plumbing facilities

schools

units
cts of harvested
75 es.
including
os of irrigation water
welling units

FIGURE 6-14
(1950 Census of Population)

GENERAL CHARACTERISTICS

SUBJECTS PRESENTED BY TYPE OF AREA AND TABLE NUMBER

[Sex not indexed separately as practically all tables include distributions by sex]

Subject	State		Standard metropolitan areas, urbanized areas, and urban places of 10,000 or more	Urban places of 2,500 to 10,000	Places of 1,000 to 2,500	Counties		
	Total	Urban-rural				Total	Rural nonfarm	Rural farm
	Table	*Table*	*Table*	*Table*	*Table*	*Table*	*Table*	*Table*
Summary	10	10	10	11		12		
Age	15	15	33	38	40	41	48	49
By color	15	15	33	[1]38		41	[1]48	[1]49
1940–1950	15	15	33			41		
By color	15	15						
1880–1950, by color	16							
Citizenship	17	17	34			42		
1930–1950	17							
Class of worker of employed persons	28	28	35	39		43		
By color	[1]28a	[1]28a	[1]36			[1]44		
1940–1950	29							
Country of birth	24	24	[2]34a	[2]38		[2]42		
Education:								
School enrollment, by age	18	18	34			42		
1910–1950	19							
Years of school completed	20	20	34	38		42	48	49
By color	20	20	[1]36			[1]44	[1]48a	[1]49a
1940–1950	20							
Families, unrelated individuals, and households	22	22	34			42		
Income in 1949 of families and unrelated individuals	32	32	37	39		45	[3]46	
By color	[1]32a	[1]32a	[1]37a			[1]45a		
Industry of employed persons	30	30	35	39		43		
By color	[1]30a	[1]30a	[1]36			[1]44		
1940–1950	31							
Institutional population	22	22	34			42		
Labor force:								
Employment status	25	25	35	39		43	48	49
By color	25	25	36			44	[1]48a	[1]49a
1940–1950	27							
Labor force, 1940–1950, and gainful workers, 1920–1930, by color	26							
Marital status	21	21	34	38		42		
By color	21	21	[1]36			[1]44		
1940–1950	21							
Married couples	22	22	34			42		
By color			[1]36			[1]44		
Nativity	17	17	34	38		42	48	49
1930–1950	17							
Occupation:								
Experienced civilian labor force	28	28						
Employed persons	28	28	35	39		43	48	49
By color	[1]28a	[1]28a	[1]36			[1]44	[1]48a	[1]49a
1940–1950	29							
Experienced unemployed persons	28	28	35			43		
Race	14	14	34, [4]47	38	40	42, [4]47	48	49
1880–1950	14							
Residence in 1949	23	23	34			42		
By color	[1]23	[1]23						
Urban-rural residence:								
Rural-farm population in places of 1,000 to 2,500					40			
Urban-farm population	13	13	34			42		
1930–1950, by color	13	13						
1950 population based on old urban-rural definition	13	13				50	50	50
By age and color	15	15				50	50	50
For urban-farm population	13	13				50		

[1] For Southern States only.
[2] Southern States excluded.
[3] For urban and rural-nonfarm parts of counties combined.
[4] For selected cities and counties.

FIGURE 6-15
(1950 Census of Population)

DETAILED CHARACTERISTICS

SUBJECTS PRESENTED BY TYPE OF AREA AND TABLE NUMBER

[Sex not indexed separately as all tables include distributions by sex]

Subject	State		Standard metropolitan areas		Cities		
	Total	Urban-rural	250,000 or more	100,000 to 250,000	250,000 or more	100,000 to 250,000	50,000 100,00
	Table	Table	Table	Table	Table	Table	Tabl
AGE *cross-classified with—*							
Citizenship, by color	55				55	55	
Color, by single years of age	51	52			51		
Education:							
Kindergarten enrollment, by single years of age and color [1]	61	61			61	61	
School enrollment, by single years of age and color [1]	62	62			62	62	
School enrollment, by single years of age, 1940–1950	62						
Year of school in which enrolled, by single years of age and color [1]	63	63			63	63	
Years of school completed for persons 5 to 24 years old, by single years of age and color [1]	64	64	64		64		
Years of school completed for persons 5 to 24 years old, by single years of age, 1940–1950	64						
Years of school completed for persons 25 years old and over, by color [1]	65	65	65	65	65	65	
Years of school completed for persons 25 years old and over, 1940–1950	65						
Income	89	²89	89				
Industry of employed persons	82		82				
Labor force:							
Employment status, by color [1]	66	66	66	66	66	66	
Employment status, by hours worked, school enrollment and color [1]	71	71	71				
Labor force status, by marital status and color [1]	70	70	70	70			
Labor force status, 1940–1950	69						
Status of employed persons	67	67	67	67	67	67	
Status of persons not in the labor force, by color [1]	68	68	68	68	68	68	
Marital status and presence of spouse, by color [1]	57	57	57	57	57	57	
Marital status, 1890–1950	56						
Nativity, by color	54						
Nativity of the white population	53	53	53	53	53	53	
Nativity of the white population, by single years of age	51				51		
Occupation of employed persons, by color [1]	76		76				
Quasi-household population, by color [1]	60	60	60	60			
Race	53	53	53	53	53	53	
Relationship to household head, by color [1]	58	58	58	58			
OCCUPATION *cross-classified with—*							
Age of employed persons, by color [1]	76		76				
Class of worker of employed persons	77		77	77			
Detailed occupation of the experienced civilian labor force and of employed persons	73		73	73	73	73	
Detailed occupation of employed persons, 1940–1950	74						
Income of the experienced civilian labor force	78		78				
Industry of employed persons (major occupation group only)	84		84				
Occupation of the experienced civilian labor force and of employed persons		75					
Race of employed persons	77		77	77			
INDUSTRY *cross-classified with—*							
Age of employed persons	82		82				
Class of worker of employed persons	83		83	83			
Detailed industry of the experienced civilian labor force and of employed persons	79		79	79	79	79	
Detailed industry of employed persons 1940–1950	80						
Income of the experienced civilian labor force	86		86				
Industry of employed persons							
Occupation of employed persons (major occupation group only)	84		84				
Race of employed persons	83		83	83			
Weeks worked in 1949 by the experienced civilian labor force	85		85				
TOTAL INCOME IN 1949 OF PERSONS *cross-classified with—*							
Age	89	²89	89				
Class of worker of the experienced civilian labor force	92	²92	92				
Family status	90	²90	90				
Income, by color [1]	88	88					
Industry of the experienced civilian labor force	86		86				
Occupation of the experienced civilian labor force	78		78				
Race	87	²87	87	87	87	87	
Type of income	93	²93	93				
Weeks worked in 1949	91	²91	91				
OTHER SUBJECTS							
Quasi-household population, by color [1]	59	59	59	59	59	59	
Quasi-household population, 1940–1950	59						
Relationship to household head, by color [1]	59	59	59	59	59	59	
Relationship to household head, 1940–1950	59						
Wage or salary income of the experienced labor force in 1949	94		94		94	94	
Wage or salary income of the experienced labor force, 1939–1949	94						
Weeks worked in 1949, by labor force status	72		72	72			

[1] Statistics by color shown for areas containing 50,000 nonwhite inhabitants or more; for urban-rural areas, separate statistics by color shown for Southern States only.

² For urban and rural-nonfarm parts of States combined.

FIGURE 6-16

U. S. DEPARTMENT OF COMMERCE
SINCLAIR WEEKS, *Secretary*

BUREAU OF THE CENSUS
ROBERT W. BURGESS, *Director*

A STATISTICAL ABSTRACT SUPPLEMENT

COUNTY AND CITY DATA BOOK
1952

Statistics included: For 1950, Agriculture, Area and Population, Banking, City Government Finances and Employment, Construction, Education, Family Income, Housing, Labor Force, Vital Statistics, and other subjects; for 1947 and 1950, Manufactures; for 1948, Trade and Services; and Climate.

Prepared under the direction of
MORRIS B. ULLMAN
in the Office of the Assistant Director
for Statistical Standards

UNITED STATES GOVERNMENT PRINTING OFFICE
WASHINGTON, D. C.
1953

FIGURE 6-16 (Continued)

COLUMN HEADINGS

County List—COLUMN HEADINGS FOR TABLES 1, 2, AND 3: STATES, STANDARD METROPOLITAN AREAS, AND COUNTIES

Asterisk (*) denotes items for which figures are shown for States, standard metropolitan areas, counties, and cities

Items 1–14 — AREA AND POPULATION

County	U.S. rank in population	Population, 1950		Non-white	Area and density, 1950		Urban-rural residence, 1950			Age, 1950			Migration, 1950[1]	Potential voters, 1950
		Total			Land area in square miles	Population per square mile	Urban population	Rural nonfarm population	Rural farm population	Persons under 5 years old	Persons 65 years old and over	Median age	Lived in different county or abroad in 1949	Citizens, 21 years old and over
		Number, Apr. 1	Increase, 1940 to 1950											
	1*	2*	3*	4*	5*	6*	7	8	9	10*	11*	12*	13*	14*
			Percent	Percent								Years		

Items 15–31 — VITAL STATISTICS, FAMILY INCOME, EDUCATION

Vital statistics, 1950				Number of families, 1950	Income in 1949 of families, 1950			Education, 1950								Institutional population, 1950
					Median family income	Percent having incomes—		Total persons 7 to 17 years old	School enrollment				Persons 25 years old and over			
Live births	Deaths	Infant deaths	Marriages			Less than $2,000	$5,000 or more		Persons 7 to 13 years old in school		Persons 14 to 17 years old in school		Median school years completed	Percent who completed—		
									Number	Percent	Number	Percent		Less than 5 grades	High school or more	
15*	16*	17*	18	19*	20*	21*	22*	23*	24*	25*	26*	27*	28*	29*	30*	31*
					Dols.											

Items 32–47 — LABOR FORCE

Labor force, 1950															
Persons 14 years old and over				Employed persons by selected major industry groups											
Total	Number in civilian labor force	Males	Females	Total employed[1]	Agriculture	Mining	Construction	Manufacturing	Transportation, communication and other public utilities	Wholesale and retail trade	Finance, insurance, and real estate	Business and personal services, excluding private households	Professional and related services	Percent of employed—	
		Percent in total labor force	Percent in total labor force											In agriculture	In manufacturing
32*	33*	34*	35*	36*	37	38	39*	40*	41*	42	43*	44*	45*	46	47*

Items 48–65 — HOUSING

Total dwelling units, 1940	Housing, 1950																
	All dwelling units						Occupied dwelling units							Nonfarm dwelling units			
	Total number	Median number of rooms per unit	Percent of dwelling units—				Total number	Median number of persons per unit	Percent of dwelling units—					Median value of one-dwelling-unit structures,[2] owner occupied	Renter-occupied	
			In one-dwelling-unit detached structures[1]	In structures built in 1940 or later	With hot running water, private toilet and bath, and not dilapidated	Vacant, available			Owner occupied	Occupied by non-white households	With central heating	With mechanical refrigerator	With radio	Total number		Median contract monthly rent	Median gross monthly rent
48*	49*	50*	51*	52*	53*	54*	55*	56*	57*	58*	59*	60*	61*	62*	63*	64*	65*
															Dols.	Dols.	Dols.

City List—COLUMN HEADINGS FOR TABLE 4: CITIES OF 25,000 INHABITANTS OR MORE—Continued

Asterisk (*) denotes items for which figures are shown for States, standard metropolitan areas, counties, and cities

Items 266-280 — TRADE AND SERVICES

Retail trade, 1948								Wholesale trade, 1948			Personal, business, and repair services, 1948			
Number of stores	Sales, entire year	Active proprietors of unincorporated businesses, Nov.	Paid employees, workweek ending nearest Nov. 15	Food group		Eating and drinking places		Number of establishments	Sales, entire year	Paid employees, workweek ending nearest Nov. 15	Number of establishments	Receipts, entire year	Active proprietors of unincorporated businesses, Nov.	Paid employees, workweek ending nearest Nov. 15
				Number of stores	Sales, entire year	Number of stores	Sales, entire year							
266*	267*	268*	269*	270*	271*	272*	273*	274*	275*	276*	277*	278*	279*	280*
	1,000 dols.				1,000 dols.		1,000 dols.		1,000 dols.			1,000 dols.		

Items 281-297 — MANUFACTURES, CONSTRUCTION, ELECTRIC CONSUMPTION

All manufacturing establishments (Census), 1947						Value of construction authorized, 1950					New dwelling units authorized, 1950				Electric energy use and bills,[1] 1950	
Number	Value added by manufacture	All employees		Production workers		All building construction	New residential building	New nonresidential building	Additions, alterations, and repairs	Valuation	Number, by type of structure				Average annual use by residential customers[2]	Typical net monthly electric bill (100 kwh.) as of Jan. 1, 1951
		Number (average for year)	Salaries and wages, total	Number (average for year)	Wages, total						In all types	In 1-family structures	In 2-family structures	In multi-family structures		
281*	282*	283*	284*	285*	286*	287	288	289	290	291	292	293	294	295	296	297
	1,000 dols.		1,000 dols.		1,000 dols.	1,000 dols.	1,000 dols.	1,000 dols.	1,000 dols.	1,000 dols.					Kwh.	Dols.

Items 298-313 — GOVERNMENT FINANCES AND EMPLOYMENT

City government finances, 1950														City government employment, Oct. 1950	
General revenue					General expenditure										
Total	Taxes		Aid received	Charges and miscellaneous	Total	Total less provision for debt retirement	Total operation	Operation—selected items				Capital outlay	Gross debt, total	Total employees	Total payroll
	Total taxes	Property						Public safety	Schools	Public welfare	Health and hospital				
298	299	300	301	302	303	304	305	306	307	308	309	310	311	312	313
1,000 dols.	1,000 dols.	1,000 dols.	1,000 dols.	1,000 dols.	1,000 dols.	1,000 dols.	1,000 dols.	1,000 dols.	1,000 dols.	1,000 dols.	1,000 dols.	1,000 dols.	1,000 dols.	Number	1,000 dols.

Items 314-333 — BANKING, SCHOOLS, HOSPITALS, CLIMATE

Banking,[1] 1950		Post Office gross receipts, 1950	City school systems, 1949-1950						Hospitals, 1950				Climate						
Bank deposits as of Dec. 30	Bank debits to deposit accounts		Total expenditure	Elementary and secondary schools	Teachers	Enrollment	Average salary of teachers	Average expenditure per pupil	Number	Beds	Admissions	Personnel	Mean temperature		Record temperature		Mean annual precipitation	Mean annual percent of possible sunshine	Mean annual degree days, 65° base
													January	July	Highest	Lowest			
314*	315	316	317	318	319	320	321	322	323	324	325	326	327	328	329	330	331	332	333
1,000 dols.	1,000 dols.	1,000 dols.	1,000 dols.	Number	Number		Dols.	Dols.			Thousands		°F.	°F.	°F.	°F.	Inches		

5. Wards. Only the total 1950 population of wards in cities over 5,000 is published. Block statistics on housing may be built up into ward totals. In some instances, rough approximations can be established between wards and census tracts.

The student should consult the 1960 Census for lists of standard metropolitan statistical areas and lists of census tract areas and of block statistics cities.

Many reports are issued by the Bureau of the Census in the interval between decennial censuses. These can be located by reference to the monthly list of census publications, cumulated twice a year into the *Catalog of United States Census Publications*. The title page and specimen sheets are reproduced as Figure 6-13.

It will pay you well to spend some time familiarizing yourself with the areas used by the Bureau of the Census because this will enable you to use many kinds of census data which would be meaningless otherwise.

Some detailed definitions of key census terms as used in the 1960 Census are reproduced in Figure 6-12. Also reproduced for your convenience is a table showing the general characteristics reported in 1950 by various areas (Fig. 6-14). A similar table is reproduced for detailed characteristics of population (Fig. 6-15). Finally, we have reproduced samples of column heads showing data to be found in the *County and City Data Book 1952*, (Fig. 6-16). The 1956 edition was issued in 1957. New editions follow each census.

REFERENCES

1. Young, P., *Scientific Social Surveys and Research*. Englewood Cliffs, N.J.: Prentice-Hall, Inc., 1956. pp. 470-72.

2. Park, R. E., "The Urban Community as a Spatial Pattern and a Moral Order" in R. E. Park, *Human Communities*. New York: The Free Press of Glencoe, Inc., 1952. pp. 165-77.

3. Duncan, O. D., R. P. Cuzzort, and B. Duncan, *Statistical Geography*. New York: The Free Press of Glencoe, Inc., 1961. pp. 14-28.

4. Hawley, A. H., *Human Ecology: A Theory of Community Structure*. New York: Copyright 1950, The Ronald Press Company.

5. Quinn, J. A., *Human Ecology*. Englewood Cliffs, N. J.: Prentice-Hall, Inc., 1950.

6. Queen, S., and D. B. Carpenter, *The American City*. New York: McGraw-Hill Book Company, Inc., 1953. pp. 95-205.

7. Anderson, W. A., and E. C. Lindeman, *Urban Sociology*. rev. ed. New York: F. S. Crofts & Co., 1935.

8. Hallenbeck, W. C., *American Urban Communities*. New York: Harper & Brothers, 1951.

9. Riemer, S., *The Modern City*. Englewood Cliffs, N.J.: Prentice-Hall, Inc., 1952.

10. Quinn, J. A., "Tropical Summary of Current Literature on Human Ecology," *American Journal of Sociology*, Vol. 46, 1940. pp. 191-226.

11. Hatt, P. K., and A. J. Reiss, Jr., eds., *Cities and Society*. 2d ed. New York: The Free Press of Glencoe, Inc., 1957.

12. Dobriner, W., ed., *The Suburban Community*. New York: G. P. Putnam's Sons, 1958.

13. Hatt, P. K., and A. J. Reiss, Jr., eds., *Reader in Urban Sociology*. New York: The Free Press of Glencoe, Inc., 1951.

14. Dickinson, R. E., *City, Region, and Regionalism: A Geographical Contribution to Human Ecology*. London: Oxford University Press, 1947.

15. Taylor, G., *Urban Geography*. 2d ed. London: Methuen & Co., Ltd., 1951.

16. James, P. E., "The Geographical Study of Population," in P. E. James and C. F. Jones, eds., *American Geography: Inventory and Prospect*. Syracuse, New York: Syracuse University Press, 1954.

17. Wright, J. J., and E. T. Platt, *Aids to Geographical Research*. 2d ed. New York: Columbia University Press, 1947.

18. Mayer, H. M., and C. F. Cohn, *Readings in Urban Geography*. Chicago: University of Chicago Press, 1959.

19. Kinneman, J. A., *The Community in American Society*. New York: Appleton-Century-Crofts, Inc., 1947. pp. 41 ff.

20. Hoyt, H., *The Structure and Growth of Residential Neighborhoods in American Cities*. Washington, D.C.: Federal Housing Administration, U.S. Government Printing Office, 1939.

21. Harris, C. D., and E. L. Ullman, "The Nature of Cities," in P. K. Hatt and A. J. Reiss, Jr., eds., *Cities and Society*. 2d ed. New York: The Free Press of Glencoe, Inc., 1957. pp. 237-47.

22. Ogburn, W. F., "Inventions of Local Transportation and the Patterns of Cities," *ibid.*, pp. 274-82.

23. Dickinson, R. E., "The Regional Relations of the City," *ibid.*, pp. 260-73.

24. Duncan, O. D., and B. Duncan, "Residential Distribution and Occupational Stratification," *ibid.*, pp. 283-96.

25. Firey, W., "Sentiment and Symbolism as Ecological Variables," in P. K. Hatt and A. J. Reiss, Jr., eds., *Reader in Urban Sociology*. New York: The Free Press of Glencoe, Inc., 1951. pp. 233-44.

26. Davie, M. R., "The Pattern of Urban Growth," *ibid.*, pp. 244-59.

27. McKenzie, R. D., *et al.*, *The Metropolitan Community*. New York: McGraw-Hill Company, Inc., 1933. pp. 191-212.

28. Federal Housing Administration, *The Structure and Growth of Residential Neighborhoods in American Cities*. Washington, D.C.: U.S. Government Printing Office, 1939.

29. Jones, V., *Metropolitan Government*. (Chicago: University of Chicago Press, 1942.

30. "Local Government Organization in Metropolitan Areas: Its Relation to Urban Development" in C. Woodbury, ed., *The Future of Cities and Urban Redevelopment*. Chicago: University of Chicago Press, 1953. Chap. 5.

31. Esser, G. H., Jr,, "Economic Aspects of Annexation," *Public Management*, August and September, 1957.

32. Scott, S., and L. Keller, *Annexation? Incorporation? A Guide for Community Action*. (Bureau of Public Administration) Berkeley, Calif.: University of California Press.

33. Government Affairs Foundation, *Metropolitan Communities: A Bibliography with Special Emphasis on Government and Politics.* Public Administration Service, 1956. pp. 162-79.

34. Jones, V., B. Hudson, and L. D. Johnston, eds., *Metropolitan Communities: Supplement for 1955-57*. Chicago: Public Administration Service, 1960. pp. 95-102.

35. Schmidt, C. F., *Handbook of Graphic Presentation*. New York: The Ronald Press Company, 1954. pp. 184, 298-301.

36. Wood, R. C., *Suburbia, Its People and Their Politics*. Boston: Houghton Mifflin Company, 1959.

37. Schattschneider, E. E., V. Jones, and S. K. Bailey, *A Guide to the Study of Public Affairs*. New York: Holt, Rinehart and Winston, Inc., 1952. Chap. 3.

38. Key, V. O., Jr., and C. Silvermann, "Party and Separation of Powers: A Panorama of Practice in the States" in C. J. Freidrich, ed., *Public Policy.*

Vol. 4. Cambridge: Harvard University Press, 1954. pp. 382-412.

39. Zeller, B., ed., *American State Legislatures: Report of the Committee on American State Legislatures of the American Political Science Association*. New York: Thomas Y. Crowell Company, 1954.

40. Dauer, M. J., and R. G. Kelsey, "Unrepresentative States," *National Municipal Review*, December 1955.

41. Merry, G. B., "Minority Rule: Challenge to Democracy, " *Christian Science Monitor*, October 2, 6, 9, 13, and 16, 1958.

42. _____, "How Minorities Help Shape Congress," *ibid*., June 2, 4, 11, and 16, 1959.

43. Strout, R. L., "The Next Election is Already Rigged," *Harper's Magazine*, November 1959.

44. Baker, G. E., *Reapportionment and Redistricting of State Legislatures*, New York: The National Municipal League, 1959.

45. Nelson, H. J., "The Vernon Area, California—A Study of the Political Factor in Urban Geography," *Annals of the Association of American Geographers*, Vol. 42, June 1952. pp. 177-91.

46. Duffus, R. L., *Mastering A Metropolis: Planning the Future of the New York Region*. New York: Harper & Brothers, 1930.

47. Foley, D. L., "Census Tracts and Urban Research," *Journal of the American Statistical Association*, December 1953, pp. 740-42.

Chapter VII

HOW TO USE CENSUS DATA IN THE STUDY OF CONGRESSIONAL AND LEGISLATIVE DISTRICTS IN METROPOLITAN AREAS

The purpose of this chapter is to suggest some quick ways in which a student studying congressional districts or state legislative districts located in the larger metropolitan areas may assemble and analyze data indicating their demographic, social, and economic characteristics. The methods described here may be applied to the study of other areas not coterminous with cities or counties.

It is difficult to secure data for many districts because they are made up of parts of large cities or of metropolitan counties. Census reports can more easily be used for the study of districts that consist of single counties or of several counties. (See Fig. 7-1.) For these districts the *County and City Data Book, 1956* is a ready source of data that can be used as indicators of the social and economic characteristics of the population. If more detail is desired, the regular census reports on population and housing can be used because most data are reported by counties. Excerpts from the principal reports of the 1950 Census of Population and the *County and City Data Book, 1952* are reproduced in Chapter VI.

If a district contains only part of a county or if it is made up of towns, as in some New England states, the student will have to be ingenious and imaginative in seeking out data that can be adapted to the area he is studying. No one should be content with data inferior to the best that is available and manageable. Frequently, however, because of exorbitant costs in time and money, it is necessary and sometimes desirable to use second-best data in a second-best manner. In this chapter, an attempt is made to show what can be done with census data on social and economic characteristics of the population in studies of metropolitan congressional districts, state legislative districts, wards, neighborhoods, or other segments smaller than cities or counties.

The short cuts suggested in this chapter should not be used as a substitute for more rigorous and time-consuming methods if the student intends to use the data for purposes other than those suggested in this book. Even though the methods described here are sufficient for his purposes,

the student should be familiar with other analyses of census tract data. In communities where typologies of subareas have been established, the resulting delimitation of these areas should be used wherever appropriate.

The principal methods of typological analysis have been described, compared, and tested by application to data for other communities by Van Arsdol, Schmid, Camilleri, and MacCannell in their study, "Methods of Differentiating Urban Social and Demographic Areas" (1). See also Shevky and Williams, *The Social Areas of Los Angeles: Analysis and Typology* (2); Shevky and Bell, *Social Area Analysis: Theory, Illustrative Application and Computational Procedures* (3); and Tryon, *Identification of Social Areas by Cluster Analysis* (4).

Our purposes, however, are different, and we do not have time for detailed computations. Therefore, let us first examine the size, shape, and constituent divisions of some typical congressional districts. Figure 7-1 is an excerpt from a 42" x 52" map of congressional districts in the United States issued by the Bureau of the Census. A map of the congressional districts in each state may also be found in the *Congressional Directory*. The larger map, however, contains insets showing the boundaries of metropolitan congressional districts and of congressional districts composed of towns. Figure 7-1 refers the user to an inset for Massachusetts which we reproduce as Figure 7-2 to illustrate a New England district composed of towns. The student is also referred to an inset for New York City, Figure 7-3. In this inset the boundaries of the twenty-two congressional districts within New York City are outlined.

We shall take two Manhattan districts, the New York Sixteenth and the New York Twenty-first, to illustrate how available census data may be organized and analyzed. Two districts, rather than one, are used because the data take on significance only when compared with those for other districts, or with the data for Manhattan, New York City, the New York sector of the New York-Northeastern New Jersey Metropolitan Area, or with the entire metropolitan area.

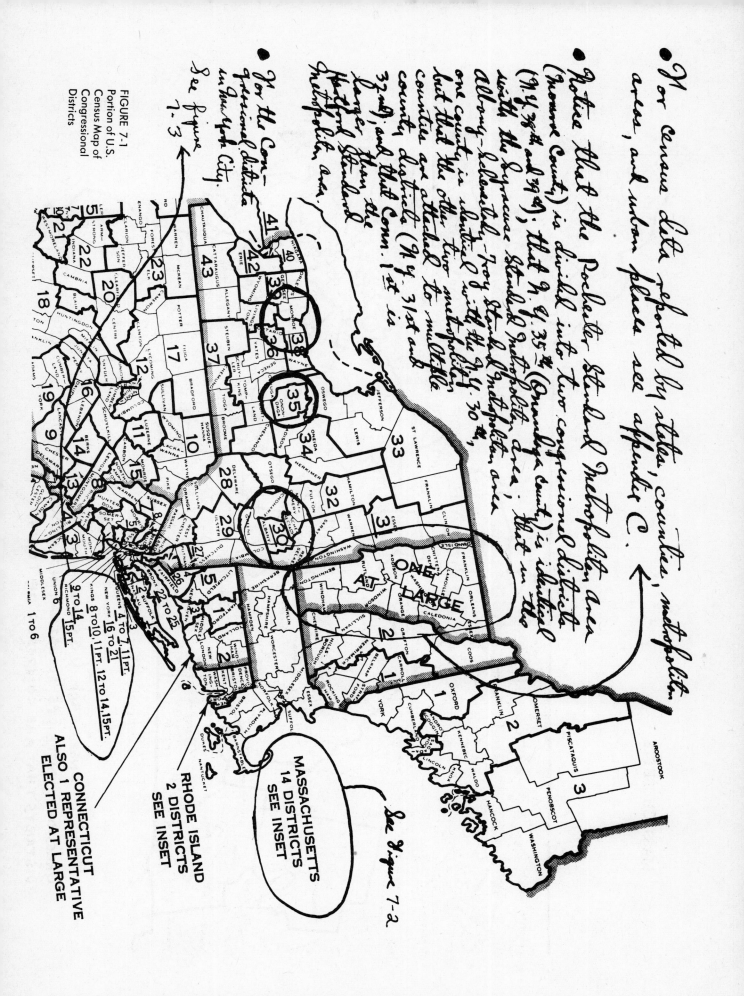

• For census data reported by states, counties, metropolitan areas, urban places, see chapter 6.

• Notice that the Rochester standard metropolitan area (Monroe County) is divided into two congressional districts (N.Y. 38th and 39th); that N.Y. 35th (Onondaga County) is identical with the Syracuse standard metropolitan area; that in the Albany-Schenectady-Troy standard metropolitan area one county is identical with the N.Y. 30th, but that the other two counties are attached to multiple counties; and that Conn. 1st is a large metropolitan area.

• For the Congressional districts in New York City. See figure 7-3.

FIGURE 7-1
Portion of U.S.
Census Map of
Congressional
Districts

See figure 7-2

MASSACHUSETTS
14 DISTRICTS
SEE INSET

RHODE ISLAND
2 DISTRICTS
SEE INSET

CONNECTICUT
ALSO 1 REPRESENTATIVE
ELECTED AT LARGE

ONE AT LARGE

MASSACHUSETTS

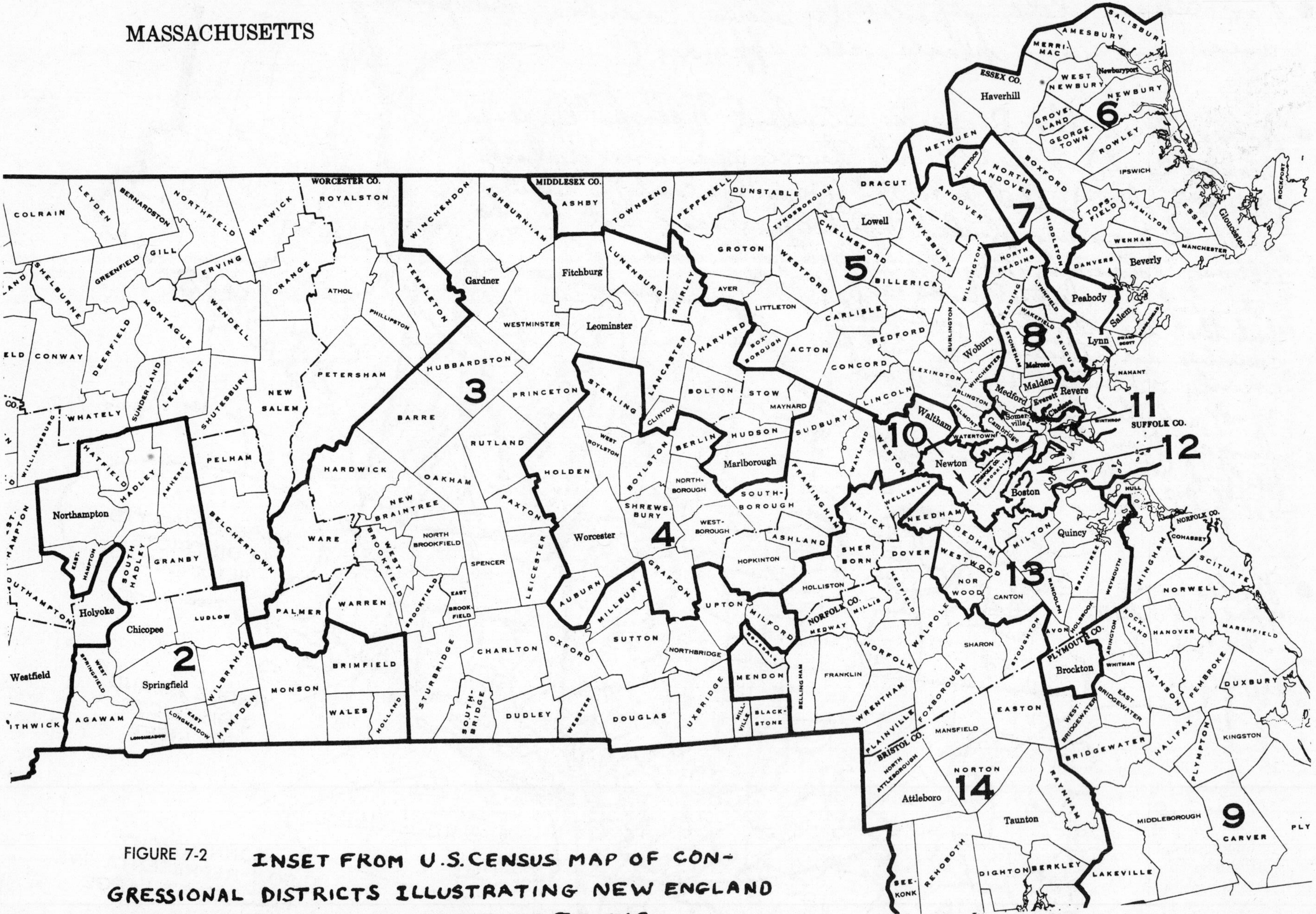

FIGURE 7-2 INSET FROM U.S. CENSUS MAP OF CON-
GRESSIONAL DISTRICTS ILLUSTRATING NEW ENGLAND
DISTRICTS THAT ARE COMPOSED OF TOWNS

FIGURE 7-3

INSET FROM U.S. CENSUS MAP OF
CONGRESSIONAL DISTRICTS SHOWING THE DISTRICTS
WITHIN NEW YORK CITY

• A more detailed description of boundary lines will be found in the Con-gressional Directory See figure 7-4.

• Notice the shape of the 4th, 5th, 11th and 12th districts

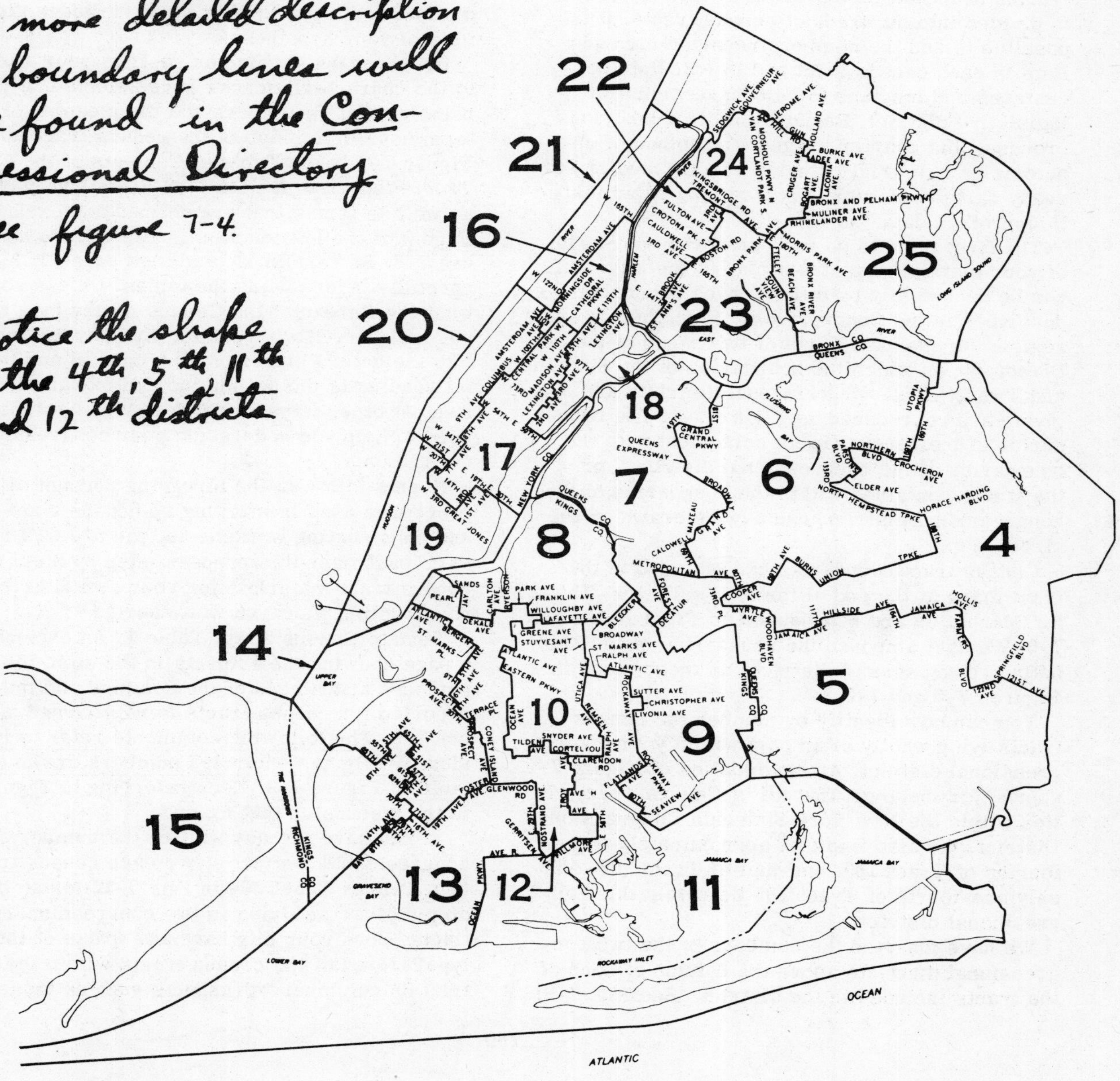

NEW YORK, N.Y.

Fortunately, the Bureau of the Census reports certain population and housing data for subareas of the larger cities and their suburban fringe. These subareas are called census tracts. See Chapter VI for the definition of a census tract given by the Bureau of the Census. Many additional cities and suburban areas have been tracted since 1950, and data for these are reported in the 1960 Census. However, the illustrations taken from the 1950 Census are equally applicable to the 1960 reports. For the New York City tract data, see the *U.S. Census of Population: 1950* (5).

Separate bulletins of the 1950 Census were published for sixty-two cities. For forty-three of these cities, adjacent areas were also tracted. The student can determine whether his city and its environs have been tracted by looking at the list of tracted areas at the end of the "Introduction" to any census tract bulletin.

Each of the larger boroughs of New York City is divided into hundreds of census tracts. It is possible to add the numbers reported for each item in each census tract and to calculate percentages and medians for a congressional or legislative district. Because this is a laborious process, this chapter suggests a method of characterizing a district by using certain medians already calculated, supplemented by a rapid inspection of other data.

The first thing to do is to draw the boundaries of your district on a street map of the city. This can be done easily by following the boundaries as described in the *Congressional Directory* or state register or manual. Parts of two pages of the *Directory,* on which the boundaries of the Sixteenth and Twenty-first congressional districts are given, are reproduced as Figure 7-4. The boundaries of the census tracts coincident with the boundaries of the congressional districts, or of the tracts contained within the boundaries of the congressional district, can now be drawn on the street map.

Census tract boundaries can be found in the tract maps at the end of the P-D bulletins. Those for Manhattan are reproduced as Figures 7-5 and 7-6. We have imposed the boundaries of the Manhattan congressional districts on these maps in Figures 7-5 and 7-6.

You can now identify by number the census tracts lying wholly or in part within your congressional district. An examination of Figure 7-5 shows, for instance, that all of Census Tract 216 lies within the New York Sixteenth Congressional District. We also find that approximately three-fourths of Tract 189, one-half of Tract 196, and only one-fourth of Tract 185 lie within this congressional district.

We have inserted the numbers of the two congressional districts above the column of each of the tracts included in the district. (See Fig. 7-9)

We have treated all tracts with half or more of their area in either district as if they were wholly within the district. See Figure 7-9 (reference No. 1), and the similar notations in the other census tract tables, Figures 7-12, 7-13, 7-14, 7-22. Worksheets were then prepared on which all census tracts within the district are listed by number. See the first column in Figures 7-10, 7-11, 7-15, 7-16.

We are now ready to record whatever observations of census tract data we may want to record. We have made only a few observations to illustrate how the data may be handled by methods short of machine calculations. When you make your own survey, it is up to you to determine whether any characteristic recorded by census tracts may be politically important. One of the purposes of this workshop assignment is to lead you to make significant hypotheses about the relationship between your congressman and his district and, upon further study, to judge the validity of your hypotheses.

By no means should you restrict your attention to the characteristics we have selected. It is imperative that you understand the meaning of every term used in the stub of the census tract tables. Figure 7-7 is the Table of Contents of the *Census Tract Statistics.* It lists five tables you may use, as well as terms that are defined and explained. Page 2 of the Introduction is reproduced as Figure 7-8. Be certain to read also pages 1, 3, and 4 carefully before using the tables. Unless you know what the Bureau of the Census means by a term, you will very likely read too little or too much into the data. Furthermore, a careful and thoughtful reading of the definitions and explanations will suggest other ways in which census data may be used to help you understand your congressman's constituents.

Having followed the foregoing account of the procedure used in marking up census tract tables and constructing worksheets, you are now ready to go back over this process, step by step, using census tract materials for your own district, and constructing your own worksheets.

Turn to Census Tract Table 1. An excerpt from a page showing the subjects in the stub, the tract numbers at the head of the columns and the data reported for census tracts is reproduced as Figure 7-9. The following comments refer to items identified by the encircled numbers drawn on the table in Figure 7-9. Keep referring to Figure 7-9 in the discussion that follows.

1. You have already written the number of the congressional district above each census tract. (See Census Tract 204 in Fig. 7-12 for an example of a tract lying in two congressional districts. Does your city have any tracts of this type?) Now list the census tracts within the district on columnar worksheets such as those in

Italian fronts November and December 1944; official observer Bikini Atom Test; elected to the Seventy-eighth Congress; reelected to the Seventy-ninth, Eighty-first, Eighty-second, and Eighty-third Congresses.

FIFTEENTH DISTRICT.—RICHMOND COUNTY. Kin~~~~~~~~ of Advisory ~~~~~~~~ Community Chest a line beginning at a point where Bay Ridge A~~~~ of Visiting Nurses Associa-New York Bay, thence easterly along Bay ~~~~~~~ber Staten Island Rotary Club; ~~~~re), to Secor ~~~~~~ Sixty-fifth ~~~~~~ate School; director and vice president ~~~~~~~ of Universalist Church; member Gras-~~~~ fund rais~~~~~ of Staten Island Cancer Committee and November ~, 1952. ~~~~mpaign; elected to the Eighty-third Congress

SIXTEENTH DISTRICT.—NEW YORK COUNTY: That portion within and bounded by a line beginning at a point where Lexington Avenue extended northward meets the Harlem River, thence southerly along Lexington Avenue to One Hundred and Nineteenth Street, thence westerly to Fifth Avenue, thence southerly to Frawley Circle, to One Hundred and Tenth Street, thence westerly along One Hundred and Tenth Street and Cathedral Parkway to Central Park West, to One Hundredth Street, thence westerly to Columbus Avenue, to One Hundred and Third Street, to Amsterdam Avenue, to Cathedral Parkway, thence easterly to Morningside Drive, thence along Morningside Drive to the intersection of One Hundred and Twenty-second Street, Morningside Drive and Amsterdam Avenue, thence northerly along Amsterdam Avenue to West One Hundred and Sixty-fifth Street, thence easterly along West One Hundred and Sixty-fifth Street extended to the waters of the Harlem River, and through the waters of the Harlem River to the place of beginning. Population (1950), 336,441.

ADAM CLAYTON POWELL, Jr., Democrat, of New York City; born in New Haven, Conn., November 29, 1908; education: B. A. degree, Colgate University, 1930; M. A. degree, Columbia University, 1932; D. D. degree, Shaw University, 1934; 1947, LL. D., Virginia Union University; studied 4 months in Europe, North Africa, and Asia Minor; minister of the Abyssinian Baptist Church, 1937, organized 1808, membership over 10,000, budget $95,000, property worth $750,000; first Negro councilman of the city of New York, 1941; member of the Phi Upsilon Kappa Society, honorary fraternity in philosophy; Alpha Phi Alpha Fraternity, Masons, I. B. P. O. E. of the W., Y. M. C. A.; in the community—

TWENTY-FIRST DISTRICT.—NEW YORK COUNTY: That portion within and bounded by a line beginning at a point where Cathedral Parkway extended westerly meets the Hudson River, thence easterly along Cathedral Parkway to Morningside Drive, thence northerly along Morningside Drive to the intersection of Morningside Drive, West One Hundred and Twenty-second Street and Amsterdam Avenue, thence northerly along Amsterdam Avenue to West One Hundred and Sixty-fifth Street, thence easterly along West One Hundred and Sixty-fifth Street extended to the waters of the Harlem River and the dividing line between the county of New York and the county of Bronx, thence in a northerly and westerly direction along said dividing line to the Hudson River, and southerly through the waters of the Hudson River to the place of beginning. Population (1950), 317,307.

JACOB K. JAVITS (elected on tickets of Republican Party and Liberal Party), Republican, of New York City; born on the lower East Side of New York City, May 18, 1904; attended Public School No. 20; moved to Brooklyn and later to Washington Heights, and was president of his class at George Washington High School and a member of the first graduating class in 1920; after working several years and taking supplementary courses at Columbia University at night was graduated from the New York University Law School in 1926; admitted to the bar the following year and became a partner of the law firm of Javits & Javits; honorary LL. D. degree from Lincoln University, June 1953; lecturer and author of a series of articles on a liberal political and economic philosophy for the Republican Party; active in New York City fusion campaigns; before Pearl Harbor was a special assistant to the Chief of Chemical Warfare Service and in charge of control division with world-wide administrative responsibilities; remained in that service until March 1942 when he went into the Army as a major and became assistant to the Chief of Operations of Chemical Warfare; served in the European Theater of Operations in 1943 and in the Pacific in 1944; received the Legion of Merit and Army Commendation Ribbon; discharged as a lieutenant colonel in June 1945, and resumed the practice of law; married Marion Ann Borris, 1947; daughter, Joy Deborah, born September 12, 1948; son, Joshua Moses, born January 2, 1950; member of American Legion, Veterans of Foreign Wars, and Jewish War Veterans; director of the Association of Committees for Inter-American Placement, an association engaged in specially training college men and women for work in Latin America; served in Eightieth Congress; reelected to Eighty-first, Eighty-second, and Eighty-third Congresses.

FIGURE 7-4

[Handwritten annotation, upper right:] Use these boundary descriptions to outline the district on a good street map. Then outline census tracts along the congressional district boundary lines. Congressional districts can then be overlaid upon the census tract map as in figures 7-5 and 7-6.

[Handwritten annotation, middle right:] This is what the Congressman himself has to say about his own background. See A Guide to the Study of Public Affairs, p. 58

[Handwritten annotation, bottom:] From The Congressional Directory, 83rd Congress, 2nd Session (1954), pp. 95 and 98.

FIGURE 7-5

NEW YORK, N. Y., BY CENSUS TRACTS
Part 4.—Tracts in Manhattan Borough

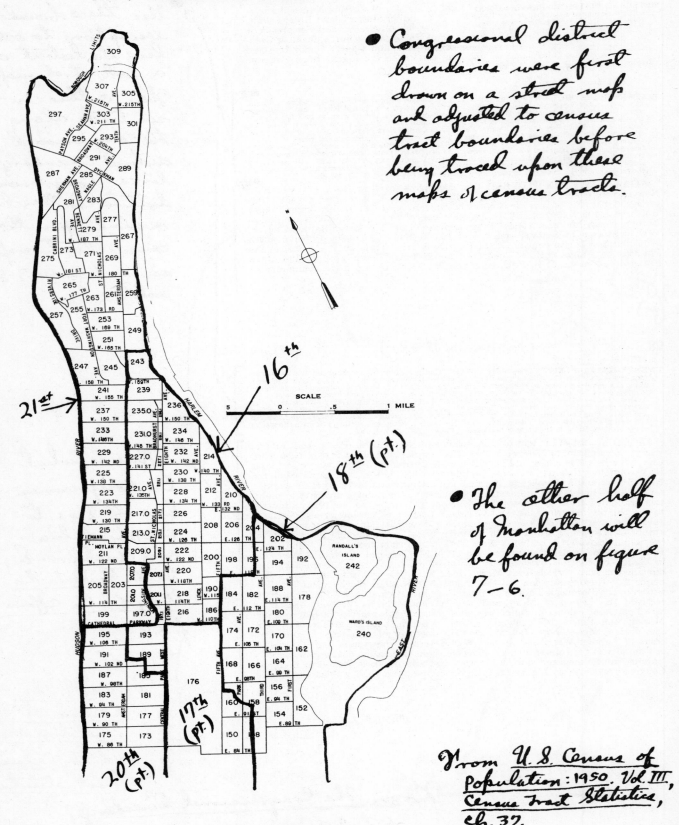

• Congressional district boundaries were first drawn on a street map and adjusted to census tract boundaries before being traced upon these maps of census tracts.

• The other half of Manhattan will be found on figure 7-6.

From *U. S. Census of Population: 1950. Vol. III, Census Tract Statistics,* ch. 37.

FIGURE 7-6

NEW YORK, N.Y., BY CENSUS TRACTS
Part 5.—Tracts in Manhattan Borough

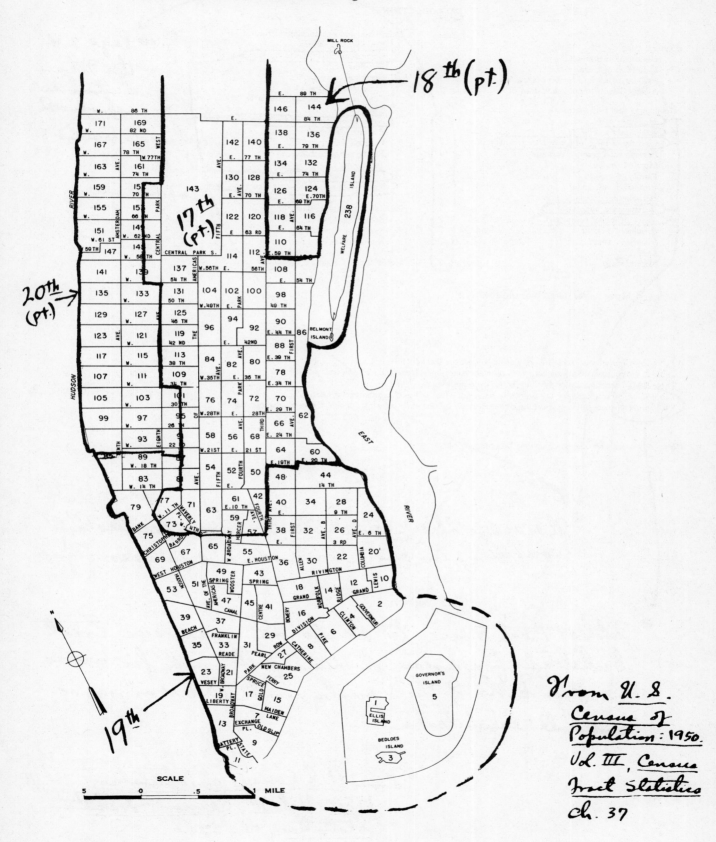

From U.S.
Census of
Population: 1950.
Vol. III, Census
Tract Statistics
Ch. 37

FIGURE 7-7

CONTENTS

INTRODUCTION

TABLES

Map of tracted area appears following last page of tables.

IV

• Page 2 of this Introduction is reproduced as figure 7-8

• Here are the items that we specifically consider in our illustrative analysis.

• Tables 4 and 5 are to be found in census tract bulletins for areas in the South and for areas in other parts of the country with 10,000 or more nonwhite inhabitants.

From *U.S. Census of Population: 1950. Vol. III, Census Tract Statistics*, ch. 37

FIGURE 7-8

STATISTICS FOR CENSUS TRACTS

Chapter B of each State part of *Population*, Volume II, *Characteristics of the Population*. Similar information of the housing items may be found in the Series H–A bulletins, which are preprints of the State chapters of *Housing*, Volume I, *General Characteristics*. Those publications contain more detailed definitions, an evaluation of the data on various items, and discussion of comparability with data on the same, or similar, subjects from the 1940 Census and from other sources.

Median.—The median, a type of average, is presented in connection with the data on years of school completed, family income, number of persons per dwelling unit, and rent or value of dwelling unit which appear in this bulletin. The median is the value which divides the distribution into two equal parts—one-half of the cases falling below this value and one-half of the cases exceeding this value.

Race and nativity.—Three major race categories are distinguished in this bulletin, namely, white, Negro, and other races. Negro and other races taken together comprise the category "Nonwhite." Persons of Mexican birth or ancestry who were not definitely Indian or of other nonwhite race were classified as white. Included as Negro are persons of mixed white and Negro parentage and persons of mixed Indian and Negro parentage unless the Indian blood very definitely predominates or the individual is accepted in the community as an Indian. All other nonwhite races are classified in the residual category "Other races" in this report.

In the presentation of housing statistics, occupied dwelling units are shown separately for nonwhite heads of households.

A person born in the United States or any of its Territories or possessions, or born in a foreign country of parents who were American citizens, is counted as native.

In view of the fact that a major portion of the nonwhite population is to be found in the South and in large urban centers in the North and West, data are shown separately for the nonwhite population in these areas only. For all tracted areas in the South and those tracted areas in the North and West with 10,000 or more nonwhite inhabitants, selected population and housing items are shown for nonwhites in each tract with 250 or more nonwhite persons.

Country of birth of foreign-born white.—The classification by country of birth is based on international boundaries as formally recognized by the United States in April 1950.

Persons with Spanish surname.—White persons of Spanish surname living in five southwestern States (Arizona, California, Colorado, New Mexico, and Texas) were distinguished separately for the first time in the 1950 Census. For tracted areas with 10,000 or more white persons of Spanish surname in these States, data for selected population and housing characteristics are presented for each tract with 250 or more white persons with Spanish surname.

Married couple.*—A married couple is defined as a husband and his wife enumerated as members of the same household or quasi household. Married couples are classified as "with own household" if the husband is head of the household.

Family.*—A family, as defined in the 1950 Census, is a group of two or more persons related by blood, marriage, or adoption and living together; all such persons are regarded as members of one family.

Unrelated individual.*—Unrelated individuals are persons (other than inmates of institutions) who are not living with any relatives. In this bulletin, statistics on unrelated individuals are limited to those 14 years old and over.

*Data based on 20-percent sample. For estimates of sampling variability and a method of obtaining improved estimates, see the section on "Reliability of sample data."

Household.—A household includes all the persons who occupy a dwelling unit. A person living alone in a dwelling unit or a group of unrelated persons sharing the same living accommodations as parners is counted as a household.

The count of households excludes groups of persons living as quasi households, that is, living in quarters not classified as dwelling units, for example, in houses with at least five lodgers or in hotels, institutions, labor camps, or military barracks.

The average population per household is obtained by dividing the population in households by the number of households. It excludes persons living in quasi households.

Institutional population.—The institutional population includes those persons living as inmates in such places as homes for delinquent or dependent children, homes and schools for the mentally or physically handicapped, places providing specialized medical care, homes for the aged, and prisons and jails. Staff members and their families are not included in the institutional population.

Years of school completed.*—Figures on educational attainment refer only to progress in "regular schools." Such schools are public, private, or parochial schools, colleges, universities, or professional schools, either day or night, that is, those schools where enrollment leads to an elementary or high school diploma or to a college, university, or professional school degree. Training in a vocational, trade, or business school was excluded unless the school was graded and considered part of the regular school system. The median number of school years completed is expressed in terms of a continuous series of numbers representing years completed. For example, the completion of the first year of high school is indicated by 9 and of the last year of college by 16.

Residence in 1949.*—Residence in 1949 is the usual place of residence one year prior to the date of enumeration and was used in conjunction with residence in 1950 to determine the numbers of persons who had changed residence from 1949 to 1950.

Income in 1949.*—Income, as defined in the 1950 Census, is the sum of the money received, less losses, from the following sources: wages or salary; net income (or loss) from the operation of a farm, ranch, business, or profession; net income (or loss) from rents or receipts from roomers or boarders; royalties; interest, dividends, and periodic income from estates and trust funds; pensions; veterans' payments, armed-forces allotments for dependents, and other governmental payments or assistance; and other income such as contributions for support from persons who are not members of the household, alimony, and periodic receipts from insurance policies or annuities. The figures in this report represent the amount of income received by families and unrelated individuals before deductions for personal income taxes, social security, bond purchases, union dues, etc.

Receipts from the following sources were not included as income: money received from the sale of property unless the recipient was engaged in the business of selling such property; the value of income "in kind," such as food produced and consumed in the home, free living quarters; withdrawals of bank deposits; money borrowed; tax refunds; gifts; and lump-sum inheritances or insurance payments.

Age.—The age classification is based on the age of the person at his last birthday as of the date of his enumeration, that is, the age of the person in completed years.

Marital status.—This classification of persons 14 years old and over relates to marital status at the time of enumeration. Persons classified as "married" comprise, therefore, both those who have been married only once and those who have remarried after having been widowed or divorced. Persons reported as separated are classified as married.

From U.S. Census of Population: 1950. Vol. III, Census Tract Statistics, ch. 37

FIGURE 7-9

NEW YORK CITY

Table 1.—CHARACTERISTICS OF THE POPULATION, BY CENSUS TRACTS: 1950—Con.

[Asterisk (*) denotes statistics based on 20-percent sample. For totals of age groups from complete count, see table 2.   Median not shown where base is less than 500]

Manhattan Borough—Con.

Subject	Tract 210	Tract 211	Tract 212	Tract 213.0	Tract 213.1	Tract 214	Tract 215	Tract 216	Tract 217.0	Tract 217.1	Tract 218	Tract 219	Tract 220	Tract 221.0	Tract 22
SEX, RACE, AND NATIVITY															
Total population, 1950	8,477	13,519	13,081	6,380	2,576	1,286	3,660	16,767	3,071	2,863	13,224	7,608	13,167	1	
Male	4,075	6,633	5,665	2,840	1,180	557	1,728	7,667	1,168	1,276	5,979	3,535	5,912		
Female	4,402	6,886	7,416	3,540	1,396	729	1,932	9,100	1,903	1,587	7,245	4,073	7,255		
White	150	10,798	65	175	12	2	3,309	265	1,327	8	233	5,830	118		
Native	133	7,927	51	119	12	2	2,598	205	1,050	6	180	4,757	7		
Foreign born	17	2,871	14	56	...	...	711	60	277	2	53	1,073			
Nonwhite	8,327	2,721	13,016	6,205	2,564	1,284	351	16,502	1,744	2,855	12,991	1,778	13,		
Negro	8,315	1,878	13,002	6,203	2,561	1,284	302	16,472	1,722	2,855	12,964	1,763	13,		
Other races	12	843	14	2	3	...	49	30	22		27	15			
Total population, 1940	(1)	12,003	12,959	(1)	(1)	1,707	3,586	15,738	(1)	(1)	13,874	6,803			
White	...	11,409	124	...	...	1	3,526	942	...	...	495	6,350			
Nonwhite	...	594	12,835	...	...	1,706	60	14,796	...	...	13,379	45			
COUNTRY OF BIRTH OF THE FOREIGN-BORN WHITE															
England and Wales	1	129	...	2	...	...	38	2	15		6				
Scotland	...	51	...	2	...	...	11	...	3						
Northern Ireland	...	17	...	...	...	...	...	...	...						
Ireland (Eire)	...	671	2	17	...	...	120	6	117		3				
Norway	...	22	...	...	...	...	2	...	...						
Sweden	...	19	1	...	...	...	7	...	2						
Denmark	...	20	...	...	...	...	5	...	...						
Netherlands	...	15	...	...	...	...	3	1	3						
France	1	48	...	...	...	...	24	4	5						
Germany	1	300	5	3	...	...	62	1	16						
Poland	1	103	1	4	...	...	36	3	11						
Czechoslovakia	...	45	...	...	...	...	3	1	6						
Austria	...	122	...	...	...	...	17	2	5		1				
Hungary	...	43	...	...	...	...	14	2	3						
Yugoslavia	...	10	...	...	...	...	1	...	...						
U. S. S. R.	3	149	...	4	...	...	53	2	...		1				
Lithuania	...	6	...	...	...	...	1	...	1						
Finland	1	16	...	...	...	...	3	...	1						
Rumania	...	9	...	...	...	...	6	...	...						
Greece	...	137	...	12	...	...	45	1	7						
Italy	2	130	1	2	...	...	50	1	9						
Other Europe	...	102	1	2	...	...	46	1	7						
Asia	...	159	...	...	...	...	33	3	7						
Canada—French	...	33	...	1	...	...	1	...	...						
Canada—Other	2	96	1	...	...	...	19	...	...						
Mexico	...	37	...	...	...	...	7	...	...						
Other America	3	359	2	6	...	...	98	24	...						
All other and not reported	1	23	1	1	...	...	6	1	...						
MARRIED COUPLES AND HOUSEHOLDS															
Married couples,* number	2,410	2,600	1,975	1,430	515	185	755								
With own household	2,360	2,350	1,530	1,150	430	160	695								
Without own household	50	250	445	280	85	25	60								
Families and unrelated individuals*	2,760	6,275	5,910	2,755	1,170	560	1,46								
Families	2,670	3,335	3,205	1,780	750	295	9								
Unrelated individuals	90	2,940	2,705	975	420	265									
Households, number	2,488	3,789	3,732	1,934	730	373	1,								
Population in households	8,477	12,019	12,141	6,195	2,371	1,243	3,								
Population per household	3.41	3.17	3.25	3.20	3.25	3.33									
Institutional population	...	...	44	...	...	...									
*YEARS OF SCHOOL COMPLETED															
Persons 25 years old and over	4,685	8,975	8,300	4,535	1,600	770									
No school years completed	20	190	285	25	70	35									
Elementary: 1 to 4 years	100	550	1,510	360	290	155									
5 and 6 years	205	750	1,550	645	240	150									
7 years	155	455	980	370	70	70									
8 years	260	1,565	1,175	655	250	95									
High school: 1 to 3 years	955	1,075	1,310	845	280	125									
4 years	1,510	1,805	945	1,000	160	80									
College: 1 to 3 years	615	860	195	265	65	1									
4 years or more	745	1,490	110	200	15	1									
School years not reported	120	535	240	170	135	5									
Median school years completed	12.4	11.0	7.7	9.5	8.2	7.									
*RESIDENCE IN 1949															
Persons 1 year old and over, 1950	8,325	13,310	12,865	6,410	2,470	1,2									
Same house as in 1950	7,970	11,410	11,685	5,885	1,995	1,									
Different house, same county	140	705	375	290	200										
Different county or abroad	55	750	225	125	85										
Residence not reported	160	445	580	110	190										
*INCOME IN 1949															
Total families and unrelated individuals	2,760	6,275	5,910	2,755	1,170										
Less than $500	150	1,185	1,125	325	190										
$500 to $999	65	470	970	285	150										
$1,000 to $1,499	75	545	885	265	130										
$1,500 to $1,999	215	485	780	285	150										
$2,000 to $2,499	430	540	815	390	160										
$2,500 to $2,999	305	410	420	280	95										
$3,000 to $3,499	250	465	2	320	75										
$3,500 to $3,999	285	395	105	145	20										
$4,000 to $4,499	215	30	95	95	20										
$4,500 to $4,999	145	150	55	30	25										
$5,000 to $5,999	325	240	35	110	5										
$6,000 to $6,999	155	185	10	20	10										
$7,000 to $9,999	75	175	20	10	...										
$10,000 or more	45	70	...	5	...										
Income not reported	125	655	320	200	140										
Median income dollars	3,155	2,116	1,395	2,155	3,650	1,									

[1] Not available; see p. 6.

(Handwritten annotations:)

8

1

10

3

4 See figures 7-10 and 7-11

See figures 7-10 and 7-11

5 See figures 7-15 and 7-16

2

8

6 See figures 7-15 and 7-16

9

7 See figures 7-15 and 7-16

From U. S. Census of Population: 1950. Vol. III. Census Tract Statistics ch. 37

N.Y. 16th Cong. Dist. (Manhattan)
Race and Foreign Born
FIGURE 7-10

CENSUS TRACT	WHITE	10%-40% NEGRO	40-60% NEGRO 40-60% WHITE	10%-40% WHITE	NEGRO	OVER 20% OF WHITES ARE FOREIGN BORN	PRINCIPAL COUNTRIES OF ORIGIN
185 (¼)	✓ (circled)					✓ (circled)	EIRE - GER. - LATIN AM.
186					✓	–	
189 (¾)	✓					✓	EIRE - GER. LATIN AM.
190					✓	–	
196 (½)		✓				–	
197.1					✓	–	
198					✓	–	
200					✓	–	
201.1					✓	–	
204 (½)				✓		–	
206					✓	–	
207.1					✓	–	
208					✓	–	
209.0				✓		–	
209.1					✓	–	
210					✓		
212					✓		
213.0					✓		
213.1					✓		
216					✓		
217.0			✓			ETC.	ETC.
217.1					✓		
218					✓		
220					✓		
221.0			✓				
221.1					✓		
222					✓		
224					✓	ETC.	ETC.
226					✓		
227.0					✓		
227.1					✓		
228					✓		
230					✓		
231.0					✓		
231.1					✓		
232					✓		

AND IN THE SAME MANNER FOR CENSUS TRACTS 234, 235.0, 235.1, 236, 239 AND 243

N.Y. 21st Cong. Dist. (Manhattan)
Race and Foreign Born
FIGURE 7-11

Census Tract	White	10%-40% Negro	40-60% Negro 40-60% White	10%-40% White	Negro	Over 20% of White are Foreign Born	Principal Countries of Origin
197.0	X	X	X	X		X	X
199	✓					✓	GER. - USSR.
201.0	✓					✓	EIRE - GER.
203	✓						
205							
207.0	✓						
211		✓				✓	EIRE, GER.-LATIN AM.
215	✓						
219		✓					
223	✓					✓	EIRE - LATIN AM. - GER.
225		✓				✓	EIRE - GER - U.S.S.R.
229			✓				
233				✓			
237			✓				
241		✓					
245		✓					
247	✓						
249		✓				ETC.	ETC.
251	✓						
253	✓						
255	✓						
257	-	-	-	-	-	-	-
259	-	-	-	-	-	-	-
261	✓						
263	✓						
265	✓						
267	✓						
269	✓					ETC.	ETC.
271	✓						
273	✓						
275	✓						
277	✓						
279	✓						
281	✓						
283	✓						
285	✓						

AND IN THE SAME MANNER FOR CENSUS TRACTS 287-309

FIGURE 7-12

NEW YORK CITY

Table 3.—CHARACTERISTICS OF DWELLING UNITS, BY CENSUS TRACTS: 1950—Con.

[Asterisk (*) denotes statistics based on 20-percent sample.   Median not shown where base is less than 100]

Manhattan Borough--Con.

Subject	Tract 200	Tract 201.0	Tract 201.1	Tract 202	Tract 203	Tract 204	Tract 205	Tract 206	Tract 207.0	Tract 207.1	Tract 208	Tract 209.0	Tract 209.1	Tract 210	Tract 211	Tract 212	Tract 213.0
All dwelling units	1,597	683	1,924	1,147	527	1,127	1,615	2,365	1,640	2,279	2,986	1,648	628	2,495	3,820	?	
Owner occupied	62	39	25	32	28	21	9	77	4	30	83	8	7	18			
Nonwhite owners	60	...	20	4	...	7	...	70	...	29	75	6	7	1ᵃ			
Renter occupied	1,518	641	1,833	1,094	495	1,052	1,591	2,252	1,594	2,241	2,890	1,631	615	2			
Nonwhite renters	1,443	9	1,795	321	6	609	41	2,198	39	2,210	2,705	1,093	605				
Vacant nonseasonal not dilapidated, for rent or sale	10	3	1	10	3	7	8	21	5	...	6	3					
Other vacant and nonresident	7	...	65	11	1	47	7	15	37	8	7	5					
TYPE OF STRUCTURE																	
1 dwelling unit, detached (includes trailers)	2	2	6	2	1	5	2	6	3	3	6						
1 dwelling unit, attached	16	6	36	11	...	288	6	22	86	11	30						
1 and 2 dwelling unit, semidetached	...	...	...	...	...	17	...	12	...	...							
2 dwelling unit, other	28	...	...	...	4	16	2	22	...	...							
3 and 4 dwelling unit	332	...	6	65	3	16	...	175	...	38							
5 dwelling unit or more	1,219	675	1,876	1,063	519	785	1,605	2,128	1,551	2,221							
CONDITION AND PLUMBING FACILITIES																	
Number reporting	1,465	664	1,778	1,048	521	1,043	1,543	2,135	1,598								
No private bath or dilapidated	917	8	1,222	277	6	179	37	720	16								
No running water or dilapidated	412	5	1,209	67	2	103	10	196	1								
* YEAR BUILT																	
Number reporting	1,100	695	1,795	1,100	510	1,070	1,555	2,255	1								
1940 or later	...	...	...	...	...	...	...	...									
1930 to 1939	...	...	10	...	...	...	55	10									
1920 to 1929	5	...	90	25	...	15	10	440									
1919 or earlier	1,095	695	1,695	1,075	510	1,055	1,490	1,80									
All occupied dwelling units	1,580	680	1,858	1,126	523	1,073	1,600										
NUMBER OF PERSONS IN DWELLING UNIT																	
1 person	276	73	244	286	68	242	230										
2 persons	430	195	459	355	150	314	50ᵃ										
3 persons	285	199	353	196	157	213	4ᵃ										
4 persons	242	125	328	125	89	118	7										
5 and 6 persons	269	78	335	116	57	138											
7 persons or more	78	10	139	48	2	48											
Median number of persons	2.8	2.9	3.1	2.3	2.8	2.4											
PERSONS PER ROOM																	
Number reporting	1,535	672	1,814	1,091	516	1,048											
1.01 or more	458	17	365	170	59	21ᵃ											
* HEATING FUEL																	
Number reporting heating equipment	1,575	690	1,830	1,060	545	1,0											
Central heating	1,565	670	1,755	610	520	9											
Coal	985	615	1,095	325	300	7											
Utility or bottled gas	275	5	280	125	15	2											
Liquid fuel	255	35	295	35	195												
Other fuel	5	...	10	...	5												
Not reported	45	15	75	125	5												
Noncentral heating	5	20	55	275	25												
Coal	5	...	20	215	10												
Utility or bottled gas	...	...	25	50	...												
Liquid fuel	...	5	5	...	10												
Other fuel	...	...	...	10	5												
Not reported	...	15	5	...													
Not heated	5	...	20	175	...												
* REFRIGERATION EQUIPMENT																	
Number reporting	1,505	645	1,825	1,095	500	1,0											
Mechanical	670	640	1,210	630	490	3ᵃ											
Ice	830	...	540	340	5	5ᵃ											
Other or none	5	5	75	125	5												
* TELEVISION																	
Number reporting	1,515	625	1,810	1,070	535	1,0											
With television	165	40	175	125	15												
CONTRACT MONTHLY RENT																	
Renter occupied; and vacant nonseasonal not dilapidated units, for rent—Number reporting	1,447	597	1,737	1,027	478	1,0											
Less than $10	...	...	...	...	...												
$10 to $19	15	...	...	261	...												
$20 to $29	113	3	237	493	4	4											
$30 to $39	469	35	564	204	39	3ᵃ											
$40 to $49	472	75	396	50	61												
$50 to $59	202	79	225	6	72												
$60 to $74	135	128	254	3	143												
$75 to $99	57	195	59	8	130												
$100 or more	4	82	2	2	29												
Median rent dollars	42.60	71.98	41.20	24.62	66.11	27											
VALUE OF ONE-DWELLING-UNIT STRUCTURES																	
Owner occupied;[1] and vacant nonseasonal not dilapidated units, for sale—Number reporting	2	...	4	1	...												
Less than $3,000	...	...	...	...	...												
$3,000 to $3,999	...	...	...	...	...												
$4,000 to $4,999	...	...	...	...	...												
$5,000 to $7,499	...	...	...	...	...												
$7,500 to $9,999	...	...	...	1	...												
$10,000 to $14,999	...	...	...	...	...												
$15,000 or more	...	...	3	...	...												
Median value dollars	...	...	...	...	...												

[1] Restricted to 1-dwelling-unit properties.

(handwritten annotations)

①

⑭ See figures 7-15 and 7-16

⑤ See figures 7-15 and 7-16

⑬ See figures 7-15 and 7-16

From U.S. Census of Population: 1950, Vol. III. Census Tract Statistics, ch. 37

FIGURE 7-13

NEW YORK CITY

Table 4.—CHARACTERISTICS OF THE NONWHITE POPULATION, FOR SELECTED CENSUS TRACTS: 1950—Con.

[Tracts listed are those which contain 250 or more nonwhite persons. Asterisk (*) denotes statistics based on 20-percent sample. For totals of age groups from complete count, see table 2. Median not shown where base is less than 500]

Manhattan Borough—Con.

Handwritten column annotations: 21 16 16 16 16 21 16   ...   16 21 16 16 16 16 21 16

Subject	Tract 225	Tract 226	Tract 227.0	Tract 227.1	Tract 228	Tract 229	Tract 230	Tract 231.0	Tract 231.1	Tract 232	Tract 233	Tract 234	Tract 235.0	Tract 235.1	Tract 236	Tract 237	Tract 238	Tract 239
MARITAL STATUS																		
Male, 14 years old and over	562	4,684	2,670	873	4,459	2,277	6,213	3,548	1,250	5,519	2,494	3,169	3,08_	1._				
Single	143	1,310	688	230	1,340	701	1,947	925	342	1,740	720	892	817					
Married	393	3,009	1,826	576	2,742	1,442	3,883	2,324	816	3,441	1,639	2,075	2._					
Widowed or divorced	26	365	156	67	377	134	383	299	92	338	135	202						
Female, 14 years old and over	706	5,995	3,306	1,184	5,593	2,726	7,656	4,442	1,698	7,160	3,107	4._						
Single	187	1,471	772	255	1,455	691	1,967	1,080	382	1,696	779							
Married	414	3,497	1,976	697	3,064	1,639	4,311	2,541	1,008	4,135	1,886							
Widowed or divorced	105	1,027	558	232	1,074	396	1,378	821	308	1,329	4							
* MARRIED COUPLES																		
Married couples, number	300	2,070	1,370	405	1,770	1,180	2,940	1,920	575	2,715								
With own household	225	1,345	955	300	1,125	830	1,965	1,285	510	2,200								
Without own household	75	725	415	105	645	350	975	635	65	51_								
*YEARS OF SCHOOL COMPLETED																		
Persons 25 years and over	1,035	8,635	5,030	1,580	8,395	3,960	11,375	6,985	2,315	10								
No school years completed	10	255	25	25	140	30	205	20	20									
Elementary: 1 to 4 years	75	1,335	345	205	945	265	1,045	450	310									
5 and 6 years	105	1,225	500	400	1,280	405	1,790	1,005	495									
7 years	65	1,100	380	180	880	325	1,320	655	165									
8 years	175	1,215	750	240	1,125	885	1,815	995	43_									
High school: 1 to 3 years	160	1,615	970	335	1,715	785	2,565	1,300	43									
4 years	220	910	1,050	95	1,220	765	1,705	1,380	3_									
College: 1 to 3 years	85	260	330	15	395	215	300	420										
4 years or more	55	150	245	5	325	150	230	415										
School years not reported	85	570	435	80	370	135	400	345										
Median school years completed	9.8	8.1	9.9	7.7	8.7	9.0	8.6	9.5										
* RESIDENCE IN 1949																		
Persons 1 year old and over, 1950	1,470	13,020	6,555	2,510	11,410	5,965	16,405	8,925										
Same house as in 1950	1,135	11,690	5,665	2,320	10,410	5,240	15,045	8,105										
Different house, same county	185	710	320	55	345	400	770	3_										
Different county or abroad	80	160	120	20	340	75	280											
Residence not reported	70	460	450	115	315	250	310											
EMPLOYMENT STATUS AND MAJOR OCCUPATION GROUP																		
Male, 14 years old and over	562	4,684	2,670	873	4,459	2,277	6,_											
Labor force	463	3,524	2,210	603	3,316	1,760	_											
Civilian labor force	463	3,522	2,202	603	3,314	1,757												
Employed	422	3,116	1,977	540	2,960	1,595												
Unemployed	41	406	225	63	354	162												
Not in labor force	99	1,160	460	270	1,143	51_												
Female, 14 years old and over	706	5,995	3,306	1,184	5,593	2,7_												
Labor force	412	2,881	1,851	529	3,048	1,4												
Civilian labor force	411	2,878	1,851	529	3,048	1,_												
Employed	381	2,676	1,730	490	2,815	1,_												
Unemployed	30	202	121	39	233													
Not in labor force	294	3,114	1,455	655	2,545	1												
Male, employed	422	3,116	1,977	540	2,960													
Professional, technical, and kindred workers	30	96	124	...	156													
Managers, officials, and props., incl. farm	49	145	113	16	127													
Clerical and kindred workers	48	290	311	51	381													
Sales workers	15	134	81	15	78													
Craftsmen, foremen, and kindred workers	36	267	188	39	264													
Operatives and kindred workers	87	754	431	108	718													
Private household workers	5	39	23	10	37													
Service workers, except private household	122	853	555	210	849													
Laborers, except mine	24	471	135	82	307													
Occupation not reported	6	67	16	9	4_													
Female, employed	381	2,676	1,730	490	2,81													
Professional, technical, and kindred workers	45	88	130	6	13													
Managers, officials, and props., incl. farm	9	20	19	2	_													
Clerical and kindred workers	48	130	217	24	18													
Sales workers	7	51	52	9	_													
Craftsmen, foremen, and kindred workers	6	36	26	7														
Operatives and kindred workers	146	936	570	150	8													
Private household workers	62	918	424	205	1,0													
Service workers, except private household	54	414	278	78	4													
Laborers, except mine	1	36	8	2														
Occupation not reported	3	47	6	7														
* INCOME IN 1949																		
Total families and unrelated individuals	670	6,320	3,390	1,105	6													
Less than $500	90	1,215	375	305	1													
$500 to $999	55	780	220	110														
$1,000 to $1,499	105	670	355	115														
$1,500 to $1,999	75	995	485	235														
$2,000 to $2,499	80	905	515	140														
$2,500 to $2,999	30	440	270	40														
$3,000 to $3,499	45	220	265	40														
$3,500 to $3,999	20	105	165	15														
$4,000 to $4,499	35	135	100	15														
$4,500 to $4,999	5	40	50	5														
$5,000 to $5,999	15	75	100	...														
$6,000 to $6,999	5	30	35															
$7,000 to $9,999	25	25	5															
$10,000 or more	...	5	25															
Income not reported	85	680	425															
Median income .... dollars	1,783	1,578	2,046	1,_														

Handwritten note:

• Tables 4 and 5 of the Census Tract Statistics can be used for a more detailed analysis in congressional districts with a large Negro population. If, for instance, the median income for the non-white population in a given tract is lower than the median for the entire population of the tract, the white population has a higher median income than the nonwhites.

From U. S. Census of Population: 1950, Vol. III, Census Tract Statistics, ci. 37

FIGURE 7-14

NEW YORK CITY

Table 5.—CHARACTERISTICS OF DWELLING UNITS OCCUPIED BY NONWHITE PERSONS, FOR SELECTED CENSUS TRACTS: 1950—Con.

[Tracts listed are those which contain 250 or more nonwhite persons.   Median not shown where base is less than 100]

Subject	Tract 188	Tract 189	Tract 190	Tract 193	Tract 196	Tract 197.1	Tract 198	Tract 199	Tract 200	Tract 201.1	Tract 202	Tract 204	Tract 205	Tract 206	Tract 207.1	Tract 208	Tract 209.0	Tract 209.1
Total dwelling units	98	94	2,185	332	330	825	951	73	1,503	1,815	325	616	41	2,268	2,239	2,780	1,099	
CONDITION AND PLUMBING FACILITIES																		
Number reporting	92	82	2,039	286	313	722	896	67	1,380	1,692	314	599	39	2,061	2,130	?		
No private bath or dilapidated	54	20	621	100	36	507	391	4	889	1,192	100	98	6	683	1,49?			
No running water or dilapidated	53	2	548	64	23	507	113	1	402	1,179	18	65	...	188	1..			
NUMBER OF PERSONS IN DWELLING UNIT																		
1 person	9	...	...	...	...	...	...	...	262	238	87	134	3?					
2 persons	23	34	483	104	79	237	289	24	404	451	86	161	1?					
3 persons	19	31	672	124	98	282	320	25	275	345	56	119						
4 persons	21	...	...	...	...	...	...	...	234	318	33	77						
5 and 6 persons	17	16	547	60	79	183	167	17	260	330	31	87						
7 persons or more	9	13	483	44	74	123	175	7	68	133	32	38.						
Median number of persons	...	...	3.4	3.0	3.4	3.1	3.1	...	2.8	3.1	2.4	?						
PERSONS PER ROOM																		
Number reporting	98	91	2,127	301	327	810	915	66	1,461	1,773	31?							
1.01 or more	34	23	504	65	78	162	372	19	435	359								
CONTRACT MONTHLY RENT																		
Renter-occupied units reporting	91	68	2,045	280	311	773	862	48	1,371	1,70?								
Less than $10	1	...	8	...	...	1	11	...	1									
$10 to $14	...	...	1	1	...	1	1	1	1									
$15 to $19	11	2	9	2	7	3	9	2	13									
$20 to $29	62	7	534	51	160	90	135	...	104									
$30 to $39	8	7	957	86	111	325	379	3	41?									
$40 to $49	4	17	345	42	19	155	197	6	4									
$50 to $74	5	25	174	88	13	186	104	20										
$75 or more	...	10	17	10	1	13	26	16										
Median rent dollars	...	...	34.42	39.50	28.78	38.50	36.76	...										
VALUE OF ONE-DWELLING-UNIT STRUCTURES																		
Owner-occupied units reporting[1]	...	2	...	...	...	...	3	..										
Less than $2,000	...	...	...	...	...	...	...											
$2,000 to $2,999	...	...	...	...	...	...	...											
$3,000 to $3,999	...	...	...	...	...	...	...											
$4,000 to $4,999	...	...	...	...	...	...	...											
$5,000 to $9,999	...	...	...	...	...	...	1											
$10,000 to $14,999	...	...	...	...	...	...	2											
$15,000 or more	...	...	...	...	...	...	...											
Median value dollars	...	...	...	...	...	...	...											

Subject	Tract 210	Tract 211	Tract 212	Tract 213.0	Tract 213.1	Tract 214	Tract 215
Total dwelling units	2,329	676	3,716	1,883	727	372	120
CONDITION AND PLUMBING FACILITIES							
Number reporting	2,265	581	3,509	1,804	687	343	111
No private bath or dilapidated	15	31	1,361	101	127	25	1?
No running water or dilapidated	14	14	1,322	20	15	24	..
NUMBER OF PERSONS IN DWELLING UNIT							
1 person	47	86	555	199	127	52	
2 persons	657	177	1,007	593	213	92	
3 persons	614	140	838	411	127	99	
4 persons	598	114	562	323	105	48	
5 and 6 persons	363	117	551	273	100	56	
7 persons or more	50	42	203	84	55	25	
Median number of persons	3.3	3.0	2.9	2.9	2.7	2.9	
PERSONS PER ROOM							
Number reporting	2,313	661	3,654	1,857	708	36?	
1.01 or more	274	115	685	335	211	5?	
CONTRACT MONTHLY RENT							
Renter-occupied units reporting	2,299	621	3,555	1,805	667		
Less than $10	...	...	6	1	...		
$10 to $14	...	1	3	...	2		
$15 to $19	...	17	33	23	4		
$20 to $29	3	219	1,064	199	80		
$30 to $39	992	157	1,797	481	377		
$40 to $49	282	81	484	586	98		
$50 to $74	1,017	132	157	498	9?		
$75 or more	5	14	11	17	?		
Median rent dollars	44.98	34.18	33.24	42.89	3?		
VALUE OF ONE-DWELLING-UNIT STRUCTURES							
Owner-occupied units reporting[1]	...	...					
Less than $2,000	...	..					
$2,000 to $2,999	...						
$3,000 to $3,999	...						
$4,000 to $4,999	...						
$5,000 to $9,999	...						
$10,000 to $14,999	.						
$15,000 or more							
Median value dollars							

[1] Restricted to 1-dwelling-unit properties.

See comment on figure 7-13

From U. S. Census of Population: 1950, Vol. III, Census Tract Statistics, ch. 37

N.Y. 16TH CONG. DIST. (MANHATTAN)
FIGURE 7-15

Census Tract	Population per Household	Median School Year Completed	Median Income	Median Rent	Median Value of One Unit Houses	Overcrowding 0-10%	10-20%	20%+	
185 (¼)	(3.21)	(8.3)	($2290)	($35.26)	(X)			(✓)	1
186	3.83	12.4	1523	36.74	X			✓	2
189 (¾)	3.06	8.6	2252	44.11	X			✓	3
190	3.88	7.9	1526	34.57	X			✓	4
196 (½)	3.51	8.0	1503	30.91	X		✓		5
197.1	3.24	9.4	1702	38.83	X		✓		6
198	3.19	8.1	1786	38.18	X			✓	7
200	3.28	9.4	1795	42.60	X			✓	8
201.1	3.47	9.2	1725	41.20	X			✓	9
204 (½)	2.91	7.9	1455	27.79	X			✓	10
206	3.15	7.7	1525	33.10	X			✓	11
207.1	3.25	8.2	1725	36.93	X			✓	12
208	3.39	7.7	1281	36.18	X			✓	13
209.0	3.04	8.6	1863	34.04	X			✓	14
209.1	2.89	8.3	2086	45.26	X		✓		15
210	3.41	12.4	3155	43.28	X		✓		16
212	3.25	7.7	1395	33.26	X		✓		17
213.0	3.20	9.5	2155	42.56	X		✓		18
213.1	3.25	8.2	3650	36.05	X			✓	19
216	3.73	9.0	1730	43.57	X			✓	20
217.0	3.13	8.9	1625	34.40	X		✓		21
217.1	3.48	8.6	2000	36.75	X			✓	22
218	3.81	8.5	1715	39.34	X		✓		23
220	3.53	8.8	1490	38.49	X			✓	24
221.0	3.47	11.7	2286	47.08	X		✓		25
221.1	2.76	9.4	1989	36.99	X		✓		26
222	2.75	9.3	1690	39.09	X			✓	27
224	2.85	8.1	1493	37.16	X			✓	28
226	3.20	8.1	1578	35.11	X			✓	29
227.0	2.79	9.9	2026	46.64	X			✓	30
227.1	3.01	8.3	1438	32.41	X		✓		31
228	3.04	8.7	1276	37.95	X		✓		32
230	3.93	8.6	1578	44.87	X			✓	33
231.0	3.14	9.4	1789	49.00	X			✓	34
231.1	3.09	8.3	1663	34.17	X		✓		35
232	3.24	8.2	1567	36.13	X		✓		36

CONTINUED

CENSUS TRACT	POPULATION PER HOUSE-HOLD	MEDIAN SCHOOL YEAR COMPLETED	MEDIAN INCOME	MEDIAN RENT	MEDIAN VALUE OF ONE UNIT HOUSES	OVERCROWDING 0-10%	10-20%	20%+
234	3.14	9.2	$1894	$38.39	x		✓	
235.0	3.30	11.9	1956	50.38	x		✓	
235.1	3.18	9.0	2163	35.90	x		✓	
236	3.17	11.0	2023	36.37	x		✓	
239	3.38	11.2	2040	47.30	x		✓	
243	3.49	10.3	1791	43.42	x		✓	

Figures 7-10, 7-11, 7-15, and 7-16. If more than half of a tract lies in a congressional district, count it as if the entire tract were in the district. Count tracts lying half in one district and half in another in both districts. Tract 185, which is predominantly in the Twentieth District, is listed on our worksheets but it is not included in the analysis. All entries for such tracts are circled to keep us from counting them.

2. (Refer to Fig. 7-9.) Check each tract to see if all or a sizeable portion of the population is living in institutions. (See Fig. 7-8 for the definition of the term "institutional population.") All such tracts should be excluded from further consideration and so marked on your worksheets. Examples are Tract 238 (Welfare Island) and Tract 240 (Ward's Island) in the Seventeenth and Eighteenth congressional districts, respectively.

3. (Refer to Fig. 7-9). A quick inspection of the number of Negroes living in a census tract will enable you to characterize it as predominantly white, predominantly Negro, or as falling somewhere in between. We have set up five categories on the worksheets reproduced as Figures 7-10 and 7-11: (a) predominantly white with less than 10 percent Negro; (b) predominantly white with 10 to 40 percent Negro; (c) a balanced tract in which the proportions of the Negro and white populations range from 40 to 60 percent; (d) predominantly Negro with 10 to 40 percent white; and (e) predominantly Negro with less than 10 percent white.

To save time required by machine calculations, we have classified the tracts by a quick, but, we hope, careful comparison of the number of Negroes to the total population. Ten percent of the population can easily be determined by dropping the last digit in the number or by using it to round off the preceding digit. It should be noted that Tables 4 and 5 of Volume III, *Census Tract Statistics* (reproduced as Figs. 7-13 and 7-14) provide data on selected population and housing characteristics of nonwhites in census tracts with 250 or more nonwhite persons.

The worksheets reproduced as Figures 7-10 and 7-11 clearly show that almost all the tracts in the Sixteenth Congressional District are predominantly Negro, and that most of those in the Twenty-first are predominantly white.

4. (Refer to Fig. 7-9.) We have checked on the worksheets (Figs. 7-10 and 7-11) those tracts in which more than 20 percent of the population are foreign born. In the next column we have listed in the order of magnitude the two or three countries of origin of the foreign born.

5-7. (Refer to Fig. 7-9.) Here are three measures that have already been calculated by the Bureau of the Census. Median rent and median value of one-unit-dwellings will be found in Table 3 (Fig. 7-12). They are transcribed onto worksheets by census tracts in the respective congressional districts (Figs. 7-15 and 7-16). Then the medians are arranged in ascending order from the lowest to the highest (Figs. 7-17, 7-18).

The median and quartile points have been indicated on these arrays. Notice, for example, that with respect to the average size of households, over one-fourth (Q_1) of the tracts in the Sixteenth District have larger average housholds than one-half of the tracts (median) in the Twenty-first District, and that over half of the tracts (median) in the Sixteenth have larger households than three-fourths (Q_3) of the tracts in the Twenty-first District. Examine the array of other measures to see if there are similar differences between these two adjacent congressional districts.

NY. 21st Cong. Dist. (Manhattan)
FIGURE 7-16

	①	②	③	④	⑤	⑥	⑦			
CENSUS TRACT	POPULATION PER HOUSE-HOLD	MEDIAN SCHOOL YEAR COMPLETED	MEDIAN INCOME	MEDIAN RENT	MEDIAN VALUE OF ONE UNIT HOUSES	OVERCROWDING				
							0-10%	10-20%	20%+	
197.0	*	*	*	--	--		--			1
199	2.64	12.5	$2325	$72.46	x		✓			2
201.0	3.02	14.2	2242	71.98	x	✓				3
203	2.93	16.2	1067	66.11	x		✓			4
205	2.81	14.7	2377	94.73	x	✓				5
207.0	2.50	15.8	2915	70.97	x	✓				6
211	3.17	11.0	2116	43.07	x		✓			7
215	2.97	9.3	2426	38.31	x		✓			8
219	3.72	8.0	2161	32.15	x		✓			9
223	3.71	9.1	2233	42.47	x			✓		10
225	3.31	10.4	2345	52.50	x		✓			11
229	3.60	9.6	2002	50.61	x		✓			12
233	3.29	10.4	2075	47.39	x		✓			13
237	3.26	11.7	2352	46.63	x		✓			14
241	2.97	12.1	2531	56.41	x		✓			15
245	3.14	10.0	2429	47.64	x		✓			16
247	3.27	12.2	3061	63.03	x		✓			17
249	3.23	8.6	1843	38.22	x		✓			18
251	2.83	9.5	2390	42.40	x		✓			19
253	3.16	8.9	3031	46.73	x		✓			20
255	2.96	12.4	3006	59.53	x	✓				21
257	--	--	--	--	-	--	--			22
259	--	--	--	--	-	--	--			23
261	3.59	8.9	3118	42.30	x		✓			24
263	3.17	10.5	2991	51.27	x		✓			25
265	3.32	11.1	3154	52.66	x		✓			26
267	2.93	11.4	4500	65.25	x			✓		27
269	3.26	8.8	2665	44.58	x		✓			28
271	3.11	10.2	3274	53.79	x		✓			29
273	2.69	12.3	4185	60.33	x		✓			30
275	2.71	12.7	5460	85.27	x	✓				31
277	3.10	9.9	3379	46.09	x		✓			32
279	2.92	11.4	3522	47.95	x		✓			33
281	2.86	12.3	4688	73.29	x		✓			34
283	2.88	11.4	3550	46.69	x			✓		35
285	2.96	9.4	3478	44.93	x			✓		36
287	2.88	12.3	4154	56.16	x		✓			37
289	3.14	12.0	*	81.53	x		✓			38
291	3.19	9.1	3348	42.60	x			✓		39
293	3.07	9.0	3629	43.86	x			✓		40

(CONTINUED)

N.Y. 21st Cong. Dist. (Manhattan)
FIGURE 7-16 (Continued)

① CENSUS TRACT	② POPULATION PER. HOUSE-HOLD	③ MEDIAN SCHOOL YEAR COMPLETED	④ MEDIAN INCOME	⑤ MEDIAN RENT	⑥ MEDIAN VALUE OF ONE UNIT HOUSES	⑦ OVERCROWDING 0-10%	10-20%	20%+	
295	2.90	11.4	$4025	$52.69	X		✓		1
297	3.76	*	*	45.96	X	*	*	*-	2
301	*	*	*	*	X	*	*	*	3
303	2.94	11.7	4053	48.76	X			✓	4
305	*	*	*	*	X	*	*	*	5
307	2.86	12.5	5125	64.48	X		✓		6
309	2.98	11.1	3744	46.76	X			✓	7
									8

Is there a relationship between size of household, median income, median rent, and occupational profile?

The data in the arrays (Figs. 7-17 and 7-18) are cast into frequency distribution tables in Figure 7-19. A glance at the data organized in this way brings out the differences between the two congressional districts. Read the section on frequency distributions in any elementary statistics textbook and then read Chapter 1 in Key, *A Primer of Statistics for Political Scientists* (6).

The differences between the two districts are even more clearly revealed when the data organized into frequency tables are presented graphically. Figures 7-20 and 7-21 are rough paired frequency histograms (see Key). Both the frequency tables and the histograms show a concentration of census tracts in the Sixteenth Congressional District in the lower frequency classes and a wider range of the tracts in the Twenty-first Congressional District. Do these characteristics have political significance in these districts?

8. (Refer to Fig. 7-9.) The asterisk (*), as the headnote explains, indicates that the data were secured from a 20 percent sample of the population. See pp. 4 and 5 of the "Introduction" to *Census Tract Statistics* for an explanation of the procedure and of the sampling variability to which the data are subject. If you wish at this point to read more about sampling, start with Chapter 6 in Key.

9-10. (Refer to Fig. 7-9.) Sex and residence the previous year are two characteristics of population that have not been analyzed in our study. They are mentioned here to emphasize the fact that an alert and imaginative student will find many kinds of data in the census volumes that

may have general political significance or that may be significant in his own district.

The ratio of females to males can be roughly estimated in the same manner that data on race and nativity were handled. (See notes 3 and 4.)

A highly mobile population may mean that a different class of people are moving into the district, that the relative importance of certain characteristics is changing, or that a concerted effort should be made by at least one of the candidates to get the newcomers to register as voters. Note that the category of previous residence in a different county may refer to residence in one of the other four boroughs of New York City.

Comments 11 and 12 refer to items on Table 2 (Fig. 7-22); these comments correspond to items identified by circled numbers on Figure 7-22. Comments 13 and 14 refer to Table 3 (Fig. 7-12).

11. What is the political significance of the age distribution of a population? Is it particularly important in your congressional district? How would you handle the age data in Table 2?

12. (Refer to Fig. 7-22.) An occupational profile of an area is one of the most important clues to the social status of its inhabitants. We suggest that the device used on the worksheet reproduced as Figure 7-23 will provide a rough but quick profile. One simply ranks the three leading occupations among the males in each census tract as shown and summarizes them at the bottom of the worksheet (not shown). The significance of the profile becomes apparent when that for the Sixteenth Congressional District is compared with that for the Twenty-first Congressional District. See Figure 7-24.

13. (Refer to Fig. 7-12.) Note that there are not enough owner-occupied one-dwelling-unit

WORKSHEET
FIGURE 7-17

POPULATION PER HOUSEHOLD 16TH DIST.			21ST DIST.			MEDIAN SCHOOL 16TH DIST.			YEAR COMPLETED 21ST DIST.		
2.75			2.50			7.7			8.0		
2.76			2.64			7.7			8.6		
2.79			2.69			7.7			8.8		
2.85			2.71			7.9			8.9		
2.89			2.81			7.9			8.9		
2.91			2.83			8.0			9.0		
3.01			2.86			8.1			9.1		
3.04			2.86			8.1			9.1		
3.04			2.88			8.1			9.3		
3.06			2.88			8.2			9.4		
3.09 ← Q_1			2.90 ← Q_1			8.2 ← Q_1			9.5 ← Q_1		
3.13			2.92			8.2			9.6		
3.14			2.93			8.3			9.9		
3.14			2.93			8.3			10.0		
3.15			2.94			8.3			10.2		
3.17			2.96			8.5			10.4		
3.18			2.96			8.6			10.4		
3.19			2.97			8.6			10.5		
3.20			2.97			8.6			11.0		
3.20			2.98			8.6			11.1		
3.24 ← Median			3.02 ← Median			8.7 ← Median			11.1 ← Median		
3.24			3.07			8.8			11.4		
3.25			3.10			8.9			11.4		
3.25			3.11			9.0			11.4		
3.25			3.14			9.0			11.4		
3.28			3.14			9.2			11.7		
3.30			3.16			9.2			11.7		
3.38			3.17			9.3			12.0		
3.39			3.17			9.4			12.1		
3.41 ← Q_3			3.19 ← Q_3			9.4 ← Q_3			12.2 ← Q_3		
3.47			3.23			9.4			12.3		
3.47			3.26			9.4			12.3		
3.48			3.27			9.5			12.3		
3.49			3.29			9.9			12.4		
3.51			3.31			10.3			12.5		
3.53			3.32			11.0			12.5		
3.73			3.59			11.2			12.7		
3.81			3.60			11.7			14.2		
3.83			3.71			11.9			14.7		
3.88			3.72			12.4			15.8		
3.93			3.76			12.4			16.2		

WORKSHEET
FIGURE 7-18

MEDIAN INCOME		MEDIAN RENT	
16TH DIST.	21ST DIST.	16TH DIST.	21ST DIST.
$1276	$1067	$27.79	$32.15
1281	1843	30.91	38.22
1395	2022	32.41	35.31
1438	2075	33.10	42.30
1455	2116	33.26	42.40
1490	2161	34.04	42.47
1493	2233	34.17	42.60
1503	2242	34.40	43.07
1523	2325	34.57	43.86
1525 ← Q_1	2345 ← Q_1	36.11 ← Q_1	44.58
1526	2352	35.90	44.93 ← Q_1
1567	2373	36.06	45.96
1578	2390	36.13	46.09
1578	2426	36.18	46.63
1625	2429	36.37	46.69
1663	2531	36.74	46.73
1690	2665	36.75	46.76
1702	2915	36.93	46.79
1715	2991	36.99	47.39
1725	3006 ← Median	37.16 ← Median	47.64
1725 ← Median	3031	37.95	47.95 ← Median
1730	3061	38.18	50.61
1786	3118	38.49	51.27
1789	3154	38.83	52.50
1791	3274	39.09	52.66
1795	3348	39.31	52.69
1863	3379	41.20	53.79
1894	3478	42.56	55.25
1956	3522	42.60	56.16
1989	3550	43.28 ← Q_3	56.41
2000 ← Q_3	3629 ← Q_3	43.22	59.53
2023	3744	43.57	60.63 ← Q_3
2026	4025	44.11	63.03
2040	4053	44.87	64.48
2086	4154	45.26	66.11
2155	4185	46.64	70.97
2163	4500	47.08	71.98
2252	4688	47.30	72.46
2286	5125	49.00	73.29
3155	5460	50.38	81.53
3650			85.27
			96.73

WORKSHEET
FIGURE 7-19

POPULATION PER HOUSEHOLD

	16TH	21ST
2.50 - 2.74		4
2.75 - 2.99	6	16
3.00 - 3.24	16	11
3.25 - 3.49	12	5
3.50 - 3.74	3	4
3.77 - 3.99	4	1

MEDIAN INCOME

	16TH	21ST
$ 1000 - 14.99	7	1
1500 - 1999	23	1
2000 - 2499	9	13
2500 - 2999		4
3000 - 3499	1	9
3500 - 3999	1	4
4000 - 4499		4
4500 - 4999		2
5000 - 5499		2

MEDIAN SCHOOL YEARS COMPLETED

	16TH	21ST
7.0 - 7.9	5	
8.0 - 8.9	18	5
9.0 - 9.9	11	8
10.0 - 10.9	1	5
11.0 - 11.9	4	9
12.0 - 12.9	2	10
13.0 - 13.9		
14.0 - 14.9		2
15.0 - 15.9		1
16.0 - 16.9		1

MEDIAN RENT

	16TH	21ST
$ 25.00 - 29.99	1	
30.00 - 34.99	8	1
35.00 - 35.99	18	2
40.00 - 44.99	8	8
45.00 - 49.99	5	10
50.00 - 54.99	1	6
55.00 - 59.99		4
60.00 - 64.99		3
65.00 - 69.99		1
70.00 - 74.99		4
75.00 - 79.99		
80.00 - 84.99		1
85.00 89.99		1
90.00 94.99		1

Frequency Distribution Tables

FIGURE 7-20

GRAPHIC PRESENTATION
FREQUENCY DISTRIBUTION
CENSUS TRACTS MEDIANS

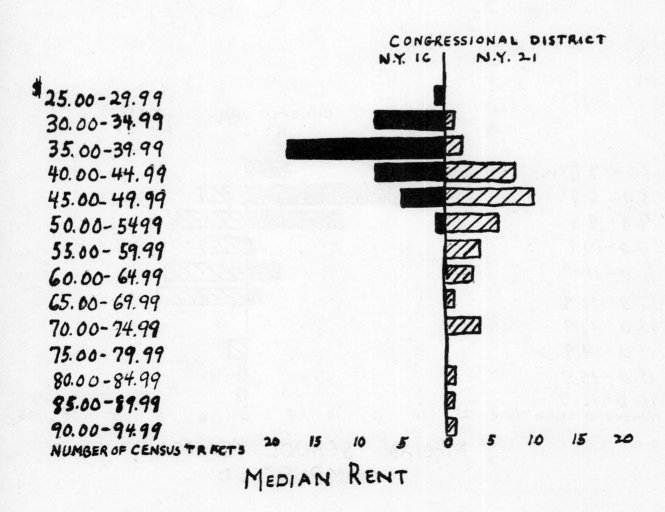

MEDIAN INCOME

MEDIAN RENT

FIGURE 7-21

GRAPHIC PRESENTATION
FREQUENCY DISTRIBUTION
CENSUS TRACTS MEDIANS

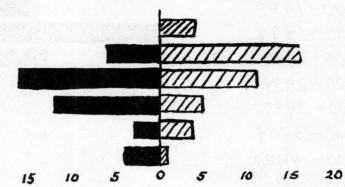

CONGRESSIONAL DISTRICTS
N.Y. 16   N.Y. 21

2.50 - 2.74
2.75 - 2.99
3.00 - 3.24
3.25 - 3.49
3.50 - 3.54
3.75 - 3.99

20   15   10   5   0   5   10   15   20

POPULATION PER HOUSEHOLD

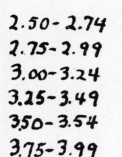

This is not a median but a mean

CONGRESSIONAL DISTRICT
N.Y. 16   N.Y. 21

7.0 - 7.9 Yrs.
8.0 - 8.9
9.0 - 9.9
10.0 - 10.9
11.0 - 11.9
12.0 - 12.9
13.0 - 13.9
14.0 - 14.9
15.0 - 15.9
16.0 - 16.9

NUMBER OF CENSUS TRACTS   25   20   15   10   5   0   5   10   15   20   25

MEDIAN SCHOOL YEARS COMPLETED

FIGURE 7-22

STATISTICS FOR CENSUS TRACTS

Table 2.—AGE, MARITAL STATUS, AND ECONOMIC CHARACTERISTICS, BY SEX, BY CENSUS TRACTS: 1950—Con.

Manhattan Borough--Con.

Subject	Tract 210 Male	Tract 210 Female	Tract 211 Male	Tract 211 Female	Tract 212 Male	Tract 212 Female	Tract 213.0 Male	Tract 213.0 Female	Tract 213.1 Male	Tract 213.1 Female	Tract 214 Male	Tract 214 Female	Tract 215 Male	Tract 215 Female	Tract 216 Male	Tract 216 Female	Tract 217.0 Male	Tract 217.0 Female
AGE																		
All classes	4,075	4,402	6,633	6,886	5,665	7,416	2,840	3,540	1,180	1,396	557	729	1,728	1,932				
Under 5 years	1,043	1,053	550	451	560	601	222	241	151	117	59	42	132					
Under 1 year	146	162	90	95	124	126	43	66	31	30	11	12	35					
1 to 4 years	897	891	460	356	436	475	179	175	120	87	48	30						
5 to 9 years	422	424	392	359	440	468	169	188	86	81	28	36						
5 years	104	103	83	86	92	82	30	41	13	14	7							
6 years	112	111	91	69	91	92	32	40	23	17	5							
7 to 9 years	206	210	218	204	257	294	107	107	50	50	16							
10 to 14 years	146	165	308	341	417	421	139	161	66	84	38							
10 to 13 years	132	138	247	268	350	351	119	117	55	64	33							
14 years	14	27	61	73	67	70	20	44	11	20	5							
15 to 19 years	89	117	377	414	423	467	127	158	68	77	?							
15 years	18	26	64	60	87	91	19	25	14	15								
16 and 17 years	43	52	148	153	170	148	58	60	22	25								
18 and 19 years	28	39	165	201	166	228	50	73	32	37								
20 to 24 years	143	401	659	671	393	662	204	271	104	137								
25 to 29 years	646	822	788	724	517	772	263	394	109	163								
30 to 34 years	629	549	600	656	485	678	286	485	126	186								
35 to 39 years	417	328	535	599	460	711	363	460	112	161								
40 to 44 years	243	173	507	504	414	649	344	345	120	11?								
45 to 49 years	125	92	494	475	428	564	255	277	71	1?								
50 to 54 years	68	76	406	435	387	464	180	18?	73									
55 to 59 years	48	58	314	358	250	352	110	124	32									
60 to 64 years	24	48	278	308	213	244	83	105	26									
65 to 69 years	21	46	191	243	157	175	56	74	19									
70 to 74 years	7	25	142	162	66	95	18	39	9									
75 to 84 years	4	18	78	156	40	85	20	27	7									
85 years and over	...	7	14	31	6	8	1	4	1									
21 years and over	2,370	2,612	4,912	5,208	3,762	5,343	2,161	2,752	796									
White	66	84	5,195	5,603	39	26	70	105	2									
Under 5 years	12	18	405	340	...	2	1	4	...									
5 to 9 years	7	9	312	294	3	1	6	2	...									
10 to 14 years	2	2	253	274	3	...	3	4										
15 to 19 years	3	2	313	341	1	...	9	5										
20 to 24 years	...	3	548	521	3	...	6	11										
25 to 29 years	14	23	577	518	10	2	6	9										
30 to 34 years	12	12	417	504	3	2	2	10										
35 to 39 years	4	5	369	455	3	4	4	9										
40 to 44 years	2	3	368	429	2	1	5	9										
45 to 49 years	2	1	386	405	2	...	7	6										
50 to 54 years	3	...	339	381	3	5	5	8										
55 to 59 years	...	4	276	324	1	4	7	9										
60 to 64 years	3	1	246	275	2	1	5	6										
65 to 69 years	1	...	169	215	2	1	1	4										
70 to 74 years	1	...	130	150	1	...	3	4										
75 years and over	...	1	87	177	...	2	...	5										
Nonwhite	4,009	4,318	1,438	1,283	5,626	7,390	2,770	3,435										
Under 5 years	1,031	1,035	145	111	560	599	221	237										
5 to 9 years	415	415	80	65	437	467	163	18?										
10 to 14 years	144	163	55	67	414	421	136	15?										
15 to 19 years	86	115	64	73	422	467	118	1?										
20 to 24 years	143	398	111	150	390	662	198	2?										
25 to 29 years	632	799	211	206	507	770	257											
30 to 34 years	617	537	183	151	482	676	284											
35 to 39 years	413	323	166	144	466	707	359											
40 to 44 years	241	170	139	75	412	648	339											
45 to 49 years	123	91	108	70	426	564	248											
50 to 54 years	65	76	67	54	384	459	175											
55 to 59 years	48	54	38	34	249	348	103											
60 to 64 years	21	47	32	33	211	242	78											
65 to 69 years	20	46	22	28	155	174	55											
70 to 74 years	6	25	12	12	65	95	15											
75 years and over	4	24	5	10	46	91	21											
MARITAL STATUS																		
Persons 14 years old and over	2,478	2,787	5,444	5,808	4,315	5,996	2,330	2,99?										
Single	186	260	2,232	1,868	1,347	1,555	520	60?										
Married	2,265	2,342	2,929	2,993	2,571	3,130	1,691	1,901										
Widowed or divorced	27	185	283	947	397	1,311	119	490										
EMPLOYMENT STATUS AND MAJOR OCCUPATION GROUP																		
Persons 14 years old and over	2,478	2,787	5,444	5,808	4,315	5,996	2,330	2,994										
Labor force	2,18?	896	3,787	2,465	3,055	3,012	1,966	1,678										
Civilian labor force	2,178	895	3,777	2,464	3,052	3,010	1,956	1,678										
Employed	2,061	852	3,424	2,305	2,600	2,767	1,739	1,506										
Private wage and salary workers	1,163	517	2,855	2,040	2,216	2,370	1,395	1,287										
Government workers	783	320	309	183	312	370	278	169										
Self-employed workers	115	15	257	77	71	27	65	46										
Unpaid family workers	...	...	3	5	1	...	1	4										
Unemployed	117	43	353	159	452	243	217	172										
Not in labor force	289	1,891	1,657	3,343	1,260	2,984	364	1,316										
Employed	2,061	852	3,424	2,305	2,600	2,767	1,739	1,50?										
Professional, technical, and kindred workers	228	242	473	437	70	233	74	127										
Managers, officials, and props., incl. farm	137	27	360	100	132	23	101	23										
Clerical and kindred workers	494	277	365	619	243	154	231	189										
Sales workers	91	21	201	101	60	32	60	30										
Craftsmen, foremen, and kindred workers	166	12	403	28	233	43	165	32										
Operatives and kindred workers	368	140	625	533	603	896	440	455										
Private household workers	2	48	15	109	20	911	11	373										
Service workers, except private household	401	66	725	325	788	411	454	259										
Laborers, except mine	161	5	178	10	408	42	179	5										
Occupation not reported	13	14	79	43	43	22	24	13										

(handwritten annotations)

See figure 7-23

Notice that data are presented for males and females in this table. Occupational rankings in figure 7-23 are for males only. You may find it necessary to make a profile for females also.

From U.S. Census of Population: 1950. Vol. III. Census Tract Statistics, ch. 37

FIGURE 7-23
N.Y. 16TH CONG. DIST. (MANHATTAN)
PRINCIPAL OCCUPATIONS - MALE

OCCUPATION	185(¼)	186	189(¼)	190	196(½)	147.1	198	200	201.1	204(¼)	206	207.1	208	209.0	209.1
PROFESSIONAL, TECH, ETC									1						
MANAGERS, OFFICIALS, ETC									2						
CLERICAL, ETC.						3								3	
SALES WORKERS															
CRAFTSMEN, ETC.	③		3							3					
OPERATIVES, ETC.	②	1	2	2	2	2	2	1		1	2	1	2	2	2
PRIVATE HOUSEHOLD															
SERVICE WORKERS	①	2	1	1	1	1	1	2		2	1	2	1	1	1
LABORERS		3		3	3		3	3			3	3	3		

OCCUPATION	210	212	213.0	213.1	216	217.0	217.0	218	220	221.0	221.1	222	224	226	227.0
PROFESSIONAL, TECH, ETC.															
MANAGERS, OFFICIALS, ETC.															
CLERICAL, ETC.	1		3			3	3		3	3	3				3
SALES WORKERS															
CRAFTSMEN, ETC.															
OPERATIVES, ETC.	3	2	2	1		2	2	2	1	2	2	2	2	2	2
PRIVATE HOUSEHOLD															
SERVICE WORKERS	2	1	1	2		1	1	1	1	1	1	1	1	1	1
LABORERS		3					3		3			3	3	3	

OCCUPATION	227.1	228	230	230.0	231.1	232	234	235.0	235.1	236	238	243
PROFESSIONAL, TECH. ETC.												
MANAGERS, OFFICIALS												
CLERICAL, ETC.		3	3	3			3	3	3	3	3	3
SALES WORKERS												
CRAFTSMEN, ETC.												
OPERATIVES, ETC.	2	2	2	2	2	2	2	2	2	2	2	2
PRIVATE HOUSEHOLD												
SERVICE WORKERS	1	1	1	1	1	1	1	1	1	1	1	1
LABORERS	3				3	3						

FIGURE 7-24

Occupational Profiles for Males

in New York 16th & 21st Congressional Districts

Number of census tracts in which the largest number of males, the second largest number and the third largest number were in the indicated occupations.

Occupation	New York 16th Congressional District			New York 21st Congressional District		
	1st	2nd	3rd	1st	2nd	3rd
Professional, teacher, etc.	1			5	5	5
Managers, officials, etc.				17	5	4
Clerical, etc.	1	1	18	1	5	13
Sales workers					2	9
Craftsmen, etc.			2	6	6	8
Operatives, etc.	6	33	1	4	12	3
Private household					1	
Service workers	33	6		8	5	1
Laborers			17			

structures in any census tract in either congressional district for a median value to be reported.

14. (Refer to Fig. 7-12.) The extent of overcrowding is suggested for the congressional district by classifying the census tracts into three groups: (a) those with less than 10 percent of the dwelling units reported as having 1.01 or more persons per room; (b) those with 10 or 20 percent; and (c) those with more than 20 percent. See the comments in notes 3 and 4.

Fortunately, census tract data in most cities have already been analyzed and interpreted by such agencies as planning commissions, councils of social agencies, health departments, civic groups, religious groups, and college departments. An early search for reports, published or unpublished, of such agencies may save you from duplicating their calculations and provide insights into the significance of the data. Such reports may also furnish you with additional data to supplement those contained in census reports.

The Bureau of the Census has issued a bibliography of many reports for tracted areas (7).

REFERENCES

1. Van Arsdol, M. D., C. F. Schmid, S. F. Camilleri, and E. H. MacCannell, "Methods of Differentiating Urban Social and Demographic Areas," *Papers Presented at the Census Tract Conference*. U.S. Bureau of the Census, Working Paper No. 7, December 29, 1958. pp. 1–10.
2. Shevky, E., and M. Williams, *The Social Areas of Los Angeles: Analysis and Typology*. Berkeley, Calif.: University of California Press, 1949.

3. Shevky, E., and W. Bell, *Social Area Analysis: Theory, Illustrative Application and Computational Procedures*. Stanford, Calif.: Stanford University Press, 1955.

4. Tryoon, R. C., *Identification of Social Areas by Cluster Analysis*. Stanford, Calif.: Stanford University Press, 1955.

5. U.S. Bureau of the Census, *U.S. Census of Population: 1950*. Vol. III, *Census Tract Statistics*. Washington, D.C.: U.S. Government Printing Office, 1952. Chap. 37.

6. Key, V. O., Jr., *A Primer of Statistics for Political Scientists*. New York: Thomas Y. Crowell Company, 1954.

7. U.S. Bureau of the Census, *Census Tract Publications Since 1950: An Annotated Bibliography*. Washington, D.C.: U.S. Government Printing Office, August 1954.

Chapter *VIII*

THE POPULATION OF THE LOCAL COMMUNITY

It has been well said that the city is the people.* Each chapter of this work is concerned with the characteristics of people.

In this chapter, however, we shall restrict our attention to the number, sex, age, and certain social characteristics of the population of local communities and their spatial distribution. We shall also be concerned with changes in these characteristics. This means that we shall be concerned with <u>births</u>, <u>deaths</u>, and <u>migrations</u>—the only means of changing the number of people in an area. Economic characteristics of population will be considered in Chapter IX.

GENERAL WORKS ON DEMOGRAPHY

Population is discussed in every text on urban sociology, rural sociology, and human ecology. See Ericksen, *Urban Behavior* (1); Quinn, *Human Ecology* (2); and Riemer, *The Modern City* (3). For a more extended discussion, see Hawley, *Human Ecology* (4). In Queen and Carpenter, *The American City* (5), demographic data are scattered through the text, but only migration is systematically discussed (in Chapter 13).

Recent editions of texts on municipal government also include a chapter on the characteristics of urban populations. See, as examples, Anderson and Weidner, *American City Government* (6); Pate, *Local Government and Administration* (7); and Adrian, *Governing Urban America* (8).

The two standard texts on population published in the United States are Thompson, *Population Problems* (9) and Landis, *Population Problems: A Cultural Interpretation* (10). See also Thompson and Whelpton, *Population Trends in the United States* (11) and U.S. National Resources Committee, *The Problems of Changing Population* (12).

The single best introductory discussion of techniques of research in population studies is Smith, *Fundamentals of Population Study* (13). See also Goode and Hatt, *Methods in Social Research* (14) and Hagood, *Statistics for Sociologists* (15). Although it is designed for those who are interested in estimating future populations, Stanbery's *Better Population Forecasting for Areas and Communities* (16), will be suggestive and helpful to students of current population statistics. See also

*See H. S. Churchill, *The City is the People*. New York: Harcourt, Brace & World, Inc., 1954.

two methodological papers by Hoover, in Berman, Chinitz, and Hoover, *Projection of a Metropolis; Technical Supplement to the New York Metropolitan Region Study* (17).

More advanced discussions of demographic techniques will be found in Jaffe, *Handbook of Statistical Methods for Demographers* (18) and, for areal analysis, in Duncan, Cuzzort, and Duncan, *Statistical Geography* (19).

It is impossible to understand demographic changes in a local community outside the context of regional and national developments. See Bogue, *The Population of the United States* (20), Taeuber and Taeuber, *The Changing Population of the United States* (21), and reports on the populations of various states. See also Bogue and Beagle, *Economic Areas of the United States* (22).

BIBLIOGRAPHICAL SOURCES

The Office of Population Research of Princeton University and the Population Association of America publish a quarterly bibliography of current materials under the title *Population Index*. Books, pamphlets and articles are classified under the following heads:

   I. General
  II. Formal Demography
 III. Mortality
  IV. Fertility
   V. Marriage, Divorce and the Family
  VI. Migration
 VII. Regional Studies
VIII. Characteristics
  IX. Policy
   X. Administration and Method
  XI. References and Compendia

Authors and countries are separately indexed. References to the United States are also listed by major classifications and by regions, states, and cities. Always check the index under "United States" <u>to see if your community or other communities in your metropolitan area are listed.</u>

In addition to this bibliography, each issue of *Population Index* carries a short essay on some aspect of demography, a few notes of news in the field, and a section of statistics. The latter usually are about countries and will not ordinarily help one in the study of local communities. Frequently, however, the short essay will provide

FIGURE 8-1

POPULATION INDEX

APRIL
1954

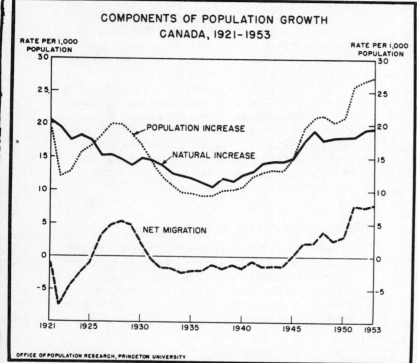

COMPONENTS OF POPULATION GROWTH
CANADA, 1921-1953

RATE PER 1,000 POPULATION

POPULATION INCREASE

NATURAL INCREASE

NET MIGRATION

OFFICE OF POPULATION RESEARCH, PRINCETON UNIVERSITY

PORTUGAL

FRANCE

SP

NETHERLAN

VOL. 20 NO. 2

OFFICE OF POPULATION RESEARCH, PRINCETON
UNIVERSITY; AND POPULATION ASSOCIATION
OF AMERICA, INC.

United States

598 Alexander, John W.
An economic base study of Madison, Wisconsin. University of Wisconsin, Bureau of Business Research and Service, Wisconsin Commerce Papers, Vol. 1, No. 4. Madison, Wis., 1953. 98 pp.

599 Barton, Thomas F.
Cities with a population decline in southwestern Indiana, 1940-1950. Proceedings of the Indiana Academy of Science 62:250-255. 1952.°

600 Beegle, J. Allan, and Thaden, J. F.-
Population change in Michigan with special reference to rural-urban migration, 1940-50. Michigan State College, Agricultural Experiment Station, Department of So-

sion.
Maryland popu
1970. Publicatio
1953. 35 pp.

609 Metropol
pany.
Large popu
cal Bulletin

610 Natio
Growth
ness Eco
63 pp.
Twen
politan
Gomp

611
Cou

Characteristics - 979, 994-998, 1
1016, 1023, 1026.
Policy - 781, 1049.
Administration and Method - 106
References and Compendia - 1068
Regions:
New England - 631.
North Central - 915.
South - 1021.
States:
Arizona - 607.
Connecticut - 807.
Florida - 603, 605.
Indiana - 599, 606.
Kansas - 632.
Maryland - 608.
Massachusetts - 1029.
Michigan - 600, 961.
Minnesota - 9
North Carolina - 749,
Pennsylvania - 908.
Rhode Island - 614.
South Dakota - 906.
Virginia - 999, 1000.
Wisconsin - 952.
Cities:
Boston, Mass. - 779.
Chicago, Ill. - 737.
Hickman, Ky. - 960.
Indianapolis, Ind. - 823, 825.
Madison, Wis. - 598.
New York, N. Y. - 611, 805, 844, 1006.
Philadelphia, Pa. - 612.
Washington, D. C. - 854.

INDEX OF COUNTRIES

SOUTH AMERICA

Argentina - 803.
Brazil - 633-637, 730, 776, 789, 893, 899,
924, 951, 1002.
British Guiana - 733, 958.
Chile - 795.
Colombia - 638, 869, 947, 974.
Ecuador - 874.
French Guiana - 1022
Peru - 639.
Venezuela

N
Po
Spa
Swe
104
Switz
United
Engla
809,
Great
Norther
Scotland
Yugoslavia

U.S.S.R. - 693

background and interpretation that will help you understand trends in the larger area of which your community is a part. Figure 8-1 is a reproduction of the title page of the issue of April, 1954, along with sample pages of the Bibliography and of the Index of Countries.

Other general bibliographical sources are *Current Geographical Publications* (see Fig. 6-1) and *Sociological Abstracts* (09: Demography and Ecology). The professional journals in sociology will also contain lists of current publications and book reviews. All of these, however, will probably be listed and classified in *Population Index*.

The Study of Population (23), edited by Hauser and Duncan, is a critical and descriptive introduction to the literature on demography. It contains bibliographical essays on demography as a science, on the development and current status of development of demography in the various countries of the world, on the principal aspects of demography studied by demographers, and on the study of population in the various social sciences. (A list of chapters that are especially recommended to the student of local politics and government are given in the references following this chapter.)

Although it is selective on the basis of relevance to the metropolitan community, the student will find an extensive bibliography on population in Government Affairs Foundation, *Metropolitan Communities: A Bibliography* (24) and in the 1955-1957 Supplement (25). Over 500 books, articles, pamphlets, and official reports are classified under the following topics: general references, characteristics, trends, current patterns of population distribution, migration, social and economic consequences of population changes, and population estimates and projections. The first volume also contains a list of agencies, journals, bibliographies, and other sources of information. See the Index for references to particular states and communities.

PRINCIPAL SOURCES OF DATA

The decennial census of the United States is the principal source of American population data. For most communities it is the only source. See Chapter VI of this text for a description of the areas for which population data are reported. Figures 6-13, 6-14 and 6-15 show the type of data to be found in the various volumes of the 1950 censuses of population and housing.

You may find that somebody or some agency has already recast population data from the census into a form significant for your own purposes. Frequently such reports will save you much labor and will enable you to use your time on other parts of the community survey.

To judge from recent publications, most studies of this kind have come from planning agencies, councils of social agencies, university research bureaus, chambers of commerce, and state departments of labor. The following are examples:

Arizona
City of Phoenix and County of Maricopa, Advance Planning Task Force, *Population Growth of the Phoenix Urban Area*, April 1959.
California
Thompson, W. S., *Growth and Changes in California's Population*, Los Angeles: The Haynes Foundation, 1955.
U.S. Department of Commerce, *Future Development of the San Francisco Bay Area, 1960-2020*, Washington, D.C.: U.S. Government Printing Office, 1959.
Connecticut
Burnight, R. G., and N. L. Whetten, *Studies in the Population of Connecticut, I. Population Growth, 1900-1950*, Storrs, Conn.: University of Connecticut Press, Storrs Agricultural Experiment Station, Bulletin 288, July 1952.
Hartford, Conn.: Commission on the City Plan, *The People of Hartford, 1940-1950*, Hartford, Conn., 1952 (mimeographed).
Florida
Maclachlan, J. M., *Florida's Population, 1920-1950; The Urban Trend and Political Representation*, Civic Information Series, No. 11, Gainesville, Fla.: University of Florida Press, 1952.
Georgia
Metropolitan Planning Commission, *We're Feeling Like a Million*, Atlanta, Ga., 1959.
Illinois
Chicago Community Inventory, "A Few Facts about Chicago's Suburbs," Chicago: University of Chicago Press, 1954.
Wirth, L., and E. H. Bernert, *Local Community Fact Book of Chicago*, Chicago: University of Chicago Press, 1949.
Northeastern Illinois Metropolitan Area Planning Commission, *Population Preview*, Chicago, 1960.
Lohman, K. B., *Cities and Towns of Illinois: A Handbook of Community Facts*, Urbana, Ill.: University of Illinois Press, 1951.
Indiana
Barton, T. F., *Population Growth of Indiana Cities, 1940-1950*, Proceedings of the Indiana Academy of Sciences 61:171-175, 1951.
Kansas
Morgan, J. D., *Some Controlling Forces in Kansas Population Movements*, viii, Lawrence, Kan.: University of Kansas, 1953.
Louisiana
Smith, T. L., and H. L. Hitt, *The People of Louisiana*, Baton Rouge, La.: Louisiana State University Press, 1952.
New Orleans Census Tract Committee and Tulane University, Urban Life Research Institute, Joint Editorial Committee, *1950 New Orleans Population Handbook*, New Orleans, La., 1953.
Maryland
Maryland State Planning Commission, *Population of Maryland, Baltimore City and Counties, 1790-1949*, Publication No. 60, IX, Baltimore, Md., 1949.
Michigan
Detroit Metropolitan Area Regional Planning Commission, *The Centers of Population of Detroit Standard Metropolitan Area and the City of Detroit 1930, 1940, and 1950*, Detroit, Mich., 1953.
Michigan Planning Commission, St. Clair County, *We*

the People of St. Clair County, 1953. Maryville, Mich., 1953.

Thaden J. F., *Contribution of Natural Increase and of Migration to Michigan's Population Changes*, Michigan Agricultural Experiment Station, Quarterly Bulletin 34 (1): 9-16, August 1951.

Minnesota

Twin Cities Metropolitan Planning Commission, *Metropolitan Population Study*, Saint Paul, Minn., 1959.

New Jersey

Brush, J. E., *The Population of New Jersey*, New Brunswick, N. J.: Rutgers University Press, 1956.

New York

Jaffe, A. J., ed., *Puerto Rican Population of New York City*, Columbia University, Bureau of Applied Social Research, New York: Columbia University Press, 1954.

New York City Planning Commission, Division of Research, *New York City: A Study of Its Population Changes*, Population Report 1, New York, July 1, 1951.

Soper, W. W., and E. W. Flinton, *Population Trends Affecting Education: the Buffalo School Survey, A Supporting Document*, Albany, N.Y.: New York State University, Bureau of Statistical Services, 1951.

Westchester County Department of Planning, *Westchester Population: 1920-2000*, Population Report 1, White Plains, N.Y., 1952.

Pennsylvania

Pennsylvania Planning Commission, Delaware County, *Population Characteristics*, Information Bulletin No. 4, Media, Penna., 1954.

Philadelphia Planning Commission, *The Population of Philadelphia and Its Metropolitan Area: General Characteristics and Trends*, Public Information Bulletin No. 6-a, Philadelphia, 1953.

Rhode Island

Mayer, K. B., *Economic Development and Population Growth in Rhode Island*, Brown University Papers, 28, Providence, R.I.: Brown University Press, 1953.

Texas

Texas Legislative Council, *Texas at Mid-century: An Interpretation of Census Data*, Austin, Tex., 1953.

Houston City Planning Commission, *Population, Land Use and Growth*, 1959.

Washington

Landis, P. H., *The People of Washington, 1890-1950*, Bulletin 535, Pullman, Wash., 1952.

Robinson, D., *Washington State Statistical Abstract*, XI, Seattle, Wash.: University of Washington Press, 1952.

Schmid, F., W. E. Kalbach, V. A. Miller, and J. Shanley, *Population and Enrollment Trends and Forecasts: State of Washington*, Seattle, Wash.: Washington State Census Board, 1953.

Seattle City Planning Commission, "Land Area and Population Density of the Seattle Standard Metropolitan Area," *Current Planning Research*, No. 7, October 19, 1951.

Seattle City Planning Commission, "Growth by Annexation, City of Seattle: 1869-1953," *Current Planning Research*, No. 11, June 1, 1951.

Wisconsin

Milwaukee Board of Public Land Commissioners, *Population Changes by Census Tracts, City of Milwaukee, 1920-1950*. Milwaukee, Wis., 1953.

Madison City Plan Commission, *Madison's Population*, 1959.

Data on births and deaths can be secured from local or state health departments. In some states annual population estimates are issued by a state agency for counties, cities, and townships.

The U.S. Bureau of the Census makes special population counts at the request and expense of governmental units. See the *Municipal Year Book*, 1960, pp. 30-35, for a description of the scope and method of the special census and of the populations reported in special censuses between 1950 and 1959 for 481 places with populations in 1950 of 5,000 or more. The names of the governmental areas where special censuses have been taken will also be listed in the *Catalog of United States Census Publications*.

THE SIGNIFICANCE OF POPULATION DATA

The population of a community, or of its parts, has many significances. Some of these will become evident as you study your community. It is clear that a populous community will have problems and resources unknown to a small, isolated community. Rapid population growth means, at the least, that new public and private services are required; a decline in population means, among other things, that public and private facilities will be vacant and unused. See Halterman, *The Impact of Population Growth in the South Coastal Area of Santa Barbara County* (26).

Population is used in many states as the legal basis for classifying units of local government. Frequently the duties and powers of these units vary from class to class. Anderson and Weidner discuss the classification of cities as a means of avoiding constitutional prohibitions against special legislation. For examples, see the *Final Report* of the New Jersey Joint Legislative Committee to Study the Effect of the 1950 Census on Certain Statutes (Trenton, June 22, 1953).

Population is often used in formulas for the apportionment of state aid to local governments. This is one of the principal reasons why some communities have a special census taken during the period between the regular decennial censuses. The special census taken in San Diego, California, in March 1952 showed that the population of the city had increased from 334,387 in 1950 to 434,924. This was an increase of 30 percent in twenty-three months. One result of this official census was to increase considerably the amount of state aid received under per capita grants.

It has often been observed that the size of a city is related to its political tendency. See Gallup, *The Political Almanac* (27). Compare city voting statistics with national and state figures. Compare the vote in cities over 100,000 population in your state with cities under 25,000.

The number of inhabitants in a particular area is frequently divided into another quantity to secure a per capita measure of growth, needs, resources, costs. The magnitude of governmental problems and of social and economic activities is assumed to vary with the size of the population. Per capita indexes for several cities are often used as a basis for comparing cities with each other. The following warning is quoted from the *Municipal Year Book:*

The usefulness of such an index is severely limited by the fact that population is only a very crude measure of problem-magnitude. Fire risk, for instance, is related directly to the amount and type of burnable property and only indirectly to population. The per capita fire risk will therefore vary with valuation per capita and types of property, and per capita fire loss is only a very approximate measure of adequacy of service.

Measures of cost per capita are even more limited in their usefulness. Since they fail to measure the level of service they are in no sense indexes of efficiency. A high per capita cost may indicate (1) that population does not adequately measure problem-magnitude, that is, that climatic, structural, economic, social, or other extragovernmental factors affected the problem; (2) that the level of service provided is high; or (3) that the activity is being inefficiently administered. However, if care is taken to compare cities which are similar in type and situation, and if allowance is made for unusual conditions, then per capita statistics can be useful.*

Only a few instances of the importance of the number of inhabitants are given here. Observe in your reading and interviews how frequently population data and per capita comparisons are made and how such material is used in the actual administration of federal, state, and local governments.

DEFINITION OF POPULATION

The population reported in official censuses is the number of people residing in a particular place:

According to usual census practice, which dates back to 1790, each person enumerated in the 1950 census was counted as an inhabitant of his usual place of residence or usual place of abode, which is generally construed to mean the place where he lives and sleeps most of the time. This place is not necessarily the same as his legal residence, voting residence, or domicile, although in the vast majority of cases, these different bases of classification would be identical.**

In metropolitan areas, however, the place where a person "lives...most of the time," i.e., works, is entertained, goes to school, may not be the same as the place where he and his family "sleep most of the time." When population figures are used, it should be remembered that they refer to the nighttime and not to the daytime population of an area.

Municipal Year Book. Chicago: International City Managers' Association, 1950.
**U.S. Bureau of the Census, *U.S. Census of Population: 1950*. Vol. I, Number of Inhabitants, p. vii. The introductory comments define and illustrate the various terms and bases of classification.

The daily movement of people from places of residence to places of work, trade and recreation is one of the characteristics that distinguishes modern metropolitan communities from the urban communities of the last century. Commutation and the attendant problems of motor and rail transportation are likely to be of major political and administrative concern to most communities, whether they are large central cities or suburbs. Wilfred Owen has summarized the discussions of these problems by city planners, architects, businessmen, politicians, scholars, and city, state and federal administrators in *Cities in the Motor Age* (28). See also Breese, *The Daytime Population of the Central Business District of Chicago* (29) and Foley's article, "Urban Daytime Population: A Field for Demographic Ecological Analyses," in *Social Forces* (30).

Other references will be found in *Metropolitan Communities*, pp. 272-274, and in the 1955-1957 Supplement, pp. 139-140.

For the first time in the history of the census, data collected on a sample basis in 1960 is reported on <u>place of work</u> as well as on <u>place of residence</u>. The number of people working inside and outside the county of residence are reported for each county, for urban places of 10,000 or more, for urbanized areas, and for standard metropolitan statistical areas (SMSA). More specific data are reported for census tracts.

Many state employment agencies made commutation surveys in 1957 and 1958. Check with the local office of your state agency to see if one has been made for the labor market area in which your community is located.

The student should note at least the following elements of population data for his area: (a) total population given in the latest and in all previous censuses; (b) the amount of increase and decrease between censuses; and (c) the percentage changes in population. The principal source of data on the number of inhabitants is the U.S. Census. For 1960, these data are published as Chapter A of the respective state volumes of *U.S. Census of Population: 1960*. Vol. II, *Characteristics of Population*. Chapters A for all the states are also published as a separate compendium in Vol. I, Part A, *Number of Inhabitants*. Figure 8-2 reproduces examples of relevant tables for the state of Georgia.

Do not use the data before reading the definition of terms at the beginning of the chapter. The footnotes to tables are especially important because they call attention to changes in areas and in the definitions of terms from census to census. However, the historical use of statistical data is necessary to an understanding of the growth and changes in your community. Figure 8-3 shows the kind of data you can get from each census since 1790.

FIGURE 8-2   Number of Inhabitants

Table 4.—POPULATION IN INCORPORATED AND UNINCORPORATED PLACES ACCORDING TO SIZE: 1960

Size of place and urban-rural classification	All places		Incorporated places		Unincorporated places	
	Number	Population	Number	Population	Number	Population
Total	613	2,216,911	592	2,140,779	21	76,132
500,000 or more	...	...	...	...	...	...
250,000 to 500,000	1	487,455	1	487,455	...	...
100,000 to 250,000	2	266,024	2	266,024	...	...
50,000 to 100,000	3	196,280	3	196,280	...	...
25,000 to 50,000	5	155,431	5	155,431	...	...
20,000 to 25,000	6	133,509	6	133,509	...	...
10,000 to 20,000	17	235,912	16	219,003	1	16,909
5,000 to 10,000	29	204,885	26	184,372	3	20,513
2,500 to 5,000	61	221,017	55	200,818	6	20,199
2,000 to 2,500	22	49,854	20	45,320	2	4,534
1,500 to 2,000	39	66,495	32	54,588	7	11,907
1,000 to 1,500	60	73,736	58	71,666	2	2,070
500 to 1,000	90	61,906	90	61,906	...	...
200 to 500	154	49,814	154	49,814	...	...
Under 200	124	14,593	124	14,593	...	...
In urbanized areas	24	1,103,234	24	1,103,234	...	...
500,000 or more	...	...	...	...	...	...
250,000 to 500,000	1	487,455	1	487,455	...	...
100,000 to 250,000	2	266,024	2	266,024	...	...
50,000 to 100,000	3	196,280	3	196,280	...	...
25,000 to 50,000	1	35,633	1	35,633	...	...
20,000 to 25,000	2	45,495	2	45,495	...	...
10,000 to 20,000	3	36,944	3	36,944	...	...

Size of place and urban-rural classification	All places		Incorporated places		Unincorporated places	
	Number	Population	Number	Population	Number	Population
In urbanized areas—Con.						
5,000 to 10,000	2	12,086	2	12,086	...	...
2,500 to 5,000	3	12,807	3	12,807	...	...
2,000 to 2,500	1	2,251	1	2,251	...	...
1,500 to 2,000	4	6,700	4	6,700	...	...
1,000 to 1,500	1	1,213	1	1,213	...	...
500 to 1,000	...	...	...	...	...	...
200 to 500	1	346	1	346	...	...
Under 200	...	...	...	...	...	...
Other urban territory	107	807,789	97	750,168	10	57,621
25,000 to 50,000	4	119,798	4	119,798	...	...
20,000 to 25,000	4	88,014	4	88,014	...	...
10,000 to 20,000	14	198,968	13	182,059	1	16,909
5,000 to 10,000	27	192,799	24	172,286	3	20,513
2,500 to 5,000	58	208,210	52	188,011	6	20,199
Rural territory	482	305,888	471	287,377	11	18,511
2,000 to 2,500	21	47,603	19	43,069	2	4,534
1,500 to 2,000	35	59,795	28	47,888	7	11,907
1,000 to 1,500	59	72,523	57	70,453	2	2,070
500 to 1,000	90	61,906	90	61,906	...	...
200 to 500	153	49,468	153	49,468	...	...
Under 200	124	14,593	124	14,593	...	...

Table 5.—POPULATION OF INCORPORATED PLACES OF 10,000 OR MORE FROM EARLIEST CENSUS TO 1960

[Minus sign (–) denotes decrease]

Incorporated place and census year	Population	Increase over preceding census		Incorporated place and census year	Population	Increase over preceding census	
		Number	Percent			Number	Percent
ALBANY:				AUGUSTA--Con.			
1960	55,890	24,735	79.4	1920	52,548		
1950	31,155	12,100	63.5	1910			
1940	19,055	4,548	31.4	1900			
1930	14,507	2,952	25.5	1890			
1920	11,555	3,365	41.1	1880			
1910	8,190	3,584	77.8				
1900	4,606	598	14.9				
1890	4,008	792					
1880	3,216						
1870	2,101						
1860							
AMERICUS:							

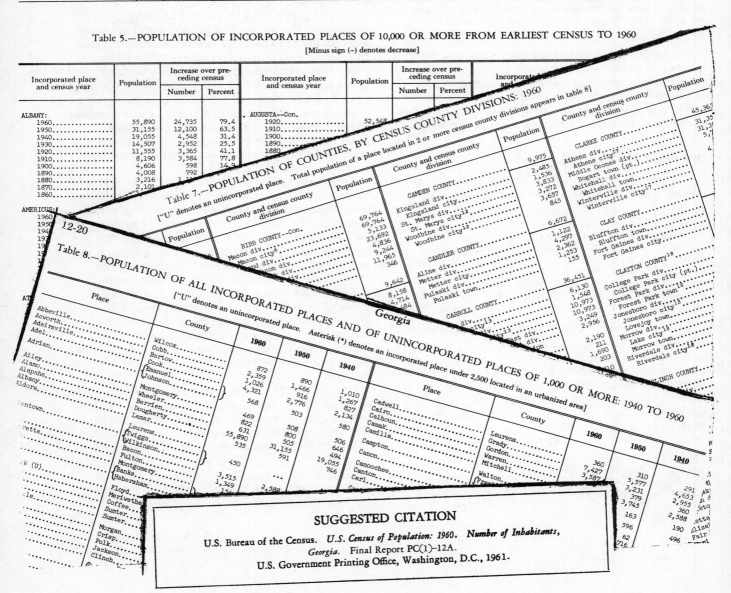

Table 7.—POPULATION OF COUNTIES, BY CENSUS COUNTY DIVISIONS: 1960

[Total population of a place located in 2 or more census county divisions appears in table 8]
["U" denotes an unincorporated place.]

Table 8.—POPULATION OF ALL INCORPORATED PLACES AND OF UNINCORPORATED PLACES OF 1,000 OR MORE: 1940 TO 1960

["U" denotes an unincorporated place. Asterisk (*) denotes an incorporated place under 2,500 located in an urbanized area]

12-20

Georgia

SUGGESTED CITATION

U.S. Bureau of the Census. *U.S. Census of Population: 1960. Number of Inhabitants, Georgia.* Final Report PC(1)–12A. U.S. Government Printing Office, Washington, D.C., 1961.

Inquiries Included in Each Population Census, 1790 to 1960

CENSUS OF 1960

Address; name; relationship to head of household; sex; race; month and year of birth; marital status; whether residence is on farm; place of birth—in which State, U. S. Possession, or foreign country; if born outside U. S., language spoken in home before coming to U. S.; country of birth of parents; length of residence at present address, where resided five years earlier; educational attainment; school or college attendance, and whether public or private school; times married and date of first marriage; of women ever married, how many children ever borne; employment status; hours worked in week preceding enumeration; date last worked; occupation, industry, and class of worker; place of work—which city or town (and whether in city limits or outside), county, State; means of transportation to work; weeks worked in 1959; earnings in 1959; other income in 1959; veteran status—which war and present service.

CENSUS OF 1950

Address; whether house is on farm; name; relationship to head of household; race; sex; age; marital status; State (or foreign country) of birth; if foreign born, whether naturalized; employment status during week preceding enumeration; hours worked; occupation, industry, and class of worker; whether living in same house a year ago; whether living on farm a year ago; if not in same house, county and State of residence a year ago; country of birth of parents; educational attainment; school attendance; if looking for work, how many weeks has he been looking; number of weeks worked in 1949; earnings in 1949; other income in 1949; veteran status—which war and present service; for persons who worked last year but not in current labor force, occupation, industry, and class of worker on last job; if ever married, whether married more than once; duration of present marital status; if female and ever married, number of children ever borne.

CENSUS OF 1940

Address; home owned or rented; value or monthly rental; whether on a farm; name, relationship to head of household; sex; race; age; marital status; school or college attendance; educational attainment; place of birth—if U. S., State, Territory, or Possession—if foreign born, country in which birthplace was situated on January 1, 1937; citizenship of foreign born; county and State of residence five years earlier and whether on farm or in place of 2500 or more inhabitants; employment status during week of March 24-30, 1940; if at work, whether in private or nonemergency government work, or in public emergency work (WPA, NYA, CCC, etc.); if in private or nonemergency government work, number of hours worked during week of March 24-30; if seeking work or on public emergency work, duration of unemployment up to March 30; occupation, industry, and class of worker; number of weeks worked in 1939; wage or salary income in 1939 and whether received other income of $50 or more; place of birth (State, Territory, possession, or foreign country) of father and mother; language spoken in home in earliest childhood; veteran status, or whether wife, widow or under-18 child of veteran; whether has Social Security number, and if so whether deductions were made from all or part of wages or salary; usual occupation, industry, and class of worker; of women ever married—whether married more than once, age at first marriage, and number of children ever borne.

CENSUS OF 1930

Name; address; relationship to head of family; home owned or rented; value or monthly rental; radio set; whether family lives on a farm; sex; race; age; marital status; age at first marriage; school attendance; ability to read and write; place of birth of person, father, and mother; if foreign born, language spoken in home before coming to U.S.; year of immigration; naturalization; ability to speak English; occupation, industry, and class of worker; whether actually at work previous day (or last regular working day); whether a veteran of U.S. military or naval forces, which war. Special schedule used for further detail on unemployment.

CENSUS OF 1920

Address; name; relationship to head of family; home owned or rented; if owned, free or mortgaged; sex; race; age; marital status; year of immigration to the U.S.; naturalized or alien; if naturalized, year of naturalization; school attendance; place of birth of person, father, and mother; for each of these reporting foreign birth, what was mother tongue (native language); ability to speak English; occupation, industry, and class of worker.

CENSUS OF 1910

Address; name; relationship to head of family; sex; race; age; marital status; number of years of present marriage; mother of how many children and number now living; place of birth of person, father, and mother; for foreign born persons, year of immigration to U. S.; whether naturalized or alien; ability to speak English; if not, language spoken; occupation, industry, and class of worker; if an employee, number of weeks out of work during year; ability to read and write; school attendance; home owned or rented; if owned, is it free or mortgaged; whether a survivor of Union or Confederate Army or Navy; whether blind or deaf and dumb.

CENSUS OF 1900

Address; name; relationship to head of family; sex; race; age; marital status; number of years married; mother of how many children and number now living;

place of birth of person, father, and mother; if person is foreign born, year of immigration to the U.S.; number of years in the U. S.; whether naturalized; occupation, trade, or profession of persons 10 years old and over; months not employed; months attended school; ability to write or read; ability to speak English; home owned or rented; if owned, whether free of mortgage.

CENSUS OF 1890

Address; number of families in house; number of persons in house; number of persons in family; name; whether a soldier, salior or marine during Civil War (Union or Confederate) or widow of such person; relationship to head of family; white, black, mulatto, quadroon, octoroon, Chinese, Japanese, or Indian; sex; age; marital status; whether married during year; mother of how many children, and number now living; place of birth of person, father, and mother; if person is foreign born, number of years in the U. S.; whether naturalized; whether papers have been taken out; profession, trade, or occupation; months unemployed during census year; ability to read and write; ability to speak English; if not, language or dialect spoken; whether suffering from acute or chronic disease, with name of disease and length of time afflicted; whether defective in mind, sight, hearing, or speech, or whether crippled, maimed, or deformed, with name of defect; whether a prisoner, convict, homeless child, or pauper; home rented, or owned by head or member of family; if owned by head or member, is it free from mortgage; if head of family is a farmer, is farm rented or owned by him or member of his family; if owned, is it free of mortgage; if mortgaged, give post office address of owner.

CENSUS OF 1880

Address; name; relationship to head of family; sex; race; age; marital status; born within the year; married within the year; profession, occupation, or trade; number of months unemployed during census year; whether person is sick or temporarily disabled so as to be unable to attend to ordinary business or duties; if so, what is the sickness or disability; whether blind, deaf and dumb, idiotic, insane, maimed, crippled or bedridden; attended school within the year; ability to read and write; place of birth of person, father, and mother.

CENSUS OF 1870

Address; name; age; sex; color (including Chinese and Indian); citizenship for males over 21; profession, occupation, or trade; value of real estate; value of personal estate; place of birth; whether father and mother were foreign born; born within the year; married within the year; attended school within the year; for persons 10 years old and over whether able to read and write; whether deaf and dumb, blind, insane, or idiotic.

CENSUS OF 1860

Name; address; age; sex; color (white, black, or mulatto) for each person; whether deaf and dumb, blind, insane, or idiotic; all free persons required to give value of real estate and of personal estate owned; profession, occupation, or trade for each male and female over 15; place of birth (State, Territory, or country); whether married within the year, whether attended school within the year; whether unable to read and write for persons over 20; whether a pauper or convict.

CENSUS OF 1850

Name; address; age; sex; color (white, black, or mulatto) for each person; whether deaf and dumb, blind, insane or idiotic; all free persons required to give value of real estate owned; profession, occupation, or trade for each male person over 15; place of birth; whether married within the year; whether attended school within the year; whether unable to read and write for persons over 20; whether a pauper or convict.

CENSUS OF 1840

Name of head of family; address; number of free white males and females in 5-year age groups to 20, 10-year age groups from 20 to 100, and 100 years old and over; number of slaves and free colored persons in six broad age groups; number of deaf and dumb; number of blind; number of insane and idiotic in public or private charge; number of persons in each family employed in each of seven classes of occupations; number of schools and number of scholars; number of white persons over 20 who could not read and write; number of pensioners for Revolutionary or military service.

CENSUS OF 1830

Name of head of family; address; number of free white males and females in 5-year age groups to 20, 10-year age groups from 20 to 100, and 100 years old and over; number of slaves and free colored persons in six broad age groups; number of deaf and dumb under 14, 14 to 24, and 25 years and upward; number of blind; foreigners not naturalized.

CENSUS OF 1820

Name of head of family; address; number of free white males and females under 10 years of age, 10 and under 16, 16 and under 26, 26 and under 45, and 45 years and upward; number of free white males between 16 and 18 years; foreigners not naturalized; male and female slaves and free colored persons under 14 years, 14 and under 26, 26 and under 45, and 45 and upward; all other free persons, except Indians not taxed; number of persons (including slaves) engaged in agriculture, commerce, and manufactures.

CENSUS OF 1810

Name of head of family; address; number of free white males and females under 10 years of age, 10 and under 16, 16 and under 26, 26 and under 45, and 45 years and upward; all other free persons, except Indians not taxed; number of slaves.

CENSUS OF 1800

Name of head of family; address; number of free white males and females under 10 years of age, 10 and under 16, 16 and under 26, 26 and under 45, and 45 years and upward; all other free persons, except Indians not taxed; number of slaves.

CENSUS OF 1790

Name of head of family; address; number of free white males of 16 years and up, including heads; free white males under 16; free white females, including heads; all other free persons; number of slaves.

FIGURE 8-3 (Continued)

13383--U.S.Dept.of Comm--DC--1960

USE OF POPULATION DATA

Illustrations of the manner in which these data may be analyzed are reproduced from the report of the Philadelphia City Planning Commission, *The Population of Philadelphia and Its Metropolitan Area: General Characteristics and Trends* (1953).

The population of the Philadelphia Standard Metropolitan Area and its constituent counties at each census from 1850 to 1950 is shown in Figure 8-4. The table shows the numerical increase or decrease as well as the percentage changes by decades, by half centuries, and for the century. It also shows the percentage distribution by decades of the metropolitan population among the counties that now make up the standard metropolitan area.

The total population of the metropolitan area, broken down by counties, is plotted by decades from 1850 to 1950 in a graph reproduced as Figure 8-5. This is an arithmetic graph showing the absolute numbers of the populations of the various counties. The slope of the line between points does not indicate the relative rate of change. In fact, the graph is designed to show two things that might more effectively have been shown on two different graphs. If the population of only two or three areas is to be plotted, an ordinary line graph can be used to show the change in size of the population from census year to census year. A graph of this kind with six lines is reproduced as Figure 8-6. In a cumulative line graph, such as that in Figure 8-5, the population of any area must be obtained by subtracting the population of all areas located below it on the graph from the sum of the population of these areas and its own population. The population of Delaware County, for example, can be obtained by subtracting the population of Philadelphia from that for Philadelphia and Delaware County combined. In a cumulative line graph of this kind the lines are misleading.

The other thing that Figure 8-5 is intended to show is the distribution of the metropolitan population among the eight counties. For this purpose it would be better to use a percentage bar chart.

The absolute size of a population at different times can be plotted on a graph with a semilogarithmic scale. Such a graph will not only show the absolute size of a population at various points of time but will also show, from the relative slope of the line, the relative rates of change of two or more populations. Irrespective of the magnitudes involved, the same percentage change will be shown on a semilog graph by the same distance on the scale. An arithmetic and a semilog graph showing the changes in the population of Kenosha and other second-class cities in Wisconsin between 1900 and 1950 are reproduced in Figure 8-6.

It is possible, of course, to calculate the percentage change and to plot the percentages. A semilog graph saves time for both the maker and

the user in that it shows both absolute size and relative rates of change.

You may wish to compare the size of the population of your community over a period of time and its rate of change with those of similar communities or of larger areas of which your community is a part. Figure 8-7 is a reproduction of a semilog graph prepared by the Indiana Economic Council for its *Economic Survey of the Terre Haute Area*, (Part I, Bulletin No. 14, July, 1951, p. 25). The plotting of the absolute population of the state, of the Terre Haute Area, and of its seven component counties for the period 1830-1950 on semilog paper enable one to compare the rates of change of the various units.

If a large number of curves are plotted on a single graph, the total impression may be confusing. One way to avoid the comingling of straight lines with dotted, broken, colored, and other kinds of lines is to plot each series on a separate semilog graph small enough so that all the graphs can be reproduced on a single page. Many more semilog graphs can be accommodated on a single page than can arithmetic graphs because in the former it is not necessary (in fact, it is impossible) to begin the scale at zero. This means that each graph need be no larger than is necessary to accommodate the curve. Figure 8-8 is reproduced from Bulletin 85 of the Regional Plan Association, *Population 1954-1957 in the New Jersey-New York-Connecticut Metropolitan Region* (November 1954) to illustrate the use of this method of charting relative population changes in the United States, in the metropolitan region, in New York City, in its five boroughs, and in sixteen suburban counties.

COMPONENTS OF POPULATION CHANGE

A population increases or decreases as a result of an excess of births over deaths or of deaths over births or because of the movement of people into or out of an area. In most instances a combination of these factors produces the net effect which is registered in the census as an increase or decrease in population.

The number of births and deaths can be secured from the local or state department of public health or from the registrar of vital statistics. The various rates that can be derived from the data are explained in Smith, Chapters 11-17, in Goode and Hatt, Chapter 18, and in Thompson, pp. 147-158 and 228-231.

Our concern at this point is with the use of the number of births and deaths to ascertain the net migration into or out of an area during the period between censuses. In the tables reproduced as Figures 8-9 and 8-10, the ''net migration for the decade 1940-1950 is found by taking the April 1, 1940, population, adding the births and subtracting the deaths April 1, 1940-March 31, 1950, and finding the difference between the result of the

FIGURE 8-4

TABLE I.

POPULATION OF THE PHILADELPHIA STANDARD METROPOLITAN AREA, BY COUNTIES; 1850 TO 1950

NUMERICAL INCREASE, PERCENTAGE INCREASE, AND PERCENTAGE OF TOTAL AREA POPULATION

YEAR	METROPOLITAN AREA	BUCKS PA.	CHESTER PA.	DELAWARE PA.	MONTGOMERY PA.	PHILADELPHIA PA.	BURLINGTON N.J.	CAMDEN N.J.	GLOUCESTER N.J.
				POPULATION					
1950	3,671,048	144,620	159,141	414,234	353,068	2,071,605	135,910	300,743	91,727
1940	3,199,637	107,715	135,626	310,756	289,247	1,931,334	97,013	255,727	72,219
1930	3,137,040	96,727	126,629	280,264	265,804	1,950,961	93,541	252,312	70,802
1920	2,714,271	82,476	115,120	173,084	199,310	1,823,779	81,770	190,508	48,224
1910	2,268,209	76,530	109,213	117,906	169,590	1,549,008	66,565	142,029	37,368
1900	1,892,128	71,190	95,695	94,762	138,995	1,293,697	58,241	107,643	31,905
1890	1,577,720	70,615	89,377	74,683	123,290	1,046,964	56,455	87,687	28,649
1880	1,293,823	68,656	83,481	56,101	96,494	847,170	53,093	62,942	25,886
1870	1,056,343	64,336	77,805	39,403	81,612	674,022	51,410	42,963	24,792
1860	903,583	63,578	74,578	30,597	70,500	565,529	45,900	31,733	21,168
1850	697,541	56,091	66,438	24,679	58,291	408,762	43,203	25,422	14,655
				NUMBER INCREASE					
1950	471,411	36,905	23,515	103,478	63,821	140,271	38,897	45,016	19,508
1940	62,597	10,988	8,997	30,492	23,443	-19,627	3,472	3,415	1,417
1930	422,769	14,251	11,509	107,180	66,494	127,182	11,771	61,804	22,578
1920	446,062	5,946	5,907	55,178	29,720	274,771	15,205	48,479	10,856
1910	376,081	5,340	13,518	23,144	30,595	255,311	8,324	34,386	5,463
1900	314,408	575	6,318	20,079	15,705	246,733	1,786	19,956	3,256
1890	283,897	1,959	5,896	18,582	26,796	199,794	3,362	24,745	2,763
1880	237,480	4,320	5,676	16,698	14,882	173,148	1,683	19,979	1,094
1870	152,760	758	3,227	8,806	11,112	108,493	5,510	11,230	3,624
1860	206,042	7,487	8,140	5,918	12,209	156,767	2,697	6,311	6,513
1850-1900	1,194,587	15,099	29,257	70,083	80,704	884,935	15,038	82,221	17,250
1900-1950	1,778,920	73,430	63,446	319,472	214,073	777,908	77,669	193,100	59,822
1850-1950	2,973,507	88,529	92,703	389,555	294,777	1,662,843	92,707	275,321	77,072
				PERCENT INCREASE					
1950	14.7	34.3	17.3	33.3	22.1	7.3	40.1	17.6	27.0
1940	2.0	11.4	7.1	10.9	8.8	-1.0	3.7	1.4	2.0
1930	15.6	17.6	10.0	61.9	33.4	7.0	14.4	32.4	46.8
1920	19.7	7.8	5.4	46.8	17.5	17.7	22.8	34.1	29.1
1910	19.9	7.5	14.1	24.4	22.0	19.7	14.3	31.9	17.1
1900	19.9	0.8	7.1	26.9	12.7	23.6	3.2	22.8	11.4
1890	21.9	2.9	7.1	33.1	27.8	23.6	6.3	39.3	10.7
1880	22.5	6.7	7.3	42.4	18.2	25.2	3.3	46.5	4.4
1870	16.9	1.2	4.3	28.8	15.8	19.2	12.0	35.4	17.1
1960	29.5	13.3	12.3	24.0	20.9	38.4	6.2	24.8	44.4
1850-1900	171.3	26.9	44.0	284.0	138.5	216.5	34.8	323.4	117.7
1900-1950	94.0	103.1	66.3	337.1	154.0	60.1	133.4	179.4	187.5
1850-1950	426.3	157.8	139.5	1,578.5	505.7	406.8	214.6	1,083.0	525.9
				PERCENT OF TOTAL AREA					
1950	100.0	3.94	4.34	11.28	9.62	56.43	3.70	8.19	2.50
1940	100.0	3.37	4.24	9.71	9.04	60.36	3.03	7.99	2.26
1930	100.0	3.08	4.04	8.93	8.47	62.19	2.98	8.04	2.26
1920	100.0	3.04	4.24	6.38	7.34	67.19	3.01	7.02	1.78
1910	100.0	3.37	4.81	5.20	7.48	68.29	2.93	6.26	1.65
1900	100.0	3.76	5.06	5.01	7.35	68.37	3.08	5.69	1.69
1890	100.0	4.48	5.66	4.73	7.81	66.35	3.58	5.56	1.82
1880	100.0	5.31	6.45	4.34	7.46	65.47	4.10	4.86	2.00
1870	100.0	6.09	7.37	3.73	7.73	63.81	4.87	4.07	2.35
1860	100.0	7.04	8.25	3.39	7.80	62.59	5.08	3.51	2.34
1850	100.0	8.04	9.52	3.54	8.36	58.60	6.19	3.64	2.10

SOURCE: U.S. CENSUS. POPULATION FIGURES ADJUSTED FOR COUNTY AREAS AS OF 1950.

PREPARED BY PHILADELPHIA CITY PLANNING COMMISSION, DIVISION OF PLANNING ANALYSIS, AUGUST 1953.

PHILADELPHIA CITY PLANNING COMMISSION, THE POPULATION OF PHILADELPHIA AND ITS METROPOLITAN AREA: GENERAL CHARAC— TERISTICS AND TRENDS (1953)

FIGURE 8-5

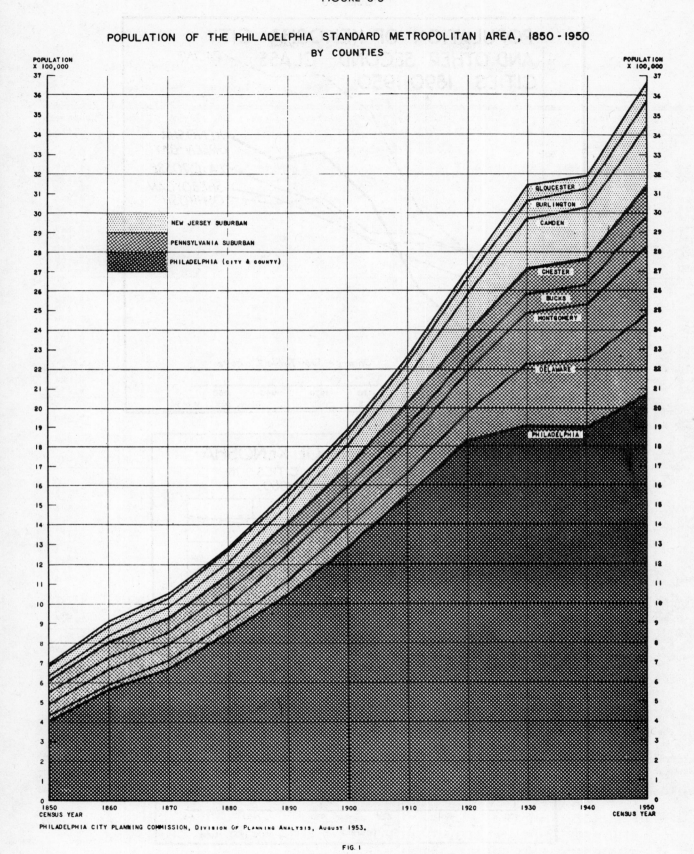

POPULATION OF THE PHILADELPHIA STANDARD METROPOLITAN AREA, 1850-1950
BY COUNTIES

PHILADELPHIA CITY PLANNING COMMISSION, Division Of Planning Analysis, August 1953.

FIG. I

**PHILADELPHIA CITY PLANNING COMMISSION, THE POPULATION OF
PHILADELPHIA AND ITS METROPOLITAN AREA: GENERAL CHARAC-
TERISTICS AND TRENDS (1953)**

FIGURE 8-6

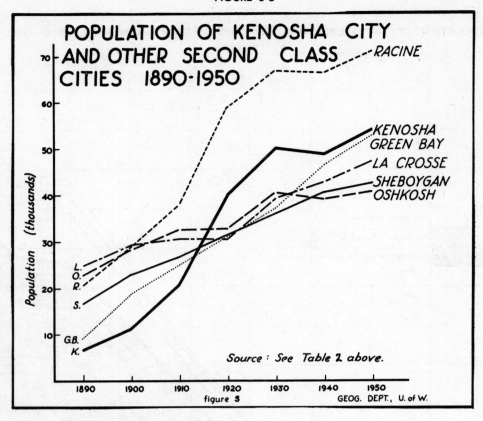

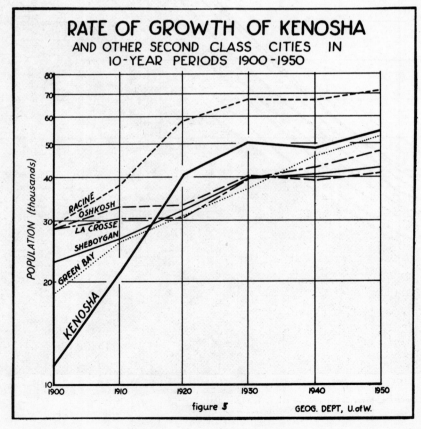

KENNETH RINDT, PART 1, PP 9, 12

"A Survey of Kenosha Economic Life and Related Aspects" (University of Wisconsin, University Extension Division, 1954)

FIGURE 8-7

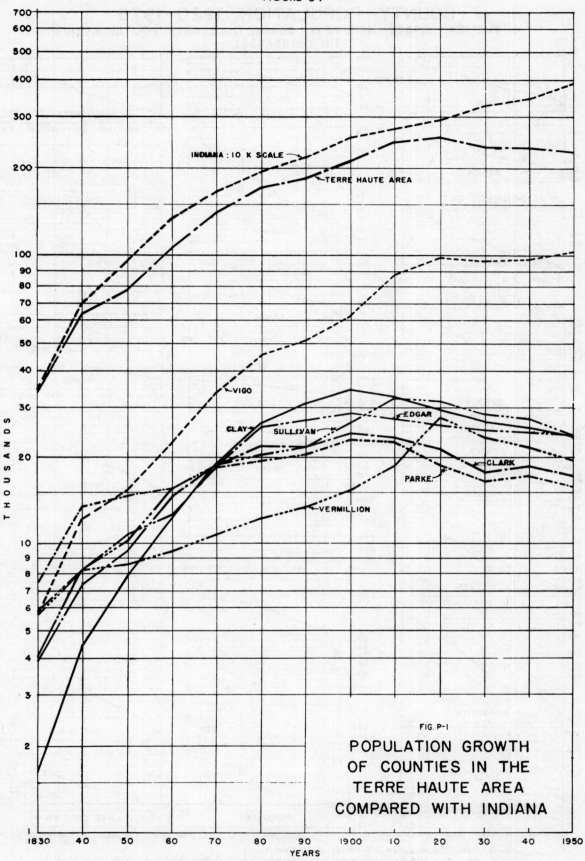

FIG. P-1

POPULATION GROWTH
OF COUNTIES IN THE
TERRE HAUTE AREA
COMPARED WITH INDIANA

INDIANA ECONOMIC COUNCIL, ECONOMIC SURVEY OF THE
TERRE HAUTE AREA PP 25

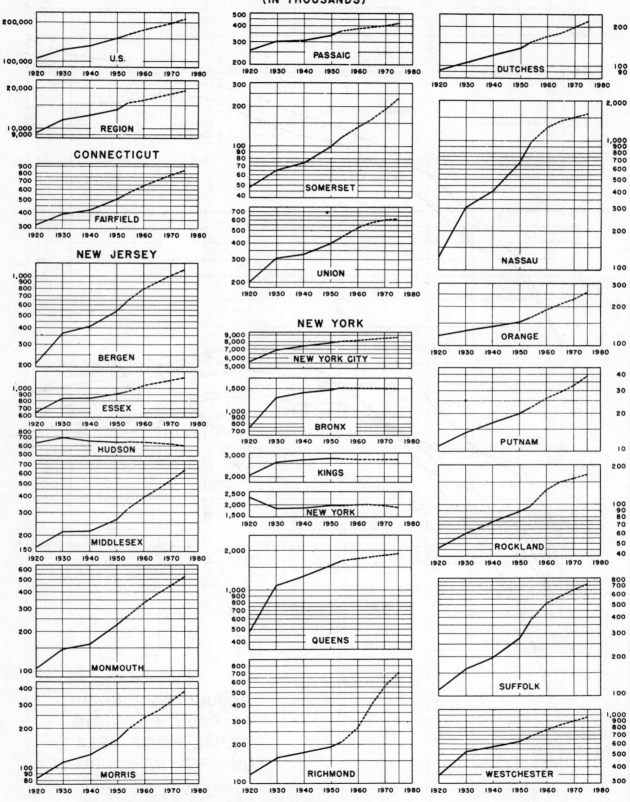

FIGURE 8-8

COUNTY POPULATION, 1920-1975
IN THE NEW JERSEY - NEW YORK - CONNECTICUT METROPOLITAN REGION
(IN THOUSANDS)

Source: 1920-1950 data from U.S. Bureau of the Census
1954-1975 estimates by Regional Plan Association Inc., 230 West 41 Street, New York 36, N.Y.

REGIONAL PLAN ASSOCIATION, POPULATION, 1954—1975,
IN THE NEW JERSEY—NEW YORK- CONNECTICUT METRO-
POLITAN REGION (1954) PP 29

above calculation and the April 1, 1950, population.*

The calculations are as simple as the following illustrations:

Net migration, as shown in Figure 8-9 and 8-10, can be computed separately for age groups. Notice that during the decade concerned there was a net loss from the District of Columbia of 39,730

Illustration A

	District of Columbia	Outside District of Columbia	Metropolitan Washington
1. Population, 1940	666,840	306,713	973,553
2. Add births, 1940-1950	172,800	126,300	299,100
	839,640	433,013	1,272,653
3. Subtract deaths 1940-1950	84,412	32,397	116,809
4. 1940 Population, plus natural increase 1940-1950	755,228	400,616	1,155,844
5. Population, 1950	805,674	664,400	1,470,074
6. Subtract 1940 Population plus natural increase, 1940-1950	755,228	400,616	1,155,844
7. Net in-migration	+50,446	+263,784	+314,230
8. Natural increase 1940-1950 (line 2 minus line 3)	88,388	93,903	182,291

Illustration B

	District of Columbia	Outside District of Columbia	Metropolitan Washington
1. Population Under 5 in 1950	74,750	87,400	162,150
2. Subtract births Less deaths, 1945-50	95,750	73,710	169,460
3. Net migration	− 21,000	+13,690	− 7,310
4. Population 5-9 in 1950	50,700	59,300	110,000
5. Subtract births 1940 to 1945 less deaths, 1940-50	69,430	48,010	117,440
6. Net migration	−18,730	+11,290	− 7,440

*Budget Office, District of Columbia Government, *Population Changes and Governmental Planning in the District of Columbia*, 1952, pp. 8-9.

Census reports of children under five years of age are adjusted for an estimated underenumeration; in 1940, white 4.7 percent, nonwhite 14.8 percent; in 1950, white 2.5 percent, nonwhite 7 percent.

Vital statistics reports of resident live births and of deaths under age one are adjusted for estimated underregistration by factors ranging from 1.6 percent in 1940 to 0.2 percent in 1950 for white, and from 2.9 percent to 2.6 percent in 1950 for nonwhite births.

FIGURE 8-9

Table III.—District of Columbia: Population Movement 1940 to 1950 by age group.*

Age (In 1950)	Age (In 1940)	Population 1940	Births 1940-1950	Deaths 1940-1950	1940 Population Plus Natural Increase	Population 1950	Net Migration
Total ...		666,840	172,800	84,412	755,228	805,674	+50,446
Under 5	Births 1945-50		99,140	3,390	95,750	74,750	-21,000
5 - 9	Births 1940-45		73,660	4,230	69,430	50,700	-18,730
10 - 14	Under 5	43,600		482	43,118	38,670	-4,448
15 - 24	5 - 14	78,334		1,211	77,123	117,196	+40,073
25 - 34	15 - 24	114,163		3,475	110,688	158,956	+48,268
35 - 44	25 - 34	140,114		6,718	133,396	134,962	+1,566
45 - 54	35 - 44	112,237		9,946	102,291	104,478	+2,187
55 - 64	45 - 54	84,559		13,603	70,956	69,146	-1,810
65 and over	55 and over	93,833		41,357	52,476	56,816	+4,340

FIGURE 8-10

Table IV.—Metropolitan Washington: Population Movement 1940 to 1950 by age groups.*

Age (In 1950)	Age (In 1940)	Population 1940	Births 1940-1950	Deaths 1940-1950	1940 Population Plus Natural Increase	Population 1950	Net Migration
Total		973,553	299,100	116,809	1,155,844	1,470,074	+314,230
Under 5	Births 1945-50		175,100	5,640	169,460	162,150	-7,310
5 - 9	Births 1940-45		124,000	6,560	117,440	110,000	-7,440
10 - 14	Under 5	73,300		719	72,581	77,170	+4,589
15 - 24	5 - 14	129,132		1,815	127,317	232,796	+105,479
25 - 34	15 - 24	166,531		4,755	161,776	298,556	+136,780
35 - 44	25 - 34	200,689		9,051	191,638	231,962	+40,324
45 - 54	35 - 44	275,166		31,817	243,349	272,824	+29,475
65 and over	55 and over	128,735		56,452	72,283	84,616	+12,333

* Budget Office, District of Columbia Government, Population Changes and Governmental Planning in the District of Columbia (1952), pp. 8-9

children who must have been accompanied by their parents. Many of these families undoubtedly moved into the suburbs—there was a net migration into the suburbs of 24,980 children born during the decade. Notice that the figures for the suburbs are secured by subtracting those for the central city from the metropolitan area figures.

Undoubtedly, however, many families moved from the metropolitan area to some other part of the country. There was a net migration from metropolitan Washington of 14,750 children born during the decade and surviving long enough to leave the area—again, with their parents, and, in many instances, with older brothers and sisters.

Almost all reports on population issued by city or county planning commissions, unofficial regional planning groups, universities, or other organizations, will contain tables, charts, and discussions of migration. Examine the bibliographical sources listed at the beginning of this chapter for such reports.

The 1950 Census reports two kinds of migration data. The special report entitled *State of Births** is of little use in a local community survey. No distinction, for example, is made between a person who left his state of birth as a young child and one who migrated during or after World War II. Furthermore, the data are not reported by localities.

In Volume II, *General Characteristics*, of the 1950 Census, residence of one year prior to the taking of the census is also reported for persons over one year of age by states (Table 23), by standard metropolitan areas, urbanized areas, and urban places of 10,000 population or more (Table 34), and by counties (Table 42). The parts of Tables 34 and 42 containing this data, together with an explanation of the term "residence," are reproduced in Figure 8-11.

Notice that the figures are based on a 20 percent sample. Many other social and economic data are based on samples rather than on a full count of the reported population. For a general understanding of the rationale of sampling, see Goode and Hatt, Chapter 14, Key, Chapter 6, and Campbell, Gurin, and Miller, *The Voter Decides* (31).

Census sampling design and the variability between a sample estimate and a complete count are described and discussed in the introduction to each census report.

In 1940, the census reported the number of people who had migrated across the boundary of a county or a large city during the period 1935-1940. Data showing some demographic, social, and economic characteristics of these migrants were also published by the U.S. Bureau of the Census in four monographs: *Population; Internal Migration 1935 to 1940, Color and Sex of Migrants*

(1943); Age of Migrants (1946); and Economic Characteristics of Migrants (1946).

Two special reports were issued by the Bureau of the Census in 1957, *Population Mobility—Characteristics of Migrants*, and *Population Mobility—Farm-Nonfarm Movers*. These reports include data for all persons who changed their residence within the year immediately preceding the 1950 Census. See also Dynes, *Consequences of Population Mobility for School and Community Change* (32).

A number of studies have been made of internal migration that are based on these census monographs and on other census data tabulated after 1940 but not published. These are the most thorough available studies of the movement of population from rural to urban areas, from one urban area to another, and from central cities to the suburbs. See Warren S. Thompson, *Migration Within Ohio, 1935-1940: A Study in the Redistribution of Population* (33); Freedman, *Recent Migrants to Chicago* (34); and Hawley, *Intra-state Migration in Michigan, 1935-1940* (35).

In *Patterns of Mobility, 1910-1950* (36), Goldstein examines the validity of city directories as a source of population data, reviews the use of such data in Washington, D.C., Tulsa, Austin, Dallas, Houston, the Illinois cities of Danville, Bloomington, Rock Island, and Moline, and in Windsor, Connecticut. Other studies are listed in a bibliography. In addition to its study of the movement of people in and out of Norristown, Pennsylvania during the first half of the twentieth century, Dr. Goldstein's work is particularly valuable as a methodological demonstration of population analysis based on data collected from city directories and from records of births, deaths, and school attendance.

The political consequences of the internal migration of population may be very great. How does migration from the central city to the suburbs influence the political tendencies of migrants? See Lubell, *The Future of American Politics* (37) for a discussion of this subject. Similarly, the migration of negroes from the South to northern industrial cities has already had important political consequences. See Lubell, pp. 90ff., for a description of this migration. Migration affects some of the deepest political cleavages in American politics: the urban-suburban conflict, the urban-rural conflict, and the sectional conflict.

Geographical mobility is also likely to affect the class structure of the community. Horizontal geographical mobility probably increases vertical social mobility because strongly marked class differentiation can be maintained only in a stable or stagnant community. Why?

The task of local party organizations in getting out the vote and assimilating new voters is made more difficult by extensive migration. How does migration affect nonvoting? What is the relation between migration and the nationalization of politics? The whole concept of local self-govern-

*P-E No. 4A, to be found in the *U.S. Census of Population: 1950*, Vol. IV, Part 4, Chap. A.

FIGURE 8-11

RESIDENCE IN 1949*

Definitions

Residence in 1949 is the usual place of residence one year prior to the date of enumeration. As indicated by the categories of table 23, residence in 1949 was used in conjunction with residence in 1950 to determine the numbers of persons who had changed residence from 1949 to 1950. Persons who changed residence in this period were classified by the type of move, viz., "Different house, same county," and "Different county or abroad." Residence abroad includes residence in all foreign countries and all Territories and possessions of the United States. The category "Same house as in 1950" includes all persons 1 year old and over who were living in the same house on the date of enumeration in 1950 as on the date one year prior to enumeration. Included in this group are persons who had never moved during the 12 months as well as persons who had moved but by 1950 had returned to their 1949 residence.

The number of persons who were living in different houses in 1950 and 1949 is somewhat less than the total number of moves during the year. Some persons in the same house at the two dates had moved during the year but by the time of enumeration had returned to their 1949 residence. Other persons made two or more progressive moves. Furthermore, persons in a different house in the same county may actually have moved between counties during the year but by 1950 had returned to the same county of residence as that in 1949.

---

*Data based on 20-percent sample. For a description of the sample, estimates of sampling variability, and a method of obtaining improved estimates, see the section on "Reliability of sample data."

U. S. BUREAU OF THE CENSUS, CENSUS OF POPULATION, 1950 CHAPTER B GENERAL CHARACTERISTICS

Comparability With Current Population Survey

For the United States as a whole, figures from the Current Population Survey of March 1950 on residence in March 1949 and preliminary sample figures on this same subject from the 1950 Census as of April 1, 1950, indicate appreciable differences both in the proportion of persons who were living in a different house in 1949 and in 1950 and in the proportion of migrants, that is, persons who were living in a different county in 1950 and 1949. The figures from the Current Population Survey indicate a greater extent of total mobility than those from the preliminary sample but a relatively smaller number of migrants. These differences apparently arise from the somewhat different periods covered by the two sets of figures, the different methods used in collecting and processing the data, and sampling variability. It is expected that further analysis of these two sets of figures will indicate more precisely the nature and sources of the differences.

GENERAL CHARACTERISTICS 37-51

Table 34.—GENERAL CHARACTERISTICS OF THE POPULATION, FOR STANDARD METROPOLITAN AREAS, URBANIZED AREAS, AND URBAN PLACES OF 10,000 OR MORE: 1950

[Asterisk (*) denotes statistics based on 20-percent sample; for totals of age groups from complete count, see table 33. Percent not shown where less than 0.1; percent and median not shown where base is less than 500]

| Subject | Portland Standard Metropolitan Area | Portland Urbanized Area | Urban places | | | | | | | | | | |
			Albany	Astoria	Bend	Corvallis	Eugene	Klamath Falls	Medford	Pendleton	Portland	Salem	Spring-field
Total population	704,829	512,643	10,115	12,331	11,409	16,207	35,879	15,875	17,305	11,774	373,628	43,140	10,807
Urban-farm population	2,335	1,087	21	7	21			6	22	3	358	76	13
RACE, NATIVITY AND CITIZENSHIP							11,204						
Male	348,401	249,411					12,356	31,999	15,240		180,339		0,765
Population per household	2,911	219,865		2.71	3.04	2.86	2.86	2.85	2.8				3.29
Institutional population			88	61	11	29	176	56	62		4,467		1
*RESIDENCE IN 1949													
Persons 1 year old and over, 1950	688,505	501,305	10,015	12,050	11,130	15,810	34,985	15,580	16,840	11,495	366,430	42,195	10,605
Same house as in 1950	520,785	376,025	7,110	8,770	7,955	10,030	23,295	10,530	11,400	7,175	276,030	29,295	6,865
Different house, same county	97,080	74,810	1,510	1,895	1,720	2,785	6,410	2,865	3,040	1,640	56,665	6,125	2,120
Different county or abroad	62,100	43,930	1,230	1,210	1,350	2,775	4,480	2,005	2,020	1,270	28,960	6,255	1,485
Residence not reported	8,540	6,540	165	175	105	220	800	180	380	1,410	4,775	520	135

37-70 OREGON

Table 42.—GENERAL CHARACTERISTICS OF THE POPULATION, FOR COUNTIES: 1950—Con.

[Asterisk (*) denotes statistics based on 20-percent sample; for totals of age groups from complete count, see table 41. Percent not shown where less than 0.1; percent and median not shown where base is less than 500]

Subject	Lake	Lane	Lincoln	Linn	Malheur	Marion	Morrow	Mult-nomah	Polk	Sherman	Tilla-mook	Uma-tilla	Union	Wal-lowa	Wasco	Wash-ington	Wheeler	Yamhill
Total population	6,649	125,776	21,308	54,317	23,223	101,401	4,783	471,537	26,317	2,271	18,606	41,703	17,962	7,264	15,552	61,269	3,313	33,484
Urban-farm population	2	97	3	31	21	176	...	675	193	...	26	22	80	...	9	156	...	83
Households, number																		
Population in households	6,528							1,187	9,701	21,618	9,124	3,833	8,011	31,250	1,812	16,948
Population per household	3.22	3.18	2.98	3.31	3.56				8,822	3,744	7,368	29,264	1,787	16,115
Institutional population	15	211	14	125	20	6,795	...	3,323	2	...			329	1,859	23	731
*RESIDENCE IN 1949																		
Persons 1 year old and over, 1950	6,460	122,415	21,140	53,160	22,625	98,750	4,660	460,955	25,615	2,175	18,140	40,610	17,440	7,145	15,055	59,815	3,265	32,550
Same house as in 1950	4,440	82,860	14,435	38,540	16,615	72,030	3,380	345,550	18,270	1,625	12,200	27,190	13,505	5,395	10,875	46,240	2,165	23,880
Different house, same county	1,120	23,080	3,480	8,045	3,010	13,010	625	72,155	3,375	155	3,170	5,915	2,395	960	2,280	5,745	485	4,560
Different county or abroad	850	14,660	2,895	5,895	2,710	12,010	600	37,570	3,795	365	2,535	5,950	1,470	730	1,820	7,280	600	3,790
Residence not reported	50	1,815	330	680	290	1,700	55	5,680	175	30	235	1,555	70	60	80	550	15	320

ment presupposes a large degree of stability of residence. At present, however, in a time of rapid automobile transportation, the availability of housing or schools, may be more determinative of residence than is the job of the head of the family. This phenomenon illustrates the extent to which some "local" problems have, in fact, been nationalized.

DISTRIBUTION OF POPULATION BY AGE, SEX, RACE, NATIVITY, EDUCATION, FAMILY, AND OTHER SOCIAL CHARACTERISTICS

The proportions of the population in various age groups is one of the factors affecting the kind of social problems a community faces. Recreation and school needs are the most obvious results of a rapid increase in the number of children and youths. See Soper and Flinton, *The Buffalo School Survey: Population Trends Affecting Education* (38). Most reports of planning agencies and councils of social agencies discuss these problems.

The following excerpts from a report of the Budget Office of the District of Columbia Government, *Population Change and Governmental Planning in the District of Columbia* (1952), illustrates the governmental consequences of the changing distribution of a community's population among age groups:

The first of the District agencies to feel the effect of an increase in birth rate is the Maternal Child Health Service of the Health Department [p. 38]....While the percentage of parents who neglect their children is small, the problems of the child who is neglected can be extremely difficult [p. 39]....Aid to dependent children [pp. 39, 41]....The serious problem of finding school rooms and teachers for the tidal wave of children born since 1945 [p. 41]....The demands of this new group of children on the Police Juvenile Bureau are just beginning to show [p. 41]....This is the age which provides the greatest participation in organized recreation, as conducted by the Recreation Department and by the Police Boys Club [p. 42]....The rate of arrests for serious crimes is higher in the age range 15 to 24 than at any other 10 years of age [p. 42]....Chronic illness and physical disability affect more people after 45. Emotional disability and alcoholism continue as serious problems [p. 44]....Needs for institutional and nursing care are particularly acute [for those over 65 years of age] [p. 45]

Age distributions were reported in the 1950 Census of Population by states, standard metropolitan areas, urbanized areas, urban places of over 1,000 and counties. For states and counties the age distributions were broken down by urban-rural, rural-nonfarm, and rural-farm populations (see Fig. 6-14). Figures 8-12 and 8-13 are a reproduction of portions of the census tables showing the age and sex distributions for the Pennsylvania Standard Metropolitan Areas, the City of Philadelphia and some census tracts in the Borough of Manhattan, New York City. An excerpt from the introduction to the census volume defining terms

and procedures is also produced as part of Figure 8-12.

The distribution of a population by age groups is usually represented graphically by a population pyramid. The pyramid is formed by drawing two sets of horizontal bar charts, joined together at the zero base line. The male population is represented by the left side and the female population by the right side of the pyramid.

Figures 8-14 and 8-15 are population pyramids for the city of Philadelphia and its suburban Delaware County. A pyramid representing absolute numbers can be quickly and easily drawn. It would consist of bars representing the number of male and female inhabitants in each age group as reported in the 1950 Census of Population. For the breakdown of age groups by sex in 1940, one would have to refer to the 1940 Census reports. (Note that the 1950 Census reports the 1940 age distribution but not by sex.)

The relative length of the bars indicates the proportion of the total population in a particular age group. If, however, the age distribution of a population is being compared at different periods of time, one should compute the percentages and plot them on the pyramid. In Figure 8-15, for example, the bars for the respective age groups in the 1940 pyramid for Delaware County may be compared with those in the 1950 pyramid. This cannot be done with the pyramids in Figure 8-14, except to compare the change in absolute numbers between the periods (see bottom pyramid).

Regardless of whether the bars represent absolute numbers or percentages, a comparison of the shapes of two or more pyramids will readily indicate differences in the age and sex composition of the population. The pyramids for both Delaware County and Philadelphia show the effects of the low birthrate during the 1930's and the high birthrate during the 1940's. They also show that there are more females than males between the ages of fifteen and forty-four.

A population pyramid is a good device to use in determining whether one area is likely to have different social and economic characteristics than other areas. In any large city or metropolitan area, different parts of the community are likely to have age and sex distributions associated with other social, economic and perhaps political characteristics.

We have pointed out that the configuration of a pyramid will indicate whether there are more males or females in a particular age group. It is possible to indicate this more precisely by means of the sex ratio. This is usually expressed as the number of males per 100 females. Most census data are reported separately for each sex. It is possible, therefore, to determine the proportion of males to females engaged in certain activities or possessing certain social and economic characteristics.

There are characteristic differences between the sex ratios and age distributions of urban,

FIGURE 8-12

PENNSYLVANIA

Table 33.—AGE BY COLOR AND SEX, FOR STANDARD METROPOLITAN AREAS, URBANIZED AREAS, AND URBAN PLACES OF 10,000 OR MORE: 1950—Con.

Area and age	1950 population							1940 population, total
	All classes			White		Nonwhite		
	Total	Male	Female	Male	Female	Male	Female	
STANDARD METROPOLITAN AREAS—Con.								
Philadelphia	3,671,048	1,798,683	1,872,365	1,565,483	1,621,638	233,200	250,727	3,199,637
Under 5 years	345,369	176,588	168,781	150,746	142,869	25,842	25,912	209,092
Under 1 year	64,012	32,851	31,161	27,805	26,011	5,046	5,150	38,581
1 and 2 years	144,750	74,066	70,684	62,898	59,549	11,168	11,135 }	170,511
3 and 4 years	136,607	69,671	66,936	60,043	57,309	9,627	9,627 }	
5 to 9 years	286,896	145,625	141,271	124,775	120,170	20,850	21,101	222,815
5 years	57,582	29,270	28,312	25,030	24,009	4,240	4,303	43,037
6 years	60,094	30,391	29,703	26,149	25,341	4,242	4,362	41,410
7 to 9 years	169,220	85,964	83,256	73,596	70,820	12,368	12,436	138,368
10 to 14 years	235,193	119,718	115,475	101,193	96,900	18,525	18,575	260,414
10 to 13 years	190,085	96,816	93,269	81,769	78,216	15,047	15,053	206,630
14 years	45,108	22,902	22,206	19,424	18,684	3,478	3,522	53,784
15 to 19 years	238,284	120,493	117,791	103,860	100,083	16,633	17,708	283,792
15 years	44,834	25,623	22,211	19,346	18,803	3,277	3,408	54,787
16 and 17 years	91,838	47,555	44,283	40,724	37,328	6,831	6,955	111,481
18 and 19 years	98,612	47,315	51,297	43,790	43,952	6,525	7,345	117,524
20 to 24 years	280,748	135,814	144,934	117,593	122,722	18,221	22,212	282,297
25 to 29 years	314,755	152,748	162,007	131,010	137,008	21,738	24,999	272,588
30 to 34 years	303,058	145,974	157,084	126,821	134,354	19,153	22,730	258,153
35 to 39 years	290,880	140,531	150,349	121,459	128,162	19,072	22,187	245,988
40 to 44 years	265,021	129,567	135,454	112,531	116,955	17,036	18,499	240,184
45 to 49 years	236,285	115,665	120,620	99,724	104,178	15,941	16,442	226,358
50 to 54 years	226,265	111,778	114,487	97,961	101,343	13,817	13,144	194,393
55 to 59 years	193,725	95,741	97,984	86,493	89,142	9,248	8,842	151,177
60 to 64 years	156,754	76,608	80,146	69,973	73,639	6,635	6,507	123,879
65 to 69 years	121,971	56,772	65,199	51,806	59,740	4,966	5,459	95,896
70 to 74 years	83,119	37,345	45,774	34,419	42,637	2,926	3,137	67,222
75 to 84 years	79,039	32,903	46,136	30,681	43,498	2,222	2,638 }	65,389
85 years and over	13,686	4,813	8,873	4,438	8,238	375	635 }	
21 years and over	2,513,767	1,211,658	1,302,109	1,063,391	1,138,715	148,267	163,394	2,166,052
Pittsburgh	2,213,236	1,096,237	1,116,999	1,028,200	1,047,775	68,037	69,224	2,082,556
Under 5 years	218,481	111,363	107,118	103,860	99,859	7,503	7,259	151,719
Under 1 year	42,526	21,584	20,942	20,095	19,463	1,489	1,479	28,082
1 and 2 years	92,427	46,916	45,511	43,677	42,397	3,239	3,114 }	123,637
3 and 4 years	83,528	42,863	40,665	40,088	37,999	2,775	2,666 }	
5 to 9 years	179,205	91,021	88,184	84,858	81,759	6,163	6,425	155,271
5 years	34,337	17,501						
6 years	36,603	18,492						
7 to 9 years	108,265	55,028						
10 to 14 years	154,765	78,819						
10 to 13 years	125,400	63,804						
14 years	29,365	15,015						
15 to 19 years	145,162	70,071						
15 years	29,042	14,538						
16 and 17 years	55,809	27,989						
18 and 19 years		27,544						

(A definitions text block overlaps the following rows; partial continuation data visible at bottom of the page:)

Area and age	Total	Male	Female	White Male	White Female	Nonwhite Male	Nonwhite Female	1940 total
...9 years	3,569	1,818						
5 years	3,705	1,907						
6 years	10,860	5,422						
7 to 9 years	16,252	8,313						
10 to 14 years	12,946	6,652						
10 to 13 years	3,306	1,661						
14 years								
15 to 19 years	17,097	8,270						
15 years	3,423	1,759						
16 and 17 years	6,781	3,344						
18 and 19 years	6,893	3,167						
20 to 24 years	19,085	9,106						
25 to 29 years	20,006	9,730						
30 to 34 years	19,775	9,644						
35 to 39 years	19,860	9,658						
40 to 44 years	19,020	9,411						
45 to 49 years	17,020	8,494						
50 to 54 years	15,844	7,805						
55 to 59 years	14,392	7,059						
60 to 64 years	12,308	6,125						
65 to 69 years	9,903	4,745		3,529	3,302			
70 to 74 years	6,858	3,329		3,577		15	17 }	5,640
75 to 84 years	6,579	2,985						
		617	413	613	5	4 }		162,569
85 years and over	1,035	418						
21 years and over	178,103	86,884	91,219	85,830	90,196	1,054	1,023	162,569

AGE

Definitions

The age classification is based on the age of the person at his last birthday as of the date of his enumeration, that is, the age of the person in completed years. The enumerator was instructed to obtain the age of each person as of the date of his visit rather than as of April 1, 1950. In most cases the age reported would have been the same on either basis.

Assignment of Unknown Ages

When the age of a person was not reported, it was estimated on the basis of other available information such as marital status, school attendance, employment status, age of other members of the family, and type of household. Age was estimated by this procedure in the 1950 Census for 0.19 percent of the population of the United States. A forthcoming report will describe in detail the method used to assign ages and will discuss the effect on specific age groups. This method of assigning unknown ages on the basis of related information was used for the first time in the 1940 Census when estimates of age were made for 0.16 percent of the population of the United States. In previous censuses, with the exception of 1880, persons of unknown age were shown in a separate category. The summary totals for "14 years and over" and "21 years and over" for earlier censuses presented in this bulletin include all persons of "unknown age" since there is evidence that most of the persons for whom age was not reported were in the age classes above these limits.

Errors in Age Statistics

A considerable body of evidence exists which indicates that age is misreported in several characteristic ways and that certain age groups are less completely enumerated than others in censuses. A comparison of age distributions from the preliminary sample of the 1950 Census with age distributions based on figures from the 1940 Census and brought up to date from official records of births, deaths, and migration suggests that the 1950 Census is no exception to this generalization. This comparison shows that for the United States as a whole there appears to be an underenumeration of children under 5 and of males between the ages of 18 and 24 years. Likewise, there appears to be a deficit of persons in the age range 55 to 64 years which is roughly offset by an excess over the number expected in the age group 65 years old and over. As additional data become available from the final 1950 tabulations and elsewhere, a more definitive analysis of these differences will be made.

FIGURE 8-13

NEW YORK CITY

Table 2.—AGE, MARITAL STATUS, AND ECONOMIC CHARACTERISTICS, BY SEX, BY CENSUS TRACTS: 1950—Con.

Manhattan Borough--Con.

Subject	Tract 217.1		Tract 218		Tract 219		Tract 220		Tract 221.0		Tract 221.1		Tract 222	
	Male	Female	Male	Female	Male	Female	Male	Female	Male	Female	Male	Female	Male	
AGE														
All classes	1,276	1,587	5,979	7,245	3,535	4,073	5,912	7,255	777	790				
Under 5 years	146	148	532	491	384	377	498	486	49					
Under 1 year	31	30	121	95	90	72	126	114	13					
1 to 4 years	115	118	411	396	294	305	372	372						
5 to 9 years	91	94	370	380	381	334	329	342						
5 years	15	20	67	65	60	53	59	86						
6 years	22	27	88	70	78	70	65							
7 to 9 years	54	47	215	245	243	211	205							
10 to 14 years	99	87	386	375	302	347	268							
10 to 13 years	88	69	312	305	243	285	214							
14 years	11	18	74	70	59	62	5							
15 to 19 years	82	97	339	470	309	379								
15 years	19	23	50	88	58	69								
16 and 17 years	30	29	152	174	126	144								
18 and 19 years	33	45	137	208	125	166								
20 to 24 years	94	159	497	710	300	423								
25 to 29 years	124	172	631	829	301	412								
30 to 34 years	129	170	590	813	301	364								
35 to 39 years	130	197	599	828	242									
40 to 44 years	106	151	536	664	286									
45 to 49 years	120	105	443	510	229									
50 to 54 years	61	55	410	413	163									
55 to 59 years	35	55	264	256	102									
60 to 64 years	19	31	162	220	106									
65 to 69 years	21	28	120	141	60									
70 to 74 years	13	14	63	91	36									
75 to 84 years	6	22	33	42	33									
85 years and over	...	2	4	12	...									
21 years and over	845	1,134	4,279	5,415	2,104									
White	3	5	112	121	2,784									
Under 5 years	...	...	14	8	283									
5 to 9 years	1	...	10	3	285									
10 to 14 years	...	...	3	9	249									
15 to 19 years	...	...	6	9	249									
20 to 24 years	...	2	6	14	266									
25 to 29 years	...	1	10	13	217									
30 to 34 years	...	...	4	9	211									
35 to 39 years	...	...	8	12	166									
40 to 44 years	...	...	8	14	229									
45 to 49 years	1	1	14	6	181									
50 to 54 years	...	...	10	8	14									
55 to 59 years	1	...	8	5	8									
60 to 64 years	...	...	2	4										
65 to 69 years	...	...	3	5										
70 to 74 years	...	...	2	2										
75 years and over	...	1	4	...										
Nonwhite	1,273	1,582	5,867	7,124										
Under 5 years	146	148	518	483										
5 to 9 years	90	94	360	377										
10 to 14 years	99	87	383	366										
15 to 19 years	82	97	333	461										
20 to 24 years	94	157	491	696										
25 to 29 years	124	171	621	816										
30 to 34 years	129	170	586	804										
35 to 39 years	130	197	591	816										
40 to 44 years	106	151	528	650										
45 to 49 years	119	104	429	504										
50 to 54 years	61	55	400	405										
55 to 59 years	34	55	256	251										
60 to 64 years	19	31	160	216										
65 to 69 years	21	28	117	136										
70 to 74 years	13	14	61	89										
75 years and over	6	23	33	54										

PENNSYLVANIA

GENERAL CHARACTERISTICS

Table 41.—AGE BY COLOR AND SEX, FOR COUNTIES: 1950—Con.

County and age	1950 population							1940 population, total
	All classes			White		Nonwhite		
	Total	Male	Female	Male	Female	Male	Female	
DELAWARE								
All ages	414,234	202,970	211,264	188,638	195,998	14,332	15,266	310,756
Under 5 years	43,896	22,555	21,341	20,887	19,592	1,668	1,749	21,142
Under 1 year	8,091	4,167	3,924	3,810	3,554	357	370	3,943
1 and 2 years	18,434	9,452	8,982	8,737	8,227	715	755	
3 and 4 years	17,371	8,936	8,435	8,340	7,811	596	624	17,199
5 to 9 years	35,666	18,076	17,590	16,642	16,140	1,434	1,450	23,119
5 years	7,442	3,823	3,619	3,541	3,346	282	273	4,396
6 years	7,603	3,842	3,761	3,550	3,452	292	309	4,350
7 to 9 years	20,621	10,411	10,210	9,551	9,342	860	868	14,373
10 to 14 years	26,476	13,547	12,929	12,200	11,657	1,347	1,272	26,168
10 to 13 years	21,364	10,934	10,430	9,848	9,408	1,086	1,022	20,830
14 years	5,112	2,613	2,499	2,352	2,249	261	250	5,338
15 to 19 years	26,400	13,255	13,145	12,096	11,844	1,159	1,301	27,652
15 years	5,139	2,576	2,563	2,301	2,313	275	250	5,541
16 and 17 years	10,278	5,167	5,111	4,646	4,612	521	499	11,053
18 and 19 years	10,983	5,512	5,471	5,149	4,919	363	552	11,058
20 to 24 years	29,294	13,981	15,313	12,945	13,995	1,036	1,318	25,231
25 to 29 years	35,161	16,673	18,488	15,569	17,157	1,104	1,331	25,026
30 to 34 years	35,363	16,971	18,392	15,944	17,177	1,027	1,215	26,204
35 to 39 years	33,096	15,992	17,104	14,903	15,913	1,089	1,191	25,980
40 to 44 years	30,586	15,100	15,486	14,054	14,421	1,046	1,065	25,146
45 to 49 years	27,238	13,392	13,846	12,491	12,887	901	959	22,640
50 to 54 years	25,710	12,922	12,788	12,035	11,989	887	799	18,538
55 to 59 years	20,739	10,329	10,410	9,749	9,927	580	483	13,753
60 to 64 years	15,844	7,744	8,100	7,362	7,731	382	369	10,971
65 to 69 years	11,819	5,443	6,376	5,126	6,031	317	345	7,984
70 to 74 years	7,977	3,435	4,542	3,267	4,350	168	192	5,674
75 to 84 years	7,605	3,076	4,529	2,928	4,353	148	176	5,528
85 years and over	1,364	479	885	440	834	39	51	
21 years and over	276,389	132,984	143,405	124,416	134,207	8,568	9,198	207,444

PENNSYLVANIA

Table 33.—AGE BY COLOR AND SEX, FOR STANDARD METROPOLITAN AREAS, URBANIZED AREAS, AND URBAN PLACES OF 10,000 OR MORE: 1950—Con.

Area and age	1950 population							1940 population, total
	All classes			White		Nonwhite		
	Total	Male	Female	Male	Female	Male	Female	
Philadelphia	2,071,605	1,001,862	1,069,743	822,467	870,170	179,395	199,573	1,931,334
Under 5 years	184,125	93,902	90,223	73,690	70,087	20,212	20,136	122,202
Under 1 year	34,472	17,576	16,896	13,666	12,903	3,910	3,993	22,371
1 and 2 years	77,531	39,567	37,964	30,810	29,280	8,757	8,684	49,421
3 and 4 years	72,122	36,759	35,363	29,214	27,904	7,545	7,459	50,410
5 to 9 years	152,429	76,930	75,499	60,935	59,277	15,995	16,222	130,156
5 years	30,057	15,139	14,918	11,859	11,588	3,280	3,330	25,157
6 years	31,807	16,038	15,769	12,775	12,446	3,263	3,323	24,294
7 to 9 years	90,565	45,753	44,812	36,301	35,243	9,452	9,569	80,705
10 to 14 years	129,442	65,398	64,044	51,539	49,747	13,859	14,297	151,711
10 to 13 years	104,543	52,991	51,552	41,750	39,957	11,241	11,595	120,506
14 years	24,899	12,407	12,492	9,789	9,790	2,618	2,702	31,205
15 to 19 years	130,116	63,531	66,585	51,919	52,902	11,612	13,683	166,271
15 years	24,814	12,347	12,467	9,931	9,800	2,416	2,667	31,770
16 and 17 years	49,803	24,836	24,967	19,995	19,590	4,841	5,377	64,762
18 and 19 years	55,499	26,348	29,151	21,993	23,512	4,355	5,639	69,739
20 to 24 years	161,511	76,601	84,910	63,412	67,226	13,189	17,684	172,599
25 to 29 years	179,643	86,638	93,005	69,668	72,412	16,970	20,593	170,219
30 to 34 years	170,054	80,615	89,439	65,441	70,769	15,174	18,670	159,802
35 to 39 years	166,695	79,092	87,603	63,818	69,230	15,274	18,373	152,209
40 to 44 years	152,834	73,681	79,153	60,073	64,092	13,608	15,061	147,576
45 to 49 years	137,886	66,849	71,037	54,115	57,812	12,734	13,225	137,522
50 to 54 years	132,171	64,740	67,431	53,852	56,995	10,888	10,436	117,889
55 to 59 years	112,353	55,051	57,302	47,876	50,262	7,175	7,040	91,927
60 to 64 years	91,104	44,200	46,904	39,142	41,859	5,058	5,045	75,357
65 to 69 years	71,610	32,851	38,759	29,177	34,549	3,674	4,210	58,397
70 to 74 years	48,042	21,257	26,785	19,128	24,381	2,129	2,404	40,306
75 to 84 years	44,266	18,051	26,215	16,451	24,193	1,600	2,022	32,680
85 years and over	7,324	2,475	4,849	2,231	4,377	244	472	4,511
21 years and over	1,446,724	688,893	757,831	573,274	625,694	115,619	132,137	1,326,413

U. S. BUREAU OF THE CENSUS, CENSUS OF POPULATION. 1950, P–D BULLETINS

FIGURE 8-14

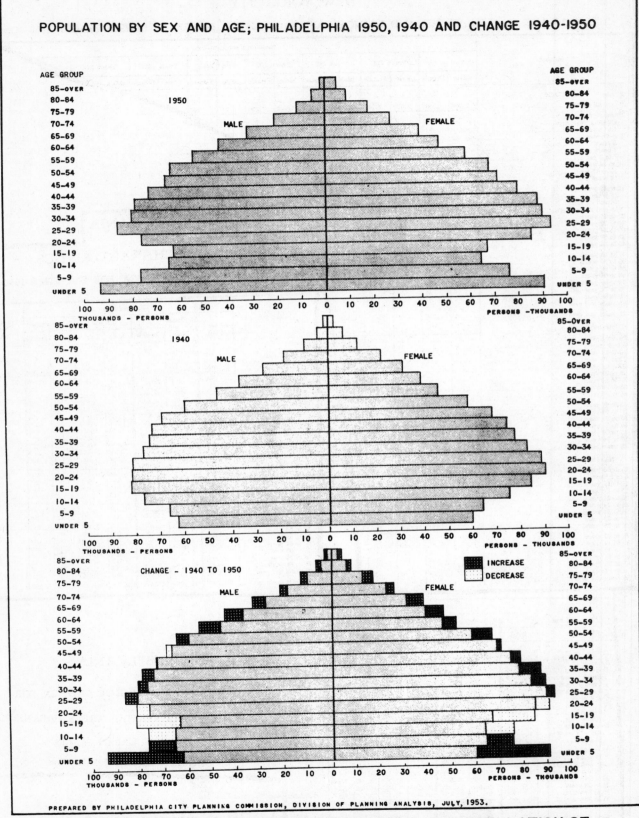

POPULATION BY SEX AND AGE; PHILADELPHIA 1950, 1940 AND CHANGE 1940-1950

PHILADELPHIA CITY PLANNING COMMISSION, THE POPULATION OF PHILADELPHIA AND ITS METROPOLITAN AREA. GENERAL CHARAC— TERISTICS AND TRENDS (1953)

FIGURE 8-15

POPULATION DISTRIBUTION BY SEX AND AGE, 1940 AND 1950, DELAWARE COUNTY

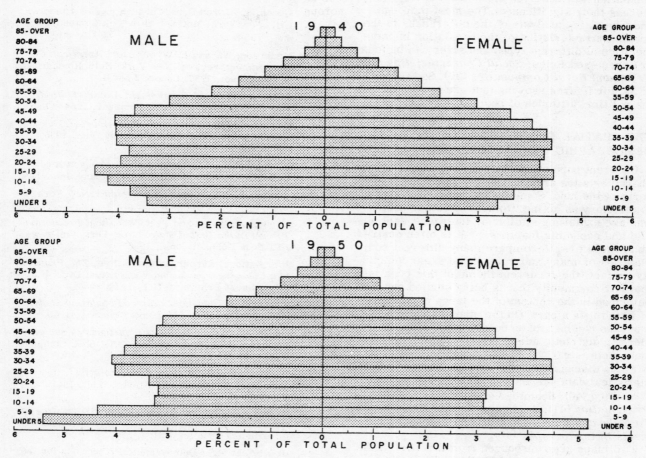

AGE GROUP, 1950	MALE		FEMALE		TOTAL	
	Persons	% of Total	Persons	% of Total	Persons	%
All Ages	202,970	49.0	211,264	51.0	414,234	100.0
Under 5	22,555	5.4	21,341	5.1	43,896	10.6
5 - 9	18,076	4.4	17,590	4.2	35,666	8.6
10 - 14	13,547	3.3	12,929	3.1	26,476	6.4
15 - 19	13,255	3.2	13,145	3.2	26,400	6.4
20 - 24	13,981	3.4	15,313	3.7	29,294	7.1
25 - 29	16,673	4.0	18,488	4.5	35,161	8.5
30 - 34	16,971	4.1	18,392	4.4	35,363	8.5
35 - 39	15,992	3.9	17,104	4.3	33,096	8.0
40 - 44	15,100	3.6	15,486	3.7	30,586	7.4
45 - 49	13,392	3.2	13,846	3.3	27,238	6.6
50 - 54	12,922	3.1	12,788	3.1	25,710	6.2
55 - 59	10,329	2.5	10,410	2.5	20,739	5.0
60 - 64	7,744	1.9	8,100	2.0	15,844	3.8
65 - 69	5,443	1.3	6,376	1.5	11,819	2.9
70 - 74	3,435	0.8	4,542	1.1	7,977	1.9
75 - 79	2,051	0.5	3,019	0.7	5,070	1.2
80 - 84	1,025	0.3	1,510	0.4	2,535	0.6
85 or Over	479	0.1	885	0.2	1,364	0.3

SOURCE: U. S. Census of Population, 1950, Vol. II, <u>Characteristics</u> <u>of the</u>
<u>Population</u>, Part 38, Pennsylvania, Chapter B.

NOTE: Population for Age Group 75-84 was divided as two-thirds and one-third
respectively for Age Groups 75-79 and 80-84 to avoid including one
ten-year group in these charts.

DELAWARE COUNTY (PENNSYLVANIA) PLANNING COMMISSION, POPULATION CHARACTERISTICS (1954)

rural-nonfarm, and rural-farm populations, of central cities and suburbs, of different types of suburbs, and of different parts of the same city. Any text on urban sociology, rural sociology, or population will describe these differences and discuss their significance. The most thorough and suggestive analysis of the differences in the social characteristics of the population in communities of different types and sizes can be found in Duncan and Reiss, *Social Characteristics of Urban and Rural Communities* (39). See Gallup, p. 39, for figures showing that age is related to the political attitudes of people.

THE SPATIAL DISTRIBUTION OF DEMOGRAPHIC CHARACTERISTICS

Different populations with different or similar characteristics are, of course, living on different parts of the land. Some human ecologists refer to territory as acting "to draw together people who are exhibiting similar or interdependent social and economic features."* It is often desirable, therefore, to compare many different communities or many subareas of the same community. In fact, the recurrent theme of this book is that any community that is being studied should be placed in the context of the large communities of which it is a part. On the other hand, most communities can be broken down into smaller areas: election districts, administrative districts, census tracts, etc.

For a discussion of the various ways of mapping statistical data see Lutz, *Graphic Presentation Simplified* (40); Schmid, *Handbook of Graphic Presentation* (41); Arkin and Colton, *Graphs—How To Make and Use Them* (42); and Robinson, *Elements of Cartography* (43).

Two maps are reproduced from a report of the City Plan Commission of Madison, Wisconsin, entitled *Madison's People,* to illustrate the use of dot maps to show the distribution of the suburban population (Fig. 8-16) and to show that different symbols can be used to indicate the spatial distribution of population growth by its source (Fig. 8-17). The territorial division used in this map is the ward. The most frequently used territorial subunit is the census tract, or some combination of tracts into social districts. See Chapter VI of this book for a discussion of the reporting of census data by tracts. Figure 8-18 is a reproduction of portions of three tables reporting census data by tracts.

REFERENCES

1. Ericksen, E. G., *Urban Behavior*. New York: The Macmillan Company, 1954. Chap. 3.

2. Quinn, J. A., *Human Ecology*. Englewood Cliffs, N.J.: Prentice-Hall, Inc., 1950. Chap. 19

———

*E. G. Erickson, *Urban Behavior*, New York: The Macmillan Company, 1954. p. 91.

3. Riemer, S., *The Modern City*. Englewood Cliffs, N.J.: Prentice-Hall, Inc., 1952. Chap. 3.

4. Hawley, A., *Human Ecology: A Theory of Community Structure*. New York: The Ronald Press Company, 1950. Chaps. 6-9 and 17.

5. Queen, S. A., and D. B. Carpenter, *The American City*. New York: McGraw-Hill Book Company, Inc., 1953.

6. Anderson, W., and E. W. Weidner, *American City Government*. rev. ed. New York: Holt, Rinehart and Winston, Inc., 1950. Chaps. 2 and 3.

7. Pate, J. E., *Local Government Administration*. New York: American Book Company, 1954. Chap. 1.

8. Adrian, C. R., *Governing Urban America*. New York: McGraw-Hill Book Company, Inc., 1955. Chap. I.

9. Thompson, W. S., *Population Problems*. 4th ed. New York: McGraw-Hill Book Company, Inc., 1953.

10. Landis, P. M., *Population Problems*. New York: American Book Company, 1943.

11. Thompson, W. S., and P. K. Whelpton, *Population Trends in the United States*. New York: McGraw-Hill Book Company, Inc., 1933.

12. U.S. National Resources Committee, *The Problems of a Changing Population*. Washington, D.C.: U.S. Government Printing Office, 1938.

13. Smith, T. L., *Fundamentals of Population Study*. Philadelphia: J. B. Lippincott Company, 1960.

14. Goode, W. J., and P. K. Hatt, *Methods in Social Research*. New York: McGraw-Hill Book Company, Inc., 1952. Chap. 18.

15. Hagood, M. J., *Statistics for Sociologists*. New York: Holt, Rinehart and Winston, Inc., 1941. Part V.

16. Stanbery, V. B., *Better Population Forecasting for Areas and Communities*. Washington, D.C.: U.S. Government Printing Office, 1952.

17. Hoover, E. M., "Demographic Projections for the Region as a Whole," "Projections of Population Change within the Region" in B. R. Berman, B. Chinitz, and E. M. Hoover, *Projection of a Metropolis: Technical Supplement to the New York Metropolitan Region Study*. Cambridge. Mass.: Harvard University Press, 1961. pp. 55-75; 103-19.

18. Jaffe, A. J., *Handbook of Statistical Methods for Demographers*. Washington, D.C.: U.S. Government Printing Office, 1951.

19. Duncan, O. D., R. P. Cuzzort, and B. Duncan, *Statistical Geography*. New York: The Free Press of Glencoe, Inc., 1961.

20. Bogue, D. J., *The Population of the United States*. New York: The Free Press of Glencoe, Inc., 1959.

21. Taeuber, C., and I. B. Taeuber, *The Changing Population of the United States*. New York: John Wiley & Sons, Inc., 1958.

22. Bogue, D. J., and C. Beagle, *Economic Areas of the United States*. New York: The Free Press of Glencoe, Inc., 1961.

23. Hauser, P. M., and O. D. Duncan, eds., *The Study of Population*. Chicago: University of Chicago Press, 1959. III "Data and Methods"; XIV "The Development and Status of American Demography";

FIGURE 8-16

POPULATION DISTRIBUTION IN DANE COUNTY

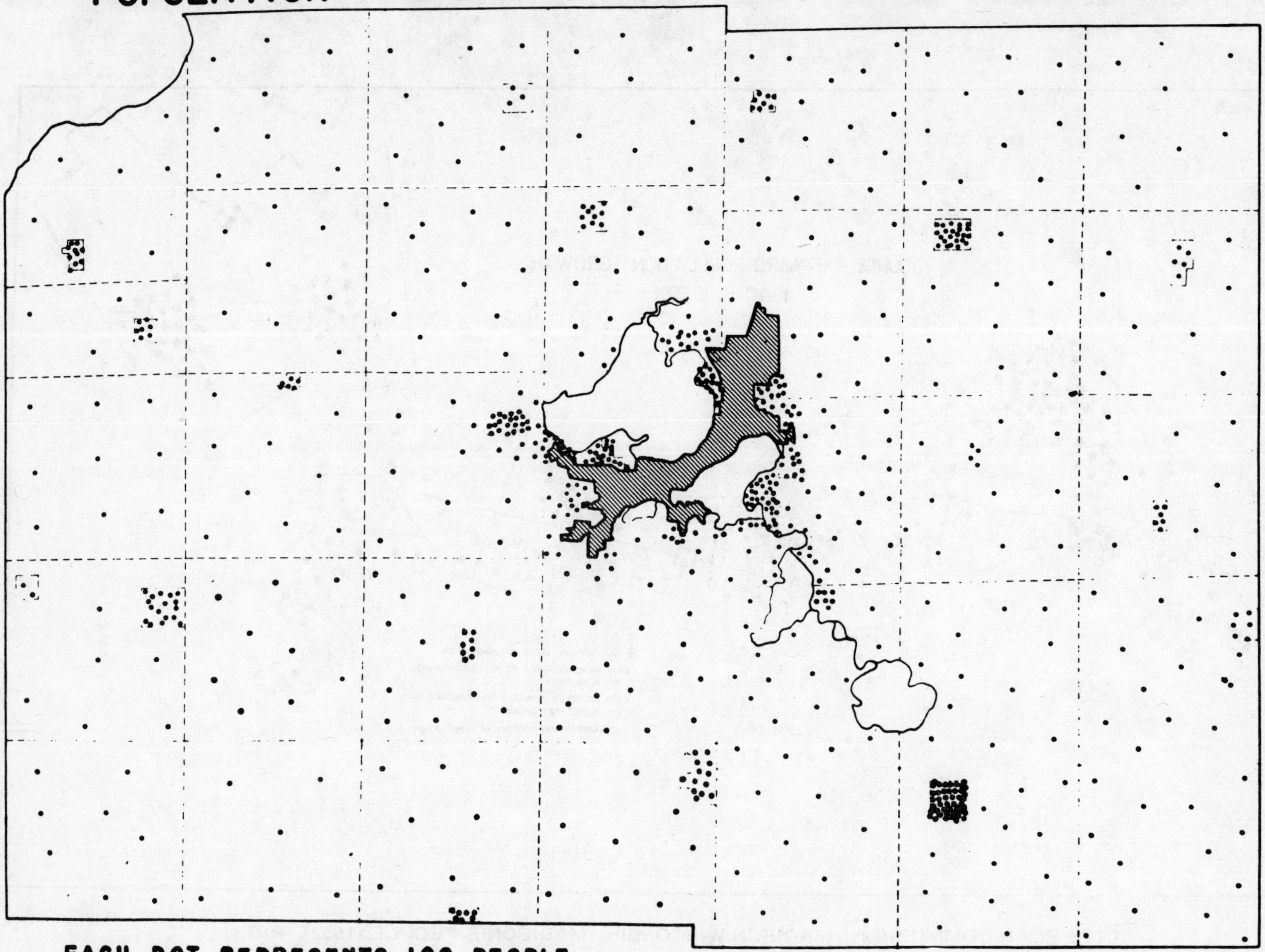

EACH DOT REPRESENTS 100 PEOPLE

CITY PLAN COMMISSION, MADISON WISCONSIN, MADISON'S PEOPLE (1952), PP13

FIGURE 8-17

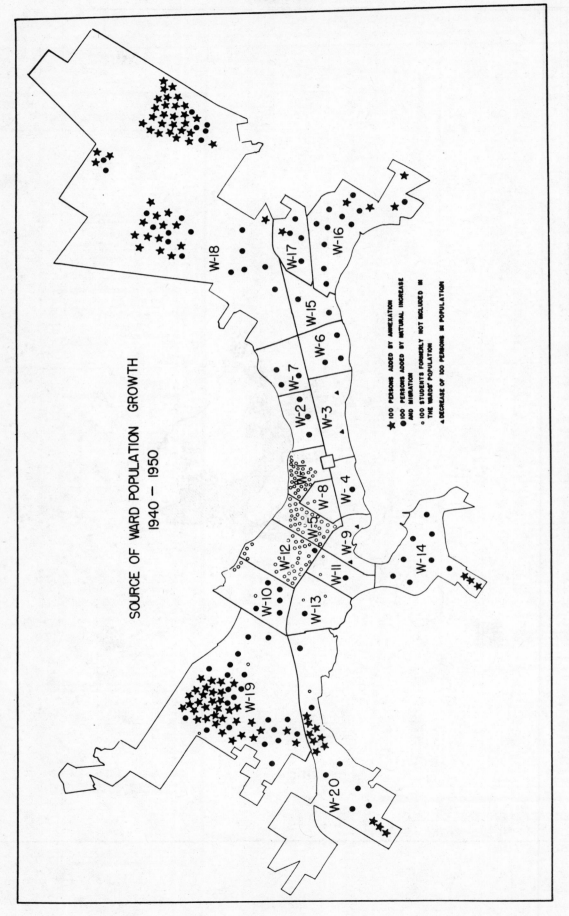

SOURCE OF WARD POPULATION GROWTH
1940 — 1950

★ 100 PERSONS ADDED BY ANNEXATION
● 100 PERSONS ADDED BY NATURAL INCREASE AND MIGRATION
○ 100 STUDENTS FORMERLY NOT INCLUDED IN THE WARDS' POPULATION
▲ DECREASE OF 100 PERSONS IN POPULATION

CITY PLAN COMMISSION, MADISON WISCONSIN, MADISON'S PEOPLE (1952), PP13

SPRINGFIELD AND ADJACENT AREA

Table 1.—CHARACTERISTICS OF THE POPULATION, BY CENSUS TRACTS: 1950

[Asterisk (*) denotes statistics based on 20-percent sample. For totals of age groups from complete count, see table 2. Median not shown where base is less than 500]

Subject	Springfield city	Tract 1	Tract 2	Tract 3	Tract 4	Tract 5	Tract
SEX, RACE, AND NATIVITY							
Total population, 1950	162,399	7					
Male	78,185	3					
Female	84,214	3					
White	156,128	7					
Native	132,591	6					
Foreign born	23,537	1					
Nonwhite	6,271						
Negro	6,173						
Other races	98						
Total population, 1940 [1]	...						
White	...						
Nonwhite	...						
COUNTRY OF BIRTH OF THE FOREIGN-BORN WHITE							
England and Wales	1,155	35					
Scotland	1,236	101					
Northern Ireland	110	...					
Ireland (Eire)	2,942	40					
Norway	50	1					
Sweden	676	13					
Denmark	46	1					
Netherlands	31	...					
France	128	2					
Germany	877	14					
Poland	2,118	566					
Czechoslovakia	99	4					
Austria	292	13					
Hungary	71	1					
Yugoslavia	7	...					
U.S.S.R.	2,051	12					
Lithuania	185	2					
Finland	117	...					
Rumania	46	...					
Greece	790	2					
Italy	4,221	26					
Other Europe	212	18					
Asia	661	93					
Canada—French	3,504	377					
Canada—Other	1,642	19					
Mexico	10	...					
Other America	101	...					
All other and not reported	159	12					
MARRIED COUPLES AND HOUSEHOLDS							
Married couples,* number	38,590	1,800					
With own household	35,695	1,670					
Without own household	2,895	130					
Families and unrelated individuals*	57,170	2,255					
Families	43,450	1,935					
Unrelated individuals	13,720	320					
Households, number	46,719	2,143					
Population in households	154,633	7,723					
Population per household	3.31	3.60					
Institutional population	836	...					
*YEARS OF SCHOOL COMPLETED							
Persons 25 years old and over	104,380	4,910	4,				
No school years completed	1,865	205					
Elementary: 1 to 4 years	5,025	380					
5 and 6 years	8,635	570	2				
7 years	5,985	395	4				
8 years	13,740	730	5				
High school: 1 to 3 years	23,245	1,085	1,0				
4 years	30,995	1,210	1,3				
College: 1 to 3 years	6,695	165	3				
4 years or more	5,945	105	1				
School years not reported	2,250	65					
Median school years completed	11.0	9.4	11.				
*RESIDENCE IN 1949							
Persons 1 year old and over, 1950	158,940	7,625	6,4				
Same house as in 1950	136,695	6,800	5,65				
Different house, same county	15,195	620	610				
Different county or abroad	5,430	140	145				
Residence not reported	1,620	65	20				
*INCOME IN 1949							
Total families and unrelated individuals	57,170	2,255	1,860				
Less than $500	5,695	185	80				
$500 to $999	3,600	85	50				
$1,000 to $1,499	3,370	80	35				
$1,500 to $1,999	3,445	100	80				
$2,000 to $2,499	4,825	180	135				
$2,500 to $2,999	5,335	200	125				
$3,000 to $3,499	6,600	245	285				
$3,500 to $3,999	4,610	220	245				
$4,000 to $4,499	4,080	140	195				
$4,500 to $4,999	2,810	160	125				
$5,000 to $5,999	4,095	215	200				
$6,000 to $6,999	2,090	95	120				
$7,000 to $9,999	2,430	120	60				
$10,000 or more	1,020	50	20				
Income not reported	3,165	100	105				
Median income dollars	3,055	3,506	3,679				

[1] Not available; see p. 6.

Table 2.—AGE, MARITAL STATUS, AND ECONOMIC CHARACTERISTICS, BY SEX, BY CENSUS TRACTS: 1950—Con.

Subject	Tract WS-43 Male	Tract WS-43 Female
AGE		
All classes	3,441	3,503
Under 5 years	386	354
Under 1 year	67	70
1 to 4 years	319	284
5 to 9 years	307	283
5 years	68	47
6 years	65	70
7 to 9 years	174	166
10 to 14 years	220	245
10 to 13 years	175	208
14 years	45	37
15 to 19 years	200	197
15 years	47	37
16 and 17 years	77	85
18 and 19 years	76	75
20 to 24 years	205	203
25 to 29 years	224	242
30 to 34 years	253	270
35 to 39 years	274	270
40 to 44 years	265	272
45 to 49 years	220	239
50 to 54 years	259	236
55 to 59 years	215	222
60 to 64 years	167	166
65 to 69 years	105	115
70 to 74 years	66	7
75 to 84 years	62	7
85 years and over	13	
21 years and over	2,293	2,3
White	3,441	3,5
Under 5 years	386	3
5 to 9 years	307	2
10 to 14 years	220	2
15 to 19 years	200	
20 to 24 years	205	
25 to 29 years	224	
30 to 34 years	253	
35 to 39 years	274	
40 to 44 years	265	
45 to 49 years	220	
50 to 54 years	259	
55 to 59 years	215	
60 to 64 years	167	
65 to 69 years	105	
70 to 74 years	66	
75 years and over	75	
Nonwhite		...
Under 5 years		...
5 to 9 years		...
10 to 14 years		...
15 to 19 years		...
20 to 24 years		...
25 to 29 years		...
30 to 34 years		...
35 to 39 years		...
40 to 44 years		...
45 to 49 years		...
50 to 54 years		...
55 to 59 years		...
60 to 64 years		...
65 to 69 years		...
70 to 74 years		...
75 years and over		...
MARITAL STATUS		
Persons 14 years old and over		2,573
Single		573
Married		1,858
Widowed or divorced		142
EMPLOYMENT STATUS AND MAJOR OCCUPATION GROUP		
Persons 14 years old and over		2,573
Labor force		2,171
Civilian labor force		2,152
Employed		2,074
Private wage and salary workers		1,631
Government workers		209
Self-employed workers		233
Unpaid family workers		7
Unemployed		402
Not in labor force		2,07
Employed		2,07
Professional, technical, and kindred workers		25
Managers, officials, and props., incl. farm		36
Clerical and kindred workers		16
Sales workers		1
Craftsmen, foremen, and kindred workers		50
Operatives and kindred workers		37
Private household workers		
Service workers, except private household		
Laborers, except mine		
Occupation not reported		

Table 3.—CHARACTERISTICS OF DWELLING UNITS, BY CENSUS TRACTS: 1950—Con

Subject	Tract 11	Tract 12
All dwelling units	1,256	1,947
Owner occupied	143	106
Nonwhite owners	7	1
Renter occupied	1,092	1,810
Nonwhite renters	83	3
Vacant nonseasonal not dilapidated, for rent or sale	16	18
Other vacant and nonresident	7	13
TYPE OF STRUCTURE		
1 dwelling unit, detached (includes trailers)	31	55
1 dwelling unit, attached	8	4
1 and 2 dwelling unit, semidetached	19	12
2 dwelling unit, other	244	196
3 and 4 dwelling unit	245	134
5 dwelling unit or more	711	1,546
CONDITION AND PLUMBING FACILITIES		
Number reporting	1,219	1,911
No private bath or dilapidated	309	210
No running water or dilapidated	169	146
*YEAR BUILT		
Number reporting	1,170	1,890
1940 or later	...	...
1930 to 1939	35	40
1920 to 1929	90	630
1919 or earlier	1,045	1,220
All occupied dwelling units	1,235	1,916
NUMBER OF PERSONS IN DWELLING UNIT		
1 person	163	403
2 persons	393	832
3 persons	252	360
4 persons	206	179
5 and 6 persons	176	116
7 persons or more	45	26
Median number of persons	2.7	2.2
PERSONS PER ROOM		
Number reporting	1,202	1,894
1.01 or more	165	111
*HEATING FUEL		
Number reporting heating equipment	1,190	1,870
Central heating	800	1,715
Coal	355	1,235
Utility or bottled gas	65	120
Liquid fuel	335	300
Other fuel	5	35
Not reported	40	25
Noncentral heating	380	155
Coal	50	20
Utility or bottled gas	35	30
Liquid fuel	295	100
Other fuel	...	5
Not reported	...	...
Not heated	10	...
*REFRIGERATION EQUIPMENT		
Number reporting	1,210	1,895
Mechanical	1,000	1,765
Ice	170	110
Other or none	40	20
*TELEVISION		
Number reporting	1,205	1,895
With television	...	10
CONTRACT MONTHLY RENT		
Renter occupied; and vacant nonseasonal not dilapidated units, for rent—Number reporting	1,062	1,787
Less than $10	3	...
$10 to $19	140	47
$20 to $29	313	184
$30 to $39	321	331
$40 to $49	119	718
$50 to $59	47	371
$60 to $74	64	83
$75 to $99	46	42
$100 or more	9	11
Median rent dollars	31.84	44.12
VALUE OF ONE-DWELLING-UNIT STRUCTURES		
Owner occupied;[1] and vacant nonseasonal not dilapidated units, for sale—Number reporting	16	19
Less than $3,000	...	...
$3,000 to $3,999	...	...
$4,000 to $4,999	3	...
$5,000 to $7,499	8	7
$7,500 to $9,999	3	5
$10,000 to $14,999	2	4
$15,000 or more	...	3
Median value dollars		

[1] Restricted to 1-dwelling-unit properties.

FIGURE 8-18

XVI "Population Composition"; XVII "Population Distribution"; XXI "Internal Migration"; XXIII "Population Estimates and Projections"; XXV "Working Force"; XXVI "Population and Natural Resources"; XXVIII "Human Ecology and Population Studies"; XXIX "Geography and Demography"; XXXII "Economics and Demography"; XXXIII "Sociology and Demography."

24. Government Affairs Foundation, *Metropolitan Communities: A Bibliography with Special Emphasis on Government and Politics*. Chicago: Public Administration Service, 1956.

25. Jones, V., B. Hudson, and L. D. Johnston, eds., *Metropolitan Communities: Supplement for 1955-57*. Chicago: Public Administration Service, 1960.

26. Halterman, J. F., *The Impact of Population Growth in the South Coastal Area of Santa Barbara County*. Santa Barbara, Calif.: University of California, 1957. (mimeograph)

27. Gallup, G., *Political Almanac*. New York: B. C. Forbes and Sons Pub. Co., 1952. pp. 30–32.

28. Owen, W., *Cities in the Motor Age*. New York: The Viking Press, Inc., 1959.

29. Breese, G. W., *The Daytime Population of the Central Business District of Chicago*. Chicago: University of Chicago Press, 1949.

30. Foley, D. F., "Urban Daytime Population: A Field for Demographic Ecological Analyses, *Social Forces*. May 1954, pp. 323–30.

31. Campbell, A., G. Gurin, and W. B. Miller, *The Voter Decides*. Evanston, Ill.: Row, Peterson & Company, 1954. pp. 227–35.

32. Dynes, R. R., *Consequences of Population Mobility for School and Community Change*. Columbus, Ohio: Ohio State University Press, 1956.

33. Thompson, W. S., *Migration within Ohio, 1935-40: A Study in the Redistribution of Population*. Columbus, Ohio: Ohio State University Press, 1951.

34. Freedman, R., *Recent Migrants in Chicago*. Chicago: University of Chicago Press, 1950.

35. Hawley, A., *Intra-state Migration in Michigan, 1935-40*. Ann Arbor, Mich.: University of Michigan Press, 1953.

36. Goldstein, S., *Patterns of Mobility, 1910-50*. Philadelphia: University of Pennsylvania Press, 1958.

37. Lubell, S., *The Future of American Politics*. New York: Harper & Brothers, 1952. Chap. 4 "The Frontier Reappears."

38. Soper, W. W., and E. F. Flinton, *The Buffalo School Survey: Population Trends Affecting Education*. Albany, N.Y.: The N.Y. State Department of Education, University of the State of New York, 1951.

39. Duncan, O. D., and A. J. Reiss, Jr., *Social Characteristics of Urban and Rural Communities*. New York: John Wiley & Sons, Inc., 1956.

40. Lutz, R. R., *Graphic Presentation Simplified*. New York: Funk & Wagnalls Company, 1949. Chap. IX.

41. Schmid, C. F., *Handbook of Graphic Presentation*. New York: The Ronald Press Company, 1954. Chap. VIII.

42. Arkin, H., and R. R. Colton, *Graphs—How To Make and Use Them*. New York: Harper & Brothers, 1940. Chap. X.

43. Robinson, A. H., *Elements of Cartography*. New York: John Wiley & Sons, Inc., 1953. Chap. IX.

Chapter IX

THE POLITICAL ECONOMY
OF THE LOCAL COMMUNITY

Even though the student of local politics may not be a professional economist, it is necessary that he understand the economic structure, functions, and changes of the city in order to comprehend its politics and government. As Coleman Woodbury says, there are at least four different yet interconnected ways of looking at the city:

1. As an economic unit or entity producing goods and services and exchanging them within its own boundaries and outside of them.
2. As a congeries of local governments and of public and quasi-public agencies, most of them corporate, legal entities with various powers, functions, and responsibilities.
3. As a gigantic physical plant: the land, buildings, streets, transit and transport lines, parks, public buildings, utilities, and other artifacts within and through which the economic, governmental, and other social activities are carried on.
4. As a social structure, or, if the term be properly qualified, a social organism made up of various groups and institutions in various stages of growth, equilibrium, and decay, and with almost numberless ties and relationships among themselves and with communities outside. (1)

This chapter is intended to suggest methods and data that a student making a local political survey can use to study the relevant economic aspects of the community. Irrespective of the extent to which the student of local politics undertakes to make an economic analysis of his own, he must understand the work of economists who have studied the city. The following texts are useful introductions:

Barlowe, R., *Land Resource Economics.* Englewood Cliffs, N.J.: Prentice-Hall, Inc,, 1958.
Ely, R. T., and G. S. Wehrwein, *Land Economics.* New York: The Macmillan Company, 1940.
Fisher, E. M., and R. M. Fisher, *Urban Real Estate.* New York: Holt, Rinehart and Winston, Inc., 1954.
Ratcliff, R. V., *Urban Land Economics.* New York: McGraw-Hill Book Company, Inc., 1949.
Renne, R. R., *Land Economics.* rev. ed. New York: Harper & Brothers, 1958.

One of the major interests of the student of politics is the role of government in the economy. We have noted time and again in earlier chapters the "economic" motives and consequences of many political issues in the local community. Nevertheless, the city and metropolitan community are often said to be the result of "market" operations in which myriads of individuals, firms, and other groups have acted to maximize their respective values. Otis D. Duncan and his colleagues state the proposition this way in *Metropolis and Region:*

Of one thing we can be sure: the metropolis is not a creation of the federal (or any other) government, nor is it an artifact of bureaucratic statistical procedures. The scientists of politics, in proof of the contrary, spend much time worrying about how to fit governments to the realities of metropolitan community structure. Actually, the metropolis was not "created" at all. It just grew— or, rather, it evolved over a period of several generations. The mechanisms of its evolution are imperfectly understood, but we have reason to think they are closely connected with the basic conditions of economic development. If this is true, then to understand the structure of a highly developed economy we must investigate the structure of its metropolitan communities; and to understand metropolitan communities we must examine them in the context of a more inclusive system. (2)

After four years of intensive study of the changing economy of the New York Metropolitan Region, Ramond Vernon, in assaying governmental policies as a factor influencing economic decisions in *Metropolis 1985,* could only assume that there was

enough response on the part of local government to continue deferring the problem (in this instance, water supply in New Jersey) in its gravest form....
Indeed, that is the basic assumption which emerges....
By one short-run measure or another, the local governments will muddle through, allowing the Region's households and enterprises to follow their own proclivities— that is, to grow more swiftly in the newer suburbs than in the older cities. (3)

In studying the government and politics of a local community, effort should be made to distinguish between decisions and policies made by governmental and political institutions and those that formal government is either unwilling or unable to influence. However, as Vernon notes (p. 166), the difficulty of integrating the "behavior... of local governments" into an "explanation of the (New York) Region's course" does not mean that governments are not, or cannot become, influential at myriad points. To act or not to act, and the scope and intensity of action, once a decision has been made, are the basic questions of politics.

Even with a wide range of effective political choice, there are many limitations in our economic, social, and political systems on the effectiveness of local governments. Acting alone, a local government is unable to do many of the things that determine whether a community will grow economically, in what direction, and at what rate. Throughout the recently completed New York Metropolitan Region Study, the dependence of local developments on regional, and of regional on national forces has been emphasized. See especially the volume by Lichtenberg entitled *One-tenth of a Nation* (4). Two recent books prepared under the auspices of Resources for the Future, Inc., also point out these relationships and suggest methods for analyzing regional and national contexts and relationships: Duncan *et al.*, *Metropolis and Region* and Perloff *et al.*, *Regions, Resources, and Economic Growth* (5).

We have already discussed the failure of metropolitan governments to consider and act on metropolitan problems. One consequence is that state and national governments are being brought into the making and execution of more of the public policies that affect the structure and functioning of our metropolitan communities.

DATA ON ECONOMIC CHARACTERISTICS

How do people in your community make a living? A thumbnail sketch of the economy of each of the larger cities in the United States, that lists their principal industries and business enterprises is to be found in Ayer's *Directory of Newspapers and Periodicals*, in the *City Directory* of your town, and in Rand McNally's *Commercial Atlas* and *Marketing Guide*. An examination of the yellow pages of the local telephone directory is likely to be instructive. The state chamber of commerce, the state department of labor, the state employment agency (find the nearest office of this agency), the district census supervisor, the commission on the city plan, and the local chamber of commerce are likely to have information about employment in the various industries and business establishments in the city.

See the profiles of fifty major cities and their relationships in Duncan, pp. 279-550. You may find among these profiles one for the metropolitan areas in which your community is located. The profiles are most valuable as illustrations of the use of secondary materials as sources to supplement statistical data. Note, for instance, the frequent use of the *Encyclopedia Americana*.

Can you rate the principal local employers according to the number of people they employ or the size of their payrolls? Conversations with

local bankers, the executive secretary of the local chamber of commerce, labor leaders, the postmaster, the freight agents of the railroads, and the tax assessor, among others, will give you a perspective on the nature of the local economy. You should be able to rate the most important industries in the city in terms of number of employees, size of payrolls, tax assessments, production, etc. Bench mark data on many of these indices are to be found in the census of manufacturers, the census of business, and the censuses of population and housing. Remember that the postwar years have been a period of rapid growth. All census data, therefore, will have to be brought up to date.

You can learn a great deal about your city by using your own eyes as you ride or walk the streets. Your problem is to learn to see your city. What kind of city is it? What do people do? What is the pattern of business, industrial, residential areas? Where are the principal traffic arteries?

The reconnaissance suggested in the foregoing paragraphs will give you something of a bird's-eye view of the economy of your community. This view will guide you in making your plans for a more intensive survey and will serve as something of a check on your conclusions. It will also save time. You may want to write a brief summary of your general observations immediately and make a list of questions and propositions you want to test.

Can you observe any of the spatial patterns mentioned in Chapter VI of this book? Your attempt to identify the areas of your city, the uses of land for commercial business, industry, wholesale markets, and for the various kinds of residential areas—slums, segregated areas, concentrations of various nationalities—brings you a long way toward an understanding of the political map of your community. See Quinn, *Human Ecology* (6), Weimer and Hoyt, *Principles of Real Estate* (7), and Fisher and Fisher, *Urban Real Estate* (8) for a discussion of the ecological distribution of economic activities. Mark up a map showing the principal industrial, wholesale, retail, and storage areas of the city.

Locate the "downtown" area (the principal shopping, financial, and hotel areas, showing the railway and bus terminals) on a map of your city. Compare "downtown" on your map with the Central Business District (CBD) as defined in the 1958 Census of Business. Figure 9-1 shows the boundaries of the CBD in Birmingham, Alabama. It contains two census tracts; all data reported by tracts can be used, if pertinent, in studying what is happening to the downtown area. Figure 9-2 illustrates data and computations indicating the changing position of the CBD during the period 1954-1958.

Draw on the map the principal traffic arteries,

FIGURE 9-1

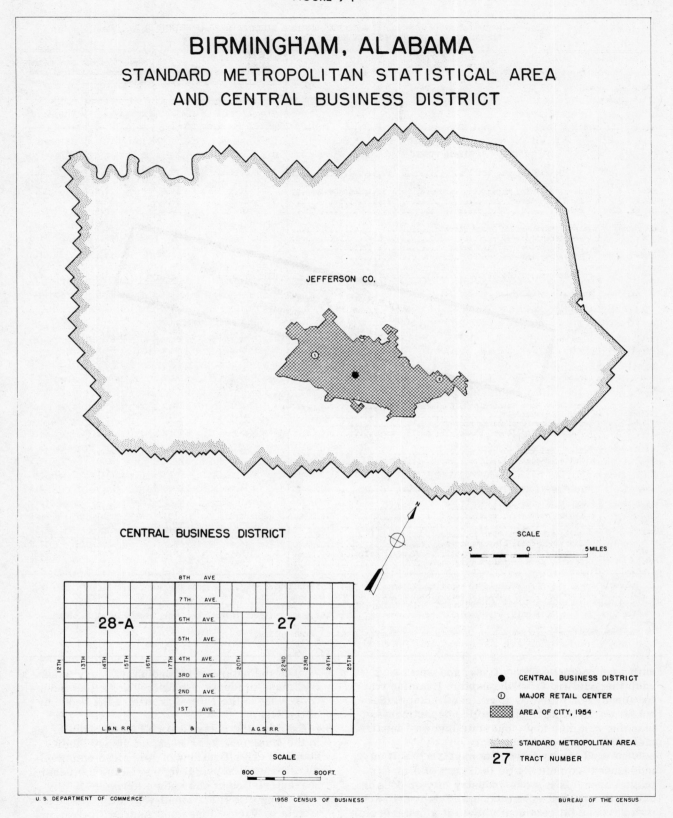

BIRMINGHAM, ALABAMA
STANDARD METROPOLITAN STATISTICAL AREA
AND CENTRAL BUSINESS DISTRICT

JEFFERSON CO.

SCALE

5   0   5 MILES

CENTRAL BUSINESS DISTRICT

	8TH AVE
	7TH AVE.
28-A	6TH AVE. 27
	5TH AVE.
	4TH AVE.
	3RD AVE.
	2ND AVE.
	1ST AVE.
L.&N. R.R.	8 A.G.S. R.R.

12TH 13TH 14TH 15TH 16TH 17TH 20TH 22ND 23RD 24TH 25TH

● CENTRAL BUSINESS DISTRICT

① MAJOR RETAIL CENTER

▦ AREA OF CITY, 1954

░ STANDARD METROPOLITAN AREA

27 TRACT NUMBER

SCALE

800   0   800 FT.

FIGURE 9-2

CENTRAL BUSINESS DISTRICT STATISTICS

Table 5.—RETAIL STORES: 1958 AND 1954 CENTRAL BUSINESS DISTRICT SALES AS PERCENT OF
BIRMINGHAM AND OF BIRMINGHAM STANDARD METROPOLITAN STATISTICAL AREA

SIC code	Kind of business	Percent of city sales in central business district		Percent of standard metropolitan statistical area sales in central business district	
		1958	1954	1958	1954
	RETAIL STORES				
	Retail stores, total[1]	34.6	38.8	26.8	30.7
52	Lumber, Building Materials, Hardware, Farm Equipment Dealers	10.5	16.6	7.8	13.5
5251	Hardware stores	17.5	29.6	10.6	20.9
52 ex. 5251	Other	07.9	10.4	6.4	09.1
53 part[2]	General Merchandise Group Stores[3]	78.8		66.1	71.2
531	Department stores	(D)		89.1	(D)
533	Limited price variety stores			48.7	64.5
539	Other general merchandise stores			13.4	(D)
54	Food Stores			8.4	08.9
55 ex. 554	Automotive Dealers			10.0	12.5
554	Gasoline Service		10.6	03.0	06.9
56	Apparel	75.7	85.4	64.0	75.2
561, 567	Men's	72.3	81.7	67.8	(D)
562,563,568	Women's	83.8	84.6	74.8	74.4
562	Ready	86.3	84.7	78.6	76.2
565	Family	59.7	86.3	43.4	74.1
566	Shoe sto	79.1	92.2	72.0	83.3
564, 569	All other	61.3	78.1	(D)	(D)
57	Furniture, Home Furnishings, Equipment Stores	60.5	74.3	49.8	62.3
5712	Furniture stores[4]	63.1	79.6	51.5	67.3
5713-15,19	Other home furnishings stores[4]	32.0	25.4	25.6	24.0
572, 573	Household appliance, radio, TV, music stores	61.0	81.2	51.2	64.0
58	Eating, Drinking places	38.6	48.0	28.9	37.3
5812	Eating places	41.1	48.6	30.9	39.5
5813	Drinking places	16.5	43.1	12.4	22.4
591	Drug Stores, Proprietary Stores	14.0	17.8	10.7	13.3
59 ex. 591	Other Retail Stores[5]	42.4	51.1	30.8	41.1
592	Liquor stores	31.8	(D)	(D)	(D)
597	Jewelry stores	85.0	87.1	72.8	81.5
594	Book, stationery stores	(D)	(D)	(D)	(D)
595	Sporting goods, bicycle stores	46.4	76.7	33.6	59.5
5992	Florists	(NA)	19.3	10.8	13.7
5996	Camera, photographic supply stores	(NA)	(D)	(D)	(D)

Standard Notes: (D) Withheld to avoid disclosure.   (NA) Not available.   ... Represents zero.
[1]Excludes nonstore retailers (mail order, direct selling, merchandise vending machine operators). Part of SIC group 53.
[2]Includes only "with payroll" establishments. Establishments "without payroll," if any, are included in the group totals.
[3]The 1954 data include only "with payroll" establishments. Establishments "without payroll," if any, are included in the group totals.
[4]Includes kinds of business not included in any of the detail lines which follow.

SUGGESTED IDENTIFICATION
U. S. Bureau of the Census. U. S. Census of Business: 1958
Vol. VII, Central Business District Report, Birmingham, Ala.--BC58-CBD8

railways, bus and subway lines, and waterways radiating outward from the center. Examine traffic surveys of your city if you can find any. (See public works departments, police departments, planning commissions, and state highway departments for material of this sort.)

What kind of city is your home town? Is it an independent community or is it part of a metropolitan area? Is it a one-industry city or does it have a diversified industrial base? Is it primarily an industrial community or is it a commercial trading center? If it is an industrial community,

what is the nature of the industry: heavy industry, mass production industry, or skilled industry? What is the rate of growth of the economy of the city?

Examine the classification of American cities in the *Municipal Year Book* and in any other standard classifications of American communities that may be useful in describing the general characteristics of your home town.

For one classification of your city, read the article by Victor Jones and Andrew Collver in the *Municipal Year Book*, 1960, "Economic Class-

ifications of Cities and Metropolitan Areas,"
pp. 69-79, and look up your city in Table VI, pp.
91 ff. (See Fig. 9-3 for an earlier edition of the
article.) Be sure to read the explanatory note on
pp. 90-91. Table VI is a good place to find a list
of cities approximately the same size as your
city.

For a discussion of the problems involved in
the classification of cities by functional specialization, see Duncan and Reiss, *Social Characteristics of Urban and Rural Communities, 1950* (9).
Standard metropolitan areas, central cities, suburbs of 10,000 inhabitants or more, and independent cities of 10,000 inhabitants or more are
classified by them in supplementary tables in
this text. See, also Reiss, "Functional Specialization of Cities," in *Cities and Society* (10).

Other classifications of cities will be found in
the following books:

Alexandersson, G., *The Industrial Structure of American
Cities.* Lincoln, Neb.: University of Nebraska Press,
1956.
Hart, J. F., "Functions and Occupational Structures of
Cities of the American South," *Annals of the Associ-
ation of American Geographers,* Vol 45, September
1955. pp. 269-286.
Nelson, H. J., "A Service Classification of American
Cities," *Economic Geography,* Vol. 31, 1955. pp. 189-
210.
Ogburn, W. F., *Social Characteristics of Cities.* Chi-
cago: International City Managers' Association, 1937.

Check these different lists to see how your
community is classified. Do the differences in
classification suggest inquiries to be pursued in
your survey?

In this connection, consider the possibility that
you may be attempting to study the wrong local
entity. A "city" or "village" may be a more or
less arbitrary legal geographical unit in a larger
community, impossible to understand by itself.
This is usually true of suburbs and satellite cities.
Much of the data used as a basis in any attempt
to define the scope of an urban community are
economic. Therefore, market areas, labor market areas, or service areas, may be more important than arbitrary legal units in helping you
make your decision.

The size of the city is related to certain other
characteristics of the community: the kinds of
services available, the extent and variety of special areas likely to develop in the community,
mass communications, the diversity of population.
See the discussion of urbanism and urbanization
in Queen and Carpenter, *The American City* (11),
in Duncan and Reiss, pp. 19-113, and in Vernon,
p. 172.

It is important to find a number of other cities
of approximately the same size and location as
your home town to use as yardsticks in measur-
ing the economic characteristics of your city.
Statistics concerning the economy of an urban

area are likely to become meaningful only when
they are compared with data for other cities of
approximately the same size. Any marked deviation from the norm should be explained. Where
discrepancies or variations appear, it may be
desirable to convert the statistics to graphs,
tables, or figures to make the differences clear.
A good point at which to begin is the table in the
Municipal Year Book in which all cities with a
population of 10,000 or more are listed in the
order of their size.

The data in Table VI of the *Municipal Year
Book,* 1961, concerning rent level, economic base,
employment-residence ratio, manufacturing ratio,
and percentage of dwelling units built between
1940 and 1950 and since 1950 may shed much
light on the nature of the community. Thus, you
might reasonably expect that Camden, New Jersey,
with a manufacturing ratio of 73 and Austin, Texas,
with a manufacturing ratio of 13, are very different kinds of urban communities. (Manufacturing
ratio is employment in manufacturing shown as
a percentage of aggregate employment. The other
terms used here are defined in the *Municipal
Year Book.*) Wichita, Kansas, with 32.4 percent
of dwellings built since 1940, is probably a very
different kind of community than Scranton, Pennsylvania, in which only 0.6 percent of dwellings
were built since 1940. Compare the statistics for
Phoenix, Arizona, and New Bedford, Massachusetts.

Look up the *Statistical Abstract,* the *County and
City Data Book,* the *Census of Housing,* the *Census of Population* (for your state), the *Census of
Manufacturers* and the *Census of Business.* Note
in the *Statistical Abstract* and the *County and
City Data Book* the bibliographies of sources of
statistical data. Do you have access to any of
these sources? Spend some time familiarizing
yourself with the scope, organization, and titles
of the census materials. See Chapter VI of this
text for a discussion of the data reported in the
censuses of population and housing and in the
County and City Data Book.

Figure 9-4 is a specimen page from the *1958
Census of Manufacturers.* In this particular table
data are presented for standard metropolitan statistical areas with 40,000 or more manufacturing
employees. Volume III of the *Census of Manufacturers* reports the following statistics:

State data for 1958: value of shipments, value added by
manufacture, employment, payrolls, man-hours, new
capital expenditures, and number of manufacturing establishments for industries and industry groups, with
historical comparisons. For the state's important
standard metropolitan statistical areas and larger counties, these data are shown by industry groups. Similar
totals for all manufacturing industries are shown for
counties, standard metropolitan statistical areas, and
cities with 10,000 or more inhabitants. The number
of establishments in each major industry group is
presented by size of establishment within county.

TABLE IV—GOVERNMENTAL AND ECONOMIC DATA FOR CITIES OVER 10,000—Continued

City	1950 Population (000 omitted)	Land Area in Square Miles	Metro Status, Rent Level	Economic Base	Employ. Residence Ratio	Mnfg. Ratio	Percent Dwelling Units Built 1940-50	Form of Govt Selec Ma	No. of Coun-	Type of Annual Election Salary	Other Elective City Offices	Utilities Owned and Operated
50,000 to 100,000—continued												
Sioux Falls, S. D. . .	53	12.7	CE2	Rm	119	36	25.5	Cç				
South Gate, Calif. .	51	7.0	SD3	Mm	81	73	51.1	M				
Springfield, Ill. . . .	82	10.5	CE2	Rm	122	38	11.0	C				
Springfield, Mo. . .	67	17.3	CE2	Rm	121	33	14.7	C				
Springfield, Ohio . .	79	12.2	CE2	Mm	145	68	11.0	)				
Stamford, Conn. . .	74	37.6	C-2	Mm		63	18.6	)				
Stockton, Calif. . . .	71	12.5	CE2	Rm	153	23	27.4					
Terre Haute, Ind. .	64	12.3	CE2	Mr	138	44	6.3					
Topeka, Kan.	79	13.1	CB2	Rm	114	32	14.5					
Troy, N. Y.	72	9.3	CB2	Mr	104	49	4.4					
Union City, N. J. . .	56	1.3	SB1	M	88	52	0.6					
Upper Darby tp, Pa.	85	. . .	. . .	. .	. .	. .	. . .					
Waco, Tex.	85	26.0	CB2	Rm	105	24	29.					
Waterloo, Iowa. . .	65	31.3	CE2	Mm	136	67	19					
Wheeling, W. Va. . .	59	10.4	CE2	Mr⁴	157¹	.⁴	4					
Wichita Falls, Tex.	68	11.8	CE2	Rm	119	26	24					
Wilkes-Barre, Pa. .	77	6.9	CE2	Mg	172	48						
Winston, Salem, N.C.	88	18.9	CE2	Mm	174	68	1'					
Woonsocket, R. I. .	50	8.6	SB2	Mm	113	74						
York, Pa.	60	4.2	CE2	Mm	190	70						
25,000 to 50,000												
Abilene, Tex.	46	10.5	IB	Rr	93	17						
Abington tp, Pa. . .	29	. . .	. .	. .	. .	. .						
Albany, Ga.	31	10.4	IB	Rr	93							
Alexandria, La. . .	35	6.2	IB	Rm	105							
Aliquippa, Pa. . . .	26	4.4	SE2	Mm	16'							
Alliance, Ohio . . .	26	4.6	SE2	Mm								
Alton, Ill.	33	6.4	SB2	M								
Amsterdam, N. Y. .	32	6.0	IE	M								
Anderson, Ind. . . .	47	9.8	IE									
Ann Arbor, Mich. .	48	7.3	IE									
Anniston, Ala. . . .	31	9.3	IE									
Appleton, Wis. . . .	34	8.2	IE									
Arlington t, Mass. .	44	. . .										
Ashland, Ky.	31	8.0										
Athens, Ga.	28	9										
Auburn, N. Y. . . .	37											
Bakersfield, Calif. .	35											
Bangor, Me.	3'											
Barberton, Ohio. . .												
Battle Creek, Mich												
Belleville, Ill. . . .												
Belleville, N. J												
Bellingham,												
Belmont t,												
Beloit, W												
Besser												
Bever												
Bev												
P												

Economic Classification of Citi and Metropolitan Areas¹

By VICTOR JONES

FIGURE 9-3   ECONOMIC CLASSIFICATION OF CITIES

SOURCE: THE MUNICIPAL
YEAR BOOK, 1953
PP. 49—57, 69—96.

Table 4.—GENERAL STATISTICS FOR STANDARD METROPOLITAN STATISTICAL AREAS WITH 40,000 OR MORE MANUFACTURING EMPLOYEES: 1958 AND 1954—Continued

(See text for explanation of column captions)

| | | 1958 | | | | | | | 1954 | |
| Code | Major industry group | Establishments, number | | All employees | | Value added by manufacture | | Capital expenditures, new ($1,000) | All employees, number | Value added by manufacture, unadjusted ($1,000) |
		Total	With 20 or more employees	Number	Payroll ($1,000)	Unadjusted ($1,000)	Adjusted ($1,000)			
		WATERBURY STANDARD METROPOLITAN STATISTICAL AREA (Consists of Waterbury City; Naugatuck Borough; and Beacon Falls, Cheshire, Middlebury, Prospect, and Wolcott Towns in New Haven County; and Thomaston and Watertown Towns in Litchfield County, Connecticut)									
	ALL INDUSTRIES, TOTAL[1]..........	[2]412	[2]144	37,235	188,885	297,253	296,922	21,547	43,029	307,565
20	Food and kindred products.............	30	6	927	4,880	15,309	15,570	394	961	10,083
23	Apparel and related products...........	13	7	968	2,565	3,112	3,033	18	1,018	2,797
26	Pulp, paper and products..............	3	3	323	1,707	2,604	2,603	159	320	1,983
27	Printing and publishing...............	25	4	749	3,723	5,267	5,267	(D)	787	4,749
32	Stone, clay, and glass products[4].......	15	6	402	1,677	2,646	2,885	86	392	2,141
33	Primary metal industries..............	20	15	6,061	34,049	54,660	59,337	7,786	7,363	65,999
34	Fabricated metal products.............	131	44	7,241	36,619	54,066	51,267	3,875	6,558	43,266
35	Machinery, except electrical[4]..........	88	18	3,639	18,471	34,654	28,056	3,790	2,983	25,561
36	Electrical machinery..................	6	5	673	2,815	3,343	3,263	221	916	6,689
38	Instruments and related products.......	12	10	4,992	21,873	33,257	33,657	784	3,773	23,179
39	Miscellaneous manufactures (including Ordnance)...........................	39	16	3,239	14,992	22,793	24,135	1,048	8,597	51,304
---	Administrative and auxiliary[5]..........	...	...	770	5,991	...	...	...	843	...

D Withheld to avoid disclosing figures for individual companies.
[1]The "All industries, total" includes figures for industry groups which have been withheld from publication in order to (a) avoid disclosing figures for individual companies in this or associated industries or areas or, (b) permit further checking of figures for smaller industry groups. Additional publishable detail will appear in the final report for the State.
[2]Does not include the number of administrative and auxiliary units.
[3]The definition of this standard metropolitan statistical area has been revised since 1954. Comparable 1954 data based on the new definition for the area were not available in time for inclusion in this preliminary release but will be included in the final report for the State.
[4]The 1958 Census of Manufactures figures include establishments classified in Industry 3273, Ready-Mixed Concrete, and establishments classified in Industry 3599, Machine Shops, that were engaged exclusively or almost exclusively in repair work. For 1954, such establishments were not classified in manufacturing but were included in the 1954 Census of Business. The 1954 and 1958 figures, therefore, are not strictly comparable. This has a relatively small effect on the statistics, except for those on number of establishments.
[5]In addition to the employment and payroll reported for operating manufacturing establishments, manufacturing concerns ordinarily reported separately for central administrative offices or auxiliary units which service the manufacturing establishments of a company (e.g., research laboratories, storage warehouses, power plants, garages, repair shops, etc.). A separate report was usually obtained for each central office or auxiliary unit if it was located at a different general location from the manufacturing establishment(s) served or if it serviced two or more manufacturing establishments and was not operated as an integral part of the establishment at the same location. Employment and payroll of central administrative offices and auxiliaries are included in the totals for the area.

1958 Census of Manufactures

FIGURE 9-4

Area Reports

(Subject to Revision)

April 1960   MC(P)-S6

CONNECTICUT

(Advance information for the State, its Standard Metropolitan Statistical Areas and Counties. This report will be superseded by a 1958 Census of Manufactures final report which, in turn, will be included in Volume III, Area Statistics.)

Figure 9-5 is a reproduction of the columnar headings of tables in the *1958 Census of Business* showing the kinds of data reported for counties and cities. Volume II reports

1958 and 1954 statistics for the State by 34 kinds of business on number of establishments and sales; 1958 statistics for the State and for standard metropolitan statistical areas by about 95 kinds of business, and for counties and for cities with 500 establishments or more by varied kind-of-business detail, on number of establishments, sales, payroll, employment, and number of proprietors of unincorporated businesses. For counties and for cities of 2,500 inhabitants or more, the same items are given for total retail trade, and number of establishments and sales by 11 kind-of-business groups.

Comparable 1954 statistics are given for counties and for cities of 2,500 or more on number of establishments, sales and payroll; for standard metropolitan statistical areas and for cities of 500 establishments or more, the 1954 figures are on number of establishments and sales.

Figure 9-6 shows the data reported on wholesale trade for all counties and for cities of 5,000 or more inhabitants. Note the statistics on types of wholesale business for counties with 100 establishments or more. The following kinds of statistics will be found in Volume IV of the *1958 Census of Business:*

Each State report presents: 1958 statistics on number of establishments, sales, payroll, employment, and number of proprietors of unincorporated businesses for total wholesale trade; and number of establishments and sales for merchant wholesalers and other wholesale types combined—for the State by about 60 kinds of business, for standard metropolitan statistical areas and counties with 100 establishments or more by varied kind-of-business detail, and totals for each county and each city of 5,000 inhabitants or more.

Also included are figures on number of establishments and sales for the State by 17 kinds of business for merchant wholesalers, manufacturers' sales branches and sales offices, merchandise agents and brokers, and other operating types combined; and 1958 and 1954 figures for the State, standard metropolitan statistical areas, and counties with 100 establishments or more, on number of establishments and sales for total wholesale trade, merchant wholesalers, and other operating types combined.

Business, personal, repair services, amusements, hotels, motels, etc., are reported in Volume VI of the *1958 Census of Business:*

Each State report presents: 1958 and 1954 statistics for the State by about 40 kinds of business on number of establishments and receipts; 1958 statistics on number of establishments, receipts, payroll, employment, and number of proprietors of unincorporated businesses for the State by about 70 kinds of business in the personal, business, and repair service trades, 30 kinds of business in the amusement trades, and hotels, motels, and tourist courts. The same items are also shown for standard metropolitan statistical areas, counties and cities with 200 establishments or more, by varied kind-or-business detail. For each county and city of 2,500 inhabitants or more, the statistics are presented for total establishments with number of establishments and receipts given for each of three major kind-of-business groups.

Comparable figures for 1954 include totals on number of establishments, receipts, and payroll for counties and for cities of 2,500 inhabitants or more; establishments and receipts for standard metropolitan statistical areas, and counties and cities with 200 establishments or more by kind-of-business major groups.

Figure 9-7 is a sample of the data on selected services reported for standard metropolitan statistical areas.

The censuses of manufacturers and business should, of course, not be used before the preface and the appendix on definitions and procedures have been carefully read. Some of the major differences between the 1954 and 1958 censuses are discussed in the preface. An exasperating feature of the censuses of manufacturers and business is the rule against publishing "any data which would disclose the operations of an individual establishment or business organization." The smaller the area reported, the greater the likelihood that data will be withheld for this reason. For an example of adjustments for nondisclosure (as well as of other adjustments of data in the censuses of manufacture and business), see Lichtenberg, Appendices A, B, and C.

Housing in one form or another is the one use of land common to each person in the community. Its economic importance is obvious. The relative quality and quantity of the important characteristics of housing are also indicators of social status. Data on housing characteristics can, therefore, be used to map the social as well as the economic structure of a community. Local planning, urban renewal, and public housing agencies are likely to have analyzed and supplemented published and unpublished census data. Parts of the publication program of the *1960 Census of Housing,* showing areas for which statistics are reported and the subjects reported, is reproduced as an appendix to this chapter.

A well-informed local real estate dealer is likely to be able to supply much rough data for a general survey of real estate values and rentals. Invite at least two dealers to mark up some maps for you.

In view of the fact that housing is a good measure of social and economic status, information concerning real estate values and rentals may indicate the economic status of people living in the various areas of the city.

Can you find any maps showing land use in your city? (See the planning commission, real estate dealers, tax assessor's office.) Study a zoning map of your city. These maps should help you form a picture of the economic status of the people living in the various sections. Lists of the assessed valuations made by the tax assessor can often be obtained at the city hall.

In the 1960 censuses of population and housing see tables for your city, county, standard metro-

RETAIL TRADE—AREA STATISTICS

FIGURE 9-5

Table 102.—RETAIL TRADE: 1958—COUNTIES;

Total Retail—Establishments, Sales, Payroll, and Personnel;

Line number	County and city	Total: Establishments: Total (number)	Establishments: With payroll (number)	Sales: Total, all establishments ($1,000)	Sales: Establishments with payroll ($1,000)	Payroll, entire year ($1,000)	Paid employees, workweek ended nearest Nov. 15: Total (number)	Paid employees: Full workweek (number)	Active proprietors of unincorporated businesses (number)	Kind-of-business group: Lumber, building matls., hardware, farm equip. dealers: Establishments (number)	Lumber…: Sales ($1,000)	General merchandise group stores*: Establishments (number)	General merchandise: Sales ($1,000)
1	ESSEX COUNTY	583	371	42,318	38,008	3,741	1,363	1,155	591	24	2,286	47	1,913
2	LAKE PLACID	83	69	5,306	5,036	601	213	182	80	1	(D)		(D)
3	SARANAC LAKE (PART)[2]	18	10	2,004	1,832	148	31	27	20	...	...		(D)
4	TICONDEROGA	67	59	8,126	7,926	804	303	255	62	5			461
5	REMAINDER OF COUNTY	415	233	26,882	23,214	2,188	816	691	429	18			1,198
6	FRANKLIN COUNTY	660	426	52,276	47,698	4,703	1,749	1,505	708				5,470
7	MALONE	174	130	21,602	20,820	2,273	766	679					
8	SARANAC LAKE (PART)[2]	109	87	9,063	8,695	971	383	322					741
9	TUPPER LAKE	79	65	6,171	5,987	565	217						726
10	REMAINDER OF COUNTY	298	144	15,440	12,196	894	383						
11	FULTON COUNTY	697	421	57,575	51,897	5,519							
12	DOLGEVILLE (PART)[3]	2	...	(D)	...	...							
13	GLOVERSVILLE	319	215	30,656	28,790								
14	JOHNSTOWN	155	101	16,323	15,117								
15	REMAINDER OF COUNTY	221	105	(D)	7,990								
16	GENESEE COUNTY	634	406	68,040									
17	BATAVIA	281	209	38,090									
18	LE ROY	88	56	7,843									
19	REMAINDER OF COUNTY	265	141										
20	GREENE COUNTY	564	346										2,300
21	CATSKILL	135											(D)
22	COXSACKIE	38											(D)
23	REMAINDER OF COUNTY												1,181
24	HAMILTON COUNTY											17	949
25	HERKIMER COUNTY											55	4,845
26	DOLGEVILLE (PART)[3]										(D)	2	(D)
27	FRANKFORT										(D)	3	(D)
28	HERKIMER									12	1,053	9	2,942
29	ILION									8	422	4	296
30	LIT									11	787	13	707
31									52	4	583	2	(D)
32									274	18	1,645	22	600
33									1,235	78	7,839	61	12,502
34								248	105	6	237	4	692
35								2,440	404	14	2,071	11	9,937
36								1,149	726	58	5,531	46	1,873
37							85,139	71,784	29,210	828	72,644	1,247	204,861
38							580	512	263	26	2,486	23	785
39							290	262	68	8	1,185	2	(D)
40							290	250	195	18	1,301	21	(D)
41	LIV					3,528	1,418	1,082	663	54	3,642	26	1,304
42	DA					920	362	290	101	10	780	...	...
43	GEN				3,278	281	117	84	48	4	139	1	(D)
44	MOU				4,293	441	168	130	89	6	412	3	(D)
45	REMA				22,975	1,886	771	578	425	34	2,311	22	1,087
46	MADISON				53,296	5,003	1,849	1,474	633	45	5,196	25	2,518
47	CANAST			5,534	5,018	489	204	137	68	8	647	4	144
48	CHITTEN			4,976	4,742	355	140	108	52	2	(D)	1	(D)
49	HAMILTO			5,025	4,971	417	164	131	43	3	(D)	2	(D)
50	ONEIDA			20,817	19,967	2,082	681	571	137	9	984	6	1,703
51	REMAINDER		165	21,074	18,598	1,660	660	527	333	23	2,831	12	464
52	MONROE COUNT		3,401	707,100	670,906	85,187	29,559	22,371	4,862	282	35,983	134	100,046
53	BROCKPORT	72	52	7,817	7,073	743	292	187	74	4	392	2	(D)
54	EAST ROCHEST	94	60	8,983	7,961	798	361	250	96	4	216	4	395
55	FAIRPORT												
56	ROCHESTER												
57	WEBSTER												
58	REMAINDER OF CO												
59	MONTGOMERY COUNTY												
60	AMSTERDAM												
61	CANAJOHARIE	63											
62	FORT PLAIN	75											
63	REMAINDER OF COUNTY	262											
64	NASSAU COUNTY	10,752											
65	BAYVILLE	41											
66	CEDARHURST	166	138	22,303	21,311	2,694	786	709	131	5	695		
67	EAST HILLS	6	6	4,772	4,772	422	90	80	6	...	...	...	...
68	EAST ROCKAWAY	68	44	6,393	5,287	546	199	156	62	1	(D)	2	(D)
69	EAST WILLISTON	13	11	3,022	(D)	300	79	56	7	2	(D)	...	...
70	FARMINGDALE	152	126	24,321	23,733	2,662	916	679	134	13	1,922	4	587
71	FLORAL PARK	200	138	24,391	23,089	2,233	743	579	189	14	1,220	9	989
72	FLOWER HILL	1	1	(D)	(D)	(D)	(D)	(D)	(D)	1	(D)	...	...
73	FREEPORT	422	310	54,761	52,149	6,321	1,826	1,516	347	20	2,253	6	2,314
74	GARDEN CITY	186	164	70,814	70,086	9,301	3,690	2,656	118	8	1,851	11	(D)
75	GLEN COVE	258	198	32,007	30,777	3,384	1,042	850	241	15	2,485	5	849
76	GREAT NECK	93	65	13,749	13,345	1,542	406	365	89	6	729	5	(D)
77	GREAT NECK ESTATES	28	28	4,513	4,513	515	160	130	27	...	...	...	...
78	GREAT NECK PLAZA	185	139	26,811	25,781	3,349	1,013	928	146	6	1,146	6	(D)

Standard Notes: ... Represents zero. (D) Withheld to avoid disclosure. (NA) Not available.

*Nonstore retailers, part of SIC major group 53, are shown separately in this table.

[2]Saranac Lake is in Essex and Franklin Counties.

[3]Dolgeville is in Fulton and Herkimer Counties.

32–11

NEW YORK

CITIES OF 2,500 INHABITANTS OR MORE—Continued

Kind-of-Business Group—Establishments and Sales

Kind-of-business group — Continued	Visible values
Food stores: Establishments (No.)	99, 7, 2, 8, 82, 120, 35, 13, 6, 66
Food stores: Sales ($1,000)	11,756, (D), (D), 2,484, 7,414, 12,667, 4,647, 2,139, 2,025, 3,856
Automotive dealers: Establishments (No.)	34, 4, 2, 2, 26, 37, 20, 6, 3
Automotive dealers: Sales ($1,000)	8,430, 533, (D), (D), 6,683, 8,993, 5,160, 1,473
Gasoline service stations: Establishments (No.)	61, 7, 1, 4, 49, 70, 16
Gasoline service stations: Sales ($1,000)	2,638, (D), (D), 454, 1,746, 3,272, 988
Apparel, accessory stores: Establishments (No.)	40, 14, 2, 8, 16, 48
Apparel, accessory stores: Sales ($1,000)	2,675, 950, (D), 865, (D)
Furniture, home furnishings, equipment stores: Establishments (No.)	20, 3, ..., 7, 10
Furniture, home furnishings, equipment stores: Sales ($1,000)	1,235, 47, ..., 728
Eating, drinking places: Establishments (No.)	142, 14, 6, 18
Eating, drinking places: Sales ($1,000)	4,559, 755, 119
Drug stores, proprietary stores: Establishments (No.)	22, 4, ...
Drug stores, proprietary stores: Sales ($1,000)	1,517, 321
Other retail stores: Establishments (No.)	90, 27
Other retail stores: Sales ($1,000)	5,222
Nonstore retailers*: Establishments (No.)	
Nonstore retailers*: Sales ($1,000)	
Line number	

SUGGESTED IDENTIFICATION

U. S. Bureau of the Census. *U. S. Census of Business: 1958*

Retail Trade, BC58-RA32, New York

U. S. Government Printing Office, Washington, D. C., 1960

FIGURE 9-6

NEW YORK

Table 102.—WHOLESALE TRADE 1958—COUNTIES; CITIES OF 5,000 INHABITANTS OR MORE

Total Wholesale Trade—Establishments, Sales, Payroll, and Personnel; Merchant Wholesalers and Other Operating Types—Establishments and Sales

County and city	Total						Merchant wholesalers		Other operating types	
	Establishments	Sales	Payroll, entire year	Payroll, workweek ended nearest Nov. 15	Paid employees, workweek ended nearest Nov. 15	Active proprietors of unincorporated businesses	Establishments	Sales	Establishments	Sales
	(number)	($1,000)	($1,000)	(dollars)	(number)	(number)	(number)	($1,000)	(number)	($1,000)
NEW YORK, TOTAL	40 125	54 627 662	2 175 784	43 192 183	405 104	19 440	31 357	24 995 772	8 768	29 631 890
ALBANY COUNTY	576	625 577	36 002	700 192	6 990	226	409	322 972	167	302 605
ALBANY	430	472 159	27 373	537 320	5 352	171	312	248 252	118	223 907
COHOES	21	10 221	673	13 059	164	7	19	(D)	2	(D)
COLONIE	16	14 049	881	17 907	170	4	7	1 556	9	12 493
WATERVLIET	8	5 772	269	6 825	83	3	6	(D)	2	(D)
REMAINDER OF COUNTY	101	123 376	6 806	125 081	1 221	41	65	62 0..	36	61 304
ALLEGANY COUNTY	37	12 311	877	20 111	282	34	29			3 249
WELLSVILLE	7	2 189	142	3 628	52	5				...
REMAINDER OF COUNTY	30	10 122	735	16 483	230	29				3 249
BRONX COUNTY (BRONX BOROUGH, PART OF NEW YORK CITY)	1 315	917 137	60 238	1 161 215	11 871					234 765
BROOME COUNTY	282	230 526	14 544	300 113						22 729
BINGHAMTON	194	120 798	9 760	195 76.						268
ENDICOTT	20	42 874	2 070	4..						(D)
JOHNSON CITY	18	24 312	1 363							(D)
REMAINDER OF COUNTY	50	42 542	1 3..							66
CATTARAUGUS COUNTY	87	40 687								8.
OLEAN	49	27 ..								
SALAMANCA	8									
REMAINDER OF COUNTY	30									
CAYUGA COUNTY										
AUBURN										
REMAINDER OF COUNTY										
CHAUTAUQUA COUNTY										302.
DUNKIRK										
JAMESTOWN										
REMAINDER OF COUNTY										8
CHEMUNG COUNTY										40
ELMIRA										8
ELMIRA HEIGHTS										8
HORSEHEADS										47
REMAIN..										

32–18

WHOLESALE TRADE—AREA STATISTICS

Table 104.—WHOLESALE TRADE: 1958—COUNTIES WITH 100 ESTABLISHMENTS OR MORE

Total Wholesale Trade—Establishments, Sales, Payroll, and Personnel; Merchant Wholesalers and Other Operating Types—Establishments and Sales; by Kind of Business

County and kind of business	SIC code	Total						Merchant wholesalers		Other operating types	
		Establishments	Sales	Payroll, entire year	Payroll, workweek ended nearest Nov. 15	Paid employees, workweek ended nearest Nov. 15	Active proprietors of unincorporated businesses	Establishments	Sales	Establishments	Sales
		(number)	($1,000)	($1,000)	(dollars)	(number)	(number)	(number)		(number)	($1,000)

ALBANY COUNTY

WHOLESALE TRADE, TOTAL		576	625 577	36 002	700 192	6 990					
MOTOR VEHICLES, AUTOMOTIVE EQUIPMENT	50	43	47 945	3 834	75 124	766		237		30	
DRUGS, CHEMICALS, ALLIED PRODUCTS	501	18	11 532	912	16 709	208		958		4	
DRY GOODS, APPAREL	502	6	3 149	88	1 710			22 570		16	
GROCERIES AND RELATED PRODUCTS	503	103	125 238	4 873	105 067			737		15	
FARM PRODUCTS—RAW MATERIALS	504	5	(D)	3 370	66 821			4 005		20	
ELECTRICAL GOODS, HEATING EQUIP, SUPPLIES	505	43	77 347	2 103	42 05.			38 598		38	12 546
HARDWARE, PLUMBING, HEATING EQUIP, SUPPLIES	506	36	20 900	7 722	145..			72 901			
MACHINERY, EQUIPMENT, SUPPLIES	507	120	71 367	1 179				90 810			682
METALS, MINERALS (EX. PETROLEUM PROD, SCRAP)	508		17 938	1 787	6..					1 195	
PETROLEUM BULK STATIONS, TERMINALS		18	69 688					977		90	
SCRAP, WASTE MATERIALS		14	8 477					921		52	
TOBACCO, TOBACCO PRODUCTS		31	40 529					4 534		36	
BEER, WINE, DISTILLED ALCOHOLIC BEVERAGES		17	13 253							404	
PAPER, PAPER PRODUCTS, EXCEPT WALLPAPER		17	10 435			11 871		842		5	
FURNITURE, HOME FURNISHINGS		22	45 30.					712		55	
LUMBER, CONSTRUCTION MATERIALS		32	8..					278		80	
OTHER MISCELLANEOUS PRODUCTS		47						4 102		100	
								42			
								391		84	
								742			
								805		9	

BRONX COUNTY

(Bronx Borough, part of New York City)

WHOLESALE TRADE, TOTAL											
MOTOR VEHICLES, AUTOMOTIVE EQUIPMENT	50										
DRUGS, CHEMICALS, ALLIED PRODUCTS	501										
DRY GOODS, APPAREL	502										
GROCERIES AND RELATED PRODUCTS	503										
FARM PRODUCTS—RAW MATERIALS											
ELECTRICAL GOODS, HEATING EQUIP											
PLUMBING, HEATING EQUIP, SUPPLIES											

SUGGESTED IDENTIFICATION. U.S. Census of Business: 1958
Wholesale Trade, BC58-WA32, New York
U.S. Bureau of the Census.
U.S. Government Printing Office, Washington, D.C. 1960

(Partial left-column labels visible through overlap:)

COR..
CO..
REM..

DELAWA..

DUTCHESS..
BEACON
POUGHKE..
REMAINDE..

ERIE COUNTY..
BUFFALO..
DEPEW..
HAMBURG..
KENMORE..
LACKAWANNA..
LANCASTER..
SLOAN..
TONAWANDA..
WILLIAMSVILLE..
REMAINDER OF COUN..

ESSEX COUNTY
SARANAC LAKE (PART)
REMAINDER OF COUNTY

FRANKLIN COUNTY
MALONE
SARANAC LAKE (PART)[1]
TUPPER LAKE
REMAINDER OF COUNTY

FULTON COUNTY
GLOVERSVILLE
JOHNSTOWN
REMAINDER OF COUNTY

GENESEE COUNTY
BATAVIA
REMAINDER OF COUNTY

		21 669
	10	9 324
6 027	17	12 345

Standard Notes: . . . . Represents zero.   (D) Withheld to avoid disclosure.   (NA) Not available.   (X) Item not applicable.

[1] Saranac Lake is in Essex and Franklin Counties.

FIGURE 9-7

SELECTED SERVICES—AREA STATISTICS

Table 103.—SELECTED SERVICES: 1958—STANDARD METROPOLITAN STATISTICAL AREAS—Continued

Establishments, Receipts, Payroll, and Personnel, by Kind of Business

SIC code	Kind of business	Establishments Total (number)	With payroll (number)	Receipts Total, all establishments ($1,000)	Establishments with payroll ($1,000)	Payroll, entire year ($1,000)	Payroll, workweek ended nearest Nov. 15 Total (dollars)	Full workweek	Paid employees, workweek ended nearest Nov. 15 Total (number)	Full workweek (number)	Active proprietors of unincorporated businesses (number)

NEW YORK STANDARD ... AREA—Continued

	AMUSEMENT, ETC.—CON.										
7949 PART	OTHER COMMERCIAL AMUSEMENTS	1 005						907	2 421	1 979	817
	AMUSEMENT PARKS, DEVICES							247	660	361	139
	CARNIVALS, CIRCUSES							904	44	34	9
	FAIRS							(D)	(D)	(D)	(D)
	TOURIST ATTRACTIONS							(D)	(D)	(D)	(D)
	COIN-OPERATED AMUSEMENT DEVICES							91	526	493	174
	OTHER							1	1 149	1 059	492
	SELECTED SERVICES, TOTAL									11 210	
	HOTELS, MOTELS, TOURIST COURTS, CAMPS										
701,703	TOTAL								1 312		75
7011,7012	HOTELS								176		20
7011	YEAR-ROUND HOTELS, 25 OR MORE GUEST ROOMS								142		4
	YEAR-ROUND HOTELS, LESS THAN 25 GUEST RMS								(D)		(D)
7012	SEASONAL HOTELS**										(D)
7013	MOTELS, TOURIST COURTS										42
7031	TRAILER PARKS										(D)
7032	SPORTING, RECREATIONAL CAMPS										(D)
	PERSONAL SERVICES										
72	TOTAL										498
721	LAUNDRIES, LDRY. SERV., CLEAN'G, DYE'G PLANTS										158
7211,7215	POWER LAUNDRIES, SELF-SERVICE LAUNDRIES										54
7211	POWER LAUNDRIES**										32
7215	SELF-SERVICE LAUNDRIES***										6
7213	INDUSTRIAL LAUNDERERS										(D)
	LINEN SUPPLY										5
7214	DIAPER SERVICE										
7212	LAUNDRIES, EXCEPT POWER AND SELF-SERVICE										20
7216,7217	CLEANING, DYEING PLANTS										79
7216	CLEAN'G, DYE'G PLANTS EX. RUG CLEAN'G*										74
7217	RUG CLEANING, REPAIRING PLANTS										5
723	BEAUTY SHOPS, INC. COMBINATION BEAUTY, BARBER	404									434
724	BARBER SHOPS	386									408
722	PHOTO. STUDIOS, INC. COMMERCIAL PHOTOGRAPHY	77									76
725	SHOE REPAIR, SHOESHINE, HAT CLEANING SHOPS	102									110
	SHOE REPAIR SHOPS	95									101
	SHOESHINE PARLORS	6									(D)
	HAT CLEANING SHOPS	1									(D)
726	FUNERAL SERVICE, CREMATORIES	92									92
727	PRESSING, ALTER., GARMENT RPR, FUR RPR, STRGE	122									128
7271	CLEANING, PRESSING SHOPS*	108									114
	GARMENT REPAIR, ALTERATION	8	6								9
7272	FUR REPAIR, STORAGE	6	4								5
729	MISCELLANEOUS PERSONAL SERVICES	92	10								92
	TURKISH BATHS, MASSAGE, REDUCING SALONS	6	2								(D)
	OTHER	86	8								(D)
	MISCELLANEOUS BUSINESS SERVICES										
73	TOTAL	391	179								322
731	ADVERTISING	39	31								23
7311	ADVERTISING AGENCIES	25	23								13
7312	OUTDOOR ADVERTISING SERVICES	6	6								
7319	MISCELLANEOUS ADVERTISING	8	6								
732	CREDIT BUREAUS, COLLECTION AGENCIES***	17	9								
7331	DUPLICATING, MAILING LIST, STENO. SERV.***	43	9								
7332	BLUEPRINTING, PHOTOCOPYING SERVICES	4	2								
734	SERVICES TO DWELLINGS, OTHER BUILDINGS	60	28								
7341	WINDOW CLEANING	21	9								
7342	DISINFECTING, EXTERMINATING SERVICES	7	7								
7349	MISC. SERVICES TO DWELLINGS, OTHER BLDGS	32	12								
735	NEWS SYNDICATES	2	...	(D)							
736	PRIVATE EMPLOYMENT AGENCIES	6	6	122							
7391	RESEARCH, DEVELOPMENT, TESTING LABORATORIES	10	6	178							
7392	BUSINESS, MANAGEMENT CONSULTING SERVICES	51	13	1 207							
7399	DETECTIVE AGENCIES, PROTECTIVE SERVICES	6	4	(D)							
	INTERIOR DECORATING	16	2	161							
	SIGN PAINTING SHOPS	34	10	515							
	EQUIPMENT RENTAL	11	11	852							
	AUCTIONEERS' ESTABLISHMENTS (SERVICE ONLY)	1	1	(D)							
	PHOTOFINISHING LABORATORIES	13	7	(D)							
	TELEPHONE ANSWERING	2	2	(D)							
	OTHER	76	38	7 188							61

Standard Notes: ... Represents zero. (D) Withheld to avoid disclosure. (NA) Not available.
*See kind-of-business descriptions for treatment of plant outlets:
**Data for establishments with no payroll are excluded; such establishments are included only at the next broader kind-of-business level.
***This is not the complete title. See Appendix for complete 1958 kind-of-business classification titles.

politan statistical area or urbanized area dealing with "economic characteristics of population," i.e., employment status, family income, industry group of employed persons, occupations. See Figures 9-8, 9-9, and 9-10.

APPROACHES TO ECONOMIC ANALYSES OF COMMUNITIES

The student who is surveying the politics and government of a community will not make "economic base studies" nor "input-output analyses." He will find, however, that businessmen, city planners, and economists have based many of their proposals for public and private policies upon assessments of the recent and future growth of the community. In order to understand and evaluate such proposals as well as the economic factors that might influence the politics of their consideration, the student should understand the economic theories and methodologies employed in community economic studies.

For a review of the export-base theory, the sector theory, and the input-output access theory, see Perloff, pp. 55-106, and Chapin, *Urban Land Use Planning* (12), pp. 81-151. A convenient book of readings is *The Techniques of Urban Economic Analysis* (13), edited by R. W. Pfouts. It contains the series of articles on the urban economic base originally published by R. B. Andrews in *Land Economics* during 1953-1956, as well as criticisms by J. Gillies, W. Grigsby, H. Blumenfeld, C. M. Thiebout, R. W. Pfouts, E. T. Curtis, and C. E. Ferguson. It also contains articles on input-output analysis by W. Isard, R. Kavesh, A. Gottlieb, and C. M. Thiebout.

Duncan and his associates in *Metropolis and Region* have applied these approaches in their own particular mix to the study of the economic structure of metropolitan areas and their regional relationships. Note especially their use of location quotients and the construction of industrial profiles.

Compare Duncan's classification of the inputs and outputs of metropolitan communities by regions of origin and destination (pp. 227-247) with the classification in the New York Metropolitan Region Study of industries into "national-market" and "local-market" activities. For the latter, see Lichtenberg; Berman, Chinitz, and Hoover, *Projection of a Metropolis* (14); Hall, *Made in New York* (15); Robbins and Terleckyj, *Money Metropolis* (16); and Chinitz, *Freight and the Metropolis* (17).

The New York Metropolitan Region Study is also valuable for its analysis of the changing distribution of economic activities within the metropolis. Certainly for the short run and for much of the long run, these intrametropolitan changes (often called suburbanization) affect the politics of the metropolitan area and its component cities, counties, and special districts. See Hoover and Vernon, *Anatomy of a Metropolis* (18); Segal, *Wages in the Metropolis* (19); Vernon, *Metropolis 1985;* Berman, Chinitz and Hoover, *Projection of a Metropolis* pp. 79-102; and Wood and Almendinger, *1400 Governments* (20).

Each volume in the New York Metropolitan Region Study contains several highly valuable methodological appendices. These should be examined carefully for suggestions and cautions on the use of published data, especially census data. See also Solomon and Bilbija, *Metropolitan Chicago: An Economic Analysis* (21), especially the technical appendix on sources and methods of estimation.

There are many local economic surveys and monographs in which these and other approaches and techniques are illustrated and critically evaluated. See the list in Government Affairs Foundation, *Metropolitan Communities: A Bibliography* (22), and in the supplement for 1955-1957 (23). In addition to general references, items are classified under the following headings: location and function of cities, regional location of industry, economic structure of cities, functional uses of land, market areas, real estate values and valuations, housing supply and demand, and municipal service costs. There is also a separate section on public finance.

POLITICAL SIGNIFICANCE OF ECONOMIC DATA

After identifying the economic characteristics of your community you should make an attempt to find out if they are politically significant. For example: heavy industry and mass production industry seem to result in a tendency toward industrial unionism but skilled industry is favorable to the development of craft unions. Does industry in your city predispose labor toward industrial or craft unionism? Consult the yellow pages of your telephone directory under "Labor Organizations" for addresses. What do labor leaders say about this question?

Census data on employment may shed light on the balance between industrial and nonindustrial employment in your city. As the political attitudes of white-collar workers are apt to differ markedly from those of industrial workers, the significance of the relative amounts of commercial and service employment in the community may be great. It is especially important to compare these statistics for your city with the employment data for other cities of the same size. You can test the importance of any differences you may find if it can be shown that your city is atypical politically, i.e., is more Democratic or more Republican than other cities of its size. Examine the tables in the *Municipal Year Book* showing the manufacturing

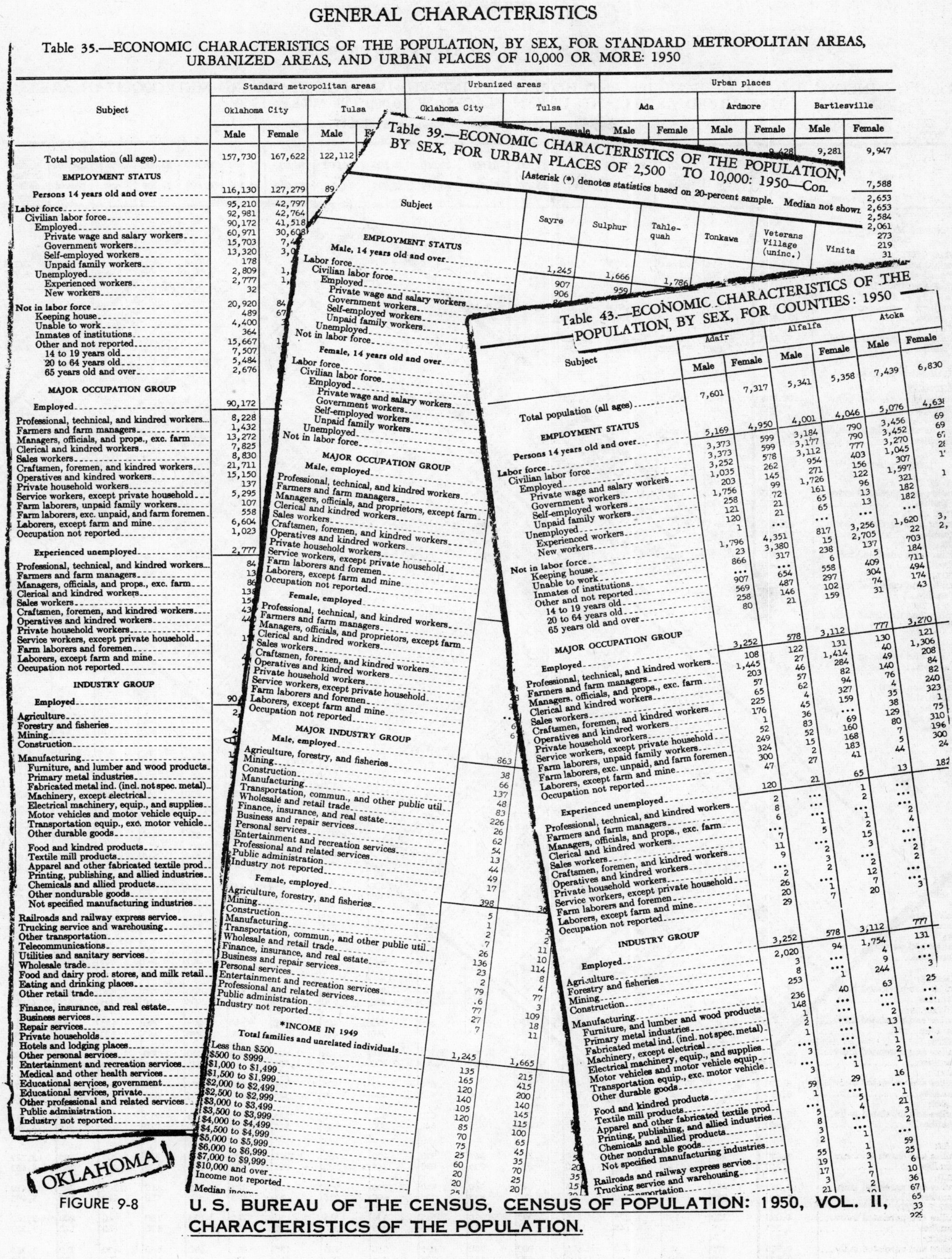

Table 35.—ECONOMIC CHARACTERISTICS OF THE POPULATION, BY SEX, FOR STANDARD METROPOLITAN AREAS, URBANIZED AREAS, AND URBAN PLACES OF 10,000 OR MORE: 1950

| Subject | Standard metropolitan areas | | | | Urbanized areas | | | | Urban places | | | | | |
| | Oklahoma City | | Tulsa | | Oklahoma City | | Tulsa | | Ada | | Ardmore | | Bartlesville | |
	Male	Female	Male	F...				Female	Male	Female	Male	Female	Male	Female
Total population (all ages)	157,730	167,622	122,112								9,428		9,281	9,947
EMPLOYMENT STATUS														
Persons 14 years old and over	116,130	127,279	89,...											7,588
Labor force	95,210	42,797												2,653
Civilian labor force	92,981	42,764												2,653
Employed	90,172	41,518												2,584
Private wage and salary workers	60,971	30,608												2,061
Government workers	15,703	7,4...												273
Self-employed workers	13,320	3,0...												219
Unpaid family workers	178													31
Unemployed	2,809	1,...												
Experienced workers	2,777	1,...												
New workers	32													
Not in labor force	20,920	84...												
Keeping house	489	67...												
Unable to work	4,400													
Inmates of institutions	364													
Other and not reported	15,667	1...												
14 to 19 years old	7,507													
20 to 64 years old	5,484													
65 years old and over	2,676													
MAJOR OCCUPATION GROUP														
Employed	90,172													
Professional, technical, and kindred workers	8,228													
Farmers and farm managers	1,432													
Managers, officials, and props., exc. farm	13,272													
Clerical and kindred workers	7,825													
Sales workers	8,830													
Craftsmen, foremen, and kindred workers	21,711													
Operatives and kindred workers	15,150													
Private household workers	137													
Service workers, except private household	5,295													
Farm laborers, unpaid family workers	107													
Farm laborers, exc. unpaid, and farm foremen	558													
Laborers, except farm and mine	6,604													
Occupation not reported	1,023													
Experienced unemployed	2,777													
Professional, technical, and kindred workers	84													
Farmers and farm managers	13													
Managers, officials, and props., exc. farm	86													
Clerical and kindred workers	138													
Sales workers	156													
Craftsmen, foremen, and kindred workers	43...													
Operatives and kindred workers	44...													
Private household workers														
Service workers, except private household	1...													
Farm laborers and foremen														
Laborers, except farm and mine														
Occupation not reported														
INDUSTRY GROUP														
Employed	90...													
Agriculture	2,...													
Forestry and fisheries														
Mining														
Construction														
Manufacturing														
Furniture, and lumber and wood products														
Primary metal industries														
Fabricated metal ind. (incl. not spec. metal)														
Machinery, except electrical														
Electrical machinery, equip., and supplies														
Motor vehicles and motor vehicle equip.														
Transportation equip., exc. motor vehicle														
Other durable goods														
Food and kindred products														
Textile mill products														
Apparel and other fabricated textile prod.														
Printing, publishing, and allied industries														
Chemicals and allied products														
Other nondurable goods														
Not specified manufacturing industries														
Railroads and railway express service														
Trucking service and warehousing														
Other transportation														
Telecommunications														
Utilities and sanitary services														
Wholesale trade														
Food and dairy prod. stores, and milk retail														
Eating and drinking places														
Other retail trade														
Finance, insurance, and real estate														
Business services														
Repair services														
Private households														
Hotels and lodging places														
Other personal services														
Entertainment and recreation services														
Medical and other health services														
Educational services, government														
Educational services, private														
Other professional and related services														
Public administration														
Industry not reported														

Table 39.—ECONOMIC CHARACTERISTICS OF THE POPULATION, BY SEX, FOR URBAN PLACES OF 2,500 TO 10,000: 1950—Con.

[Asterisk (*) denotes statistics based on 20-percent sample. Median not shown]

Subject	Sayre	Sulphur	Tahle-quah	Tonkawa	Veterans Village (uninc.)	Vinita
EMPLOYMENT STATUS						
Male, 14 years old and over						
Labor force	1,245	1,666	1,786			
Civilian labor force						
Employed	907	959				
Private wage and salary workers	906					
Government workers						
Self-employed workers						
Unpaid family workers						
Unemployed						
Not in labor force						
Female, 14 years old and over						
Labor force						
Civilian labor force						
Employed						
Private wage and salary workers						
Government workers						
Self-employed workers						
Unpaid family workers						
Unemployed						
Not in labor force						
MAJOR OCCUPATION GROUP						
Male, employed						
Professional, technical, and kindred workers						
Farmers and farm managers						
Managers, officials, and proprietors, except farm						
Clerical and kindred workers						
Sales workers						
Craftsmen, foremen, and kindred workers						
Operatives and kindred workers						
Private household workers						
Service workers, except private household						
Farm laborers and foremen						
Laborers, except farm and mine						
Occupation not reported						
Female, employed						
Professional, technical, and kindred workers						
Farmers and farm managers						
Managers, officials, and proprietors, except farm						
Clerical and kindred workers						
Sales workers						
Craftsmen, foremen, and kindred workers						
Operatives and kindred workers						
Private household workers						
Service workers, except private household						
Farm laborers and foremen						
Laborers, except farm and mine						
Occupation not reported						
MAJOR INDUSTRY GROUP						
Male, employed						
Agriculture, forestry, and fisheries	863					
Mining	38					
Construction	66					
Manufacturing	137					
Transportation, commun., and other public util.	48					
Wholesale and retail trade	83					
Finance, insurance, and real estate	226					
Business and repair services	26					
Personal services	62					
Entertainment and recreation services	54					
Professional and related services	13					
Public administration	44					
Industry not reported	49					
	17					
Female, employed						
Agriculture, forestry, and fisheries	398					
Mining						
Construction	5					
Manufacturing	1					
Transportation, commun., and other public util.	2					
Wholesale and retail trade	7					
Finance, insurance, and real estate	26	11				
Business and repair services	136	10				
Personal services	23	114				
Entertainment and recreation services	2	8				
Professional and related services	79	4				
Public administration	6	77				
Industry not reported	77	3				
	27	109				
	7	18				
		11				
***INCOME IN 1949**						
Total families and unrelated individuals	1,245	1,665				
Less than $500						
$500 to $999	135	215				
$1,000 to $1,499	165	415				
$1,500 to $1,999	120	200				
$2,000 to $2,499	140	140				
$2,500 to $2,999	105	145				
$3,000 to $3,499	120	115				
$3,500 to $3,999	85	100				
$4,000 to $4,499	70	65				
$4,500 to $4,999	75	45				
$5,000 to $5,999	25	35				
$6,000 to $6,999	60	25				
$7,000 to $9,999	20	70				
$10,000 and over	20	25				
Income not reported	25	20				
Median income						

Table 43.—ECONOMIC CHARACTERISTICS OF THE POPULATION, BY SEX, FOR COUNTIES: 1950

| Subject | Adair | | Alfalfa | | Atoka | |
	Male	Female	Male	Female	Male	Female
Total population (all ages)	7,601	7,317	5,341	5,358	7,439	6,830
EMPLOYMENT STATUS						
Persons 14 years old and over	5,169	4,950	4,001	4,046	5,076	4,63...
Labor force	3,373	599	3,184	790	3,456	69...
Civilian labor force	3,373	599	3,177	790	3,452	69...
Employed	3,252	578	3,112	403	3,270	67...
Private wage and salary workers	1,035	145	954	156	1,045	28...
Government workers	203	99	271	122	1,597	1...
Self-employed workers	1,756	72	1,726	96	321	
Unpaid family workers	258	21	161	13	182	
Unemployed	121	21	65	13	182	
Experienced workers	120		65			3,...
New workers	1				1,620	
Not in labor force	1,796	4,351	817	3,256	22	2,...
Keeping house	23	3,380	15	2,705	703	
Unable to work	866	317	238	137	184	
Inmates of institutions		654	558	409	711	
Other and not reported	907	487	297	304	494	
14 to 19 years old	569	146	102	74	174	
20 to 64 years old	258	21	159	31	43	
65 years old and over	80					
MAJOR OCCUPATION GROUP						
Employed	3,252	578	3,112	777	3,270	121
Professional, technical, and kindred workers	108	122	131	130		1,306
Farmers and farm managers	1,445	27	1,414	40	49	208
Managers, officials, and props., exc. farm	203	46	284	140	84	84
Clerical and kindred workers	57	57	82	76	240	82
Sales workers	65	62	94	4	323	
Craftsmen, foremen, and kindred workers	225	45	327	35	1	
Operatives and kindred workers	176	36	159	38	75	
Private household workers	1	83		129	310	
Service workers, except private household	52	52	69	80	196	
Farm laborers, unpaid family workers	249	15	160		300	
Farm laborers, exc. unpaid, and farm foremen	324	2	168	5	24	
Laborers, except farm and mine	300	27	183	44		
Occupation not reported	47		41			
	120	21	65	13		18...
Experienced unemployed						
Professional, technical, and kindred workers	2		1			
Farmers and farm managers	8		2			2
Managers, officials, and props., exc. farm	6		1			4
Clerical and kindred workers		5	1			
Sales workers	7		15			3
Craftsmen, foremen, and kindred workers	11		2			2
Operatives and kindred workers		3	2		12	
Private household workers		5			7	3
Service workers, except private household	26		1			
Farm laborers and foremen	20		7		20	
Laborers, except farm and mine	29					
Occupation not reported						
INDUSTRY GROUP						
Employed	3,252	578	3,112	777		
Agriculture	2,020		94		1,754	131
Forestry and fisheries	8	1			9	
Mining	253		244			3
Construction	236	40	63			25
Manufacturing	148					
Furniture, and lumber and wood products	2		2		13	
Primary metal industries	1		1			
Fabricated metal ind. (incl. not spec. metal)					1	
Machinery, except electrical	3		1			2
Electrical machinery, equip., and supplies	3				16	
Motor vehicles and motor vehicle equip.						
Transportation equip., exc. motor vehicle	59	29				
Other durable goods	1		5		21	
Food and kindred products			1		2	
Textile mill products	5					
Apparel and other fabricated textile prod.			1			59
Printing, publishing, and allied industries	2		1			25
Chemicals and allied products	55	3	1		6	
Other nondurable goods	19		2		9	
Not specified manufacturing industries					10	
Railroads and railway express service	17		1		36	
Trucking service and warehousing	3	2			67	
					65	
					33	
					2...	

FIGURE 9-8

U. S. BUREAU OF THE CENSUS, CENSUS OF POPULATION: 1950, VOL. II, CHARACTERISTICS OF THE POPULATION.

OKLAHOMA

FIGURE 9-9

GENERAL CHARACTERISTICS

Table 37.—INCOME IN 1949 OF FAMILIES AND UNRELATED INDIVIDUALS, FOR STANDARD METROPOLITAN AREAS, URBANIZED AREAS, AND URBAN PLACES OF 10,000 OR MORE: 1950

[Statistics based on 20-percent sample. Median not shown where base is less than 500]

Area	All classes	Less than $500	$500 to $999	$1,000 to $1,499	$1,500 to $1,999	$2,000 to $2,499	$2,500 to $2,999	$3,000 to $3,499	$3,500 to $3,999	$4,000 to $4,499	$4,500 to $4,999	$5,000 to $5,999	$6,000 to $6,999	$7,000 to $9,999	$10,000 and over	Income not reported	Median income (dollars)
STANDARD METROPOLITAN AREAS																	
ATLANTIC CITY:																	
Families and unrelated indiv	48,525	7,615	3,900	4,575	3,860	4,495	3,980	4,105					210		1,020	4,530	2,228
Families	34,405	3,295	1,670	2,610	2,730	3,575	3,345	3,							930	2,795	2,788
NEW YORK-NORTHEASTERN NEW JERSEY (N. J. PORTION):																	
Families and unrelated indiv	1,079,175	88,145	37,695	43,645	51,610	80,155	91,10							585		74,165	3,463
Families	893,620	43,355	18,105	25,865	34,050	61,555	76,									52,550	3,835
TRENTON:																	
Families and unrelated indiv	74,945	8,885	3,905	3,625	3,885	5,680	3,935									375	3,237
Families	56,335	2,600	1,355	1,785	2,190	3,											3,836
URBANIZED AREAS																	
ATLANTIC CITY:																	
Families and unrelated indiv	39,795	6,645	3,265	3,645	3,15												
Families	27,865	2,910	1,295	2,115													
TRENTON:																	
Families and unrelated indiv	59,340	5,615	2,615	2,575													3,276
Families	47,240	2,175	1,090	1,35													3,8
URBAN PLACES																	
ASBURY PARK:																	
Families and unrelated indiv	7,005	960															
Families	4,370	330															
ATLANTIC CITY:																	
Families and unrelated indiv	25,450	4,645															
Families	15,970	1,7															
BAYONNE:																	
Families and unrelated indiv	23,760																3,472
Families	20,380																3,698
BELLEVILLE:																	
Families and unrelated indiv	9,4															585	3,679
Families	8,															495	3,934
BERGENFIELD:																	
Families and unrelated indiv																625	4,411
Families															230	410	4,545
BLOOMFIELD:																	
Families and unrelated in															515	990	3,806
Families															505	740	4,057
BRIDGETON:																	
Families and unrel															130	350	2,480
Families															95	190	3,019
BURLINGTON:																	
Families an														115	70	165	2,881
Families														140	70	135	3,121
CAMDEN:																	
Fami												1,470	1,565	525	1,390	2,927
												1,455	1,515	495	890	3,241
COL...												110	165	105	295	3,184
												110	160	105	195	3,391
DOVER:																	
											315	350	3,731
											305	290	3,975
EAST ORANGE:																	
Families and unrelated indiv							2,215	2,920	2,210	1,970	1,330	2,690	1,520	2,220	1,580	2,590	3,441
Families							1,550	2,285	1,830	1,670	1,150	2,420	1,400	2,080	1,395	1,820	4,005
EAST PATERSON:																	
Families and unrelated indiv							250	390	690	370	425	270	550	275	290	125	265	3,916
Families							225	375	670	360	410	270	540	270	285	120	245	3,990
ELIZABETH:																	
Families and unrelated indiv	36,2						2,860	2,900	3,700	3,160	2,620	1,920	3,240	2,050	2,300	1,370	2,050	3,442
Families	29,570						2,135	2,380	3,260	2,900	2,360	1,835	3,115	2,025	2,245	1,325	1,350	3,792
ENGLEWOOD:																	
Families and unrelated indiv	8,370				475	505	515	690	495	505	350	650	425	645	960	655	3,674
Families	6,415				205	315	390	615	450	490	325	635	405	635	920	430	4,426
FAIR LAWN:																	
Families and unrelated indiv	7,090	33		100	115	275	435	670	625	620	525	1,150	655	715	450	350	4,619
Families	6,680	205		70	95	250	410	640	600	610	515	1,140	650	710	440	315	4,765
FORT LEE:																	
Families and unrelated indiv	3,880	315	120	155	170	280	265	320	270	260	165	370	255	345	205	385	3,727
Families	3,240	185	45	70	130	230	235	290	245	225	165	370	255	330	205	260	4,133
GARFIELD:																	
Families and unrelated indiv	8,255	425	190	265	315	695	940	1,410	700	750	435	825	510	410	120	265	3,413
Families	7,670	285	160	210	280	610	855	1,335	690	715	435	820	510	410	120	235	3,493
GLOUCESTER CITY:																	
Families and unrelated indiv	4,035	320	190	225	210	395	410	585	330	315	190	285	135	180	40	200	3,122
Families	3,385	170	105	145	150	365	355	535	325	310	190	270	135	170	40	120	3,320
HACKENSACK:																	
Families and unrelated indiv	9,925	875	475	440	675	900	780	865	810	735	435	865	490	640	430	510	3,325
Families	7,725	400	180	185	405	630	645	725	735	700	415	830	465	625	415	370	3,845

FIGURE 9-10

HOUSING—GENERAL CHARACTERISTICS

Table 21.—FINANCIAL CHARACTERISTICS OF URBAN AND RURAL-NONFARM DWELLING UNITS, FOR STANDARD METROPOLITAN AREAS AND CONSTITUENT COUNTIES, URBANIZED AREAS, AND URBAN PLACES OF 10,000 OR MORE: 1950

[Median not shown where base is less than 100]

VIRGINIA

	Standard metropolitan areas											
	Norfolk-Portsmouth					Richmond				Roanoke		
Subject	The area	Norfolk city	Portsmouth city	South Norfolk city	Norfolk County	Princess Anne County	The area	Richmond city	Chesterfield County	Henrico County	The area	Roanoke city	Roanoke County
Total dwelling units	117,096	56,122	20,796	3,054	26,709	10,415	91,733	66,434	9,152	16,147	36,433	27,219	9,214
CONTRACT MONTHLY RENT													
Renter-occupied dwelling units	64,582	34,731	11,529	1,441	12,342	4,539	40,647	34,586	2,180	3,881			
Less than $10	2,144	1,120	374	74	422	154	2,246	1,976	141				
$10 to $14	6,511	4,256	1,553	167	422	113	5,167	4,831	18_				
$15 to $19	4,637	3,063	997	119	335	123	4,466	4,162					
$20 to $24	4,562	2,362	1,259	183	599	159	3,500						
$25 to $29	5,469	2,468	1,792	142	906	161	3,1__						
$30 to $34	7,647	2,804	1,580	114	3,023	126							
$35 to $39	7,346	2,784	1,026	296	3,028	21_							
$40 to $49	7,784	4,723	1,213	213	1,222								
$50 to $59	5,653	3,576	939	35									
$60 to $74	4,887	3,137	280	106									
$75 to $99	3,400	2,504	106										
$100 or more	1,293	833											
Rent free or not reported	3,249	1,10_											
Median rent ... dollars	34.30												

Vacant nonseasonal not dilapidated dwelling units, for rent

Less than $10
$10 to $19
$20 to $29
$30 to $39
$40 to $49
$50 to $59
$60 to $74
$75 to $99
$100 or more
Rent free or not reported
Median rent ... dollars

GROSS MONTHLY RENT

Renter-occupied dwelling units
Less than $10
$10 to $14 ... 3_
$15 to $19
$20 to $24 ... 5,9_
$25 to $29 ... 4,5_
$30 to $34 ... 9,30_
$35 to $39 ... 12,51_
$40 to $49 ... 6,866
$50 to $59 ... 5,559
$60 to $74 ... 4,427
$75 to $99 ... 1,639
$100 or more ... 4,036
Rent free or not reported
Median rent ... dollars ... 40.09

VALUE OF ONE-DWELLING-UNIT STRUCTURES

Owner-occupied dwelling units[1]	38,322	
Less than $2,000	2,965	
$2,000 to $2,999	2,290	
$3,000 to $3,999	3,098	
$4,000 to $4,999	2,843	
$5,000 to $5,999	3,588	1,218
$6,000 to $7,499	7,840	2,459
$7,500 to $9,999	6,092	2,858
$10,000 to $14,999	4,823	2,691
$15,000 to $19,999	1,875	1,196
$20,000 or more	1,566	946
Not reported	1,342	387
Median value ... dollars	6,659	7,76_

Vacant nonseasonal not dilapidated dwelling units, for sale only ... 492

Less than $3,000	9
$3,000 to $3,999	14
$4,000 to $4,999	10
$5,000 to $7,499	196
$7,500 to $9,999	162
$10,000 to $14,999	45
$15,000 or more	34
Not reported	2_
Median value ... dollars	7,__

MORTGAGE STATUS

Owner-occupied dwelling units
Mortgaged
Not mortgaged
Not reported

[1] Restricted to 1-dwe_
[2] Restricted to uni_

Table 21.—FINANCIAL CHARACTERISTICS OF URBAN AND RURAL-NONFARM DWELLING UNITS, FOR STANDARD METROPOLITAN AREAS AND CONSTITUENT COUNTIES, URBANIZED AREAS, AND URBAN PLACES OF 10,000 OR MORE: 1950—Con.

[Median not shown where base is less than 100]

Subject	Urbanized areas			Alexandria	Bristol	Charlottes-ville	Danville	Urban places	
	Norfolk-Portsmouth	Richmond	Roanoke						Fred_
Total dwelling units			31,413	18,753		7,277	__3	58	

Data fragments (partial, overlapping):
4,266 ... 9 ... 8 / 30 / 45 / 35 / 24 / 39 / 18 / 12 / 11 / 2 / 44 / 41.57 / 40.36 / 13,087 / 10,581 / 2,506 / 98 / 60 / 38 / 201 / 440 / 666 / 207 / 157 / 125 / 27 / 13 / 559 / 27.03

11,943 / 11,452 / 28 / 408 / _510 / 764 / 66.90 / _4,724 / 10_

46-44

Table 24.—FINANCIAL CHARACTERISTICS OF DWELLING UNITS, FOR URBAN PLACES OF 2,500 TO 10,000: 1950

Subject	Abingdon	Alta-vista	Appa-lachia	Arlington-Five Forks-Kenwood (uninc.)	Ashland	Base_ (uni_)
CONTRACT MONTHLY RENT						

Fragments: 565 / 37 / 117 / 102 / 77 / 46 / 21 / 7 / 335 / 20 / 107 / 79 / 25 / 31 / 20 / 343 / 27 / 90 / 102 / 49 / 27 / 11 / 355 / 79 / 56 / 25 / 38 / 18 / 310 / 17 / 38 / 77 / 31 / 13 / 593 / 266 / 172 / 56 / 22 / 15 / 28 / 3

26.66 / 112 / 22.21 / 23.47 / 19.75 / 30.68 / 553 / 4 / 63 / 91 / 70 / 76 / 51 / 45 / 17 / 3_ / 333 / 34 / 3 / 40 / 85 / 64 / 48 / 18 / 335 / 346 / 10

Table 25.—CHARACTERISTICS OF DWELLING UNITS, FOR PLACES OF 1,000 TO 2,500: 1950

[Average not shown where base is less than 100]

	Urban, rural nonfarm, and rural farm						Occupied dwelling units				Urban and rural nonfarm				Rural farm dwelling units
Incorporated or unincorporated place	All dwelling units by occupancy and tenure				All dwelling units by condition and plumbing facilities				Persons per room		Occupied by non-white	Total dwelling units	Contract monthly rent[1]		Value of one-dwelling-unit structures[2]	
	Total	Owner occupied	Renter occupied	Vacant nonseas. not dilap. for rent or sale	Other vacant and nonresident	Number reporting	No private bath or dilapidated	No running water or dilapidated	Total	Number reporting	1.51 or more			Number reporting	Average monthly rent (dollars)	Number reporting	Average value (dollars)

Fragments of data rows:
237 / 288 / 61 / 1 / 9 / 191 / 88 / 97 / 118 / 63 / 239 / 285 / 324 / 237 / 283 / 323 / 20 / 9 / 22 / 240 / 278 / 327 / 275 / 416 / 43 / 92 / 142 / 264 / 177 / 21.65 / 8.97 / 30.67 / 168 / 151 / 121 / 168 / 2,637 / 8,608 / 7,162 / 9,351 / 179 / 140 / 13.83 / 26.57 / 179 / 248 / 7,055 / 5,692 / 72 / 115 / 271 / 270 / 43 / 18 / 372 / 50 / 156 / 6,9__ / 389 / 392 / 414 / 844 / 45.52 / 32.81 / 226 / 54 / 5 / 61

Allie_ / Amher_ ...

U. S. BUREAU OF THE CENSUS, CENSUS OF HOUSING: 1950, VOL. I, GENERAL CHARACTERISTICS OF HOUSING

ratios of your city and comparable cities, and see how these ratios are calculated.

How do you determine whether or not your city is an industrial or a commercial center? Some tests are: industrial and commercial employment (employment ratio); assessed valuations of commercial and industrial property; total wages paid in industrial and commercial employment. Statistics for commercial employment can be found in the census of business bulletins on retail trade which show the number of establishments, yearly sales, yearly payrolls, number of paid employees, number of stores, and total sales by nine categories.

The major indices of economic activity in your community are: payrolls, resident labor force, bank clearances, volume of business at the post office, gross retail sales, family incomes, manufacturing ratio, building permits for new construction, employment, value added by manufacture, the grand list, and consumption of electric power.

One insight into the economy of your town is provided by an examination of the tax base of the city government. What percentages of the grand list are provided by industrial and commercial properties on the one hand, and by residential property on the other hand? Consult local fiscal officers about the relation between public costs for schools, health, highways, police, and fire protection and the taxes paid by the average family. To what extent is the city dependent on industrial and commercial establishments for its tax revenues?

The composition of the working force of your community is significant, but it should be remembered that any differences in this respect between your community and other communities are never more than a matter of degree, sufficient only to give you leads for investigation. The political inclinations of workers are influenced by the way they are organized in unions, and labor organization is in turn influenced by the type of employment. Service trades and occupations are likely to account for a major part of the employment in any community and must be taken into consideration in any study of the economic base of the politics of your community.

It is important to see the community as a whole in the study of the economic basis of politics. If the central city is "filled up" with no room for new industrial or residential construction, rapid growth is likely to take place in the fringes of the city. This expansion of satellite towns is really part of the growth of the area and may result in a change of the functions of the central city, in commercial uses of vacated industrial buildings, or in changes in the character of the population. Do commercial concerns take over industrial plants in the central city? Have there been significant changes in the total as-

sessed valuation of commercial and industrial properties?

Certain industries are likely to be more stable than others. What are the employment characteristics of industry in your town? Unemployment is doubtless the economic factor to which the political system is most sensitive. See state employment office for statistics.

Is there any evidence that there has been a significant migration of industry from the central city to the suburbs, or from the city to some other part of the country? Or what are the patterns of growth? What new industries have moved into the city in recent years? Is employment growing, declining, or stagnant? Is there a housing shortage? How much unemployment is there in your city? There is a very great difference between the politics of a boom town and that of a depressed area.

Any city over 25,000 which does not vote Democratic ought to be studied carefully. What special factors are there in the nature of the economy that may account for a deviation from the usual urban Democratic pattern? It may be necessary to look beyond the city itself to find the explanation. Thus, New York State politics is greatly conditioned. by the long-standing conflict between upstate areas and New York City. In upstate New York, the cities tend to take on the political complexion of the whole area in which they are located.

Income is apt to be closely related to political alignment. Ordinarily one would expect that the most useful source of this information is "family income" tables reported in the census. But there is evidence that people under-reported their income in 1950. There are, however, many other related indices. Housing, rents, crowding, home furnishings, years of schooling, occupations, and even religious affiliation are related more or less closely to income.

REFERENCES

1. Woodbury, C., *A Framework for Urban Studies: An Analysis of Urban-metropolitan Development and Research Needs* Washington, D.C.: National Academy of Sciences, National Research Council, Highway Research Board, 1959. p. 9.

2. Duncan, O. D., *et al.*, *Metropolis and Region*. Baltimore: Johns Hopkins Press, 1960. p. 4.

3. Vernon, R., *Metropolis 1985*. Cambridge, Mass.: Harvard University Press, 1960. p. 189.

4. Lichtenberg, R. M., *One-tenth of a Nation*. Cambridge, Mass.: Harvard University Press, 1960.

5. Perloff, H. S., *et al.*, *Regions, Resources, and Economic Growth,* Baltimore: Johns Hopkins Press, 1960.

6. Quinn, J. A., *Human Ecology*. Englewood Cliffs, N.J.: Prentice-Hall, Inc., 1950. Chap. 20.

7. Weimer, A. M., and H. Hoyt, *Principles of Real Estate*. 3d ed. New York: The Ronald Press Company, 1954. Chaps. 17-19.

8. Fisher, E. M., and R. M. Fisher, *Urban Real Estate*. New York: Holt, Rinehart and Winston, Inc., 1954. Chaps. 13 and 14.

9. Duncan, O. D., and A. J. Reiss, Jr., *Social Characteristics of Urban and Rural Communities*. New York: John Wiley & Sons, Inc., 1954. pp. 215-370, 387-409.

10. Reiss, A. J., Jr., "Functional Specialization of Cities" in P. K. Hatt, and A. J. Reiss, Jr., eds., *Cities and Society*. New York: The Free Press of Glencoe, Inc., 1957. pp. 555-75.

11. Queen, S. A. and D. B. Carpenter, *The American City*. New York: McGraw-Hill Book Company, Inc., 1953. Chap. 3.

12. Chapin, F. S., Jr., *Urban Land Use Planning*. New York: Harper & Brothers, 1957.

13. Pfouts, R. W., ed., *The Techniques of Urban Economic Analysis*. West Trenton, N.J.: Chandler-Davis Publishing Company, 1960.

14. Berman, B. R., B. Chinitz, and E. M. Hoover, *Projection of a Metropolis: Technical Supplement to the New York Metropolitan Region Study*. Cambridge, Mass.: Harvard University Press, 1961. pp. 1-3.

15. Hall, M., ed., *Made in New York: Case Studies in Metropolitan Manufacturing*. Cambridge, Mass.: Harvard University Press, 1960.

16. Robbins, S. M., and N. E. Terleckyj, *Money Metropolis*. Cambridge, Mass.: Harvard University Press, 1960.

17. Chinitz, B., *Freight and the Metropolis*. Cambridge, Mass.: Harvard University Press, 1960.

18. Hoover, E. M., and R. Vernon, *Anatomy of a Metropolis*. Cambridge, Mass.: Harvard University Press, 1959.

19. Segal, M., *Wages in the Metropolis*. Cambridge, Mass.: Harvard University Press, 1960.

20. Wood, R. C., and V. V. Almendinger, *1400 Governments*. Cambridge, Mass.: Harvard University Press, 1961.

21. Solomon, E., and Z. C. Bilbija, *Metropolitan Chicago: An Economic Analysis*. New York: The Free Press of Glencoe, Inc., 1959.

22. Government Affairs Foundation, *Metropolitan Communities: A Bibliography with Special Emphasis on Government and Politics*. Chicago: Public Administration Service, 1956.

23. Jones, V., B. Hudson, and L. D. Johnston, eds., *Metropolitan Communities: Supplement for 1955-57*. Chicago: Public Administration Service, 1960.

U. S. DEPARTMENT OF COMMERCE
BUREAU OF THE CENSUS
WASHINGTON 25, D. C.

January 1961 (rev.)

PUBLICATION PROGRAM FOR THE 1960 CENSUS OF HOUSING

The results of the 1960 Census of Housing will be published as soon as they are tabulated and assembled. The preliminary and advance statistics will be superseded by final reports and volumes as described below. Announcements and order forms will be issued when the printing plans for each series are completed.

Detailed specifications showing the precise content of each table in Volume I, States and Small Areas, and in the housing portion of the Census Tracts Reports are available upon request.

PRELIMINARY REPORTS

Housing Unit Counts for Places of 10,000 or More. 55 reports, Series HC(P1). A report for each State, the District of Columbia, Virgin Islands, Guam, Puerto Rico, and a United States summary. The reports include total housing units based on 1960 preliminary counts obtained in the field offices, and the 1950 dwelling unit count, for each place of 10,000 inhabitants or more. These preliminary reports will be superseded by final statistics in advance and final reports.

Series completed
May-September
1960

ADVANCE REPORTS

State Reports. 52 reports, Series HC(A1). A report for each State and the District of Columbia giving selected housing characteristics for all standard metropolitan statistical areas and places of 10,000 inhabitants or more, and a United States summary. The statistics include housing units by tenure, color, and vacancy status; number of rooms; number of persons; contract rent; value of property; and condition and plumbing facilities. This information is issued in advance of publication in final reports.

November 1960-
March 1961

Standard Metropolitan Statistical Areas--Selected Characteristics. About 100 reports, Series HC(A2). A report for each of about 100 standard metropolitan statistical areas of 250,000 inhabitants or more in the United States and one in Puerto Rico. Each report will contain data on tenure, color, vacancy status, condition and plumbing, number of rooms, units in structure, year structure built, heating equipment, number of persons, year moved into unit, value of property, and gross and contract rent. The statistics are issued in advance of publication in final reports.

May-October
1961

Components of Inventory Change--Selected Characteristics. 18 reports, Series HC(A3). A report for each of 17 standard metropolitan statistical areas and the United States, giving inventory changes from 1950 to 1959, including demolitions, new construction, conversions, etc. In addition, selected characteristics may be shown. The statistics are issued in advance of publication in final reports. .

Date of issue
to be
announced

Standard Metropolitan Statistical Areas and Counties--Selected Equipment and Facilities. 51 reports, Series HC(A4). A report for each State and the District of Columbia. Each report will contain data on heating equipment, clothes washer and dryer, home food freezer, telephone, automobiles available, air conditioning, and radio and television sets. These statistics are issued in advance of publication in final reports.

May-October
1961

FINAL REPORTS

Census Tracts. About 175 reports, Series PHC(1). These reports will present information on both housing and population subjects. There will be one report for each of about 175 tracted areas in the United States and Puerto Rico. Among the housing characteristics to be given are tenure, color, vacancy status, number of persons, persons per room, year moved into unit, type of structure, year built, condition and plumbing facilities, automobiles available, heating equipment, value of property, and rent. Population items will include age, race, marital status, employment characteristics, income, years of school completed, etc.

April-September 1961

Selected characteristics of housing units with nonwhite household heads will be shown for tracts containing at least 100 such units. Selected data will also be shown for census tracts with 400 or more units occupied by white household heads with Spanish surnames in Arizona, California, Colorado, New Mexico, and Texas. In the other States similar data will be published for each census tract with 400 units or more occupied by household heads of Puerto Rican birth or parentage provided the entire tracted area contains 5,000 persons or more of Puerto Rican birth or parentage. This series of reports is described also in the publication program for the 1960 Census of Population.

Volume I--States and Small Areas. 55 reports, Series HC(1). One report for each State, the District of Columbia, Virgin Islands, Guam, Puerto Rico, and a United States summary. Information will be presented for the States as a whole and for the following area groupings: urbanized areas, standard metropolitan statistical areas by counties and urban places over 50,000, urban balance of the SMSA, rural total of the SMSA, places of 25,000 to 50,000 inhabitants, places of 10,000 to 25,000 inhabitants, places of 2,500 to 10,000 inhabitants, places of 1,000 to 2,500 inhabitants, counties not included in SMSA's, nonfarm housing, and occupied farm housing in rural portions of counties.

The amount of information to be shown will vary with the area groupings-- occupancy characteristics, such as tenure, color, vacancy status, population per occupied housing unit, number of persons, and persons per room; structural characteristics, such as number of rooms, number of bedrooms, type of structure, year built, condition and plumbing facilities; equipment and facilities, such as heating equipment, cooking and heating fuels, air conditioning, source of water, sewage disposal, radios, television, automobiles available, etc.; financial characteristics, such as contract rent, gross rent, and value.

June 1961-January 1962

Selected characteristics of housing units with nonwhite household heads will be shown for SMSA's and urban places containing at least 100 such units. Selected data will also be shown for SMSA's and urban places with 400 or more units occupied by white househeold heads with Spanish surnames in Arizona, California, Colorado, New Mexico, and Texas. In the other States similar data will be published for SMSA's and urban places with 400 or more units occupied by household heads of Puerto Rican birth or parentage. These reports subsequently will be assembled and bound in buckram.

Volume II--Metropolitan Housing. About 200 reports, Series HC(2). One report for the United States and geographic divisions, a separate report for each standard metropolitan statistical area with 100,000 or more inhabitants, and a separate report for the San Juan SMSA in Puerto Rico. Cross-classifications of housing and household characteristics for analytical use will be presented separately for owner-occupied and renter-occupied housing units. There will be separate tables for each city of 100,000 inhabitants or more in the SMSA.

September 1961-April 1962

Subjects to be covered include value, rent, income, number of rooms, condition and plumbing, household composition, number of persons, type of structure, etc. For SMSA's or cities with 25,000 or more housing units occupied by nonwhites, selected characteristics will be shown for those units. Selected statistics will also be shown for cities and SMSA's with 25,000 or more housing units occupied by white household heads with Spanish surnames in Arizona, California, Colorado, New Mexico, and Texas. In the other States similar data will be published for cities and SMSA's with 25,000 or more housing units occupied by household heads of Puerto Rican birth or parentage. These reports subsequently will be assembled and bound in buckram.

FINAL REPORTS

<u>Volume III--City Blocks.</u> About 425 reports, Series HC(3). One report for each city with 50,000 inhabitants or more in the 1950 census or in a subsequent special census conducted by the Bureau, and reports covering about 200 places that have specially requested inclusion in the block statistics program. Information to be shown includes condition and plumbing facilities, average rooms, average contract rent, average value, total population, housing units occupied by nonwhites, and persons per room.   March-August 1961

Statistics will be published also for "block" cities in Puerto Rico.   October 1961

<u>Volume IV--Components of Inventory Change.</u>
    <u>Part 1. 1950 to 1959, United States and Selected Metropolitan Areas.</u>
     18 reports, Series HC(4A). One report for the United States and one for each of 17 standard metropolitan statistical areas (14 with 1,000,000 inhabitants or more, and 3 smaller areas which had been included in the 1956 National Housing Inventory program). These reports will present measures of the source of the 1959 inventory and disposition of the 1950 inventory in terms of such changes as new construction, conversion, merger, and demolition. Characteristics will be shown for the units involved in each type of change and also for units which were not involved in change. In addition, some characteristics such as information on "recent movers" may be shown for the total inventory.   Date of issue to be announced

    <u>Part 2. 1956 to 1959, United States and Selected Metropolitan Areas.</u>
     10 reports, Series HC(4B). One report for the United States and one for each of 9 standard metropolitan statistical areas which were included in the 1956 National Housing Inventory. These reports will show measurements of change since 1956. Characteristics will be shown for the units involved in each type of change.   Date of issue to be announced

<u>Volume V--Residential Finance.</u> This report comprises the following 3 parts:

<u>Part 1. Homeowner Properties, United States.</u>

<u>Part 2. Homeowner Properties, Selected Metropolitan Areas.</u>
 A separate report for each of 17 standard metropolitan statistical areas (14 with 1,000,000 inhabitants or more, and 3 smaller areas which had been included in the 1956 National Housing Inventory program).

<u>Part 3. Rental and Vacant Properties, United States.</u>

All 3 parts of the report will present data on method of financing purchase of property, the size of the outstanding mortgage debt, and detailed tabulations on such mortgage characteristics as amount of loan, interest rate, government insurance status, method and amount of mortgage payments, and type of lender. Also shown in each of the 3 parts will be such property characteristics as value, purchase price, year built, year acquired, taxes and number of units in property.   Date of issue to be announced

For one-dwelling unit homeowner properties, owner characteristics include household composition, veteran status, color of family head, and income. Computed characteristics include ratio of amount of loan to purchase price, outstanding debt as percant of market value, purchase price as percent of market value, and for one-dwelling unit homeowner properties, the ratio of purchase price to family income and the percentage relationship of mortgage payments to family income. Cross tabulations of the mortgage, property, and owner characteristics and ratios and percentages will be shown. Separate tables will be provided for recent transactions, i.e., mortgages made or assumed and properties acquired in 1957-59.

<u>Volume VI--Rural Housing, Economic Subregions.</u> This report will contain analytical tables for about 120 subregions and the United States, showing inter-relationships between selected housing and household characteristics of occupied units. Statistics will be presented separately for nonfarm and for farm units.   August 1962

SUPPLEMENTARY REPORTS

<u>Special Reports for Local Housing Authorities.</u> 139 reports, Series HC(S1).
One report for each participating locality, made at cost for local housing
authorities and other agencies.   This series was requested by, and planned
in cooperation with, the Public Housing Administration.   Items shown will
be all housing units and housing units classified as substandard by PHA   March-May
criteria, by color and tenure of occupants; number of rooms, condition,   1961
plumbing facilities, number of persons, persons per room, presence of eld-
erly persons, presence of nonrelatives, and selected characteristics for
primary families by color and tenure of occupants; the same for housing
units with head 65 years or over; distribution and median for gross rent
and for contract rent for substandard units occupied by primary families,
by color of head; income of primary renter families in substandard housing
units by number of persons in family, by color; income of primary renter
families in substandard units by rent income ratio, by color.

- - - - - - - - - - - - - -

USCOMM--DC